QUEER CINEMA IN THE WORLD

QUEER CINEMA

in the World

KARL SCHOONOVER
ROSALIND GALT

Duke University Press   Durham and London   2016

Library of Congress Cataloging-in-Publication Data
Names: Schoonover, Karl, author. | Galt, Rosalind, author.
Title: Queer cinema in the world / Karl Schoonover and Rosalind Galt.
Description: Durham : Duke University Press, 2016. |
Includes bibliographical references and index.
Identifiers: LCCN 2016021422 (print) | LCCN 2016023364 (ebook)
ISBN 9780822362463 (hardcover : alk. paper)
ISBN 9780822362616 (pbk. : alk.paper)
ISBN 9780822373674 (e-book)
Subjects: LCSH: Homosexuality in motion pictures. | Homosexuality and
motion pictures. | Motion pictures—Political aspects. | Mass media
and gays—Political aspects.
Classification: LCC PN1995.9.H55 S37 2016 (print) |
LCC PN1995.9.H55 (ebook) | DDC 791.43/653—dc23
LC record available at https://lccn.loc.gov/2016021422

Cover art: *Pojktanten/She Male Snails*, 2012, photo by Minka Jakerson,
Courtesy of Ester Martin Bergsmark.

— To our loves —

CONTENTS

ACKNOWLEDGMENTS

This book is the result of collaborative thinking. It is an experiment in co-authorship, as the names on its front cover declare. But even more than in other projects, we feel indebted to the people who have stimulated, debated, and encouraged the thinking between its covers. This has been a truly queer collaboration whose many participants have nurtured and transformed how we think about cinema and the world.

This project benefited at a critical stage from the support of the Arts and Humanities Research Council (AHRC), which funded a series of symposia and queer film events as part of the Global Queer Cinema (GQC) research network. This network could not have happened without the dedication of the brilliant Laura Ellen Joyce. During the life of this grant, we were able to work with an inspiring group of queer scholars, filmmakers, and programmers, including Cüneyt Çakırlar, the late Suzy Capó, Rohit Dasgupta, David Eng, Campbell X, Gayatri Gopinath, Catherine Grant, Samar Habib, Jim Hubbard, Stephen Kent Jusick, Kam Wai Kui, Michael Lawrence, Song Hwee Lim, Shamira Meghani, Nguyen Tan Hoang, Sridhar Rangayan, John David Rhodes, B. Ruby Rich, Brian Robinson, Deborah Shaw, Juan Suárez, and Patricia White. The conversations and work that was shared at these symposia was invaluable for revisions to the book. More important, the symposia generated a rare atmosphere of intellectual exchange, antihierarchical thinking, and friendship. We have tried to bring some of that spirit into this volume.

Many filmmakers and artists generously shared their work and their time with us, and we thank Karim Aïnouz, Clara Bodén, Jayan Cherian, Igor Grubić, Maryam Keshavarz, Daniel McIntyre, Mitsuyo Miyazaki, Anurupa Prakash, Noman Robin, Navid Sinaki, and Apichatpong Weerasethakul. We also thank Ollie Charles and Droo Padhiar at Peccadillo Pictures. J. B. Capino, Sarah Hodges, Cynthia Yu-Hua Li, Lin Shu-yi, Karolina Szpyrko, and Marta Wasik were generous with their time, experiences, and personal archives of queer cinema. Caine Youngman and Nick Bullock generously allowed us to reproduce their photographs.

So many people nourished this project along the way by sharing their scholarship, engaging us in intellectually inspiring conversations about queer cinema, and providing moral support when it was needed. They include Dudley Andrew, Augusto Arbizo, Hongwei Bao, Rosa Barotsi, Tonci Kranjcevic Batalic, Ariella Ben-Dov, Shoshana Cohen Ben-Yoar, Mark Betz, Gilberto Blasini, Anthony Bonet, Chris Cagle, Jih-Fei Cheng, Nayda Collazo-Llorens, Jeffery Conway, Nick Davis, Vilma De Gasperin, Cheryl Dunye, Richard Dyer, João Ferreira, Matthew Flanagan, Bishnupriya Ghosh, Shohini Ghosh, Ivan Girina, Bex Harper, Kenneth Harrow, Dan Herbert, Lucas Hilderbrand, Homay King, Eunah Lee, Helen Leung, Bliss Cua Lim, Eng-Beng Lim, Katharina Lindner, Denilson Lopes, Sanda Lwin, Rafael Maniglia, Douglas Martin, Candace Moore, Ros Murray, Matilde Nardelli, Nancy Nicol, David Wallace Pansing, Victor Perkins, Flavio Ribeiro, Connor Ryan, Ingrid Ryberg, Bhaskar Sarkar, Mina Shin, Marc Siegel, Gerald Sim, Tracey Sinclair, Eliza Steinbock, James Tweedie, Patricia Villalobos Echeverría, Michael Wade, Jean Walton, Phyllis Waugh, Thomas Waugh, Cynthia Weber, Helen Wheatley, Jennifer Wild, Josette Wolthuis, and Bryan Wuest.

The anonymous readers offered generous responses to the manuscript, and their advice generated some crucial revisions. Their enthusiasm for the necessity of the project was sustaining, as was the help of Shannon McLaughlin, Brendan O'Neill, and Nicole Rizzuto, who were integral to its intellectual development. Peter Limbrick provided vital support, scholarly and otherwise.

We presented portions of this book in several talks and seminars, and we gratefully acknowledge the hospitality of our hosts: Jackie Stacey, Monica Pearl and the participants at the Manchester University Sexuality Summer School; the Cornerhouse Cinema in Manchester; Elena Gorfinkel, Patrice

Petro, and Tami Williams at University of Wisconsin, Milwaukee; Anna Stenport, Lilya Kaganovsky, Julie Turnock, and Lauren Goodlad at the University of Illinois, Champaign-Urbana; Natalia Brizuela at the University of California, Berkeley; Barbara Mennel and Amie Kreppel at the University of Florida; Jon Binnie and Christian Klesse at the Queer Film Festivals as Activism Conference at Manchester Metropolitan University; Conn Holohan at the National University of Ireland, Galway; Skadi Loist at the University of Hamburg; Stefano Baschiera at Queen's University, Belfast; and Karla Bessa and Marcos Antonio Rocha at the Curto O Gênero Festival in Fortaleza, Brazil. In each of these places, we encountered engaged audiences who posed questions that helped us hone our arguments. We also experienced unprecedented hospitality from the scholars, curators, and students who shared meals with us, showed us bats and alligators, and invited us to dance parties.

Heartfelt thanks go to colleagues and students at our home institutions, who have supported the book in ways big and small: at the University of Warwick, José Arroyo, Charlotte Brunsdon, Stella Bruzzi, Jon Burrows, Howard Chiang, Ilana Emmet, Tracey McVey, Dee Marco, Rachel Moseley, Alastair Phillips, and Charlotte Stevens; at the University of Sussex, Thomas Austin, Anjuli Daskarolis, Sarah Maddox, Sally Munt, Rachel O'Connell, Sue Thornham, and Amelia Wakeford; and at King's College, London, Chris Berry, Sarah Cooper, Victor Fan, Russell Goulbourne, Lawrence Napper, Michelle Pierson, and Sarah Rowe, as well as our incomparable graduate assistant Kelly Samaris.

Thanks also go to the staff at the British Film Institute; the British Library; the Bodleian Library; Jane Lawson at the Vere Harmsworth Library, University of Oxford; the Pacific Film Archive; the University of California, Berkeley; and K. C. Price at Frameline. Everyone at BFI Flare: London LGBT Film Festival welcomed us year after year, and we especially thank Brian Robinson for including us. Cine-City: The Brighton Film Festival provided a fantastic home for several queer film programs, and Nicky Beaumont, Tim Brown, and Frank Gray all helped us to make things happen. The Brighton and Hove City Council let us screen lots of unrated experimental films without batting an eye. The National Theatre espresso bar contributed a good amount of mid-afternoon energy (caffeinated and electric).

Courtney Berger understood the stakes of this project from early on and has made Duke University Press the ideal home for the book. We are grateful for her support, her unfaltering sense of the project's direction, and her careful shepherding of the process. Sandra Korn has smoothed the way at every stage, and our thanks go also to Sara Leone and Susan Deeks for their support and hard work during the book's production.

The discussion of film festival branding in chapter 2 was published as "Queer or Human? Film Festivals, Human Rights and Global Film Culture," *Screen* 56, no. 1 (Spring 2015): 121–32. Part of our discussion of *Undertow* in "Hypotheses on the Queer Middlebrow," in *Middlebrow Cinema,* ed. Sally Faulkner (London: Routledge, 2016), led us to our argument on the film in chapter 1. Small sections of the discussion of Apichatpong in chapter 6 appear in a different version in "Slowness as Intimacy in Apichatpong's *Mekong Hotel*," *In Media Res* (December 2012), http://mediacommons.futureofthebook.org /imr/2012/12/12/slowness-intimacy-apichatpong-s-mekong-hotel. We are grateful to *Screen*, Routledge, and *In Media Res* for the permission to publish these earlier pieces in their present form.

Finally, we thank Lloyd Pratt and Adrian Goycoolea for their boundless patience and goodwill toward a queer collaboration that took over all of our lives. They are our heroines. Without them, you would not be reading these words.

INTRODUCTION
Queer, World, Cinema

Maryam Keshavarz's film *Circumstance* (2011) uses a scene of film consumption to expose the international fault lines of politics and sexuality. The film is set in contemporary Tehran and centers on two young Iranian women, Atafeh and Shireen, who are in love but are compelled to hide their relationship. With their friends Joey and Hossein, the women visit a back-room video store to buy Western movies (figure I.1). They come across Gus Van Sant's *Milk* (2008) and begin to discuss its politics. For Joey and Hossein, *Milk* matters primarily not as a story of gay rights but as a story of political activism and an inspiring example of grassroots organizing for the youth of Iran. Thus, Joey proclaims, "This film is not about fucking. It is about human rights!" to which Atafeh responds, "Fucking is a human right." The question of how to read a film such as *Milk* and what a "gay" film might signify internationally is explicitly played out in this exchange. If fucking is a human right, then queerness takes its place on a certain kind of

Fig. I.1: A video store provides space to discuss human rights in *Circumstance*.

world stage. But is that space of "human rights" the only one in which non-Western queerness can be made palpable in cinema? Or, is it ethnocentric to demand that non-Western queer desire be understood in terms of Western gay identity politics? Is it right, as Joey implies, to appropriate American gay rights struggles for other political causes and in other cultural contexts? These questions that *Circumstance* poses textually have proved equally contentious in the film's critical and scholarly reception. The film has been both welcomed as a positive account of lesbian desire in Iran and critiqued as an Islamophobic product of an ethnocentric Western logic.[1] In both cases, the film cannot help but provoke the question of queers in the world and of cinema's role in queer world politics.

Circumstance anticipates the challenges involved in representing queerness cross-culturally. The film is perhaps unusually aware of the pitfalls of such translocation, since Keshavarz shot in Lebanon with a fake script to protect her cast and crew from authorities. Cinema as an institution and a practice is not a neutral mediator of lesbian representation for Keshavarz but has a quite material politics that is then encoded into the film itself. But this impetus to thematize cinema textually can be seen in a striking number of contemporary queer films that allude meta-textually to cinema's institutional spaces. This recurrence of the social apparatus of cinema as a textual motif alerts us to cinema's unique role in sustaining and making evident queer counterpublics. Video stores, for example, are often posed as sites of cultural intersection, and they figure the messy intermingling of community identity and individual desire across such disparate films as *The Watermelon Woman* (Cheryl Dunye, dir., 1996), *Fire* (Deepa Mehta, dir., 1996), *Nina's Heavenly*

Fig. I.2: A scene of communal film consumption in *The Blossoming of Maximo Oliveros.*

Delights (Pratibha Parmar, dir., 2006), *J'ai tué ma mère/I Killed My Mother* (Xavier Dolan, dir., 2009), and *Parada/The Parade* (Srđjan Dragojević, dir., 2011). Communal film consumption occupies a privileged space of queer longing in *Ang pagdadalaga ni Maximo Oliveros/The Blossoming of Maximo Oliveros* (Auraeus Solito, dir., 2005; figure I.2), *Bu San/Good Bye, Dragon Inn* (Tsai Ming-liang, dir., 2003), *Ni na bian ji dian/What Time Is It There?* (Tsai Ming-liang, dir., 2001), and the short *Last Full Show* (Mark V. Reyes, dir., 2005). The locations in which queer people access cinema have even become the subject of several recent documentaries that have focused on queer film festivals and their audiences, such as *Acting Out: 25 Years of Film and Community in Hamburg* (Cristina Magadlinou, Silvia Torneden, and Ana Grillo, dirs., 2014) and *Queer Artivism* (Masa Zia Lenárdic and Anja Wutej, dirs., 2013). Cinema makes queer spaces possible, but at the same time, what cinema means in these films is rarely prescriptive. It is a space that is never quite resolved or decided, at once local and global, public and private, mainstream and underground; it produces spaces of dominance and resistance.

Of course, for the video store as much as the queer film festival, reception often depends on translation.[2] *Circumstance* features a scene of translation in which, later in the narrative, the four friends are employed to dub *Milk* into Farsi (figure I.3). Watching them record over the original English dialogue, the viewer might be tempted to see the scene as a metaphor for the translatability of sexuality and politics, but the conclusions we are intended to draw are by no means clear. Are these Iranian youths copying American

Fig. I.3: *Circumstance*'s protagonists dub the American film *Milk* into Farsi.

sexual identities and misappropriating a Western politics of coming out? Or are they writing over—more literally, speaking over—that American text, replacing it with an Iranian idiom? Or is the process of translation more ambivalent?[3] Through its dramatization of translation, the film is able to articulate simultaneously not only Iranian versus American cultural politics, but also the women's spoken and unspoken desires and their public and covert identities. The viewer's ability to see the layering of visible identity and hidden meanings simultaneously is enabled by the fact that *Circumstance* itself is a film. The multilayered meanings of this scene are produced by its use of cinematic spaces and forms: the separate production of sound and image in the dubbing scenario creates virtual spaces for the articulation of same-sex desire. The film thus exploits both the theme of transnational cinema and the formal complexities of cinematic narration, and in that exploration it interrogates the stability conventionally granted to distinctions of public and private, straight and queer, Euro-American and Iranian. To understand queerness in the world, then, *Circumstance* tells us that we have to think not just about the representations on-screen but about the cinematic apparatus itself, its mechanisms of articulation, and its modes of transnational circulation.

This book draws critical attention to the place of queer cinema in the world: what might or could the world mean to queers, and what does queer cinema mean for the world? By bringing the reader to the intersection of queer politics and world cinema, it asks both how queer films construct ways of being in the world and what the political value is of the worlds that queer cinema creates. To propose a queer world cinema is to invite trouble.

The combination of terms provokes a series of anxieties about the certainty of knowing and the privilege of position; it raises fears of mistranslation, of neocolonial domination, of homogeneity and the leveling of difference. It suggests the forcing of meaning or the instrumentalization of film aesthetics in support of a limiting identity politics. In researching and presenting this project, we have encountered all of these concerns, often underwritten by a sense among those involved in queer film culture that the terms "world," "queer," and "cinema" should not be spoken together by those sensitive to global politics and cultural difference. Despite our agreement with the political and aesthetic stakes of this reluctance, we are placing these terms together in a risky venture. Our willful evocation of queer/world/cinema insists that queer cinema enables different ways of being in the world and, more than this, that it creates different worlds.

Cinema is always involved in world making, and queerness promises to knock off kilter conventional epistemologies. Thinking queerness together with cinema thus has a potential to reconfigure dominant modes of worlding. We use this term "worlding" to describe queer cinema's ongoing process of constructing worlds, a process that is active, incomplete, and contestatory and that does not presuppose a settled cartography. Any utterance about the world contains a politics of scale that proposes particular parameters for that world, and we insist on de-reifying the taken-for-granted qualities that these parameters often possess. We see film texts as active in this process. Worlding necessarily includes (though is not limited to) the many processes and concepts that have gained traction in thinking about the planet's cultures: globalization, transnational identification, diaspora, postcolonialism, internationalism, ecology, cosmopolitanism, and so on. We argue that queer cinema elaborates new accounts of the world, offering alternatives to embedded capitalist, national, hetero- and homonormative maps; revising the flows and politics of world cinema; and forging dissident scales of affiliation, affection, affect, and form.[4]

We need all three terms—queer, world, and cinema—to make this argument. There is an emerging literature on globality within queer theory that takes on neoliberal economics, the complicity of "queer" in homonationalism and globalization, and the limitations of Western models of LGBT identity to engage the gendered and sexual life worlds of the global South. This scholarship is important to our project, but it misses what is unique about cinema and its ability to nourish queer spaces that are not reducible to capital, both textually and institutionally. Similarly, a critical awareness of the global frame has challenged and revised the traditional rubrics of film studies, inflecting national, generic, and industrial studies with categories such as the transnational, diasporic, the exilic, and migrant. However, these studies too often have been partitioned away from the innovations of queer theory, leaving an overly hetero account of the shapes of the cinematic world. Finally, scholarship on queer cinema forms a crucial basis for our analysis, from pathbreaking studies of lesbian and gay representation to criticism of the New Queer Cinema (NQC), queer experimental film, film festivals, and more. We draw widely on this archive, but despite significant studies of national and regional cinema, queer film studies has yet to fully engage the challenges of the global. These three foundational concepts—queer, world, and cinema—provide theoretical pathways into our argument. Each term is contested, and when brought together they prompt us to ask what kinds of global communities are produced (or precluded) by queer film consumption and how presiding visions of the global depend on the inclusion or exclusion of queer lives. In this introduction, we map the stakes, for us, of queer cinema in the world.

What's Queer about Cinema?

Cinema might appear more stable as a concept than either queer or world, but this book is as much a work of film theory as of queer critique, and the meanings of cinema cannot be taken for granted. The queer worlds we explore are made available through cinema's technologies, institutional practices, and aesthetic forms, which together animate spaces, affective registers, temporalities, pleasures, and instabilities unique to the cinematic sensorium. It is crucial to affirm that cinema is not simply a neutral host for LGBT representations but is, rather, a queerly inflected medium. To adapt Jasbir Puar's terminology, we understand cinema as a queer assemblage.[5]

Part of what makes popular cinema popular is the queer pleasures of spectatorship. The ease with which audiences identify and desire across expected lines of gender is what gives classical Hollywood, for example, its seductive and transgressive appeal.[6] We can develop Alexander Doty's account of queer pleasures in classical cinema if we think about how Hollywood's narration of point of view asks all spectators to adopt the perspectives of various and often incommensurate personae within even the same scene. Few audience members are allowed a perfectly reflective or narcissistic relationship to the bodies on-screen. In fact, one of the infamous debates of canonical feminist film theory surrounds Laura Mulvey's use of the word "transvestite" to describe how Hollywood films demand that a female spectator oscillate her identification, often adopting a position in discourse aligned with male agency and the male gaze.[7] While these debates were sometimes accused of heterocentrism, they nonetheless point to how the basic operation of the Hollywood text requires a certain gender mobility.[8] If these ambidextrous affinities render all spectatorship potentially queer, cinematic traditions have developed variegated ways to play with this capacity. Of course, mainstream cinemas have means of damping down queer identificatory structures via the gaze, especially Hollywood itself (as Mulvey has taught us), but as with feminist film theory's critique of the gendered gaze, the site of ideological struggle is the structure of the image rather than simply its content. We see this tension in the films of Ferzan Özpetek: both *Hamam/Steam: The Turkish Bath* (1997) and *Mine Vaganti/Loose Cannons* (2010) play with the gendered ambiguity of the desiring gaze, shuttling between same-sex and opposite-sex identifications.

The dynamism of the cinematic image pushes against the reification of meaning, as it keeps the signifier in motion, never fixing terms of relationality. Maria San Filippo has argued for "the bisexual space of cinema" as a potentiality, constituted by "textual *sites* (spatio-temporal locations) and spectatorial *sights* (ways of seeing) that indicate how sexuality as well as gender is irreducible to and always already in excess of dominant culture's monosexual, heterocentrist paradigm."[9] Not all films activate bisexual space, but cinema's sensory apparatus constantly alludes to its potential. This dynamic spatiality pushes against normative sexualities and genders but also against the sedimented systems of the globalized world. For instance, the Egyptian filmmaker Youssef Chahine links sexuality, critiques of globalization, and film aesthetics in an interview. When Joseph Massad asks Chahine how he interrelates his aesthetic sense with his political message, Chahine responds that politics are inevitable in cinema. After critiquing the inequalities of the supposed open market of globalization, he notes that what is happening in the world "even influences your sex life; what happens in bed depends upon what is happening in politics."[10] Or, as Benigno Sánchez-Eppler and Cindy Patton put it, "Sexuality is intimately and immediately felt, but publicly and internationally described and mediated."[11] Politics infuses sex, and cinema is the place where this intertwining of the intimate and the public can be visibly registered. Cinema does not merely offer a convenient institutional space of distribution and exhibition in LGBT film festivals and cosmopolitan art houses. Rather, it produces queer identification, desire, and figurability as a constituent feature of the medium.

It is important to stipulate this queer stratum of the cinematic so that when we consider how to define queer cinema, we are not tempted merely to instrumentalize identities or representational content. Corralling a category of "queer cinema" is tricky. Some scholars have found it crucial to distinguish an identitarian strand of lesbian and gay cinema from a more radical (or at least anti-identitarian) queer practice.[12] We might define queer films in this way, or with reference to queer directors, or again as those films viewed by queer audiences. But who is excluded when these logics are imposed as the prerequisite for defining queer cinema? Each of these common-sense approaches is undone by its insistent privileging of Western or other dominant practices of cinema. Thus, filmmakers outside the West may not be "out" as gay and, indeed, may not find the rhetoric of visibility useful or relevant for their sense of self. Similarly, any presumption of what a queer audience might look like is often underwritten by insidious cultural assumptions. Madhava Prasad writes that whereas reception studies see Western spectators as complex and autonomous in their interpretations of texts, ethnographic studies understand non-Western spectators as reading only and exactly what the text directly presents.[13] This is equally a problem for queer world cinema, which is too rarely granted complexity in its reception contexts.

Sometimes films are queer in certain contexts and not in others. Perhaps because of our interest in these questions of knowledge (How do we know queer cinema when we see it? Will we always recognize queer films as queer?), we are alert to those moments in which foreign films are claimed as queer or imagined as not queer. Many of the films canonized as contemporary world cinema engage with queer issues or feature queer characters, but they are infrequently analyzed by queer film studies or recognized by their straight advocates as queer endeavors. For example, within Thailand Apichatpong Weerasethakul is regarded as gay, and his artistic practice is understood as queer. However, he has been embraced in the West by mainstream critics and proponents of art cinema as an international auteur.[14] His films are more likely to be screened in world cinema venues (Cannes, Venice, Berlin, New York's Museum of Modern Art) than in LGBT film festivals. Similarly, some critics have accused the Taiwanese director Tsai Ming-liang of overusing sexually ambiguous characters as a way to cater to foreign audiences, whereas recent scholarship has engaged with the complexity of his affiliations to queerness, sexual acts, and film style.[15] As Fran Martin puts it, "His films' obsessive and ultimately denaturalizing focus on sexual behaviours rather than sexual identities does seem to preclude a reading of his cinema as straightforwardly 'gay' in the sense of sexual identity politics."[16] So while it is clear that the remit of queer film must be expanded, how to

Fig. I.4: Same-sex intimacy is visible in classic Hindi films such as *Razia Sultan*.

do this is fraught with epistemological instabilities that are as geopolitical as they are sociological.

From its start, queer film studies has included those seemingly straight films that LGBT audiences have made indelibly queer. In fact, one well-known anthology—*Queer Cinema: The Film Reader*—is largely concerned with reception issues.[17] For scholars of Indian cinema such as Rajinder Dudrah and Gayatri Gopinath, popular Hindi films often flaunt homosocial bonds in ways that invite re-coding by audiences looking for same-sex intimacies on-screen (e.g., *Sholay* [Ramesh Sippy, dir., 1975], *Pakeezah* [Kamal Amrohi, dir., 1972]).[18] The only slightly submerged networks of forbidden desire in films such as *Mughal-e-Azam* (K. Asif, dir., 1960) and *Razia Sultan* (Kamal Amrohi, dir., 1983; figure I.4) become the means by which queer audiences have adopted mainstream cinema as their own. Stanley Kwan similarly mines the history of popular Chinese cinema for queer subtexts and pleasures in his documentary *Yang ± Yin: Gender in Chinese Cinema* (1996). More recently, in *Pop!* (2012), the Iranian artist Navid Sinaki deploys found footage from prerevolutionary popular Persian cinema to reveal a persistence of alternate desires in Iranian culture. This re-coding of "straight" films as queer is not simply a private practice with a discrete semiotics: queer appropriation contaminates a wider cultural perception of popular cinema. Queer film criticism has always had to address the question of how to define the boundaries of queerness across a perplexing multitude of texts and audiences.

Yet another approach to queer film methodology is a textual focus that defines queer films as those that depict queer people diegetically. Although

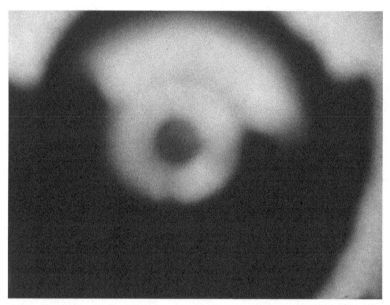

Fig. 1.5: In *Kajitu*, shooting through a glass apple produces strikingly graphic abstract images.

we will be closely concerned with all manner of queer figures and representations, a definition that demands representations of queers excludes artists who work in other registers and forecloses on the queerly expressive potential of cinematic sounds and images. For instance, an experimental film such as *Kajitu/Some Days Ago* (Nakamura Takehiro, 2008) is largely abstract in its images, but by shooting through a glass ball it enables the spectator to see the queer potential of the lens to transfigure nature by warping normative regimes of visuality (figure I.5). Film scholars are alive to the queer potential of abstraction. Juan Suárez, for example, persuasively writes on queer textures, grain, and glitter in the American underground films of Jack Smith, as well as the political radicality of color-saturated tropicalist style in the work of the Brazilian artist Hélio Oiticica.[19] In a different vein, Song Hwee Lim analyzes Tsai Ming-liang's "undoing of anthropomorphic realism, which partly explains why his representations (of queer sexuality, for example) are not always amenable to identity politics." For Lim, Tsai's characteristic art-cinematic quality of temporal drift sustains a queer representational logic found as much in the relationship of stillness to movement as it is in gay characters.[20] These examples illustrate the significance of queer abstraction in histories of art cinema and the avant-garde, but they also insist on the limits of a politics of representation and on queer cinema's participation in what Rey Chow terms "the radical implications of cinema's interruption of the human as such."[21]

A final possibility for definition lies in thinking queer cinema in terms of its staging of sexuality, gendered embodiment, and nonheteronormative sex. Teresa de Lauretis's memorable attempt to define queer textuality insists that queerness inheres in a formal disruption of referentiality at the level of the signifier and, further, that "a queer text carries the inscription of sexuality as something more than sex."[22] De Lauretis is attempting to balance a semiotic account of queerness's anti-normative potential that would focus on its decentering of dominant regimes of representation with an anxiety that such abstraction might lose sight of a crucial link to dissident sexuality. Her "something more" speaks to feminist theory's account of cinema as an apparatus of desire, endlessly reconstituting what Jacqueline Rose called sexuality in the field of vision. Cinematic images of desiring bodies cannot be thought without attention to this apparatus. Queer film theory is always a feminist project for us, and this book maintains a deep investment in cinema as a principal technology of gender and sexuality. De Lauretis's use of the word "sex" here speaks at once of sex acts and of a resistance to the binary of sexual difference; hence, it may include queer genders, such as genderqueer and trans experience. Limiting our focus to sex acts as a necessary quality of textual queerness, de Lauretis allows us to address a crucial tension that is revealed when we propose sex as a determining facet of queer cinema.

On the one hand, representation of same-sex or other dissident sex acts is for many spectators a defining pleasure of queer cinema. The gay Filipino melodrama *Walang Kawala/No Way Out* (Joel Lamangan, dir., 2008), for instance, quite self-consciously interrupts its narrative for a slow-motion montage in flashback of its central couple having sex. That sex sells is not exactly news, but the organization of cinema's sexual pleasures can help us understand the affective force of queer film cultures. Deborah Shaw has pointed out that sometimes we go to movies because we really want to see two girls kissing, and this deceptively simple idea discloses the potential of the erotic to remake the cinematic desire machine.[23] A film such as *The Hunger* (Tony Scott, dir., 1983) may not seem queer in the way de Lauretis intends, but its iconic sex scene circulates in the lesbian cultural imaginary in ways that go beyond the limits of the film's narrative. Its queer fandom is well documented.[24] More recently, Campbell X's *Stud Life* (2012) includes scenes of lesbian sex that challenge cinematic conventions of gender expression and embodiment. In their eroticized depiction of the top and bottom

Fig. I.6: *Stud Life*'s sex scenes illustrate the cinematic potential of showing sex.

dynamic and BDSM power exchange, these scenes assert the political necessity of queer monstration. Here, the political aim of extending representation beyond mainstream fantasies about white femme lesbians is achieved in and through sex acts: cinema's ability to *show* sex tethers the voyeuristic pleasures of erotic spectacle to the counterpublic logic of visibility. The titular stud is butch, black, kinky, and located not in a bourgeois fantasy space but in working-class London. As in the same director's erotic short *Fem* (2007), *Stud Life*'s camera appears most confident and comfortable when it displays the femme body and embodies the butch gaze. Both films succeed in their most sexually explicit sequences because they make the viewer re-see the black lesbian body (figure I.6).

On the other hand, the demand that queer films depict sex acts also risks endorsing a Western cultural privileging of visibility and publicness. This impetus can be linked to neocolonial representational impulses that imperiously call for the exposure of the ethnic other as a queer body open to colonization by the West. Non-Western or nontraditional sexualities may not always fare well when viewed through a Western lens of visibility. Queer film scholarship has always been attentive to practices of not showing, from Patricia White's writing on invisibility to Catherine Grant's reading of the Argentine director Lucrecia Martel's *La mujer sin cabeza/The Headless Woman* (2008), which reveals the film's queerness not in any overt visioning of sex but, instead, in its framing and looking relations.[25] Ann Cvetkovich outlines the geopolitics

Fig. I.7: *Girlfriend, Boyfriend* couples queer intimacy to political rebellion.

of this issue, stating that "it has been extremely important for queer studies to move across historical and geographic boundaries, away from the recent history of gay and lesbian identities and communities in the Western metropolis. In such contexts, what counts as (homo)sexuality is unpredictable and requires new vocabularies; affect may be present when overt forms of sexuality are not."[26] As an attempt to refute a Western optical regime, Cvetkovich's shift to affect proves crucial when framing queer cinema globally.

To illustrate this point, consider the Taiwanese historical drama *Girlfriend, Boyfriend* (Yang Ya-che, dir., 2012), in which gay desires between two school friends are registered insistently but not explicitly alongside a political narrative of student protest. The film is set in 1985, when Taiwan is under martial law, and the draconian discipline of the school allegorizes the country's repressive polity. Rebellious Aaron has had his head shaved as punishment for speaking out, locating bodily shame as a locus of political control. In one scene, Aaron and his friend Liam sit together intimately, touching arms, while kids dance with sparklers behind them. Aaron says, "One person dancing alone is a rebellion, but if the whole school dances together, that's the will of the people." He draws a fake tattoo on Liam's arm, writing, "We are waves welling up from the same ocean." Queer intimacies are here linked to rebellious Taiwanese nationalism, and both a political sense of solidarity and a queer desire are written—literally—on the body. The moment is replete with affect, but its desire will not turn into visible sex. Instead, queer revolutionary hope and the nostalgic evocation of teenage desires flow into a radical narrative of Taiwanese history, replete with the potential and losses of the democracy movement (figure I.7).

Girlfriend, Boyfriend exemplifies a queer affective structure in which cinema theorizes a relationship between spectator and screen, between the individual and the collective, or, in other words, between subjectivity and historical change. Queer cinematic affect can emerge in the political *jouissance* of capturing how non-normative sex feels, but it can equally harness the life worlds of queer feelings whose relationship to the body and its acts travel along other pathways. There is thus a structuring tension in thinking queer world cinema between a reticence to reify certain regimes of sexual representation and the counter impulse to value cinema's monstrative potential to show queer sex. If this tension is to be productive, we may need to expand de Lauretis's terms and think of sexuality in queer cinema as potentially more than, less than, or sometimes exactly coterminous with sex.

If queer cinema cannot depend on queer characters, directors, representations, or audiences, how can it be specified? We return to Eve Kosofsky Sedgwick's universalizing and minoritizing discourses to think through the trouble with defining queer cinema.[27] A universalizing discourse takes as axiomatic that it is helpful to think universally; that understanding the systems, structures, and discourses of "queer cinema" is a necessary first step for any critical analysis. In this reading, just as it would be restrictive to view world cinema as simply the accretion of films from different countries, with no regard for circuits and systems of power, it is similarly limiting to think queer cinema as merely a collection of queer-oriented texts. This is precisely the trap set by the questions of category outlined earlier. However, a minoritizing discourse reminds us of the need for specificity. Too often, universalizing concepts reiterate dominant power structures, whether of gay male culture, mainstream taste categories, or neo-imperialism. Minoritizing discourse insists on both the cultural heterogeneity and the radical impulses of LGBT cultures, redirecting research away from what is already familiar. Just as Sedgwick refuses to choose between these modes of thought, we resist taxonomizing logics that are always at once too broad and too narrow.

In place of a neat definition of queer cinema, we propose a radically promiscuous approach, and we insist that our polemic can be found in the logic of a capacious corpus. We are unwilling to relinquish the category of queer to charges that openness equals conceptual looseness and a dissipation of power. In fact, we believe that capaciousness is necessary so as not to determine in advance what kinds of films, modes of production, and reception might qualify as queer or do queer work in the world. Thus, this book analyzes unpredictable intersections of queer plus cinema plus world, jostling side by side feminist videos, trashy heist movies, modernist art films, and homophobic melodramas. We maintain a radical openness on the question of what queer films might look like and where we might find them. Such an openness makes several related political claims:

- It understands the force of queerness as active across the field of cinema, so it refuses to draw bright lines between LGBT films and queer films or between positive and negative representations of queer living, or to stipulate particular modes of identification for filmmakers.
- It contains a theory of what constitutes the cinematic: we acknowledge how diffuse the cinematic has become but insist on its generative potential across platforms, viewing protocols, and institutional contexts. We do not limit queer cinema to traditional theatrical settings or to commercial production.
- It demands that we locate queerness not only in formally transgressive films (which privilege certain culturally dominant canons of world cinema) but equally in popular, debased, and generic forms.
- Conversely, it leaves open the possibility that experimental and non-representational image practices speak in politically coherent ways and offer socially relevant insight to the lives of queer people.
- It draws on queer theory but does not limit queer cinema to those filmmakers with access to or investment in Western theories of sexuality and gender.
- It takes part in an anti-imperialist stance that de-privileges the Western queer film canon and works to upend Eurocentric ways of thinking cinema.
- It resists hierarchies of production value, taking seriously cheaply made films and the political economy of perpetually minoritized audiences. Many of the films we discuss escape the conventional tripartite divisions of First, Second, and Third Cinemas and thus offer important correctives to the constitution of contemporary world cinema.
- It approaches the cinema image as meaning in motion and thus recognizes an inherent semantic instability in even the most overt representations of sex.

In constructing our corpus, then, we asked an apparently simple question: where in the world is queer cinema? We find the locations of queer cinema to be particularly fruitful sites of negotiation: since there is little infrastructure devoted exclusively to the exhibition of queer film or media, a provisional inventory of the spaces—whether bricks and mortar or imagined communities—in which queer cinema happens can help elucidate the existence of queer cinema in the world. Queer cinema is conventionally found at the film festival or in art-house theaters, but it is also to be found in mainstream theaters and in local language-based markets. Its history includes the community center, the porn theater, and the lesbian potluck. Queer cinema is certainly to be found in the video store, which Lucas Hilderbrand has argued forms both an archive and an affective community, constituted in the degradations of tapes paused and rewound hundreds of times.[28] It is found in bootlegging and tape-sharing communities; on bit torrent sites; in pirated video CDs in China; in underground DVD markets in Iran and Egypt; among gray-market distributors; in queer movie clubs in Croatia organized on Facebook; and at market stalls in Nigeria, Mexico, and Vietnam. It is found through specialist distributors such as Peccadillo and TLA Video; and in video-on-demand (VOD) sites targeted to queer and diasporic audiences. Finally, queer cinema flourishes on social media, on video-sharing sites such as YouTube and Vimeo.

The online economy of queer cinema is heterogeneous. YouTube hosts serious transnational web series such as *The Pearl of Africa* (Johnny von Wallström, dir., 2014), a Swedish documentary about the Ugandan trans activist Cleopatra Kombugu, but it is, of course, also the home of fan-made supercuts of same-sex kisses in Thai movies and off-air recordings of older gay movies such as Lino Brocka's *Macho Dancer* (1988). Many of the popular South Asian and Southeast Asian films we analyze are more easily accessed on YouTube or through file-sharing sites than on DVD. The social media film distribution company Distrify illustrates how the industry is catching up with online circulation, but it also provides telling insights into how queer cinema is moving in the world. Embedded in Facebook or on LGBT websites, Distrify enables international audiences to share links, view trailers, stream entire films, and access local cinema listings. Films can be rented in 150 countries, paid for in twenty-three currencies, and viewed in eight languages. The company tracks clicks as a way to broker distribution deals and cites the views of Nigerian films by Nigerian diasporic audiences as an example of a demographic it learned about through this kind of analysis.[29] Even as the first wave of queer VOD, such as Busk, disappears, new models of international mobility are emerging.

By broadening the field of inquiry in this way, we aim to respond to the call of many film scholars, who ask, as Ramon Lobato puts it, "Where is contemporary cinema located, and how is it accessed?"[30] Lobato himself begins to answer that question by arguing that "formal theatrical exhibition is no longer the epicenter of cinema culture."[31] Instead, he argues for our attention to be turned to the unregulated, ungoverned, and largely unstudied means by which films travel to and among viewers. Lobato contends that studying world cinema requires focusing on "informal distribution," which includes pirating, covert file sharing, bootlegging, gray-market trading, and so on. When these practices are seen together as an informal economy of film consumption, they constitute neither a niche nor a marginal market. Instead, the informal economy is "the key driver of distribution on a global scale" and must be central to the study of cinema.[32] If, as Lobato argues, "informal circulation has not shown up in our data sets and research frameworks because they have been calibrated in a way that renders these movements invisible," then we might say that the industrial film historian has been doubly blinded to queer cinema (and its audiences). This is the case, first, because queer cinema has been long excised from official records and public exhibition (due to the application of obscenity standards and other institutions of homophobia), and second, because it has been largely consumed informally via secret networks, delivered in plain envelopes and shared through bootlegging networks.[33]

It is helpful, then, to consider alongside queer cinema's many material and virtual spaces the equally revealing list of some of the places where queer cinema is not. Despite the proliferation of screens (on trains, in hospital rooms, on the street) characteristic of the contemporary media landscape, we rarely see queer images in these public spaces. In many locations, state censorship means that cinemas, public libraries, and online services are allowed no LGBT content. Queer films may be sequestered in video stores and DVD stalls, available only to those who ask the right questions. They may be categorized with porn in online rental sites, hidden behind paywalls or age restrictions. Google's auto-fill feature blacklists many gay-oriented search terms, making queer searching incrementally more difficult. Some cell phone companies block LGBT sites, locking down the queer portions of the web. Areas that are underserved by digital projection or without high-speed Internet connections may lack access even to popularly circulating gay movies.

Although the Internet has expanded the media texts available to many people, including those living in repressive regimes, we have been careful to recognize how a Western middle-class sense of availability can shape the terms of access. Even Lobato cautions against privileging "internet users and patterns of activity most commonly found in the USA and other first world nations."[34] Daniel Herbert writes, "If we take it that 'film' is a particular technology for the capture and presentation of moving images, and that 'cinema' more broadly describes the social arrangements through which moving images are produced, circulated, and consumed, then over the last several decades, cinema has not 'died' but rather proliferated and transformed."[35] Queer cinema by necessity has been at the forefront of this transformation, but it is also imperiled by institutionalized and often state-sanctioned homophobia. For instance, the paucity of committed queer film archives and university collections renders the preservation and circulation of queer cinema precarious. The explosion of political spaces online must be weighed against the seemingly boundless encroachment of surveillance and against the covert degradation of the public sphere in its migration to corporatized social media platforms.

Queerness is thus complexly embedded in the spaces of world cinema, and, we propose, it plays an intrinsic part in its development. We primarily focus on contemporary queer cinema, from the 1990s onward, a choice that enables us to consider closely the historical situation of globalization and the forms of worldliness that have emerged in this period. Yet we want to complicate a notion of queer cinema that considers only its most recent manifestations, with Barbara Mennel contextualizing the current "explosion" of queer cinema historically.[36] There is a danger in supposing that queer cinema goes global only in the contemporary era, leaving the rest of the world presumptively heterosexual until the effects of Western-style globalization enable a queer cultural discourse. By contrast, our account of cinema as an inherently queer medium asks readers to think about film history as always already queer. We turn to key international queer filmmakers, theorists, and texts from earlier eras to demonstrate how much contemporary world cinema builds on the queer histories embedded in the medium. Even the most conventional histories of cinema are replete with queers, from F. W. Murnau and Rainer Werner Fassbinder to Dorothy Arzner and Lucrecia Martel. Thus, we consider Sergei Eisenstein, Pier Paolo Pasolini, and Toshio Matsumoto to be important interlocutors from the Soviet Union, Italy, and Japan, respectively, as are groundbreaking queer-themed films such as *Ba wang bie ji/Farewell My Concubine* (Chen Kaige, dir., 1993) from China and *La Cruel Martina/The Cruel Martina* (Juan Miranda, dir., 1989) from Bolivia.

So in the same way that Dipesh Chakrabarty's *Provincializing Europe* asks readers to reorient their understanding of the world without reference to Europe as a center, we reframe world cinema both without privileging Europe and without a presumption of heterosexuality as a determinant of the cinematic experience.[37] *Queer Cinema in the World* argues that cinema has always been queer and thus that the worlds made by cinema have always been queer worlds. What would film history look like if we oriented ourselves to films such as *Fukujusô/Pheasant Eyes* (Jirô Kawate, dir., 1935), a Japanese silent film about same-sex desire between two sisters-in-law? Romit Dasgupta points out the way in which this film prefigures Deepa Mehta's *Fire*, locating lesbian desire in a domestic setting and turning to familial intimacies as a place where women might find fulfillment beyond the strictures of marriage.[38] The film was based on a story written by Nobuko Yoshiya, who lived with her female partner, and yet even recently her family did not agree to reprint her work in a lesbian collection. Both textually and extratextually, *Pheasant Eyes* creates queer spaces, but the heteronormatizing institutions of family and film historiography constantly threaten its visibility. Across both time and space, queer narratives can create contiguities and affinities; it requires renewed attention to see the shapes of this queer cinematic world.

Returning to the present, we argue that queer cinema makes new forms of worldliness visible, thinkable, and malleable. The spectacular growth of queer filmmaking and queer film consumption around the world in the mid-1990s occurred in parallel with the supposed death of cinema. Far from being exhausted, cinema has emerged as a privileged platform for articulating queer experiences of and responses to globalization. An evocative example of queer cinema's symbolic labor in the world can be found among the activities LGBT activists in Indonesia created to observe the International Day against Homophobia (IDAHO) in 2008. Alongside public discussion, street actions, and a radio appearance, the group People like Us—Satu Hati (PLUSH) took an ambulant medical clinic to Pantai Sundak, a village on the south coast of Java. As the Indonesian LGBT network reported, "The group went there together with a medical clinic team while distributing rice, milk powder, second-hand clothes and school supplies. They staged a playback show and even screened the film *Iron Ladies* as an educational tool. The villagers were delighted and became sensitized of LGBT issues along the way."[39] *Satree lek/The Iron Ladies* (Yongyoot Thongkongtoon, dir., 2000) will be discussed in chapter 4, but what stands out for us here is both the use of a *Thai* popular trans sports movie in *Indonesia* as part of a *globalized* anti-homophobia campaign, and the apparently disjunctive combination of cinema with urgent medical needs in a location that is ill served by the state. Of course, as we have seen, such global transits are not always positive: the worldliness of cinematic space is highly contested and frequently instrumentalized for reactionary politics—but never with any completeness. So although we maintain some cynicism toward world cinema as a category, we are reluctant to dismiss it as a neoliberal frenemy.

What is so curious about queer global film culture is the persistence of the *idea* of cinema as an effective means of worlding and of participating in the world politically. In an era in which many take instant digital interconnectivity for granted, why is this old medium still understood as a key means of worlding, of connecting to global politics, and of experiencing the category of the human? Why do queers still go to movies? Cinema persists in queer culture as a site of political ferment, a volatile public stage on which protest can be expressed and ideas disseminated. It also provides spaces in which to nourish more diffuse experiences of affinity, belonging, and intimacy, where spectatorship provokes the formation of unexpected collisions and coalitions. We might consider *Hei yan quan/I Don't Want to Sleep Alone* (Tsai Ming-liang, dir., 2006), where intersecting narratives of bisexual longing and belonging fend off the otherwise precarious realities of globalization, immigrant labor, and transnational identities in contemporary Malaysia. It is the queerness of these connections that makes the terms of intimacy and the exigencies of world politics speak to one other. Or we could point to a popular film such as *Memento Mori* (Kim Tae-yong and Min Kyu-dong, dirs., 1999), which transforms the key generic elements of the globally popular East Asian horror film (longing, dystopic melancholy, surreal but extreme violence) into lesbian drama, making the genre suddenly seem inseparable from same-sex desire. The vitality of these conversations demonstrates that cinema remains a necessary instrument for seeing the world differently and also for articulating different worlds.

In the World

Inherent in our project is a complex and delicate mapping of what queerness signifies—for cinema and for international public cultures more broadly. The term has been sometimes embraced but equally often contested by activists around the world. For instance, Robert Kulpa, Joanna Mizielińska, and Agata Stasińska have argued that Western-style queer theory has a neo-imperialist quality that limits understandings of radical practice in Poland. Still, they end by insisting, "We are queer. Locally."[40] Tracing this conflicted relationship to "queer" in every community in the world is impossible, but we are closely attentive to the ways in which the term resonates, or is adapted, transformed, or repudiated altogether, in different localities and cultural contexts. It is widely used in untranslated English form—for instance in Queer Lisboa, the Lisbon film festival, and in Hong Kong, where the popular website Queer Sisters advocates for lesbians. We can hear it in local vernaculars, too: in Turkey, "queer" becomes *kuir*, and in mainland China, it is transliterated into *ku'er* (酷儿). In Taiwan and Hong Kong, a more common translation of queer is 酷異, meaning cool and different.[41] Each of these apparently simple translations conceals a complex labor of appropriation, adaptation, and transformation.

To return to Eastern Europe, we can see two politically different approaches in art and activist culture. Zvonimir Dobrovic, former head of the Queer Zagreb film festival sees queer as directly translatable, arguing that the festival "made queer an accepted term in Croatia."[42] By contrast, the organizers of the Queer Beograd Festival both use and transform the term, turning the English "queer" into the Serbian *kvar*:

> In Serbian there is no word that means queer, no way to say what we mean about queer being more than LGBT equality. For us queer means radical, inclusive, connecting to all kinds of politics and being creative about how we live in this world. So our new festival is called "Kvar," a technical term literally translating to mean "a malfunction in a machine," because in this world of capitalism, nationalism, racism, militarism, sexism and homophobia, we want to celebrate ourselves as a malfunction in this machine.[43]

At stake for each is a politics of the national that implicitly theorizes the relationship of the nation to the world. Dobrovic's sense of Croatia joining a preexisting and progressive world of queers (via the film festival) is complicated by the Belgrade collective's writing of local, post-Yugoslav, antinationalist, and antiglobalization politics into the project of queer destabilization. The vernaculars of the word "queer" thus recursively stage precisely the issues we see as animating our project: the word speaks to the radical potential and internationalist impulses, as well as to the geopolitical hierarchies and imperialist forces, bound up in world cinema's spaces.

A central goal of *Queer Cinema in the World* is simultaneously to take care when deploying the word "queer" politically and not to dodge the more promiscuous applications of that label. We stand with those activists and theorists who resist efforts to impose Western models of gender and sexual life on communities and people who define themselves otherwise. At the same time, we have reservations about seemingly anti-imperialist approaches that can foreclose on queer discursive space and thus inadvertently deem the whole world always already straight.[44] It is crucial to maintain both modes of critique, as the world is always in the process of being made. Over-specifying what counts as queer can place an unfair burden on those living in non-heterosexual and gender-dissident formations, and our use of the term is self-consciously open-ended. Puar posits queerness as a potential counterforce to the liberal discourses of the global, insisting that "queerness irreverently challenges a linear mode of conduction and transmission: there is no exact recipe for a queer endeavor, no a priori system that taxonomizes the linkages, disruptions, and contradictions into a tidy vessel."[45] Our use of queer as a conceptual rubric is thus intended as a way into a volatile discursive field rather than as an a priori claim. To ask whether globalization enables the queer to emerge as a universal figure or whether queer films can be found in every national cinema is, we consider, a flawed approach that begs a series of questions about sexuality, gender, and the spaces of the world.

At the start of the article "In Search of Sensibilities: The International Face of Gays on Film," published in the gay magazine *Manifest* in 1983, Penni Kimmel describes an occupational hazard of being a film critic: "Film reviewers are notoriously greedy. Gay film reviewers . . . can get positively grabby."[46] Across the article, Kimmel looks for what she sees as "a definite gay sensibility" in many of the films shown at that year's San Francisco International Film Festival, but she does so while mocking her own impulses as a Western critic trying to establish that queer film is in the world. "Was there enough gay sensibility to be found in the celluloid of Upper Volta?" she writes. "Would lesbian love float across the [Iron] Curtain or over the [Berlin] Wall?"[47] What does count as gay for Kimmel is surprisingly heterogeneous: a documentary on Montgomery Clift, a film about child abuse, a docudrama on sexually transmitted diseases that features naked men. She is also attuned to how the spaces created by the film festival's events amend and extend the political life of these films and the project of world cinema. For example, Harry Belafonte's autobiographical film triggered a discussion of the "persecution of gays in Cuba" to which the neither Cuban nor queer (though Caribbean and gay-allied) Belafonte replied, "All art is political. People are responsible for each other; we must protect the rights of all human beings. . . . The question is how do you politically use the art?" In that context, Kimmel notes distinctions between engaged films that enable a queer reading and more directly political films that banish "homophilia" as if homosexuality were merely "a sophisticated peacetime luxury." This snapshot of a Western critic's "world cruise for films to jolt the rods and the cones and the grey matter and still leave me feeling wonderful with the world" suggests how the search for queer films has often been a means of mapping the world.

We might connect Kimmel's grabbiness to an imperialist or neocolonial project, one that appropriates difference as yet another facet of its own methodological self-awareness. A contemporary version of this might be the encyclopedic volume *L'homosexualité au cinéma* by Didier Roth-Bettoni, which attempts to "englobe" a hitherto uncollected global history of more than five thousand LGBT films from all continents. This ambitious project nonetheless falls into some neocolonial traps when speaking of the naiveté of African films or the "obvious" taboo of homosexuality in the Arab world.[48] However, we could equally see Kimmel's discussion as presaging more politically engaged readings of world cinema. For instance, Gopinath's "scavenger" approach emulates a diasporic spectator who crosses geopolitical and historical boundaries in reading non-normative desires on-screen. Gopinath's technique itself builds on another version of queer appropriation—that of Patricia White's "retrospectatorship"—which reminds us that appropriation has been a necessary practice for queers that reaches not only to other parts of the world but also across time.[49]

A cliché retold about the 1990s model of queer cultural studies is that as a hermeneutic, it overly appropriated texts, objects, attitudes, and historical figures to queer. It was too grabby. These seemingly overeager appropriative acts defined the verb "to queer." Today in the humanities, a backlash has taken hold, and promiscuous queering can sometimes be seen as old-fashioned and misguided. Indeed, the backlash has succeeded in suggesting that all queer critical practices are inflected with a looseness of definition and critical object. In fact, these queer perspectives are now often marginalized by an undue burden of proof, which seems indirectly to reinforce the always already heterosexual imperatives of dominant descriptions of world history. Heterosexual patriarchy is a world system that naturalizes its own dominance and far-reaching proliferation as a theory of human life.[50] When we look back to the 1990s, the appropriation of the word "nation" by "queer nation" was not a nationalist or homonationalist endeavor. It was an aggressive re-coding strategy based on the sheer impossibility of imagining a world in which queerness could be a culturally productive force. As Sarah Schulman reminds us, it brought together an otherwise impossible pairing of words.[51]

In writing this book, we have resisted thinking that heterogeneity—or bringing together impossible terms—is a problem. We are not ready to give up on the possibility of reimagining a world that would be useful to more than just a tiny percentage of its inhabitants. We believe that non-Western cinemas of sexual and gender dissidence may be one place from which that world can be reimagined. Borrowing from Ernst Bloch, we replace the homogenous vision of the "crackless world picture" with the "never closed" utopian impulse that "breaks into life when the varnish cracks."[52] We remain politically committed to resisting the lure of totalities while refusing to reduce queer cultural practices to minoritized particularity.

One of the challenges of writing the book has been balancing the grabby tendency of the (usually) Western critic while not giving up on the world. On the one hand, non-Western filmmakers offer revised definitions of the world, distinctly different from either those of world cinema studies or those of commodity capitalism in the global North. But on the other hand, non-Western texts can warn of the dangers of grabbiness—and that critique needs also to be showcased. In commodity globalism, a plethora of choices is a simulacrum of difference, in which everything carries the same exchangeable value. Insofar as cinema is intertwined in the systems of global capital, it always risks such reification. Rey Chow describes contemporary culture as "caught up in . . . global visibility—the ongoing, late-capitalist phenomenon of mediatized spectacularization, in which the endeavor to seek social recognition amounts to an incessant production and consumption of oneself and one's group as images on display."[53] Similarly, Sean Cubitt takes up a critical position on dominant modes of cinematic worlding when he argues that "cosmopolitanism corresponds to informationalization because it operates in only one direction. The cosmopolitan is at home in the culture of the other, but he does not offer the other the hospitality of his own home."[54] We will see this compulsive visualization of the other at work when we consider the conflicted cinematic discourses of queer multiculturalism in chapter 1.

We insist, however, that this is not the only possible vision of the world and that cinema has long been embedded in—yet in tension with—the systems of global capital. Some recent accounts of cosmopolitanism offer valuable insight for theorizing queer cinema, even as they speak in quite a different register. In his influential book on the concept, Kwame Anthony Appiah writes,

> There are two strands that intertwine in the notion of cosmopolitanism. One is the idea that we have obligations to others, obligations that stretch beyond those to whom we are related by the ties of kith and kind, or even the more formal ties of a shared citizenship. The other is that we take seriously the value not just of human life but of particular human lives, which means taking an interest in the practices and beliefs that lend them significance. People are different, the cosmopolitan knows, and there is much to learn from our differences.[55]

This passage is, to us, strongly reminiscent of Sedgwick's foundational axiom that "people are different from one another," a way of thinking queerness and the human to which we return in chapter 1. This textual affiliation (albeit probably an unintentional iteration) opens up what processes of worlding can offer us against their more elitist, globalizing manifestations. Pheng Cheah rejects what he calls a "facile cosmopolitanism," which he aligns with market capitalism, and against which he proposes a "more rigorous . . . modality of cosmopolitanism, that is responsible and responsive to the need to remake the world as a hospitable space, that is, a place that is *open* to the emergence of peoples that globalization deprives of world."[56] Although we do not adhere closely to the discourse of the cosmopolitan, it is this attempt to remake the world as a place open to those currently deprived of world that motivates this project.

When we analyze queer films in terms of their worldliness, then, we aim to describe what it is that texts create as they intervene in worlding processes. Dudley Andrew writes, "In cinema, something as technical as 'point of view' asserts an ideological and political claim, literally orienting a culture to a surrounding world."[57] For Andrew, every film brings into being a perspective on the world, a way of looking that frames social and affective space. His understanding of point of view here is formal but never merely technical: it tells us something important about the film's world, but that thing is not quantifiable in the way that global capital wants to capture all human activity. We cannot, for example, measure the colonial gaze in *La Noire de . . . / Black Girl* (Ousmane Sembene, dir., 1966). Rather, point of view for Andrew provokes thought and calls for analysis. In a similar vein, we argue that every film constructs a world formally and that this worldliness has the capacity to recalibrate its own parameters. Worldliness can shift the terms of agency and power and has the ability to create effects in the world.

Queer Cinema in the World investigates how queer films intersect with shifting ideas of global politics and world cinema aesthetics in order to open out queer cinema's potential to disturb dominant modes of world making. The book does not aim to provide a complete overview of global queer cinema, but neither does it completely surrender the idea of the world to globalization. Instead, it makes a case for the centrality of queerness in what we understand as world cinema and for the significance of cinema in making queer worlds. The worldliness of cinema is highly contested space, fought after and instrumentalized in politically suspect ways. But the cooptation of cinematic worlds to neocolonial fantasies and consumer capitalist effects is never achieved with completeness. The dynamics of cinema allow experiences that transcend pragmatism, and the utility of cinema for political ends is always accompanied by a radical instability. So while we maintain cynicism toward the canonization of a category called "world cinema," we are also reluctant to relinquish all cinema that poses worldly questions. Despite the success of global market-driven capitalism in systematizing the world, we insist that neoliberalism does not get to own the world. In our individual and collective endeavors, we have listened to other ways of defining the world. For this reason, the essay we co-wrote in our anthology *Global Art Cinema* put forward the idea of "the impurity of art cinema" to reignite the potencies and instabilities of what we felt had become a category of film—arthouse fare— that was too easily dismissed by film scholars as decadent, overly aesthetic, and inherently compromised.[58] To use the term "global" is always a political act and yet few of us can opt out of being subject to the world. We resist a critique that would see any and all renderings of the world as inescapably complicit with globalization.

We are also concerned by an almost kneejerk unwillingness to discuss queers and the world together. In film studies, a critical awareness of the global frame has challenged and revised the traditional rubrics of film studies (inflecting them with categories such as the transnational, diasporic, the exilic, and migrancy) but these debates have often marginalized or excluded queer film. *Queer Cinema in the World* opens out conversations between critical models of queer worlding and rubrics of world cinema. The challenge is to think critiques of the global gaze/gays alongside Ella Shohat and Robert Stam's view of European spectators as "armchair conquistadors"; to read the racializing logic of the gay international against Fatimah Tobing Rony's account of the "third eye"; to compare homonationalism with Miriam Hansen's vernacular modernism; and to add White's retrospectatorship to Dudley Andrew's phases of world cinema.[59] Bringing these perspectives together is also our attempt to correct what we see as an avoidance of queer theory by film studies and film theory. Even many of the canonical studies of queer cinema speak apart from queer theory's most significant challenges to categories of identity, affect, life, and aesthetics. We propose that when thought together, these intellectual traditions rethink the world from the ground up. They simultaneously ask: what do we mean by a world? Do we need a world? If so, why? Is it politically necessary to imagine the scale/space of human living in global terms? In other words, what is having a world good for?

Scales of Worldliness

Andrei Tarkovsky asks, "Why do people go to the cinema?" and concludes that this impulse springs from "the human need to master and know the world."[60] Our impetus in foregrounding this question comes from our conviction, contrary to Tarkovsky's, that people use cinema to know the world without mastering it. For another Soviet filmmaker, Sergei Eisenstein, the question of the world was also a question of cinema, but the terms of its mastery were less certain. For Eisenstein, cinema collapses physical distance and temporal difference, perverting the proximities within which we ordinarily live. Its spatiality has little to do with what is physically contiguous; instead, Eisenstein's politics of cinematic space was, as Mary Ann Doane has noted, a politics of scale.[61] As she quotes Eisenstein, "The representation of objects in the actual (absolute) proportions proper to them is, of course, merely a tribute to orthodox formal logic. A subordination to an inviolable order of things. . . . Absolute realism is by no means the correct form of perception. It is simply the function of a certain form of social structure."[62] As much as it has the potential to reinforce a social order, naturalizing a certain mode of perception, cinema for Eisenstein also has the potential to de-reify perception by distorting scale. He alerts us to pay attention to how cinema recalibrates scale, because in that operation there is a politics of the world. We know that Eisenstein was keen to unlock cinema's potential to collide spaces and times in order to bring down oppressive hierarchies and radically reorganize the world. We might even say that cinema for him is able to *queer* scale by perverting orthodox proximetrics, collapsing distances, and drawing together various and skewed perspectives. If all cinema plays with admixtures of scale (via composition, montage, and so on), then Eisenstein asks what world we are making when we make cinema.

We draw on this reading of Eisenstein to think cinematic worldliness in terms of queer scales and spaces, juxtaposing his insights with those of recent queer film scholars who take on questions of globality. One such scholar is Helen Hok-Sze Leung, who positions the cinematic as a site in which alternate scales of political, social, and sexual identification can occur. Leung, building on Gordon Brent Ingram, identifies what she calls queer-scapes in a " 'locality of contests' between normative constitutions of identity and less acceptable forms of identification, desire, and contact."[63] Leung lays out the potential for this intersection at an early stage in the debate when she argues that New Queer Cinema should engage Third Cinema, to counter both NQC's dominant Western male point of view and the blind spot Third Cinema often had for sexuality. She points to films such as *Chou jue deng chang/Enter the Clowns* (Cui Zi'en, dir., 2002), *Fresa y chocolate/Strawberry and Chocolate* (Tomás Gutiérrez Alea, dir., 1993), and *Woubi Cheri* (Laurent Bocahut and Philip Brooks, dirs., 1998) as examples of global films that are geopolitically queer:

It is clear that many new queer cinemas are emerging, from the "margins and interstices" of global power. These films are "queer" not only in the sense that they explore sexual and gender practices outside of normative heterosexuality and the dichotomous gender system. They are queer— indeed more than a little strange—because they unsettle current notions of history and politics, while going against conventional paradigms of filmmaking. Most of all, they answer to the legacies of Third Cinema by remaining on the side of the disaffected and disenfranchised.[64]

With Leung, we insist on a mode of cinematic queerness that links sexuality and gender both to textual transgression and to a politics of worldliness. As she writes, "Such a cinema would . . . engage with and resist the decentered and dispersed forms of late capitalist domination that operate transnation- ally and across different identity formations. There are signs that a new wave of queer films, emerging from diverse locales, are moving in precisely such a direction. Not only do these films explore non-normative sexualities and gender practices from new perspectives, they do so by rendering strange— indeed queering—existent narratives of history and culture as well as the institution of filmmaking."[65] The structures and shapes of world cinema en- able new forms of transnational articulation.

One of these existing narratives is diaspora, which Gopinath redeploys as a means of mapping the vectors and transits of queer desires. Queer dia- sporic cinema allows us to see spaces of shared desire that are otherwise illegible. It also traverses historical boundaries, borrowing from White's concept of retrospectatorship. Thus, speaking of the Indian lesbian film *Sancharram/The Journey* (Ligy J. Pullapally, dir., 2004), she writes:

> The various genealogies that converge in a text like *Sancharram* can only be traced through . . . a queer diasporic frame, one that would allow us to read the multiple registers within which the film gains meaning: the local, the regional, the national, the diasporic, and the transnational. . . . The film in effect supersedes a national frame; instead it interpolates a transnational lesbian and gay viewership in its framing of the strug- gle of its heroines through these transnational discourses. *Sancharram* therefore allows us to consider the formation of a transnational lesbian/ feminist subject through the use of a regional linguistic and aesthetic idiom.[66]

Neither Leung nor Gopinath gives up on the idea of a spatial politics of trans- national identification. For both scholars, there is a political imperative continually to think beyond one's own community. In fact, Gopinath explicitly offers her transregional subject as an alternative to the consumer capitalist subject that is often disparagingly called the "global gay."[67] Here we might connect Gopinath's intervention to the practices of "self-regioning" described in Cüneyt Çakırlar's analysis of queer Turkish experimental media. Çakırlar suggests that these self-regioning practices confront the problematic appropriation of the regional, the authentic, or the local when art from outside Western Europe travels. Gopinath, Leung, and Çakırlar propose queer transnational scales without sweeping the problems of cultural translation under the carpet of global gay identity. But at the same time, and in each of these approaches, the space of queer desire is not limited to a single cultural frame.

Queer Cinema in the World takes three methodological interventions from the work of these scholars. First, it understands cinema as a place where the politics of globalization are articulated and disarticulated. Cinema is a critical means by which queerness *worlds* itself, a means by which queers negotiate local and global subjectivities. Therefore, to engage with the politics of global queerness, we must attend to its cinematicity. This process is legible at the level of individual films articulating the worldly in their form and style. For example, *Wusheng feng ling/Soundless Wind Chime* (Kit Hung, 2009) figures transnational queer desire via elliptical montages and sound bridges, graphic matches that link different times and spaces, and synthetic edits that align bodies via analogy rather than synchrony. We are interested in the spaces enabled by film form and the geopolitical questions they pose, exploring how queerness grants film a spatiality that speaks differently in the world.

Second, we have taken inspiration from the ways that Gopinath and Leung align disparate films and film practices. Leung's bold move to think NQC alongside Third Cinema shows how forceful it can be to juxtapose dissimilar spaces as a means of questioning the terms of their supposed incommensurability. We denaturalize the incongruences of different types of film because we are interested in finding resistant means of living in the world. We are unwilling to relinquish the scaling of the world to its most reactionary formations. This book thus looks to alternative scales, unusual linkages, and unexpected lineages. Third, each of these scholars brings a new critical sensitivity to the politics of exhibition and the complex circuitry of distribution (official and unofficial) that enable queer films to be seen by various audiences. Gopinath, Leung, and Çakırlar understand watching a film to be a practice that reaches across disparate times and spaces, a sensorium in which audiences connect conventionally incommensurate moments, experiences, and locations. We have privileged those queer films that partake in worlding in ways that neither obliterate difference nor make everything reconcilable to a single global sexual or political currency. We are determined to retain the scale of the worldly as a dialectical mode that enables difference to precipitate change in the world.

Subjective Investments

We are aware of our own positionality in the world systems of cinema and queer culture. By certain reckonings of identity and power, we tread carefully, for we write as two white, middle-class, cisgendered people working in elite Western universities. We are outsiders to many of the cultures we engage—and outsiders with some significant privileges. Of course, as world cinema scholars, we have a commitment to comparative research. Yet our speaking positions make a difference, and queer politics insists on the consequences of these differences. As Sedgwick notes in considering what she brought to an anti-homophobic project, identifications within lines of gender, sexuality, race, and so on require explanation every bit as much as those across definitional lines, and her different, vicarious cathexes to her subject inevitably shape the directions of analysis.[68] For Sedgwick, in writing outside one's own positionality in an anti-homophobic project, there is either no justification needed or none possible. This is only the more true when the project is global in scope. Identities are complicated things, and as coauthors we bring many intertwined perspectives to the project. One of us is Jewish, while the other's father was born in Palestine. Both of us come from culturally mixed immigrant backgrounds, and both of us have lived as immigrants. Both of us have a long-standing engagement in queer scholarship, and one of us was present at a foundational moment of queer film studies, the How Do I Look? symposium. Although we have different sexual orientations, both of us have had sex with men and with women. One of us frames their sexual identity in terms of BDSM. We both come from politically active families. One of us has a history in early AIDS activism, and the other in anti–Third World debt activism. These terrains of subjectivity all play their parts in shaping our intellectual, aesthetic, and political commitments and have surely contributed to the place from which we write.

These positionalities provide, in one reading, a map of our political investments in gender, sexuality, and geopolitics, as well as a sense of why a queer endeavor that binds the intimate and subjective with the public and collective might be important to us. Our impulse to theorize queer cinema's worldliness derives in large measure from our commitment to reimagining the world. To some degree, this polemic emerges from our desire to recon-figure what film studies names "world cinema." Film studies has adopted the rubric of world cinema, as contested and contingent as that category may be. And yet queer cinema was remaking the world long before we got to the film cultures described between this book's covers. Throughout our collab-orative research trips, screenings, and heated discussions, we have remained determined to avoid a kind of missionary impulse that we sometimes see in surveys of queer art and culture. We have not been on a mission to excavate new instances of queer sexualities around the world; nor should this book be seen as an argument for the existence of particular identity categories in par-ticular locations. Rather, we note how queer cultures have long deployed cin-ema as a means of making and unmaking the world. We find a rich discur-sive terrain of debates around queer cinema worldwide, and yet, for some reason, mainstream film studies has remained reluctant to acknowledge the centrality of these discourses in the reinvigoration and reinvention of the political life of the medium.

The book contains six chapters, each focused on a different category drawn from the apparatus of cinema. The organization is deliberately not geographical: although we spend time on case studies that delve into par-ticular national cultures, our logic is not that of the almanac or atlas. In-stead, we find queerness across the life worlds of the cinematic, attending to its existence in forms and structures that are not easily recognized by more conventional taxonomies of nation or genre. We proceed comparatively, staging encounters between films from different places and in disparate cinematic modes. The book's definition of the world derives avowedly both from film theory and from the films themselves, and our conceptualization of the chapters speaks to a commitment to cinema's capacity to reorganize the world.

Chapter 1 centers on the figure of the queer, considering how represen-tations such as the bisexual sex worker, the trans exile, and the diasporic lesbian circulate in world cinemas. Our approach is not characterological; rather, it leverages these recurring tropes to get at some central problems for thinking contemporary queer worldliness. Here, we consider debates on homonationalism, neoliberal versions of globalization, and the concept of the global gay, analyzing how films construct geopolitically hierarchized po-sitions from which to look at racialized queer bodies. We consider the politi-cal value of such a critique and its limitations, opening out the multivalences contained in scenes of translation, dramas of the European queer Muslim, and romantic comedies made by lesbians of color.

Chapter 2 takes the institution as its organizing term. It examines the queer film festival, which provides a vantage point from which to view cinema's shifting role in world politics. In 1955, André Bazin offered an early theory of the international film festival, calling it "the very epitome of a worldly affair."[69] Contemporary queer film festivals are strongly invested in the worldly nature of their programming. We read the rise of globalized queer film festivals in the 1990s alongside the simultaneous emergence of international campaigns for the decriminalization of homosexuality. A close examination of the cultural practices of some film festivals, however, complicates this human rights rhetoric, exposing how dynamically these events reimagine public spaces and audiences. Moving away from film texts to consider the material spaces, curatorial logics, publicity, and social media practices of the festival, chapter 2 proposes the queer film festival as a space of tension, at once operating in complicity with globalized capitalism and inaugurating alternative figurations of queer life.

Chapter 3 focuses on narrative and specifically deploys allegory as a way to reimagine what it means to speak in the world. Locating queer bodies at the heart of some canonical theories of political allegory, we argue that queerness is a constitutive part of imagining the world and that allegory is a central modality of its narration. We find allegory at work across geographically disparate sites of narrative cinema, from contemporary classics of art cinema such as *Fire* and *Sud pralad/Tropical Malady* (Apichatpong Weerasethakul, dir., 2004) to crucial postcolonial texts such as *Dakan/Destiny* (Mohamed Camara, dir., 1997). The chapter also reaches back historically to examine flashpoints of queer film history such as *Dog Day Afternoon* (Sidney Lumet, dir., 1975) and *Bara no sôretsu/Funeral Parade of Roses* (Toshio Matsumoto, dir., 1969), an experimental narration of Japanese modernity. Across these heterogeneous film texts, we propose allegory as a mode of queer worlding that intersects a politics of erasure with insistent utopian imaginaries that reframe the space of the public.

This utopian strain in queer visual culture leads us to Chapter 4, which addresses the apparently contradictory idea of a queer popular. Queerness is that which destabilizes systems and norms; thus, it seems opposed to cultural normalcy. Yet what are we to make of wildly popular gay-themed films such as *The Parade*, which earned practically the same box office in Serbia as *Avatar* (James Cameron, dir., 2009)? This chapter counters the need for a critical, antihomonormative queerness with popular cinema's potential for unregulated pleasures and transgressive desires. We consider a range of popular genre films, from Thai transgender sports films through comedies of tolerance and to actively homophobic genres such as Nigerian Christian melodrama. These readings demonstrate the complexity with which popular cinemas negotiate gender, sexuality, and globalization and suggest the radical potential for queerness to reconfigure the terms of the popular.

Chapter 5 turns to the more elusive terrain of register, positing that cinema captures queer modes of belonging in the world by deploying feeling and affect. The chapter deliberately brings together films with apparently mismatched registers of tone and cultural hierarchy, finding resonance across disparate genres and modes of filmmaking. We begin with melodrama, a register that is already overdetermined as queer. The audiovisual regime of emotion and surface that characterizes melodrama has been central to queer cultural theories, and we consider the global implications of melodrama's political affects in relation to Indian and Bangladeshi gay and transgender films. The chapter moves on to elaborate registers of affiliation and proximity and queer experiences of sociality and community. It analyzes the queer historical drama and the politics of touch in activist documentary, and it considers space and nature as vectors of queer intimacy, rethinking concepts such as the pastoral and animality.

The final chapter addresses cinematic temporality, making the case that the disjunctures of queer history and subjectivity can be read in film form and style. The chapter outlines the queerly temporal trajectories of contemporary world cinema, analyzing excision and disruption, slowness and boredom, asynchrony and reproduction. It studies a wide range of international art films by directors such as Zero Chou, Julián Hernández, and Karim Aïnouz, as well as radical work by Jack Lewis and John Greyson and the melodramas of Lino Brocka. By insisting on the cinematicity of queer time, it rethinks the relationship between aesthetics and politics in queer theory and contemporary world cinema.

Although our worldly scope could lead to accusations of a utopian internationalism, we do not propose a global cinematic language or even a global queer film style. However, we refuse to relinquish the world to equally fantasmatic accounts of the medium that pose it as a sinister commodifier of human life and equalizer of experience. Cinema has always been more complicated than is allowed by simple analogies between those on the screen and those in front of it. As we engage with both films and the transcultural politics that surround their exhibition, we have tried to remain attentive to how worlding is part of cinema's apparatus. Universalism remains a crucial feature of cinema's account of its own medium specificity, and this longing has particular potencies and perils for queers. As much as Tom Cruise's postapocalyptic

1

FIGURES IN THE WORLD
The Geopolitics of the Transcultural Queer ·

Queer figures populate world cinema. In films that narrate the global, clichéd characters such as the sexually vulnerable Other, the bisexual migrant, the outsider closet case, the unveiled woman, the transgender exile, the un-dutiful daughter, the immigrant son, and the lesbian backpacker abound. This chapter is about how films stage the question of the world through such queer figures, and how these figures allow films to recast the relationships of identities to intercultural difference and international space. Our analysis opens out the geopolitics of sexuality as it has been interrogated by contemporary queer theory and challenges how that theory engages with visual culture. Confronted by efforts in the late 1980s to define queer, Teresa de Lauretis asserted the mission for queer scholarly work as "to rethink the sexual in new ways, elsewhere and other-wise." De Lauretis was here engaging the implication of sexualities in issues of gender, race, ethnicity, indigeneity, generation, and class in the United States, as well as the ways that sexuality might speak about sexual acts, perversions, and cathexes, as well as orientation. She insisted that "otherwise desiring subjects" could shift the "semantic horizons" and "forms of community."[1] Thus, the queer not only raises the problem of otherness but also directs our thinking toward the "other-wise" and the "elsewhere." The process of figuring queerness, we propose, is therefore also a mode of thinking spatiality and the geopolitical landscape of the subject.

Queer scholars have used de Lauretis's argument to shake up the conventional parameters of existing academic disciplines.[2] In the process, the figurability of the queer has been contested. Here we argue that the space of otherness is not merely a new frontier of identity politics. It is also a zone for renegotiating modern subjectivity. In other words, we adapt de Lauretis's elsewhere and other-wise to rethink the relationship between the alterity of queerness and the spaces of the world. In a study of queer geographies, Kath Browne, Jason Lim, and Gavin Brown write that "sexuality—its regulation, norms, institutions, pleasures and desires—cannot be understood without understanding the spaces through which it is constituted, practiced and lived."[3] For these authors, what is at stake here is an "institutionalisation of sexualised imagined geographies . . . [which holds] the power to define who belongs and to define what bodies are allowed to do, when and where." From a film studies perspective, this analysis prompts the question of whether cinema as an institution produces geographies that center heteronormativity or whether its figures might unsettle such dominant regimes of space.

Jordana Rosenberg and Amy Villarejo advocate for the geopolitical potential of queer theory much along these lines, asking, "How might a methodology attuned to both sexuality and the specificities of capitalist crisis orient us toward a world other than the one in which we find ourselves currently mired?"[4] For Rosenberg and Villarejo, queer theory must be articulated to materialist critiques of contemporary world systems. Queer subjectivity has the potential, for them, to figure the other-wise and elsewheres of late capitalism. Or, as Roderick Ferguson puts it, "Contemporary globalization is constituted though regimes of gender and sexual normativity and the disruptions to those regimes."[5] Ferguson does not celebrate global sexual identities but argues that queer critical practices have the potential to disarm modes of being that currently dominate world systems. This means that figures of queers (and representational practices that foreground such figures) may hold the potential to expose the mechanisms of liberal capitalism's regulatory structures.

More important, however, Ferguson's work insists on the processes of racialization that form and are formed by sexual and gender normativities. Expanding on Chandan Reddy's work, he argues "that racist practice articulates itself generally as gender and sexual regulation, and that gender and sexual differences variegate racial formations. This articulation, moreover, accounts for the social formations that compose liberal capitalism."[6] Many of the films we analyze in this chapter can be seen as either participating in or problematizing this process of racialization. They stage the question of global politics explicitly through their othering of the queer figure, whether it be along the lines of race or ethnicity. The troublesome discourses of multiculturalism are a constitutive part of the liberal identities offered to the gay subject of late capitalism, and these identities take part in queer cinema's global circulation. The queer of color analysis that Ferguson and others propose demands that global studies of cinema recognize race and ethnicity as constitutive of queer subjectivities. In other words, the queer characters in these films are not merely representatives of a newly globalized field of vision. Their figuration as "others" also incites a critique that renders the segregation of white Westernized queer theory and global studies obsolete.

Neville Hoad asserts that queer theory is foundationally invested in geopolitical difference, whether it admits it or not: "In terms of colonial attempts to impose the gendered division of productive, reproductive and affective labor of a state-sanctioned monogamous heterosexuality on the world, connections between the alterity of elsewhere and the alterity of queerness become obvious."[7] These historically intermeshed alterities do not, in and of themselves, make queer figures geopolitically resistant: the settler-colonial logic of Israeli films such as *Ha-Buah/The Bubble* (Eytan Fox, dir., 2006) and *Ha-Sippur shel Yossi/Yossi* (Fox, dir., 2012) demonstrate the urgent need to theorize the geopolitical complicity of some queer figurations. But the connection Hoad asserts does ask us to think resistance to coloniality and heteronormativity in relation to each other.[8] This chapter traces a series of queer figures across world cinema, discovering them to be disruptions and provocations to—as much as confirmations of—the stable accounts of sexual and cultural identities promoted by globalization. Here we will be looking at depictions, representations, and categories of identity and being as they appear on-screen. But figuration is not only a question of character and narrative: cinema is more than a screen reflecting back existing social formations, and the figure of the queer poses a formal problem for these films as much as it provides a vehicle for representing known identities. Hence, we do not read the figure of the queer characterologically. What cinema does in its structures of point of view, identification, and narration is not inconsequential to the geopolitics of sex and gender in a globalized world.

In the 1970s, feminist film theory took a decisive step away from reflectionist models of representation to insist that the figure of woman was significantly constituted through cinematic structures of identification and desire. This intervention remains critically productive, and in a similar move this book claims that queerness today is vividly constituted through representational forms and the cinematic apparatus that produces and circulates those forms globally. Cinematic experiences of gender dissidence and non-hetero sexualities, we suggest, are brought about not only via sociologically reflective representations (e.g., LGBT characters) but also, and more significantly, through cinematic forms, narrational structures, audience address, and modes of exhibition. The entire apparatus of cinema takes part in the reproduction of sexual and gendered subjectivities. Thus, in this chapter we turn to the cinematic figuration of queerness as a locus of unique political force and historical urgency for the articulation and contestation of queerness in the world.

To understand the stakes of this claim for our contemporary moment, we must first turn back to an earlier moment of film studies to see how entangled questions of sexuality and worldliness are in the histories of thinking on cinema. In 1990, Richard Dyer published Now You See It, the first major survey of gay and lesbian films after Vito Russo's The Celluloid Closet.[9] Dyer writes that he chose to end his survey in 1980 because lesbian/gay films proliferate enormously after that date, and if the book took into consideration the 1980s, he worried, it would become simply "a book of lists." Dyer admits that using this cutoff results in a book that discusses more films "by and about men than women, and next to no representation of non-white, non-Northern/Western people."[10] Unlike Russo, who seems fairly indiscriminate about genre and mode of production while unconsciously Western in scope, Dyer is keen to acknowledge the relatively Euro-American–centric nature of his survey. Now You See It does reference some non-Western films, such as the Japanese film Funeral Parade of Roses, the Filipino director Lino Brocka and the Mexican film El lugar sin limites/Place without Limits (Arturo Ripstein, dir., 1978), and the later edition of the book expands to include international directors such as Youssef Chahine. However, Dyer writes, "The specificity of the idea of 'being' lesbian or gay means that the very different way same-sex relations are constructed and experienced in Japan or Third World countries does not come into my purview."[11] Dyer's words here reflect his insistent anti-imperialist spirit; the rest of the world appears in moments throughout the book as a limit point, and one that demands the otherwise brave undertaking maintain a modest scope and scale.

While many of Dyer's analyses remain pertinent and even urgent to our contemporary moment, justifying such limited parameters would be clearly undesirable today. As elegantly as he brackets these concerns, *Now You See It* should be understood as speaking from a different moment in queer scholarship. There is a striking tension in Dyer's approach that remains relevant to our present work. Even as he rejects the political utility of universal sexual identity categories, Dyer retains a certain investment in a transcultural existence of non-normative sex: "Even the words homosexual, homo-erotic, lesbian or gay were hard to apply outside of Western culture since the nineteenth century. Many came to argue that, while affective and/or sexual acts between persons of the same sex were indeed a universal reality, the idea that people who engaged in them belonged to a distinct group of persons (homosexuals, lesbians) was found only in modern times in the West."[12] We confront here what Eve Kosofsky Sedgwick would call the incommensurability of acts and identities as a way to make a claim for the universality of sex acts that maintains a sense of cultural relativism.

Dyer anticipates the focus on the non-Western queer as a highly contested geopolitical figure in the early twenty-first century. These debates might be summarized in the following questions. Are words such as "gay" or "queer" or "lesbian" descriptions of attractions that exist in approximately analogous terms across the world's diverse cultures? Or does the project of applying these terms globally impose Western notions of identity onto sexual and gender modalities that are misunderstood or unrecognized in the West? Dyer speaks softly but firmly to those who circulate phobic notions of a world in which queer sex does not exist or has no grounding. In the book's last paragraph, there is a striking parenthetical sentence: "(Humans could live, and do and have, in worlds without gay/lesbian identities and cultures, though not without gay/lesbian acts; but we do not live in such a world and cannot magically transport ourselves to one.)"[13] Not only are non-hetero acts universal for him, but he insists that we live in a world in which queer cultures exist everywhere in quite material ways. In a similar fashion, it would be dangerously anachronistic to think of queer cinema as unscathed by global politics or outside of debates on the geo-cultural parameters of identity categories. In writing this book, we have tried to remain sensitive to our limitations as spectators, scholars, and translators, yet at the same time we insist on the value of reading film culture transnationally and comparatively as a site where the frictions between identities and acts enter into public discourse and public experience. The Turkish filmmaker Kutluğ Ataman considers that his film *Lola + Bilidikid/Lola and Billy the Kid* (1999) draws strong responses because although "Turkish people had been watching foreign gay films for years . . . as soon as Turks make the same, they are embarrassed."[14] In a sense, then, the opposing impulses to universalize and relativize represent the highly pitched debates between those who assert gay rights globally and those who insist on cultural specificity. As worldviews, they appear irreconcilable. Yet the relationship between world cinema and national film traditions, like that between global and local modes of sexual expression, cannot be thought entirely independently from each other.

Gay for Pay, or Queer for the Gay International

A telling intersection of queer identity and geopolitics came in 2014 at the UK premiere of the Cuban/Spanish film *La Partida/The Last Match* (Antonio Hens, dir., 2013) at BFI Flare: London LGBT Film Festival. *The Last Match* describes the life of two young men in Havana who turn to sex work with older, foreign male tourists to support themselves and their families. Gradually, an attraction develops between the two friends, but it is eventually destroyed by their struggle to rise above poverty. The film enacts and depends on a privileged international gaze looking at the global South. It plays with many of the visual clichés of world cinema—its saturated colors, gritty realism, and shallow focus echo world cinema hits such as *Cidade de Deus/City of God* (Fernando Meireilles and Kátia Lund, dirs., 2002)—while leveraging a prostitution melodrama that uses the prohibition of same-sex desire as an exploitative narrational way into suspense. The Cuban protagonists offer a pleasurable insight into a world as ripe with energy and desire as it is lacking in economic opportunity. They are figures of queer poverty; desirable bodies; spectacles for the Western spectator (figure 1.1). After the screening, the film's Spanish director Antonio Hens and two of its stars took questions from the festival's audience via Skype. Originally, the trio was meant to be at the premiere, but both actors were Cuban and were denied visas to enter the United Kingdom under an intensified immigration regime. During the Q&A, Hens initially argued that he did not want the film to have a political message but went on to claim that because Cuba does not officially celebrate homosexuality, he was obliged to end the story tragically. Regardless, the film's real question, he said, was whether real love can be found in economic difficulty. These comments about the unsustainability of love without money, alongside the voyeuristic narrative, feed directly into a logic that insists capitalism is the solution to Cuba's problems.

Fig. 1.1: *The Last Match* trades in figures of queer poverty.

A puzzling series of unchecked contradictions plagued this premiere. The program notes contain a director's statement in which Hens marks his status as an outsider to Cuban culture: "I felt very much puzzled when I first learnt that it was not a shame for a teen Cuba macho to be seen in the street walking hand in hand with a tourist some decades older than him. Money was the element that subverted the logical order."[15] Yet during the Q&A, Reinier Díaz, one of the actors, admitted to his fear about Cubans' reaction to the film, given that he was shown having sex with a man. No one—least of all Hens—appeared aware of the parallels between on- and off-screen economies around "gay for pay." Moreover, the London premiere was sponsored by the multinational consulting firm Accenture. The audience was whiter and skewed more male than at any of the Flare festival's other screenings, and perhaps included many of Accenture's clientele, employees, and their friends. The audience giggled knowingly and seemed enthusiastic about the film's mixture of half-naked boys playing soccer, artfully lit scenes of sex for hire, and liberal concern for oppressed people from far-off lands. The director's unquestioned assumptions about the parameters of the political seemed largely validated both by the erotics of pathos and pity deployed by the film and the titillating questions that the festival audience asked the actors. *The Last Match* folds presumptions of Western economic prosperity as the means to personal freedom into its apparently apolitical imagery of gay affection. The global North audience had little resistance to deeming queer intimacies in the global South unsustainable, and a Western definition of sexual identity is the only one granted to both fictional protagonists and the actors who portray them. Thus, they appear to us as queer only in conditional terms, as long as they reconcile themselves to an extra-national life or to being the object of a transnational and voyeuristic desiring gaze.

The film and its premiere manifest the implication of LGBT identities in the corporatization of social life, cultural events, and a neocolonial tourist gaze. This example reveals not only film culture's complicity in neoliberalism, but also how queerness can enable the admixture of desire for foreignness, sexual liberty, and economic exchange in a way that naturalizes the hierarchies of global capital. As if responding to the problems raised by this particular screening of *The Last Match*, Michael Warner urges queer theory to think more systematically about how its definitions of sex and gender difference are written through with cultural and political biases: "As gay activists from non-Western contexts become more and more involved in setting political agendas, and as the rights discourse of internationalism is extended to more and more cultural contexts, Anglo-American queer theorists will have to be more alert to the globalizing—and localizing—tendencies of our theoretical languages."[16] Critiquing that rights discourse more sharply, Joseph Massad insists on the pernicious effect of what he terms the Gay International:

[The] Gay International incites discourse on homosexuality in the non-Western world, it claims that the "liberation" of those it defends lies in the balance. In espousing this liberation project, the Gay International is destroying social and sexual configurations of desire in the interest of reproducing a world in its own image, one wherein its sexual categories and desires are safe from being questioned. . . . The Gay International's imperialist epistemological task is proceeding apace with little opposition from the majority of the sexual beings it wants to "liberate" and whose social and sexual worlds it is destroying in the process. In undertaking this universalizing project, the Gay International ultimately makes itself feel better about a world it forces to share its identifications.[17]

In recent years, and partially in response to these provocations, queer theory has undergone a necessary geopolitical reorientation, turning its critical attention to the cultural and economic presumptions that subtend popular LGBT politics in the West.

A geopolitically inflected queer theory has emerged that participates in the critique of globalization and thus of the liberal models of gay and lesbian culture that go along with it. Inderpal Grewal and Caren Kaplan insist that "in this globalized framework of encounter and exchange, sexual identities are similar to other kinds of identities in that they are imbued with power relations. These power relations are connected to inequalities that result from earlier forms of globalization, but they have also generated new asymmetries. Our task is to examine both the specificities and the continuities within the globalization of sexual identities at the present juncture."[18] Turning queer theory's critique of power on itself, scholars of queer postcoloniality, diaspora, transnationalism, and indigeneity have insisted on the problematic status of sexual citizenship in the neoliberal world.[19] Grace Kyungwon Hong and Roderick Ferguson point out the importance of women-of-color feminism and queer-of-color critique to this project as genealogies that are often obscured by white queer studies. They might also be speaking of *The Last Match* when they point to the policing of "the difference between those who are able to conform to categories of normativity, respectability, and value, and those who are forcibly excluded from such categories." In the current moment, they argue, "Neoliberal modes of power rely on such valuations to subject the racialized poor to brutal violence through rhetorics of individual freedom and responsibility."[20] As David Eng concludes, "A renewed queer studies must insist that problems of neoliberal political economy cannot be abstracted away from the racial, gendered, and sexual hierarchies of the nation-state, but must be understood as operating in and through them."[21] In these accounts, even the radical malleability of queerness can be seen as a formation that is particularly well suited to modern capitalism.

Where the queer is a figure productive of neoliberalism, an asset in its portfolio, travel becomes the marker of differential access to both worldliness and subjectivity itself. In 2011, a travel article in the popular US gay magazine *Out* called the international gay film festival "the new circuit party."[22] Now more of a reactionary than an oppositional figure, the global gay is an incessantly mobile "circuit queen" who aids and abets the flow of postindustrial capital. The "passport gay" traverses borders with a sinister ease, defined in opposition to the service industry laborers attending to his intimate desires. Benigno Sánchez-Eppeler and Cindy Patton touch on the political stakes of this travel when they note, "Translocation itself, movement itself, now enter the picture as theoretically significant factors in the discussion of sexuality."[23] Just as queer scholars have critiqued the terms in which gay mobility can be imagined in mainstream culture, we can look to films themselves as queer bodies that are variously mobile in the world. *The Last Match* illustrates the perils of translocation not only in its narrative but also in its public circulation. That neither the fictional protagonists nor the actors in *The Last Match* can travel freely animates the stakes of transnational travel and global circulation for thinking contemporary queer subjectivities.

Eithne Luibhéid argues that "sexuality scholarship must rethink the role of migration (including as it connects with transnational capitalism and neo-imperialism) in constructing sexual identities, communities, politics, and practices."[24] This insight is equally true for scholars of queer cinema, who must consider the migrations of films, creative talent, audiences, and international funding, as well as their fictional narratives of global queerness. The agile, ethnicized bodies of the young Cubans in *The Last Match* are placed in direct tension with the global flexibility of the capitalist world (e.g., Accenture) from which they appear barred. While they cannot migrate, the film travels as a gay circuit queen or tourist normalizing the global South's marginalization through its eroticization of poverty and insistence on money's ability to make the world accessible. The aspirations of *The Last Match*'s two main characters give shape to a conflation of economic and sexual liberation. Their tragic end condemns them to what appears to be their destiny as people from the global South, alienated from neoliberalism's notion of the global citizenry. This is precisely the regime that *The Last Match* inadvertently renders visible. Its cinematic effects allow circuits of desire while maintaining and naturalizing a divide that grants life and liberty to some but condemns others to subjection or death.

The impoverished queers of *The Last Match* expose queer film culture's implication in neoliberalism: it Westernizes through commodity capitalism and obliterates difference in its path, justifying neocolonial exploitation of the global South by making resource extraction palatable and erotic. We can see this effect not only in the film's narrative representation of the transnational sex trade but equally in its international exhibition and the events that surround it. Through their intertwining of human rights advocacy with eroticized poverty voyeurism, festival films like *The Last Match* arguably serve as vehicles of late capitalist globalization and as ideological sites for the global North's reassertion of its more modern status.

The Apparitional Gay

The Last Match illustrates the implication of queer cinema in oppressive circuits of global power, but this neocolonial world is not the only one the queer festival film creates. A more ambivalent Latin American queer figure can be glimpsed in *Contracorriente/Undertow* (Javier Fuentes-León, dir., 2009), where the conflict between global audiences and homophobic "locals" provides the affective energies for a festival "crowd pleaser." This Peruvian drama won audience awards at the Sundance, Miami, and Lima film festivals and played widely at LGBT festivals, including Tokyo, Paris, and San Francisco. As a consequence of the win at Sundance, the film was distributed theatrically in Europe and in North and South America, including a limited release in the United Kingdom. The success of *Undertow* illustrates the tendency for contemporary world cinema to reinscribe neoliberal visions of relationality (a tyranny of exchange values in which all aspects of life and desire are made uniformly interchangeable, comparable, and exchangeable). The film's figuration of a ghostly queer protagonist negotiates the relationship among desire, community, and public identity. *Undertow* is set in a Peruvian fishing village, a touristic location that allows for Western fantasies of a simpler rural life, as well as a pleasurable mise-en-scène of beaches and picturesque streets. More troublingly, though, its narrative stages a reactionary humanism that quite literally kills a main queer character to produce a normative vision of happiness in a reproductive hetero marriage.

The film begins with the protagonist Miguel talking to his pregnant wife's belly, setting up an image of reproductive heteronormativity as a starting point. However, it immediately complicates this apparently monogamous setup. In addition to being married to a woman, Miguel has a secret male lover, Santiago, an out gay man who is rejected by the village as a result of his sexual orientation. Santiago is forced to live on the social margins, while Miguel is closeted and widely accepted as an upstanding family man. Miguel regularly sneaks away from his wife to have sex with Santiago in a cave. A quarter of the way through the narrative, Santiago drowns: the gay relationship is excised from everyday reality, and Santiago returns as a ghost. Queerness becomes a spectral presence, haunting the visible world of the film in a selectively diegetic fashion. There are hints of something resistant in this structure of haunting; the marginalized, yet insistent presence of queerness in a space that pretends to be straight. Still, the major narrative labor achieved by the trope of the ghost is to stage the impossibility of queer visibility. As a ghostly presence, Santiago is trapped in the village where nobody but Miguel can see or hear him, in a situation notably similar to his social ostracization before he died. In a key scene, the lovers can go for a walk out in the open—something they could never do before—because Santiago is invisible. In this retrograde fantasy of queer publicity, holding hands in public is contingent on violently expelling the actual queer (figure 1.2).

Miguel does eventually come out to his wife, but in the form of a biblical confession. He constructs his sexuality in analogy to Mark 9:45—"And if

Fig. 1.2: *Undertow*'s apparitional gay figure enables an openness only visible in cinematic space.

thy foot offend thee, cut it off"—implying that homosexuality is a sin that he must confess to cut it out of his life. The film performs the same cauterization of queerness in its final removal of Santiago from the diegesis. In the narrative climax, Miguel decides to offer Santiago's body to the sea in the local Catholic ceremony that Santiago explicitly did not believe in when he was alive. Not only his queerness but his atheism is punished by a narrative that teaches him a lesson by subjecting his body to both violent death and traditional religious rites. Of course, the ceremony that Santiago mocked as a fairy tale when he was alive transpires to be true, as the rite does work to exorcize his ghost. *Undertow* works to exorcize the ghost of queerness, returning to church, family, and traditional values. By the film's end, no outwardly queer character remains; Miguel is returned to his role as patriarch; and the heteronormative family home is restored.

In *Undertow*, the neoliberal queer subject cannot be a social outsider in a positive way, a force able to critique, disrupt, or enact change, but must be folded into the traditional community in the most punitive manner. Seen in these terms, it is noteworthy that such a conservative film won audience awards at film festivals around the world, including LGBT festivals. This international traffic illustrates the form of global mobility associated with co-opted cosmopolitanism that we describe earlier in terms of the passport gay. "In world cinema terms," writes critic Steve Rose of *Undertow*, "you can't get much further off the beaten track than this extraordinary Peruvian drama."[25] The claim of "off the beaten track" implies a backpacking vision of touristic world cinema in which the more obscure the location, the more authentic the experience. But however distant the location from the centers of critical judgment, *Undertow* provides a reassuring familiarity for global audiences. This combination of exotic globalized location and violently assimilationist content could be seen to stage precisely the neoliberal vision of the world.

This narrative reading is not, however, the whole story. Both at the formal level and in its international consumption, *Undertow* articulates a more conflicted account of globalized sexuality. The film maintains a space for desiring homosexual bodies within its frames, but only for cinema audiences. Whereas spectators can see Santiago as a ghost, the film's supporting actors perform as if they cannot see him or his physical effects on the world. Seen only by each other and by us as spectators, the apparitional gay couple carries an odd relationship to the diegesis, without the special-effects trickery of *The Invisible Man* [James Whale, dir., 1933]). More important, the couple's appearance is not established through experimental or art-house techniques, such as a split focus diopter, wipe, optical printing, jump cut, or even animation. Rather, the couple remains visible in the compositions typically found in middlebrow depictions of romance: the framing accommodates Santiago and centers him in the image. The apparitional couple is granted cinematic space through two-shots that frame them in conversation and through hand-held framing that responds to the action of their tussles on the beach.

The narrative space that *Undertow* allows for the visibility of queer desire is cinematic and privatized, inviting only the spectator and the couple to see same-sex intimacy. If we think of this couple as occupying a local, a national, and, thus, a known space of intimacy, then the apparitional publicity of their desire remains a troubling concession. However, if it is the semi-visible nature of the queer romantic couple that is essential to the film's international popularity, then we find that the space Miguel and Santiago occupy exploits different geographical orientations and scales of publicness. As such, the space in which the apparitional queer couple gains its power is virtual, cinematic, and worldly. This is a space that fully allows them to be "here" and queer as long as that here and queer remain a non-national space. In fact, in the venues of the international queer film culture (the film festival, the streaming website, file-sharing exchanges), this couple becomes less of an apparition than a fixture for queer audiences around the world. In its textual production of an intimacy that is visible only to audiences, *Undertow* indexes a mode of representation that demands to be studied in its extra-national life. The film's entrée to the world stage was via a queer world film culture. This queerly cinematic visibility should not necessarily redeem the film. The fact that queerness is viable only in an international space and through a global lens is perhaps also a problematic compromise, one reductive in its vision of queer politics. The power of a queer festival crowd pleaser like *Undertow* is to use the spaces of cinema to reanimate an otherwise invisible desire and to make it both public and worldly. However, this ability seems dependent on a formal system in which global gay visibility either ignores or actively forecloses on locally and regionally specific politics, social practices, and sexual intimacies.

A certain cynicism monopolizes the reigning critical suspicion of the global. In the long run, this critique appears unwilling to imagine a world that is not a neoliberal world or international connections that are not exploitative or neocolonial. For this approach, the fostering of affinities across geographical distance is always akin to neoliberalism's homogenizing force, with its concomitant violent imposition of equivalent values across formerly sovereign spaces. Nearly all instances of global culture are seen to operate as either agents or symptoms of neoliberalism. As now practiced, then, the anti-neoliberal critique inadvertently follows a neoliberalizing logic. It demonstrates how seemingly impossible it is to critique globalized capitalist structures without eradicating the world from sight altogether. Despite the undoubted value of this critique, we nonetheless insist on the potency of queer desires to remake the world. In other words, although we draw extensively on antineoliberal and antihomonationalist critiques, we also see alternative modes of worlding at times even in the most apparently straightforward liberal circulations of queer film culture and are unwilling to use this critical polemic to foreclose on other ways of being queer in the world.

Take, for example, the way that visuality operates in Puar's influential concept of homonationalism, which argues that in the context of the United States post-9/11, gay rights developed in a liberal fashion that helped to justify violent racism. She identifies this racist discursive field as an "optic," implying that it is often enacted visually or through visual culture.[26] Puar's paradigm counterposes the always ideological function of such an optic with "intimacies" that hold the possibility of radical change and democratic modes of being. Putting aside the implicit iconophobia of this argument, we might ask: can cinema also provide access to these radical intimacies? We claim that it does (see the discussion of time in chapter 6) and that cinema as an institutional space does more than simply concretize homonormative (and heteronormative) optics. The diverse and conflicting methodologies of film studies have always agreed on one thing: that the space of film reception remains contested and negotiated. Across the debates about spectatorship and film viewership, from psychoanalytically informed apparatus theory to reception sociologies, there has been a crucial resistance to reifying the dynamics of exhibition and viewing. As much as cinema provides a venue for normativities, it has always also nurtured spaces for resistant and intimate experience. It is ultimately too easy to view films as only commodifying a liberal definition of identity and circulating Western modes of being human.

Multiculturalism's Muslim Queer

The false pitting of "global gay visibility" against "local practices" as discursive fields has been particularly apparent in debates over cultural diversity in Western Europe. The critiques of Puar and others crucially expose the role played by the queer in multiculturalism's violent exceptionalism. The figure of the ethnic queer in particular becomes a flashpoint in the relationship between liberal Western politics and Islam. Puar is sensitive to the moments in which "the figure of the queer or homonormative ethnic is crucial for the appearance of diversity in homonormative communities. . . . Ironically, the queer ethnic is also a marker of the homophobia (and the claim that homosexuality reflects the taint of the west) of his or her racial/ethnic/immigrant community while in homonormative spaces."[27] Writing in a European context, Jin Haritaworn, Tamsila Tauqir, and Esra Erdem concur that "the new omnipresence of queers of colour" occurs in a context of Islamophobia and that "white people are once again able to identify themselves as global champions of 'civilisation,' 'modernity' and 'development.' Gay Muslims are the latest symbol of this identity."[28] Similarly, Fatima El-Tayeb argues that "while the European Muslim community as a whole is judged to present the 'wrong' (i.e., misogynist and homophobic) type of heterosexuality, feminist and queer Muslims too appear as limited by their culture, deviating from the dominant norm of liberal and progressive cosmopolitanism."[29] Although not primarily concerned with cinema, these pointed critiques of white liberalism's savior complex in relation to Muslim queers have equally pressing relevance for the study of contemporary cinema.

In thinking queerness in the world, then, it is necessary to learn to take into account these queer figures who speak about the processes of racialization on which discourses of the West depend. For El-Tayeb, Europe's sense of its own racelessness is built on excluding the migrant as foreign, and

Europeans of color create queer practices of unstable and precarious belonging. Drawing on José Esteban Muñoz's use of disidentification, El-Tayeb attempts to think queerness and race in a transnational context. We find European cinema to be a revealing locus of homonormativity; its representations of nonwhite queers are replete with what Sara Ahmed might call globalism's diversity talk.[30] Yet we insist both on cinema's ability to do more than simply reflect or exemplify dominant ideological regimes and on queerness as an affective force and a set of practices that is more heterogeneous than the logic of the Gay International would imply. Cinema as an apparatus and an institution is complexly engaged in negotiating queer subjectivities as a problem of worldliness. The queer, we argue, becomes not just an emblem, symptom, or symbol of liberalism's tolerance but a structuring figure of its contradictions.

A cluster of European films that focus on the Muslim queer can help bring out the stakes of this claim. *Mixed Kebab* (Guy Lee Thys, dir., 2012) and *My Brother the Devil* (Sally El Hosaini, dir., 2012) both deal with lives of Muslim youth on the streets of modern Western Europe, while *Fremde Haut/Unveiled* (Angelina Maccarrone, dir., 2005) centers on an Iranian lesbian who lives an insecure life as an asylum seeker. Each film is set in Western Europe—in Belgium, the United Kingdom, and Germany, respectively—and all echo the influential gay drama *My Beautiful Laundrette* (Stephen Frears, dir., 1986), staging intersectionalist dramas by showing the confluence of race, sexuality, gender, ethnicity, and religion. The films all operate within popular genres of contemporary European filmmaking. *Mixed Kebab* is a romantic drama of family versus sexual desire; *My Brother the Devil* deploys the urban gang drama (it even shares an actor with *La Haine* [Mathieu Kassovitz, dir., 1995]); and *Unveiled* attempts the realist style of the Dardenne brothers, thematizing European precarity and marginal lives. Each film speaks fluently in the liberal vernaculars of European cinema, attempting to enfold the queer Muslim into that discourse.

Mixed Kebab articulates the contradictions of liberal tolerance quite plainly. The film sets up a dichotomy from its start with a rare moment of direct address in which the film's main character introduces himself as at once Bram and Ibrahim. Both Belgian and Turkish, Westernized gay and respectful Muslim, he seems unable to merge his names and identities. By setting up his subjectivity as bifurcated, the film dooms the possibility of queering Turkish Muslim identity before its story has begun, making tensions inevitable and affinities impossible. The film cues us to the affective registers of these two worlds from the start, contrasting the bright primary

Fig. 1.3: The final scene of *Mixed Kebab* reconstitutes the family without the homophobic brother or homosexual lover.

colors of the café owned by Bram/Ibrahim's future white lover with his dark and drab family home. Whereas the white-owned café visualizes a space of gayness and truth in which each character pops out as a distinct entity, human figures here have a hard time standing out from their surroundings in the palette of dull, muddy tones used for the Muslim domestic space. As the film moves the Muslim queer between the two spaces, it burdens him with navigating liberalism's desire for both universality and cultural relativism. The figure of the Muslim queer makes plain the contradiction in modern European liberalism in which racial others must be both exemplars of and exceptions to the universal category of personhood. As Sylvia Wynter has outlined, such a European assertion of humanism at once makes racial difference invisible and racializes access to the category of the human.[31]

In the film's final scenes, Ibrahim/Bram's white lover, Kevin, has saved the life of his homophobic brother Furkan. In the final shot, Ibrahim/Bram walks down a hospital corridor with his arms around both his accepting mother and his hateful father, presented as a figure of compromise and reconciliation (figure 1.3). The homophobic brother who has been lured into radical Islam and the white Western gay remain off-screen: the film has hardly been able to hold these two in the same frame throughout, and now they are missing from its final composition. *Mixed Kebab*'s multiculturalist logic implies that gays are gays regardless of their cultural background, and they must accept their destiny and come out of the closet. It also positions white racism and anti-immigration attitudes as mere peculiarities in an otherwise just society—that is, as exceptional behavior that results in no structural damage to the category of personhood. By contrast, it presents Muslim homophobia as a menace that violences the subject. As a typical ethnic queer,

Fig. 1.4: In *Unveiled*, Fariba evades detention in Germany by taking on the identity of a male detainee.

Ibrahim/Bram must anxiously hold together these contradictions of liberalism. Liberal tolerance for queers—tolerance itself already being a harshly compromised and contingent form of acceptance—competes with cultural relativism. In the film's homonationalist logic, the queer is the Achilles' heel who reveals the racist substratum of multiculturalism's pluralism.

Angelina Maccarrone's *Unveiled* vocalizes the limits of multiculturalism even more directly, folding the Muslim queer into a cinematic discourse on European immigration and economic precarity. The film tells the story of Fariba, a lesbian who escapes Iran after being arrested for her sexuality and in Germany takes on the identity of Siamak, a male refugee who has killed himself in the detention center (figure 1.4). Forced to assume a male identity to gain a German visa, Fariba encounters the racism of provincial Germans in her new life as a day laborer in a cabbage-processing plant. She begins a romantic relationship with a white German woman (figure 1.5), but after being attacked by the local men when they discover her gender, she is arrested and deported back to Iran. The film is noteworthy first for its title. The original German-language title means "foreign skin" or "strange skin" and focuses on the gender masquerade narrative. The film's US distributor Wolfe Releasing chose the English-language title *Unveiled*, shifting focus to Fariba's religious background and leveraging a colonialist representational history of white male desire to "lift the veil" on Muslim women. The film itself oscillates between these poles, at some moments complicating identities as transitive and relational yet at others reinstating the ethnic queer as an always compromised figure of European tolerance.

Fig. 1.5: *Unveiled* depicts Fariba having sex with her white German girlfriend.

An ambiguous Orientalism haunts the film's representation of a multi-cultural Germany: Stuttgart is introduced via a montage of Turkish kebab shops, women in head scarves, sex shops, and men kissing. The film cues us to read the women in *hijab* as signifying Germany's multicultural diversity, its European tolerance for the apparently opposing signifiers of (Muslim) sexual modesty and (queer) sexual display. This background maps onto the central narrative: Fariba as a Muslim lesbian figures the stakes of liberalism, the litmus test for Europe's hospitality to the other. The narrative takes as a given the homophobia of the Iranian state, the unseen threat of the non-European forming the very basis for fashioning an authentic self. The film needs Fariba to be unveiled, her secret self revealed, so that her stripping bare can enable the spectator's pleasurable outrage. But as much as this mode of European homonationalism echoes *Mixed Kebab*'s dichotomy of European tolerance versus Muslim homophobia, *Unveiled* reveals more than this Puarian structure.

Fariba's appropriation of Siamak's identity (hiding his body in a suitcase) is an unexpectedly melodramatic narrative trope in such a naturalistic film. It echoes the Egyptian popular genre films discussed by Samar Habib, in which gender-swap stories render female homosexual desire visible in presumptively straight environments.[32] In this context, Fariba's presentation as male echoes Eliza Steinbock's proposal of trans as a conceptual rubric.[33] For Steinbock, reading cinema from a trans perspective allows us to think gender transitivity alongside the transnational, trans-species, and trans-genre. Trans becomes a new assemblage that is capable of bringing disparate contemporary struggles into alliance. *Unveiled* does not seem to be a straightforward transgender narrative in the sense that Fariba's initial choice to present as male is narrated as a circumstantial necessity. But the film does juxtapose movement across gendered borders with those across national, regional, sexual, and class ones.

Fariba disguises herself as a man to gain access to Germany and chooses to continue presenting with a male identity when she returns to Iran. The transnational and the transgender are interlinked, with gender performance a matter of life and death in both national spaces. As Sima Shakhsari argues, counterposing Michel Foucault's and Achille Mbembe's accounts of the political body, "Shuttling between life and death, the transgender refugee is caught between biopolitics and necropolitics, where her body is produced and managed through religious, medical, psychological, and geopolitical discourses, and her death is sanctioned in the state of exception as a refugee . . . and as transgender."[34] Thus, although female passengers' removal and replacement of the hijab when leaving and entering Iranian airspace proposes an expected Western discourse on repressive Islam, *Unveiled*'s most interesting moment comes with Fariba's brave decision to remove female apparel in the airplane's bathroom and return to Iran in the identity of a male political dissident (figure 1.6–1.7). We expect Siamek/Fariba to be met on arrival with torture or death. This unexpected transition, like Fariba's disposal of Siamak's body at the beginning of the film, presents narrative agency in crucial but textually intermittent departures from multicultural realism. In their suspension of verisimilitude, these scenes both acknowledge what Shakhsari describes as the fragility of the trans body, crossed as it is with biopolitical and necropolitical forces, and offer an expanded agency to the queer figure.

Our final example in this section is a film that seeks to evade the racialization described by El-Tayeb as a feature of European humanism. *My Brother the Devil* is a coming-of-age story of two brothers, Mo and Rashid, growing up in London's council estates. The British Egyptian director Sally El Hosaini describes the film as an homage to *La Haine* that adopts the style of a Gus Van Sant film (figure 1.8). The film rejects certain questions and thus evades the sociopolitical impasses that often seem certain and inevitable. For instance, it refuses to place queer sexuality and Islam in existential tension: the narrative does not punish characters for being homosexual or for being traditionalists. It also refuses to place Islam as a cause of violence against homosexuals. In fact, characters associated more closely with the homeland are more comfortable with their sexuality than those characters who repeatedly assert their Britishness.

Figs. 1.6–1.7: Two mirror shots echo in *Unveiled*, offering different images of Fariba's gender.

The film appears at first to follow the generic outline of the racialized "ghetto gangster" drama, setting up a plot in which Mo is desperate to follow his older brother Rashid into what he perceives as the glamorous life of drug dealing. The narrative dangles the melodramatic expectation of a tragic end, but then reneges on this threat by offering a happy ending in which both brothers survive their youth on the streets. The film also does not provide its audiences with a coming-out scene but, at the same time, makes it clear at the end that Rashid has not concealed his sexual life from his parents. The film remains ambiguous about whether his parents disapprove of his life with the photographer Sayyid or are simply melancholy about his leaving home and moving away from them (figure 1.9). And unlike *Mixed Kebab* and *Unveiled*, *My Brother the Devil* discourages an ethnographic gaze;

Fig. 1.8: *My Brother the Devil* draws on representational conventions of British working-class realism.

its realism is deeply subjective in places and as the film progresses turns increasingly away from offering titillation for the cosmopolitan spectator, "slumming" for erotic thrills.

The film's central analogy seems to address the same paradigm that Puar describes in her account of the queer terrorist. After Mo discovers that Rashid is in a sexual relationship with Sayyid, he returns to his neighborhood clearly shaken and despondent. When his friends ask him why he is upset and where Rashid is, he lies, saying that Rashid has become a terrorist, in an attempt to divert attention away from that sexual truth. This keen interweaving of shame and sexuality, ethnicity and expectation, reformulates the urban genre and overturns clichés about queer sexuality in nonwhite communities. How are we to read the affective force of this switch—which, like Fariba's—is a protective fiction? In these moments, queerness navigates between disruption and belonging and between the universal and the culturally specific. Elizabeth Povinelli and George Chauncey have argued that globalization studies too often ignore the effects of subjective mediation, seeing social effects as all too transparently legible from social forms. Queer theory by contrast demands that we theorize the subject. "Where," they ask, "are the intimate and proximate spaces in which persons become subjects of embodied practices and times of desire?"[35] *My Brother the Devil* poses similar questions, and in fact, for each of these films, queer subjectivity is closely tied to the embedded practices and political travails of cultural relativism. Cinema, we argue, provides a privileged space for negotiating

Fig. 1.9: In its final scene, *My Brother the Devil* allows ambiguity to suffuse its familial bond.

this intersection, where intimate spaces are geopolitically defined and where embodiment, temporality, and desire have the potential to be imaginatively reworked.

The Diasporic Lesbian

This work of imaginative reconstruction can be seen most vividly in a genre that is often perceived as debased and reactionary. Since the 1990s the market for independent queer rom-coms (romantic comedies) has burgeoned. One need only peruse LGBT film festival catalogues or video-on-demand (VOD) sites to see that this independent market for same-sex romance has boomed. From the Chinese American *Saving Face* (Alice Wu, dir., 2004) to the Brazilian *Como Esquecer/So Hard to Forget* (Malu De Martino, dir., 2010), lesbian rom-coms have become a significant niche within the circuits of queer world cinema. The rom-com seems like an unlikely venue for queer cinema, since the genre is overwhelmingly hetero—not just casually hetero like most popular cinema but committed to compulsory heterosexuality as the foundation of its narration and affective economy.[36] However, the rom-com is not simply a historically straight form; rather, it is a genre historically engaged in women's desires, speaking to female audiences, and constructing sexual fulfillment for women as a structuring principle of narrative. It is thus less surprising than it might appear that it should form such a compelling and ambivalent site for lesbian filmmaking.

Multicultural rom-coms provide a space in which the diasporic lesbian figure is able to emerge. These films center on the queer woman in what reads, at first glance, as a means of figuring core–periphery and tradition–modernity in liberal terms. On closer inspection, though, they articulate more complex intersections of race, sex, and gender oppression. Several films in a broadly rom-com mode about the sexual identities of young women emerged in the United States and United Kingdom in the 2000s, including *Nina's Heavenly Delights* (Pratibha Parmar, dir., 2006), *I Can't Think Straight* (Shamim Sarif, dir., 2008), and *Three Veils* (Rolla Selbak, dir., 2011). All directed by lesbian-identified women from diasporic backgrounds, these films engage the experiences of first- and second-generation immigrants from the Middle East and South Asia. They represent lesbian desire alongside familial obligations and broader issues of ethnicity, religion, and national or transnational politics. We see these films as rendering visible the tensions produced by liberal multiculturalism in the West, as it struggles to accommodate LGBT rights discourse into dominant narratives of race, ethnicity, and religion in the metropolis.

The films draw on conventions of the rom-com to greater or lesser degrees, but each film we focus on here deploys figures of sexual and ethnic difference to narrate anxieties around multiculturalism. As Frank Krutnik puts it, "In the case of romantic comedy, it is particularly important to stress how specific films or cycles mediate between a body of conventionalised 'generic rules' . . . and a shifting environment of sexual-cultural codifications."[37] This relationship between generic codes and sexual contexts is especially appropriate in describing the diasporic rom-com, in which the shifting cultural environment is also narrated in the diegesis and the tension among tradition/family/non-Western and modern/lesbian/Western forms the central axis of narrative conflict. Here, the rom-com genre enables the films to romanticize liberal ideologies of multiculturalism, where the imperative to overcome difference subtends each transnational narrative of encounter. *Three Veils* sets up a romance between two Middle Eastern diasporic women in Los Angeles: Amira's family is Egyptian, and Nikki's family is from Iran (her parents are Persian and Afghan). The film makes explicit the backgrounds of its protagonists, directing spectatorial attention to the relationships among ethnic and sexual identities. Similarly, in *I Can't Think Straight*, Tala is a Palestinian woman whose family lives in Jordan. She works in London and falls for the British Indian Leyla. *Nina's Heavenly Delights* is also set in the United Kingdom, but here the main characters are all Scottish, with the South Asian Nina falling in love with the white Lisa. The rom-com form enables these mixed couples to come together (and break up) in ways that negotiate, in distinctly neoliberal terms, the binaries of tradition versus modernity, East versus West, and familial obligation versus sexual desire.

All three films are open to being critiqued as homonationalist and using ethnic, racial, national, and religious difference instrumentally to create the United States or the United Kingdom as the geopolitical spaces best able to accommodate happy LGBT lives. We see this homonationalist impulse quite directly in *I Can't Think Straight*, where the narrative about an upper-middle-class Palestinian family insulates Britain from any involvement and culpability in the Palestine–Israel conflict and produces Britain instead as a land of liberty and freedom. The key vector for this freedom is queer publicity, where a successful queer life is one lived publicly and a Western vision of coming out is necessary for both narrative closure and identitarian happiness. Thus, Leyla presents Tala with an ultimatum: come out to her traditional Palestinian family or they cannot be together. The same conflict is visible in *Three Veils*, in which the closet forms a central engine of drama in Amira's story line, and in *Nina's Heavenly Delights*, in which sexual tension is produced when coming out is again the prerequisite for narrative resolution.

Of course, the rom-com as a genre demands a normative romantic couple as its end point, and all of these films end with some variant of the couple form. Only *Three Veils*, which is the least comedic and most generically mixed of the films, refuses any lesbian couple, allowing a conventional "happy ending" only to its hetero character Leila. We return to this film later, but more straightforward in terms of homonormativity is *I Can't Think Straight*'s final scene. Here Leyla and Tala are not only a couple, but they are presented enviously watching a mother with her toddler in a park, implying that the ultimate goal of their relationship is to have children together. If the rom-com's narrative demand for the couple form stages a normative model of queer life, this image of maternity doubles down on the marriage plot, aligning the lesbian relationship with a history of patriarchal visioning of women's happiness. The lesbian rom-com here apes its conservative straight equivalent, and homonormativity results in a perfect reproduction of the hetero familial imperative, including the biological reproduction demanded by that family.

The diasporic rom-com thus intertwines coming-out narratives with the homonormative couple form and insists that the West is the site where this ideal form of queer life is most easily accessed. The West in these films is more modern and not enslaved to tradition; it is a place where gay rights discourse is rendered possible. Queer relations here represent progress and modernity, in opposition to the backwardness, inflexibility, and repressiveness of Middle Eastern and South Asian cultures. This opposition is most visible in *I Can't Think Straight*, where coming-out scenes juxtapose modern Westernized homosexuality with conservative non-Western families. Leyla's mother is shocked because she is a traditional Muslim and thinks lesbianism is sinful, while Tala's mother fears for the family's social reputation. Strikingly, in both families the patriarchal father responds well to the daughter's coming out; it is the mothers who carry the weight of backward Otherness. Patriarchy is not presented as the problem here; rather, the problem is religion and social status, both articulated through female characters.[38]

The opposition of Western queer liberty with Middle Eastern repression is most violently played out in *Three Veils*. The three veils, of course, represent synecdochally three Muslim women, and the narrative forecloses on the possibility of reconciling Islamic traditions with lesbian sexuality. Amira has to choose between queerness and Islam—or, rather, the film makes her choose and presents her privileging of religion over sexual orientation as a tragic loss of selfhood (figure 1.10). Although there is a romantic ending for Leila, the film moves away from the rom-com genre into that of the social-problem film in its proliferation of punishments for its protagonists when they try to assert autonomy as women. Thus, the hetero Leila is raped by her fiancé; Nikki is an alcoholic who is revealed to have been sexually abused as a child; and Amira both refutes her sexual identity and gives up her life in the United States. In this narrative economy, queer sexuality and religious belief are themselves social problems that can be resolved only by separation. Leila is supported by her community and hence achieves a happy hetero ending with husband and baby, whereas Nikki can become a happily out lesbian only by leaving her family behind, moving to San Francisco, and becoming a writer.

The film has prompted conflicting responses. Rachel Lewis locates it as a lesbian migration film, concerned with "the geographical and psychological effects of migration and border-crossing," while Samar Habib links it to texts such as *Sukkar banat/Caramel* (Nadine Labaki, dir., 2007) and the Egyptian television series *A Woman's Cry* (2007) as "evidence of a paradigmatic shift that installs a queer Muslim subjectivity at the center of culture and scholarship."[39] Taking up the ambivalence of the film's unhappy queer Amira, Elaine Castillo considers *Three Veils* in relation to Sara Ahmed's work on queers as unhappiness causes.[40] If the conventional happy ending of the rom-com defangs queer resistance to social norms, perhaps the unhappy ending of Amira's story reveals that which cannot be neutralized by homonormativities in the middle-class West. Ahmed argues that the unhappy ending can be a "political gift" in which "the unhappiness of the deviant performs a claim for justice."[41] Castillo finds the film ambivalently progressive, both laying bare some of the difficult experiences of intersectionality and yet still pun-

Fig. 1.10: *Three Veils* makes Amira a figure of repression, forcing her to choose religion over sexuality.

ishing its heroines for daring to step out of line. The piece is symptomatic of a larger question of interpretation: do we read unhappy endings as truth telling about homophobia or as ideological traps in which queer characters inevitably function as cautionary tales? Similarly, the happy endings of the more conventionally structured rom-coms might be feted as utopian visions of transcultural bonding as easily as they are critiqued as homonationalist fairy tales.

These rom-coms are self-aware about the seductions of assimilation for diasporic queers, and they deploy genre partly as a way to push back against both racialized scripts for cinematic romance and restrictive discourses of queer belonging. Here the significance of authorship to this modality of queer cinema becomes clear. Each of these films is directed by lesbian-identified women of color, and their engagement with queer politics is equally legible through the discourse of authorship as of genre. Of course, genre and authorship often have been placed in productive tension in popular cinema (e.g., Douglas Sirk's melodramas), and we might counterpose the dominant structures of the rom-com with the more radical authorial persona of Pratibha Parmar. Known for her experimental and activist films, Parmar has consistently addressed the intersections of racial and sexual violence and the cultures of postcoloniality. An authorial approach could consider Parmar's choice of the rom-com as a deliberate play with a form that enables her to engage contemporary South Asian or Black British queerness.

Moreover, as feminist film scholarship has insisted, authorship is a more heavily weighted discourse for minority groups.[42] Given how hard it is for female filmmakers of color to get funding to make features, especially when they are queer-identified, these films represent a perspective in queer cinema that is too often marginalized. Indeed, given the paucity of features made by lesbians of color, it is striking how often the rom-com is used in this way. Dee Rees's *Pariah* (2011) successfully deploys the romance genre (although, like *Three Veils*, it is more of a romantic drama) to broker themes of class and butch identity. In the United Kingdom, Campbell X's *Stud Life* (2012) adopts the rom-com for a Black British butch–femme romance that mixes British working-class realism with various anti-normative subcultures of queer black London. If we read genre alongside the films' authorship by queer women of color, it becomes clear that the romantic comedy contains an unusual capacity to articulate pressing critiques of multiculturalism and intersectionality in ways that successfully address diverse audiences.

If we take seriously the activist aims of these rom-coms, might we think of their popular mode of address as, in itself, a pushback on the limitations of antihomonationalist politics? Robyn Wiegman has addressed this flaw in thinking the relation between critical theory and social justice:

> It seems so strange to me when scholars expend enormous energy to critique such phenomena as homonormativity and queer liberalism without exploring how struggles to undo any form of phobic exclusion can never be made immune either to the desire for accessing traditional forms and formulas of normative US life or to reinterpretation, if not reinvention, by the conservative forces that cede political ground to the minoritized existence in the process. While I might share the sense that becoming a legible state subject on the terrain of one's identity-based subjection is always dicey, I hold no belief that the critical project of saying so tells us as much as we need to know about the complicated historical itineraries in which political struggles over identity have been and continue to be remade.[43]

The rom-com occupies exactly this territory, clearly implicated in homonationalist visions of the queer state subject, yet attempting, in its wide appeal to lesbian viewers, to enact modes of social transformation that are occluded by a rigidly antinormative queer politics.

So how do these films reject or complicate homonationalism within the normative structures of the rom-com? If we return to *I Can't Think Straight*'s evocation of the United Kingdom as a place of freedom, we can

Fig. 1.11: *I Can't Think Straight* depicts elite English tradition and heritage as queer and nonwhite.

discern some ambiguity in its representations of Britishness. The film circulates some very recognizable sites of British heritage: shots of the Houses of Parliament bathed in golden light, historic Oxford colleges, a bucolic thatched cottage, and even a polo match (figure 1.11). The film clearly has one eye on an international market and is drawing on histories of touristic looking at a particular wealthy English cultural heritage. But this traditional heritage is also re-signified as queer, with a lesbian polo player, a lesbian couple enjoying the Oxford University parks, and so on. Moreover, these traditional views of Britain are also reinscribed as nonwhite: a South Asian family live in the thatched cottage, and the film's overall vision of cosmopolitan London is mostly nonwhite. Whereas many films from Europe and the United States use foreign countries as backdrops for exotic homoeroticism, these films do not locate same-sex desire in an Orientalist mise-en-scène. Rather, they reimagine traditional British locations as queer-of-color spaces.

Nina's Heavenly Delights is even more comfortable constructing queerness as not only modern and British but equally as traditional and Indian. The romance plot brings together British Indian and white women in a multicultural union, but these bonds have a history. Lisa uncovers Nina's lesbianism by peeling back old flocked wallpaper in the family's Indian restaurant to see teenage "Nina + Lorna love forever" graffiti. Sexuality is linked to Indian identity humorously through a different type of heritage image: the tattered ornamental decor of a typical British curry house. The film implies that this queerness is not only a function of non-resident Indian (NRI) identity, but is also traditionally Indian in a scene in which Nina's mother watches *Mughal-e-Azam* (K. Asif, dir., 1960) on television and enjoys a song of forbidden love. We hear the famous lyrics, "What is there to be afraid of when you are in love?" These lyrics are repeated as we see the women undressing each other. The film offers a potentially queer reference point for South Asian audiences, affirming nostalgic and transgressive modes of reading classic Hindi cinema and indicating that the film's queerness is not entirely oriented to white Western knowledge and experience.

Not unlike *I Can't Think Straight*, *Nina* grants an unapologetic British-ness to its mise-en-scène—or here, more accurately, a Scottishness. When it deploys the iconography of Scottish life and landscape, it does so not simply as a suitable backdrop to stage a disaporic narrative and its apparently hy-brid identities. Rather, it asserts Scotland as home, a place that clearly forms Nina's identity but is also formed by it. Take, for example, the framing device used to demarcate acts, chapters, or intervals of the narrative. Each of these bridges centers on the sights and sounds of Glasgow. As intimate desires and family bonds increasingly intermingle, these intervals plot out urban space: visually through panning shots across skylines of the city's characteristic ar-chitecture (monumental Victorian buildings mixed with 1960s high rises) and overcast weather, and aurally through the voiceover of the disc jockey at a local South Asian music station, describing the weather, announcing community events, and sharing dedications for the loved ones of listeners. As with *Do the Right Thing* (Spike Lee, dir., 1989), in which a DJ's voiceover and cityscapes are inflected with community intimacies and tensions, *Nina* deploys these framing sequences to complicate its assertion of national and sexual figuration.

One of the film's tenderest scenes also works to co-articulate ethnic and national allegiances and sexual identities through cinematic space. This mo-ment occurs in a video store run by Nina's best friend, the gay Asian dance aficionado Bobbi, right after he has finished demonstrating a classical Bol-lywood dance routine to a group of adoring children. Left alone in the shop together, Nina and Bobbi sit among piles of VHS and DVD boxes and next to a large poster of the iconic film *Mother India* (Mehboob Khan, dir., 1957). Nina confesses her emotional predicament to Bobbi. She seems troubled, torn among her fears about her mother's expectations, her growing love for Lisa, the legacy of her father, and her professional ambitions. The video store,

Fig. 1.12: The video store in *Nina's Heavenly Delights* allows for the intermingling of national, diasporic, and sexual identities.

as in many queer films, provides a space in which conflicted affiliations can be spoken (figure 1.12). We could say that all of these details are overdetermined: the Glasgow skyline giving way to the diasporic video store, the poster from the famous nationalist drama of maternal sacrifice underscoring a discussion of family expectation. Moreover, Nina was introduced earlier by another character, who declared, "The prodigal returns," and until recently she was in London, estranged from her family. So, when Bobbi talks to her about home, it's particularly significant. He declares, while putting his arm around her, "You're home now." For the viewer, and for Bobbi, "home" designates embracing one's gay identity publicly as much as it might refer to a constellation of belongings including Glasgow, Scotland, finding true love, being with friends, the LGBT community, and the Indian family.

Bobbi's sassy commentary seems to echo what the film cues us to ask of Nina, "Why can't you just say it?" Belonging is brought to fore, and the scene provides a culmination of the film's interrogation of home. The idea of "belonging" is finally transformed by the film from an obstructive obligation (the necessity of choosing between seemingly conflicting desires) into a utopian route to cohesion (never scarce or exclusive, platonic as well as erotic, grounded in one place and another, respectful of the past and guaranteed for the future). By its ending, *Nina* refuses to recognize any disjuncture between what is possible in Britain, in living queerly, and in being part of an Indian diasporic family.

Although its sentimentality seems clichéd at times, the montages of food preparation and consumption are early harbingers of the film's critical transformation of home and its de-reifying of identity categories. Food is a sensual force, a carrier of affect equally crucial between father and daughter as it is between two same-sex lovers (mortar and pestle grinds and combines with brute lesbian arm strength that unlocks intense sexual feelings). It is the matter of bonding and kinship, offering an alternative connective tissue other than patriarchy. This refusal to segregate family romance from sexual romance is not about incest; instead, it is the film's powerful refusal to segregate the affections of queers as outside familial relations. If heterosexuality is not discontinuous with parental relations, then why should we place queer intimacies apart from parent/child affections? Food, for the film, is a vehicle in which to transfer affections and emotions, but it is also a mode of polymorphous desire in which mixture (or in the film's own terms, "masala") allows a kind of blending that does not destroy difference or disrespect boundaries. As Nina and Lisa win a TV cooking contest, the ever attendant ghost of Nina's father is also present, brimming with smiles. In the final triumph of queer culinary arts, *Nina* gives crucial screen time to the pleasure and pride Nina's mother receives from seeing her daughter's lesbian desire made very public (broadcast live on television and on the television sets in shop windows across the country). In a final flourish, the DJ who hosts the event points at the couple and says, adapting his oft-repeated catchphrase, "It must be the garam masala. Hold me back!"

Nina's most direct signaling of a reconfigured queer Asian British identity is the final scene, a fictional Hindi film shooting in Scotland. This discourse of transnationalism draws from a trend for Hindi films to shoot in rural northern European landscapes (especially Scotland and Ireland), most notably *Ek Tha Tiger* (Kabir Khan, dir., 2012) whose locations became a tourist attraction in Dublin. *Nina*'s fictional film scene conjures a utopian queer hybrid Scottish-Indian image, with Hindi film-style dance numbers (headed up by drag queens), including Scottish Highland dancing (figure 1.13). By the scene's end, all of the film's main characters are included in the frame. David Martin-Jones argues that although the film could be seen as appropriating seemingly kitschy elements of Bollywood for Western cinema, it is better seen as creating a hybrid aesthetic from an NRI perspective.[44] So while he finds the film's fantasy elements to be problematic (because such an interracial same-sex couple would encounter more problems in reality), the film's

Fig. 1.13: *Nina's Heavenly Delights* stages a cinematic spectacle of Indian and Scottish dancing.

insistence on a collective queer utopian vision provides a counter to the restrictive homonormativity of *I Can't Think Straight*'s socially reproductive ending. Queerness here is part of a collective re-visioning of the national public rather than a process of assimilation into the private mode of citizenship that has been critiqued so effectively in the US context by David Eng.[45]

The final moments of the film also suggest the potential of the moving image to produce spaces that allow for non-normative vectors of belonging and kinship—the happy coexistence of family ties and erotic bonds that the film uses the word "masala" to sum up. In the dance sequence, true love in all its variants can reign. Crucially, the film underscores for the audience that this is a space constructed for the film camera: it is both British and Bollywood but also purely neither. Thus, the moving image provides a space of political consequence for us and for the characters on-screen (and presumably for Parmar and her cast and crew). The film admits this is a construction and, in the final moments of the sequence, reveals the green screen, cranes, cameras, and production team. The sweeping dramatic landscapes of the Scottish countryside (hills, lochs, castles) gives way to the empty walls of a film studio. This revelation does not trigger a dystopic postmodern *mise en abyme* in which a vertiginous piling up of simulacra lead us to the conclusion that everything is a performance and thus up for grabs semantically. A sincerity persists in this moment in spite of (and is made prominent to the viewer because of) the revelation of an artificial mise-en-scène. This scene thus operates similarly to moments of self-reflexivity (e.g., in the "You Were Meant for Me" sequence in *Singin' in the Rain* [Stanley Donen and Gene Kelly, dirs., 1952]), which amplify rather than reduce the affective engagement of the audience with those on-screen. Seen from this perspective, the ending offers neither false hope nor dangerously impractical fantasy. It constitutes a refiguring of the parameters (limits) of prevailing political imagination. Daniela Berghahn argues that queer diasporic figures in films function as "a master trope of hybridity," and while this may seem to burden the queer figure unfairly, she also argues that "the revelation of queer desire in diasporic family films articulates a critique of fantasies of purity, which simultaneously underpin certain traditional models of the family and national ideologies." Later in the same discussion, she holds up the self-reflectivity of *Nina's* final sequence as disrupting ideologies of ethnic and national purity as "nothing but pure fantasy." This utopianism, she finds, surmounts that of other queer diaspora classics such as *My Beautiful Laundrette*.[46] It is in this same utopian impulse that we locate the ability of queer cinema to push against the norms of figurability in the rom-com.

In the end, the rom-com as a genre may find it hard not to assent to reactionary models: its generic structure, more pointedly than that in other types of popular narrative, demands a final capitulation to fantasies of romantic normativity, typically arranged around public displays of monogamous commitment and privatized sexuality. It is the perfect genre for homonationalism and yet the rom-com, like other instances of popular cinema, provides opportunities for ideological negotiation and resistance. For audiences eager to find stories of lesbians of color on-screen, these films have provided sites of pleasure and political contestation. Where the films' accounts of diasporic communities have been perceived as inadequate, they have equally provoked extensive online discussion. The star of *Three Veils* and *I Can't Think Straight*, Sheetal Sheth, who also starred in the lesbian web series *Lips*, drew a significant lesbian fan base. These lesbian figures can offer an alternative set of identifications that work against the films' more homonationalist impulses.

Elsewhere and Otherwise

If cinema intervenes in the developing relationship between queerness and global politics, then it also challenges us to theorize queer worldliness in resistance to, outside, or despite the dominance of globalized sexual and racial hierarchies. How can human communities grapple with difference that cannot be accommodated by late capitalism's limited notions of commodity fetishism, liberal diversity, and bland interchangeability? Eve Kosofsky Sedgwick's introduction to *Epistemology of the Closet* remains one of the most profound theoretical writings (queer or otherwise) to grapple with the question of difference. She opens her introduction with the binary of minoritizing and universalizing theories of sexuality in large part to prepare the reader for the startlingly plain declaration that will begin her axiomatic statement: "People are different from each other."[47] This axiom has a renewed resonance in the age of the global gay, for it firmly refuses to fix an essential truth or political determination of sexuality. As Jason Lim puts it in an analysis of queer geographies, "In seeking to multiply the possibilities for desire and for different kinds of action, queer theories and practices attempt not to prejudge the question of what a body can do. Indeed, queer thinkers have pointed out how heteronormativity and homonormativity are belied by the diversity of desires and relationships that already characterize many people's lives, and that transcend the ideological identities and proprieties that heteronormative and homonormative institutions attempt to enforce."[48] What does this openness to difference offer to the cinematic figuration of the queer? When thinking sexuality and gender in global or transnational terms, it is surprisingly easy to forget this crucial lesson in not making assumptions.

As we have seen in overtly multicultural films such as *Mixed Kebab* and *Three Veils*, queer figures are constantly at risk of being instrumentalized for discourses of racialized difference, whether in reactionary or liberal modes of Euro-American ethnocentrism. Figures who seem at first to speak of the complexities of identity across race, ethnicity, nationality, gender, and sexuality often end up reiterating white Western scripts. As Gaurav Desai has argued with regard to representations of African queerness,

> Just as Western feminism finds itself in a "nervous condition" vis-à-vis its negotiations with non-Western practices such as incision and clitoridectomy, an antihomophobic politics finds itself unable to open up gay-affirmative spaces without running the risk of being culturally insensitive. And yet, if no "culture" is so monolithic, so homogenous, as to be fully recuperable within a singular sexual, aesthetic, economic, moral, or epistemic order, if "culture," that is, always exceeds the limits it seeks to set for itself, then what divides the "culturally sensitive" from the "culturally insensitive"? Could sensitivity to the needs and desires of some subjects mean risking insensitivity to the needs and desires of others? If so, to which subjects and voices must such a politics pay heed?[49]

Here we see the horizon of limitation for what Nancy Fraser has called a "politics of recognition," in which a liberal LGBT demand for visibility shares some commonality with an intersectionalist claim on the essential experience of marginalized subjects. In both cases, the figure of the queer is understood as having a pre-existing and authentic identity that might be adequately (or inadequately) mediated by films. But not all films subscribe to such deterministic models of subjectivity.

Our final set of examples takes films that resist what Lynne Huffer calls the epistemic authority of the foundational subject. Huffer argues that intersectional theory has appealed to queer scholars attuned to difference because it attempts to diversify the kinds of subjects who can speak, but that such theories nonetheless depend on an understanding of subjectivities as given and empirically legible.[50] By contrast, Huffer insists that, even though Sedgwick herself wrote largely about a conventionally white, male, European canon of literature, her resistance to defining any kind of essentialist queer subject holds open the potential to create different forms of subjectivity within and against dominant social systems. This resistance to a certain kind of subjectification is crucial for thinking queer subjectivity beyond the figure of LGBT visibility, and we pose world cinema as a space in which an anti-foundational understanding of the queer subject might nourish previously unimagined queer figures.

What happens when world cinema's queer figures resist being instrumentalized for dominant narratives of global gay identity? In films by directors such as Fatih Akin, Li Yu, Apichatpong Weerasethakul, and Zero Chou, queer characters appear whose sexuality is largely inconsequential and remains unremarked on by other characters. In narratives of what we are calling taken-for-granted queerness, the sexuality of queer characters does not trigger religious debate, parental strife, or separation from the straight world. The films refuse to grant queerness any tumultuous impact on the diegesis. Such point-blank queerness is aligned with the uneventful rather than with rupture or rapture.[51] For instance, *Jin nian xia tian/ Fish and Elephant* (Li Yu, dir., 2001) is often heralded as the first lesbian film from mainland China, but it does not tell a story of sexual awakening. Its protagonist Qun already knows she is gay when the narrative begins, and fending off her family's expectations that she date men is a quotidian necessity (figure 1.14). Qun and Ling do not simply refuse the dramatics of coming out of the closet; more than this, they refuse to serve as figures of the universality of queer identity or experience. At the same time, neither

Fig. 1.14: Quotidian queerness in *Fish and Elephant*.

do they demonstrate the existence of queerness as a pre-existing local, in-digenous, or non-Western formation.

Similarly, in *I Don't Want to Sleep Alone* (Tsai Ming-liang, dir., 2006), homosocial proximities gradually become homosexual intimacies, but that transition is unremarked upon diegetically. As the narrative develops, the protagonist Hsiao-kang also begins a sexual relationship with a woman, and his bisexuality goes equally unremarked. There is something of the bathetic here in the sense that the queer does not operate as a force of the revelatory, the climatic, or the confessional, and instead is commonplace. The film de-emphasizes its unfolding of Hsiao-kang's sexual object choices and locates sex as equivalent to quotidian acts of human survival, like peeing, walking, and food gathering. In one of its most visually striking shots, the three lov-ers float through the frame on an old mattress, embracing in an affectless polyamorous tableau (figure 1.15). The film's staging of the precarious lives of transnational migrant laborers in Kuala Lumpur places sexual acts in an unremarked category. The mattress speaks as much of their meager living conditions as of their sex acts, and it has already played a narrative role when Bangladeshi migrant workers use it to rescue Hsiao-kang after he has been

Fig. 1.15: *I Don't Want to Sleep Alone* uses an old mattress to animate multiple intimacies and economic precarity.

beaten up and left for dead on the street. The very ground of sexuality—the physical object on which the lovers lie—speaks vividly of economic precarity and cross-cultural solidarity and care.

In many contemporary films, characters simply exist as queer. But whereas their sexuality, no matter how fluid, remains uncontested, other social tensions simmer. In these films, queerness is not the place in which globalization becomes visible. Fatih Akin's *Auf der anderen Seite/Yaşamın Kıyısında/ The Edge of Heaven* (2007) very clearly narrates how Lotte's affair with Ayten is a problem for Lotte's German mother not because Ayten is a woman but because she is Turkish. The lovers are separated not by homophobia but by Ayten's imprisonment as an activist for the Kurdish nationalist movement. Throughout, queerness presents itself plainly, refusing to pose ontological questions such as whether same-sex love is merely an affectation of Western cultural ideals or an extension of local and indigenous social formations. As figures, Ayten and Lotte evidence the film's lack of interest in the binaries of universal–particular and global–local. For Claudia Breger, there is something valuable in the film's evasion of existing geopolitical hierarchies. She refers to Akin's claim that by making Ayten and Lotte lesbians, he aimed to escape the engrained racial connotations of the dark (male) Turk falling in love with an innocent blonde (female) Northern European. For Breger, the good feelings prompted by Ayten and Lotte's love propose an affect other than that of European racism. Thus, she writes, "*Auf der anderen Seite* does not pretend to actually solve any dilemma by dissolving complex political configurations of power and affect into queer love."[52] Although critical of the film's liberal tendencies, which she sees as potentially reinscribing inequality, Breger locates *The Edge of Heaven*'s radicality at least partly in this refusal to harness queer love instrumentally to geopolitics.

In this way, the film does not offer Ayten and Lotte's queer relationship as the answer to binaries of race, politics, or power. Instead, as Berghahn has noted, *The Edge of Heaven* offers "elective forms of kinship" between Ayten and Lotte's mother, allied in a bereavement that crosses generations, nationalities, and politics.[53] Sexuality is not what is at stake in this difficult rapprochement. Queerness is an always already given in the film; it neither necessitates melodramatic disclosures nor leads to fracturing of other social bonds. (We might think of Barbara Mennel's description of homosexuality as "not a problem to fix" in current world cinema.[54]) The non-heterosexuality of such characters contrasts with the identitarian impulses of neoliberal queer identity. We see the taken-for-granted queer as a provocation of the contemporary historical moment, which refuses to instrumentalize the queer figure either to an essential identity grounded in cultural specificity or to a critical politics of globalization that sees films only as illustrative of social formations.

What is significant for us about these taken-for-granted queers is their ability to evade the dichotomies of universalism and cultural relativism. Queer theory that is attentive to the structures of racism and postcolonial power has addressed this very issue. Fatima El-Tayeb argues for what she calls a theoretical practice of creolization, which explores the "at times tense relationship between specific circumstances and universal conditions, local applications and global connections, without aiming to dissolve them through an all-encompassing, unified model, instead allowing for the intersectional, sometimes contradictory workings of power structures and subject positions shaped though not determined by them."[55] El-Tayeb's project of creolization works to shift the frame of theoretical reference in a way that is congruent with our attempt to expand the corpus of queer world cinema beyond a Eurocentric viewpoint. Her focus on intersectional subject positions, though, belies a more grounded version of queer identity than the films we address here necessarily claim.

What if the queer could figure the world otherwise? Gloria Anzaldúa famously asserted, "Being the supreme crossers of cultures, homosexuals have strong bonds with the queer white, Black, Asian, Native American, Latino and with the queer in Italy, Australia and the rest of the planet. We come from all colors, all classes, all races, all time periods. Our role is to link people with each other."[56] This polemical passage has prompted many responses, but a renewed contemporary significance can be found in its presentation of a model for queer worldliness that is far from the debased currency of the neoliberalized passport gay. For Anzaldúa, queer bonds form a way to make or even remake worldly connections. In cinematic terms, this cross-cultural queer would not be merely passively represented, viewed by properly globalized spectators, but could form and rework the apparatus itself. Such a figure might offer new modes of cinematicity that could emerge from queer relationships to geographical as well as sexual alterity.

Throughout this chapter, we have insisted on the queer as a figure whose effects can be felt across the cinematic apparatus. More than a question of good or bad representations, this figure condenses the work of sexuality and gender dissidence in the virtual and international spaces of cinema spectatorship. Where films pose queerness as a mode of cross-cultural translation and bonding, queer figures are able to evade the identitarian traps that characterize liberal multiculturalism, enabling a shift from LGBT-identified characters to less corporeal figurations of queer worldliness. This work of cross-cultural bonding is vividly rendered in *Lilting* (Hong Khaou, dir., 2014), which describes queer experiences of loss in an immigrant family.

We can see in *Lilting* a transnational bond that, not unlike the taken-for-granted queers, both depends on and refutes the possibility of direct translation between worlds. Directed by the Cambodian British filmmaker Hong Khaou, *Lilting* is transnational in its production and cast and narrates a cross-cultural drama. *Lilting*'s narrative centers on a mother grieving the death of her gay son and her strained relationship with her son's lover. As evoked by its title, the film plays with interweaving spaces and times and uses an expressionist approach to editing to capture the temporality of mourning. Film form is far from inconsequential here. In fact, for *Lilting* form offers a space of longing as much as of loss; of presence as much as of absence. What allows this stylized space to be invested with such affects is another ghostly figure of the gay man. Here, however, the apparitional gay is figured as more self-consciously transcultural, the child of immigrants who themselves come from mixed ethnic and racial backgrounds. Whereas the ghost in *Undertow* visually manifests the closet, the figure who haunts *Lilting*'s narrative represents the longed-for possibility of an embodied and loved Chinese-Cambodian-British queer kinship.

The Chinese Cambodian mother and English son-in-law do not share a language, so the son hires a translator to help with communication. After

Fig. 1.16: The problems of translation are textualized in *Lilting*.

the son's death, and after weeks (months?) of skirting around the nature of the relationship, the son-in-law outs the relationship in a confession that the diegetic translator does not translate. The mother then confesses to the son-in-law the jealousy she harbored and her deep sadness. The translator does not translate this either, but the film provides non-Mandarin speakers with subtitles. The confrontation is left ambiguous, so that the film both has and does not have a coming-out scene. If the final scene provides any conclusion, it is in the thematic and formal overlapping of coming out with questions about the capacity of any of us to communicate our experiences of loss or to express the nature of our subjectivity. *Lilting*'s assertion of queer identity does not affirm transcultural relationships as legitimate or even knowable. However, through cinema, with its ability to overlap different voices, languages, translations, and perspectives, a union is forged between two characters who otherwise are at odds (figure 1.16). Does this ending sidestep the question of cultural translation? Or does it suggest that humans can bond without having to reconcile their culturally specific expectations for human relationships? In either case, *Lilting* ends by derailing the arc of the coming-out narrative, replacing the logic of gay identity with a cinematic space of affect and affection across cultures.

The Slovenian film *Dvojina/Dual* (Nejc Gazvoda, dir., 2013) creates a similar effect of queer transnational cinematic space, and here again we see explicitly how questions of travel and translation are animated for the viewer. The film features a relationship struck up between a Danish woman and a Slovenian woman when the Danish woman's flight is delayed in Ljubljana. In one key scene in a café, the sexual tension that has been growing between the women culminates, but not in a way that is directly experienced in the diegesis. Neither can speak the other's language, and each discloses highly personal information that the other does not understand. However, these confessions are understood by the international audience—either by those who speak both languages or, more likely, via subtitling. In contrast to the history B. Ruby Rich describes of subtitling as a perceived problem for monolingual American audiences, *Dual* depends on the process of subtitling to create a non-diegetic realm of spectatorial affect.[57] Transnational cinematic space enables same-sex desire, even when the diegetic characters cannot entirely understand one another. Here, European cinema imagines the European Union itself as a queer space, but one that is truly available only through the apparatus and exhibition of cinema. Using a figuration of queer desire, *Dual* and films like it directly address the relationship between wealthy nations such as Denmark, which have long been part of the European Union, and East European states such as Slovenia, whose accession is more recent. This figure insists on queer desire as at once a vector of transcultural communication and a form of bonding that is radically unknowable and untranslatable.

In keeping with this refusal, we are not interested in asking whether globalization enables the queer to emerge as a universal figure. Such a line of thought spatializes a progress narrative in which the West is the first to open its arms to queers, and the rest of the world eventually follows. Nor do we wish to invest local cultural formations with an essential truth status that could be deployed in support of reactionary nationalisms and coercive gender politics. Sedgwick's minoritizing and universalizing approaches to homosexuality provide a compelling rubric for negotiating the fraught politics of queer globality. A minoritizing approach sees sexual identities as exclusive and particular territories, foreign to those who do not culturally belong. A universalizing perspective, by contrast, claims that all people have something of other people in them. These two approaches are thus not simply debates about ontology but also theories about what organizes human community. More simply put, they are worldviews. In the theoretical and sociological debates surrounding global sex cultures (debates that mostly come after Sedgwick and increasingly have come to dominate queer theory and politics in the past two decades) we can see an agonistic battle between minoritizing and universalizing views. Thus, a minoritizing view such as Massad's sees queers as emerging from specific historical and geographical scenarios, whereas universalizing human rights discourse works to trouble this historicity and geographical exclusivity, suggesting that people around the world experience love in comparable ways.

But for Sedgwick, the point is not to choose between these perspectives. The cross-cultural plenitude of queerness as a political and affective affinity and the preservation of apparently indigenous forms of gender and non-heterosexual intimacy constitute a necessary dialectical tension. Indeed, she warns that when we demand a resolution of the binary either way, the result is often to make queer forms of living less viable.[58] Thus, for instance, the universalism that hopes to create equality and repeal homophobic laws can often work in practice as a form of neo-imperialism that alienates non-Western governments so that queer people in those countries become more vulnerable to state-sanctioned attack. At the same time, the minoritizing discourse that rejects universal identities can end up demanding a very particularized identity that forecloses on the imaginative and literal spaces available for queers. Universalizing thinking can erase vulnerable queers, while minoritizing thinking can foreclose on connections and alliances.

Remembering that people are different from one other and refusing to define any particular understanding of queerness in advance helps avoid imperialist visionings of the global queer. Sedgwick's list form and its architecture of difference might be adapted or even subverted to thinking the worldly. In light of the complex figurations of transcultural bonding we have explored in these films, we offer some stipulations about worldly queerness after Sedgwick:

- Some people characterize their gender or genders in locally specific terms, and others view them in universal terms.
- Some people find that identity categories offer agency, and others find them limiting.
- Some people embrace the label "queer" as liberatory, and others find it oppressive.
- Some people understand their sexuality as continuous with those around them, and others define it as foreign to those around them.
- Some people understand their sexuality as connecting them to a world of other queers, and others see it as exclusive to their culture.
- Some people connect their sexuality and/or gender identity with regional, ethnic, religious, or national backgrounds, and some do not.
- Some people have to travel to express their sexuality and/or gender, and others stay at home.
- Some people invest in the erotics of geographical otherness, and others do not.
- Some people take their sexuality and/or gender for granted and others do not.

This list deserves to be expanded, but even this provisional version illustrates how Sedgwick's paradigm can be adapted to our understanding of the queer in world cinema.

Our focus on the figure of the queer in the world has aimed to move from normative representations to those texts that evade the traps of both minoritizing and universalizing discourses. Indeed, those queer theorists who are most attentive to the exclusions of globalized LGBT identities provide insight into the different worlds that queer figures might make. Rinaldo Walcott boldly argues that "black diaspora queers have actually pushed the boundaries of transnational identification much further than we sometimes realize. Black diaspora queers live in a borderless, large world of shared identifications and imagined historical relations produced through a range of fluid cultural artifacts like film, music, clothing, gesture, and signs or symbols, not to mention sex and its dangerously pleasurable fluids."[59] Walcott takes a film, *Welcome to Africville* (Dana Inkster, dir., 1999), as the key illustration of this fluidly queer world and the diasporic reading practice that might access its heretical globalism. Chela Sandoval proposes an even more utopian vision of queer worldliness when, drawing from black, Native American, and Latino/a feminisms, as well as from anticolonial and queer theories, she states, "The afterlife of colonialism shimmers with [a] new dissident mode of global cosmopolitics."[60] While the tyranny of our current neoliberal moment might make such accounts read like distant fantasies, we consider it nevertheless crucial to listen to these dissident propositions. These shimmering queer worlds trouble globalization and heteropatriarchy in ways that resonate with the potentialities that we see in cinema. In the films we have analyzed in this chapter, we have been attentive to moments of political and intimate connectivity that could conjure such worlds. In these moments we can catch glimpses of what another queer world might look and feel like.

A WORLDLY AFFAIR
Queer Film Festivals and Global Space

Cinema makes spaces that did not exist before. Even the most fantastic of filmic spaces are connected to our lived world via an apparatus that binds exhibition space with diegetic space. Different uses of cinema, different arrangements of its *dispositif*, remake the world differently. Thus, how the institutions of global queer film culture use cinema politically is directly linked to their worlding practices. This chapter focuses on the institutional sites of queer cinema in the world, taking the queer film festival as its central example. Reading queer cinema institutionally focuses the question of how particular kinds of interdiscursive space are enabled by the cinematic apparatus and how these cinematic spaces affect the spaces available to queer politics. In other words, we consider the political potentials and limits produced by queer cinema's global circulation and consumption.

Spatiality forms a vital heuristic for us because it overlays the geopolitical with the cinematic and, moreover, understands the cinematic at the intersection of text, exhibition, and audience. Thinking global queer cinema evokes a set of spaces and scales that includes not only technologically mediated and often quasi-virtual places (the screen, diegetic worlds, intertexts) but also actual locations (the profilmic, theaters, festivals, and other institutional sites). Audiences occupy these technological and physical places in locally defined communities and in the context of the purely imagined spaces that films build through their images and sounds. Whether in the established cinephile setting of Queer Lisboa or the precarious counterpublic that the &Proud LGBT Film Festival in Yangon produces for queer youth in Myanmar, the sensorium of queer cinema remaps the world. The longtime human rights activist Aung Myo Min says, "LGBT people in Burma are always marginalized and shown as abnormal in local movies. However, [the films at &Proud] show the other side of their life, courage and contribution."[1] Or, as Ging Cristobal, project coordinator for Asia at the International Gay and Lesbian Human Rights Commission says of the festival, "When Myanmar opened its doors to the world, it also opened a window on the activism of lesbian, gay, bisexual, and transgender (LGBT) communities in the country."[2] This chapter reads the queer film festival as an institution not only for its implication in hegemonic systems but also for the places where it complicates dominant discourse and speaks back to power (including queer power), and for the resistant spaces it enables. We find such spaces across the gamut of queer film festivals, from those most mired in homonationalism to those most bravely resistant or transgressive. It is a question not of separating good objects from bad ones but, rather, of locating the queer potentiality of the institutions, counterpublics, and audiences engendered by cinema.

Film festivals in general have become the subject of renewed interest in film studies, including two recent fora in *Screen* and several anthologies.[3] Driven by the field's broader desire to address the industrial side of international cinema and to interrogate the institutional and economic circuitry of categories such as "global art cinema" and "world cinema," these studies approach the film festival as an institution that enables understanding of cinema's shifting role in world politics. As if anticipating these debates, André Bazin cynically notes that the film festival appears to the public as "the very epitome of a worldly affair."[4] From our perspective, the festival represents at once an exceptional space for films and quite a typical space in which to find queer cinema presented as such.

Today, nearly all international film festivals admit that they are in the business of worlding, and queer film festivals seem particularly eager to proclaim *both* that queers make films more worldly and that films make the world more queer. For example, in 2014 the Out in Africa South African Gay and Lesbian Film Festival screened the British film *Pride* (Matthew War-chus, dir., 2014) on its opening night. Focusing on a group of lesbians and gay men who supported striking miners in Margaret Thatcher's Britain, *Pride* understands LGBT politics in terms of solidarity across identities. Although deeply embedded in national history, the film won the Cannes Queer Palme and thus also speaks as a representative of the international. From this perspective, cinema as an institution and a medium appears to open the queer local to the world. The screen is the threshold between the limits of the national and the expansive promises of the global. To signal the transformative possibilities of this threshold, the screen presents a world in which queers can live publicly, which may be less possible to imagine beyond the theater's walls. The queer film festival is uniquely alive to the tensions between the global forces that exert themselves on cultural institutions and the potential for local practices to negotiate worlding.

In other words, the queer film festival not only reflects the world but actively makes and remakes worlds. Sometimes it does so according to reigning ideas of globalization, but not always. Certainly, it responds to the institutions of world building in which the festival's survival is implicated. Since the 1990s, queer film festivals have been faced with a pressure to reconcile a globalizing mission with a local politics of being queer in the world. In our interviews with queer film festival organizers, many programmers noted a trend toward a more international focus since the late 1990s and increasing pressures from funding bodies, audiences, and critics to provide cosmopolitan experiences. Kam Wai Kui, former director of the Transgender Film Festival in London and Amsterdam, points to a shift in Anglophone festivals from resistance among audiences to watching subtitled films to a gradual normalization of "foreign" films. Suzy Capó points to a different factor in the early days of MIX Brasil, where there was no budget for subtitling and the local audience could not be expected to understand non–Portuguese-language films. By 1996, subtitling software was available that enabled the festival not only to subtitle its own films but to make money subbing for other festivals.[5] Thus, both technological democratization and broader social changes helped usher in the era of international queer film festivals. Ragan Rhyne identifies this period as the third phase in the history of queer film festivals, "marked by the international proliferation of the gay and lesbian film festival model."[6]

The stakes of this globalizing impetus can be read in the history of the San Francisco International LGBT Film Festival, often referred to as Frameline after the organization that mounts it each year. Founded in the mid-1970s, Frameline is the world's longest-running gay and lesbian film festival and remains probably the largest, with annual sales of more than sixty thousand tickets. The festival has had the word "international" in its title since its fifth year and now calls itself "the world's destination for LGBT film." Early on, "international" designated the inclusion of a few European features: premiering the latest film of the German queer media pioneer Rosa von Praunheim or dusting off a print of *Un chant d'amour* (Jean Genet, dir., 1975), but by the 1990s the festival had begun foregrounding its role in bringing world cinema to a queer audience. Thus, for example, the opening night slot at the 1990 festival was given to *Coming Out* (Heiner Carow, dir., 1989), which it described as the first gay film from East Germany. Similarly, in 1997, Riyad Vinci Wadia, the director of *BOMGay* (1996), is described as producing "the first ever indigenously produced gay films from India."[7] In that year, the shift toward overt worlding is fully visible: the catalogue opens by announcing a sidebar on "Gender in Hong Kong Cinema," including *Gei Lo Sei Sap/A Queer Story* (Kei Shu, dir., 1997) and *Gam chi yuk yip/Who's the Woman, Who's the Man?* (Peter Ho-sun Chan, dir., 1996), timed to reflect on the handover of Hong Kong back to China that year.

By 2006, the festival had begun dividing its program into three categories that showcased its internationalism: US features, documentaries, and world cinema. The world cinema section included more familiar art-house auteur films such as François Ozon's *8 femmes/8 Women* (2002) but was also clearly invested in geographical diversity. Screenings included *Go West* (Ahmed Imamovic, dir., 2005), a Bosnian/Croatian love story set across the religious divide in the former Yugoslavia; *El favor/The Favor* (Pablo Sofovich, dir., 2003), a lesbian screwball comedy from Argentina; and *Detik Terakhir/Last Second* (Nanang Istiabudi, dir., 2005), described in familiar terms as "the first lesbian feature from Indonesia."[8] In a discourse of exception, international films are often contextualized as the first gay films from their country. The programmer K.C. Price describes a strategy of identifying "emerging zones" of queer film production, such as the showcase of Asian films held in 2002 called "Tsunami Warning" (figure 2.1) or "South America's New Queer Cinema" in 2010. In the catalogue copy for these programs, an evolutionary geography takes hold, with Western attitudes toward sexuality and queer identity setting the terms for a kind of progressive acceptance of LGBT people that sweeps across the globe, implying chronologies of cinema that see peripheral queers as belated entrants to the world.

Fig. 2.1: Frameline's 2002 Asian cinema showcase was titled "Tsunami Warning."

In this newly globalized era, however, queer cinema has become a flash-point for public debates about cultural integrity, nationalist politics, and human rights. For instance, Deepa Mehta's film *Fire* (1996) prompted controversy in India over its frank depiction of lesbianism, and the divisive and violent protests that ensued are now cited as a foundational moment for the queer rights movement in India.[9] As Jigna Desai has argued, the *Fire* controversy demonstrates how culture is burdened with managing the contradictions of the nation-state.[10] Queer film culture has borne the brunt of these contradictions, with queer film festivals around the world increasingly becoming sites of homophobic attacks. In 2010, anti-gay protestors attacked the Q! Festival in Jakarta, threatening to burn down venues if the event continued, and in 2014 Kiev's oldest cinema was firebombed during a gay festival screening. According to its founder, Manny de Guerre, Russia's Side by Side Festival is regularly threatened with violence, as are festival programmers and the owners of the venues it uses.[11] Jon Binnie speaks of the "politicization of homophobia" that has emerged in the twenty-first century alongside resurgent nationalism and religious fundamentalism, and queer film festivals provide a very public site for both LGBT cultural spaces and the vicious attacks by homophobic hate groups.[12] In John Greyson's film *Covered* (2009), one interviewee says of the first Queer Sarajevo Film Festival in 2008, "Festivals are turning into massacres."

On the other end of the political spectrum, progressive activists and scholars have critiqued queer film festivals as handmaidens of globalization. Sarah Schulman's use of film festivals as exemplifying Israeli "pinkwashing" is illustrative of cinema's central role in radical queer activism.[13] Queer film festivals, these activists argue, may seem like a neutral venue for world cinephilia, or even a positive extension of human rights politics, but they actually form a locus of state propaganda and corporate interventionist policies that align with racist and classist agendas. Thus, major festivals in San Francisco and Toronto have been protested for their acceptance of Israeli state funding, and at the Hamburg Lesbian and Gay Film Festival in 2014, protestors drowned out the speech of a local politician who garners progressive kudos through his support of LGBT rights yet works to deport undocumented Turkish immigrants. In all of these examples, queer film festivals emerge as a public battleground in a culture war that pitches local sovereignty against globalization and locates the question of queer identity or community in the very middle of the universalism-versus-cultural specificity debates. It might be easy, on the one hand, to critique these protests as betraying a certain naiveté (or utopian expectation) about how most forms of public culture are funded, or, on the other, to derive a mere critical frisson from uncovering how festivals are in bed with globalization. More pressing for us than either response is the emergence of queer film institutions as sites that are uniquely able to reveal the political assets and liabilities of thinking culture globally. In other words, festivals do more than instantiate dominant ideologies: they persistently pose questions of queer globalism for audiences. Theorizing the world is part of the work of the queer film festival.

Cinema conjures a space in which evidence for the global presence of queerness is made palpable, experiential, and realizable. In the words of the organizers of the Torino Gay Film Festival, cinema is a "fascinating machine of seduction," and that well-oiled machinery of apparatus and embodied desire enables cinema to manifest the world as a queerly intersubjective space. It is not that queer film festivals provide an empty space that can be filled up with more or less radical queer content (films, events, audiences, and so on) but, rather, that cinema itself must be theorized as a queer and worldly institution. A dynamic theoretical understanding of the medium recognizes how the experience of cinema produces complex subject effects. These effects can resist and derail as much as they enable the instrumentalization of films for neocolonial forms of cosmopolitanism. What kind of world does the festival conjure? What are the political and social potentials allowed by that this particular rendering of the world? Whose needs does this world fulfill? Identifying the exact parameters of the worlds proposed by institutional uses of queer films is critically important, then, and how these practices define the scale of the worldly delimits a political terrain of great consequence in contemporary queer politics.

Take, for example, the Painting the Spectrum festival in Guyana, the Anglophone Caribbean's only LGBT film festival. The festival is produced by a group called Society against Sexual Orientation Discrimination (SASOD), which also engages in legal advocacy and AIDS activism. The programmer Ulelli Verbeke has written about the significance of the festival in Guyana, a country where same-sex intimacy and cross-gender dressing are both illegal. She has also lauded the festival's Spectrum Night, at which attendees paint messages promoting and imagining "a society which is more embracing of sexual and gender diversity" and "expressions through poetry, song, dance, and fashion are also a much anticipated component."[14] The counterpublic spaces created for and by audiences at Painting the Spectrum arise in the integration of a globalism borrowed from past queer film festival hits with a program of regionally produced films that address pressing local issues.

So, for example, in 2014, the festival highlighted queer filmmaking from the Caribbean alongside high-profile international films, and screened documentary shorts produced by SASOD that profile LGBT Guyanans. Activist documentaries such as *Sade's Story* (SASOD, 2014) about the discrimination faced by a trans fashion designer in Guyana, and *Jessica's Journey* (SASOD, 2014) about a trans woman who left the country because she did not feel safe, played as part of a Caribbean showcase that also featured the Guyanese gay romance *Antiman* (Gavin Ramoutar, dir., 2014) and the US/Jamaican documentary *Taboo Yardies* (Selena Blake, dir., 2011). Alongside these Caribbean films, the festival screened international documentaries such as *Venus Boyz* (Gabrielle Baur, dir., 2002) and mainstream international features, including *XXY* (Lucia Puenzo, dir., 2007). This event harnesses together prestige films whose circulation already claims a worldly history with domestic productions that might not travel so easily.

In the queer film festival, and Painting the Spectrum is a good example of this structure, worlding includes not only the world(s) represented in the programmed films, but also the worlds imagined by the spaces and shapes of the event and the activities of its audiences. Its world extends to paratexts such as promotion, sponsorship, and the structure of the program (including categorizations, sidebars, juxtapositions, and even omissions). Marc Siegel has eloquently articulated the experience of the queer film festival audience: "At a queer film festival, one finds therefore not only films but a festival of encounters, whether nostalgic, erotic, or informative which combine to create a particular film viewing experience. The identity that one affirms upon entering the festival can thus become redefined to include not merely a different relation to race, gender, or sexuality, but to cinema as well."[15] Or, as Martha Gever says of the festival, "Our identities are constituted as much in the event as in the images we watch."[16] Hongwei Bao describes the creative "guerilla warfare" tactics deployed by the Beijing Queer Film Festival after being repeatedly shut down by the Chinese government, including screenings held on public trains and buses, using shared laptops and USB sticks.[17] If queer film festival audiences have the potential to nurture new modes of being, festivals themselves can push back more consequentially on the limitations of the globalized world. Indeed, we insist that their unique position in the center of struggles over LGBT subjectivities, public life, and global geopolitics gives queer film festivals the opportunity to play a role in reenvisioning queer publics.

This chapter develops a film theoretical account of the queer film festival that is able to attend to this complex space of text, paratext, context, and audience. Each queer film festival produces a different experience of being in the world for the audience, a different mode of worlding. The most culturally dominant version of this experience can be seen in a festival such as Frameline, where the spectator is presented with a panorama of queer films from all over the world and with a world in which there appear to be queers everywhere. In the analyses that follow, we examine three very different festivals—the MIX NYC Queer Experimental Film Festival, the KASHISH Mumbai International Queer Film Festival, and the Batho Ba Lorato Film Festival in Gaborone, Botswana. In concert, these festivals enable a more ambivalent accounting of transnational queer publics and of what it means to ask people to participate in cinema.

Of particular importance here is attending to the audience, not in the sense of an empirical reception study, but as a set of material practices through which queer publics are imagined, anticipated, and activated. These analyses offer contrasting modes of being public and very different scales of queer collectivity. The MIX NYC festival's uniquely interactive and inventive exhibition spaces create alternative worlds whose utopianism is contingent on their exclusivity, sealed off from the rest of the world. We associate this festival with a minoritizing politics, where despite the fluidity of queer identities the audience forms a distinct and self-consciously oppositional community. The KASHISH festival aims for the opposite effect, moving increasingly toward an integrated audience that mixes festival-goers with cineplex viewers and intermingles exclusively queer audiences with mainstream Hindi film audiences and Bombay industry insiders and movie stars. It works from a universalizing premise, dependent on a human rights discourse and the funding of nongovernmental organizations (NGOs), the United Nations, and cultural agencies from wealthy nations. Batho Ba Lorato negotiates between these poles, hailing an audience at once through universalizing and minoritizing tactics. Its programming and social media presence boldly addresses an LGBT community in Botswana while simultaneously connecting to transnational struggles for racial equality and social justice. Taken together, these festivals refute standard accounts of LGBT global politics. They demand that we pay much closer attention to how queers around the world create new venues for cultural expression and, indeed, alter the material terms in which queer life can be lived.

MIX NYC's Exceptional Worlds

Writing on the festival's Facebook page, one audience member describes the MIX NYC festival as an "aesthetically powerful radically queer deliberately inclusive fiercely political artistically subversive dangerously creative continuously improving community-building non-profit organization." These comments encapsulate the audacious nature of this queer experimental film festival based in New York. Running for twenty-five years, MIX NYC has become known not only for its showcasing of innovative and unconventional queer media works, but also for the exploratory and immersive exhibition environments in which it shows that work. In fact, the festival could be seen as building and rebuilding the idea of cinematic exhibition in particularly queer terms each year. For much of the festival's history, its venue has shifted from year to year, and a result of this constant relocation is its investment in large-scale, temporary constructed environments. This process became a cycle in which MIX NYC now tirelessly experiments with physical space as part of the annual event. The brick-and-mortar fragility of the festival led the organizers to rethink institutional spaces and imagine them as extensions to—and corollaries of—the visual and aural spaces developed in queer avant-garde film aesthetics.

Stephen Kent Jusick, director and head programmer of the MIX NYC festival, led this transformation after he realized that participatory experiments in the 2010 festival significantly increased engagement among audiences and widened how those audiences understood their participation. As Jusick sees it, the immersive and interactive atmosphere created by these built environments allowed the festival finally to live up to the ethos of a queer experimental cinema: "It became clear that there was something about the space—the world—that MIX was creating that audiences were responding to."[18] In 2010, MIX NYC gave the artist Diego Montoya the task of reworking the interior architecture of that year's venues. He reconfigured several of the festival's key public spaces with massive planes of string art that looked like multicolored intersecting spiderwebs. Another space appeared besieged by massive explosions of household junk; suspended detritus enveloped visitors in a sea of ordinariness made spectacular. Montoya said the intention of his designs for the 2010 venue was to offer "a big gay hug," and, as Jusick's words make clear, the big gay hug embraces not just a space but a world.

More recent incarnations of MIX NYC have furthered these experiments with interpenetrating spaces in which films are one among many audiovisual attractions. In 2011, Montoya, working with Bizzy Barefoot, created an assortment of intergalactic environments, including a starlit, mirrored reception area that crossed a glitzy 1970s disco with a planetarium; a subterranean space cave populated with oversize fuchsia pillows in spiky shapes resembling stalagmites and stalactites seemingly inspired by *Barbarella* (Roger Vadim, dir., 1968); and a psychedelic forest (figures 2.2–2.3). In the forest environment, attendees walked through passages crowded by walls overtaken with glowing tropical flowers and were brushed by the unavoidable gropes of dripping ferns. A powerfully queer pastoralism emanated from both the space cave and the psychedelic forest. Both locations scrambled oppositions of synthetic and organic, growing and deformed, soft and hard, and cozy and parasitic, playfully upending notions of nature and culture to propose a queerly natured environment. (We discuss the potentialities of the queer pastoral in chapter 5.)

In these tactile and participatory worlds, MIX NYC aimed to design spaces that purposely blur the difference between viewing theaters and reception areas. Whereas conventional cinema architecture carefully regulates audience members' behavior via dedicated areas for socializing, waiting, and viewing, these otherworldly locations appear designed to exploit, expand,

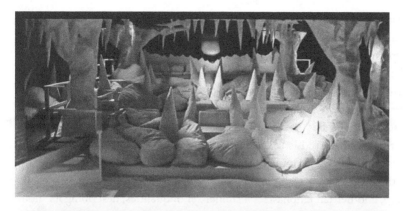

Figs. 2.2 and 2.3: Queer environments at the MIX NYC Queer Experimental Film Festival. Courtesy of MIX/Nick Bullock.

and reboot cinema's sensorium to encourage new ways of being together. These spaces, with their apparently over-the-top campy excess, are more than party decoration. Rather, they should be taken seriously as site-specific temporary installation projects in the traditions of Andy Warhol or Hélio Oiticica. Their work is to produce MIX NYC's entire environment as queer, experimental, and experiential. These immersive site-specific installations use mood as a kind of social experiment, establishing new intimacies and different ways to come together as a group and amalgamating otherwise distinctly individuated experiences. Jusick has talked about the world-making qualities of these environments both as extensions of the ethos of experimental and underground cinema practices and as a central feature of the festival's commitment to nourishing queer communities and lives. He articulates MIX NYC's aim as to "create a queer world for a week," in which the festival space becomes a "temporary autonomous zone." The MIX NYC festival thus echoes many of the qualities of early erotic film festivals in New York described by Elena Gorfinkel. Her research argues that those festivals' immersive environments fostered non-identitarian forms of being together politically, socially, and sexually.[19] In a post to the festival's Facebook page, another fan emphasizes a similar set of qualities, describing its "non-exclusivity" in this way: "It is truly SO MUCH MORE than a film festival. It is a HOME and safe space. . . . I would not be who I am today without it, and neither would many many people."

Like its precursors of the 1970s, the MIX NYC festival encourages group-viewing practices that emphasize a collective experience more than conventional movie theaters. The architecture of its temporary exhibition spaces and structure of its program aim to amplify spillover rather than reduce it. But despite upsetting the expectations of conventional viewing practices in this kind of space, this design is not a betrayal of cinema as a medium. In fact, we might say that it radically derives from the festival's keen awareness of that medium's specificity. The MIX NYC festival amplifies the odd public–private communalism of traditional cinema's spectatorship model and, moreover, infects non-cinematic experiences with that special kind of intimate public encounter, belonging, and collectivity. It reminds us that cinema remains a plastic aesthetic experience. The MIX NYC festival persists as an experimental space not only because it provides screens for avant-garde film practices and depictions of alternate sexualities, sexes, and genders but also because it remains committed to the flexible, impure, promiscuous, perverse, and even queer nature of cinema itself as a medium. The temporary architectures of these venues encourage both adventure and comfort. They serve as platforms for gender/sex deviance and as spaces of safe communion. They offer venues for encounter and wonderment, as well as of freedom from the violence imposed by regimes of normalcy.

This form of queer world making extends beyond the built environment to encompass both the programming and the international spaces of MIX. As early as 1994, international politics were on the agenda for the festival's mission. That year, they hosted a pioneering panel discussion on the expansion of queer film festivals beyond North America and Europe, "World Clique?

Queer Festivals Go Global." As Robert Reid-Pharr points out, questions of race and class were central to this debate, as well as contested cross-cultural uses of the term "queer."[20] In its implementation of cinema as a queer medium, MIX NYC has defined itself against the segregation often encountered and inadvertently fostered by the structures of other queer festivals. In other words, central to the programming and design of the festival is to erode what Jusick calls "fragmentation." The MIX NYC festival has done this by developing strategies that refuse the segregation of audiences (into gay, lesbian, or trans interest groups), of genre (narrative, nonrepresentational, personal, documentary), of media (video, celluloid film, installation art, performance, dialogue, lecture), or of realms of experience (fantasy or reality, public or private, closeted or out). Its commitment to radical queer experience also encompasses the breakdown of national and cultural boundaries, one year even attempting a live-video feed to queer artists in Iran. The stated mission of MIX NYC has always been to *mix*, and facilitating admixture has meant that the festival has escaped "ghettoizing" (Jusick's term) films from particular nations into special screenings or distinct programming strands.

Likewise, the festival's approach to globality has been unusual. It is in some ways resolutely local, tied to New York's queer urban cultures and deliberately shunning global corporate sponsorship. Instead, MIX NYC has helped to found similar festivals in other countries that take its name, such as MIX Brasil or MIX Mexico. The festivals are progeny with absolute autonomy and not colonial outposts. These other MIX festivals have entirely independent curatorial teams and policies. The MIX Copenhagen festival has, in turn, spawned MIX Aarhus and MIX Aalborg, in a queer fractal process of replication without reproduction. And while MIX NYC does sponsor community screenings, and parts of the program have traveled, Jusick emphasizes that the organization has resisted the temptation to become too transportable or transmissible in the way that other festivals syndicate themselves.[21] The MIX NYC festival is not directly exportable; rather, it offers to its collaborators a collision of media, modes of address, forms of communal intimacy, and experiential registers. As an institution, MIX maintains international connections, yet resists the kind of commodification and fragmentation that globalization demands.

Something akin to the imaginative environments of MIX NYC can be found in other queer film festivals—for instance, the Nachtbar at the Hamburg Lesbian and Gay Film Festival intervenes in city space in a comparable way. Each year, the Nachtbar is created anew. The bar is not advertised; instead, the address is provided at the opening night film, and information spreads by word of mouth. It remakes existing buildings, a practice that began in the late 1980s and emerged from the culture of squatting, in which occupying unused buildings was a mode of resistance to gentrification and the forms of capitalist life. (Both Hamburg and New York provide rich histories of gentrification and its opposition, with queer culture at the center of resistant forms of living.[22]) The Nachtbar repurposes an everyday environment and transforms it into a queer space—in 2014, it took over a school. The transformation is cheap, tacky, and resolutely non-consumerist. Found objects and homemade decorations resist the commodification of gay culture, emphasizing instead spaces that nurture queer affects, bonds, and communities. Like MIX NYC, the bar provides a setting for festival interviews, art events and performances, functioning as a queerly fantastical social space.

Most queer film festivals understand that their mission extends beyond the exhibition of films and that the social environment created by screenings and their adjacent events provides a public gathering space that perhaps is unavailable elsewhere. But both Nachtbar and MIX NYC politically charge these collective experiences in their fostering of new forms of being and being together. They nurture modes of being public that are not sanctioned elsewhere in LGBT culture, and these experiments have a consequence for their politics of the world. As one MIX NYC fan writes, "I learn so much about the human experience at large through the films, conversations, installations and shared experience of building an inclusive supportive family. My ideas of what it means to be not just queer but HUMAN are constantly being obliterated and refined through MIX. . . . My ignorance about so many facets of life has a place to be confronted, challenged and replaced with understanding and compassion." As a festival, MIX NYC is closely aware of the politics of these reimagined worlds. The theme of the 2011 festival, Planet MIX! is introduced in the program with a quote by the gay science-fiction novelist and critic Samuel Delany: "Science Fiction isn't just thinking about the world out there. It's also thinking about how that world might be—a particularly important exercise for those who are oppressed, because if they're going to change the world we live in, they—and all of us—have to be able to think about a world that works differently."[23]

The festival fits Ger Zielinski's description of queer film festivals as deviant heterotopias, "radically heterogeneous spaces, spaces of difference that lay figuratively and sometimes literally at the edges of society, its built spaces and its norms."[24] However, MIX's collectivity could also be seen as exemplifying a left-invisible privilege, given its dependence on producing its spaces and events as exceptional. Whereas fans see MIX "building an inclusive

Asia (an organization underwritten by the Ford Foundation), and the British Council (an office of the UK government that functions like the cultural side of the US State Department). It is supported by advertising and by Movies That Matter, an Amsterdam-based foundation that is part of Amnesty International and has become one of Europe's biggest players in documentary media. The grassroots organization has had a diverse group of benefactors, including major corporations such as Barclays and IBM, UNAIDS, Nomura Investment Bank, gay clubs, queer festivals in the United States, international film distributors, and a local LGBT magazine. It is also made viable by local benefactors such as the Humsafar Trust, a twenty-year-old charity that works for queers and men who have sex with men (MSM) in the area. The KASHISH festival is the first queer film festival to receive exemption from the Indian government's Ministry of Information and Broadcasting, a significant recognition of cultural status from the state that now offers a renewed strategic value in the revived Section 377 era. The KASHISH festival positions itself as a player in world culture and politics, as part of the global circuitry of queer film distribution and exhibition. It has always (and often bravely) asserted an outward-facing stance that is determinedly inclusive. Its world is a world defined by popular cinema, the film industry, and a particular brand of human rights internationalism. In simple terms, it has a majoritizing approach to imagining an audience for queer films and festival events.

On the one hand, the festival's self-descriptions emphasize visibility, human rights, and acceptance in ways that do not immediately scream radical queerness. The prominent use of "mainstream" as a verb suggests that those impulses guide how the festival understands visibility. On the other hand, the festival's curatorial choices and organization of space seem to privilege the ability of queerness to disrupt and revise mainstream culture. We can see this tension in the festival's physical location. Since its inception, KASHISH has been hosted primarily in mainstream cinemas such as the Cinemax multiplex chain (located in a mall) and, in 2014, in the glamorous art deco-style Liberty cinema. These locations could be read as a corporatizing strategy, which in addition to supplying crucial brick-and-mortar support also lend the festival a kind of legitimacy. But the mainstream location also insists on constructing queer space within and alongside ostensibly "non-queer" spaces: the audiences for KASHISH mix directly with audiences for other new movies. A similar politics is at stake in the Amsterdam Transgender Film Festival's insistence on remaining in a downtown location.[27] In this way, KASHISH creates what Skadi Loist has called "a public sphere where [various queer identities and groups] meet between programmes and are

Fig. 2.4: *Frangipani*'s images of Sri Lanka might be seen as exotic or as locally familiar.

not separated because certain programmes only show in certain venues."[28] Indeed, the festival expands that public sphere, promiscuously mixing audiences for queer and non-queer films, along with activist and entertainment films. The KASHISH festival casts a wide net, taking a universalizing approach to outreach by bringing queer films and audiences to mainstream spaces.

The same effect can be observed in the curatorial choice of the Sri Lankan gay film *Frangipani* (Visakesa Chandrasekaram, dir., 2014) as the centerpiece feature of the 2014 festival. *Frangipani* is mainstream in register, with relatively high production values and a popular art-cinema style. The director is both a well-known playwright and a human rights lawyer, and he sees the film in terms of advocacy.[29] In another exhibition context, the film might be seen to exemplify the spread of both Western gay identities and festival film style. On the queer film festival circuit, *Frangipani* is notable as the first gay film from Sri Lanka—an appellation that folds the film into a progress narrative of Westernization—and the film can be viewed in Orientalizing terms as an authentic representation of a faraway land (figure 2.4). In a Sri Lankan review, Dhanuka Bandara discusses the problem that the film was censored at home and was seen by only a tiny metropolitan audience.

Bandara raises the recurring question of engaged cinema: how to reach the masses, both in terms of a political aesthetic that can gain popular traction and in terms of overcoming state and industrial obstacles to distribution beyond urban centers.[30] So *Frangipani* is an overdetermined choice for a South Asian queer film festival, functioning in multiple registers. At KASHISH, this film's form can be read as art cinema for the educated urban audience, but it equally speaks to other love triangle melodramas that audiences might view at the Liberty or the Cinemax. In this context, its exotic "authenticity" is replaced by a much more engaged localism. The KASHISH festival locates queer audiences in a counterpublic that seeps into the official public sphere, often in the same building.

Likewise, principles of accessibility and outreach are familiar to anyone who has worked in programming or arts management, but KASHISH uses these neoliberal watchwords to construct more genuinely inclusive spaces. Most important, the festival is completely free to attend, a use of funds that immediately alters the constitution of the audience. Festival-goers include not only moneyed queers but a large number of working-class people. Programming consciously addresses diverse Indian audiences by including films in Marathi, Bengali, and other national languages, and events engage minorities such as *hijras*, who are often excluded from mainstream cultural spaces. The KASHISH festival also supports queer Indian filmmakers via prizes, filmmaking workshops, and consistent programming of a wide range of Indian and South Asian films. Part of its logic is situated within an Indian history of activist film and video, which constitutes "cinema" in a rather different way from the cinephilia of the film festival. For instance, Anurupa Prakash and Lok Prakash's documentary *Will This Change?* (2014) is the result of their work with hijras and MSM in rural Bangladesh, and the film's screening at KASHISH aims to create a space in which "outreach" nurtures solidarities and connections from social actors to audiences. (See also the discussion of activism and Bangladeshi queer communities in chapter 5.)

Despite (or perhaps through) its generic promiscuity, KASHISH works to engage filmmakers and audiences as part of a queer community that is constituted through political engagement in public space. For instance, panel discussions in 2014 considered LGBT rights and human rights. The debate is framed in human rights terms, yet these terms are not taken for granted. The value and limitations of rights discourse form live issues to be debated by heterogeneous groups of queers who otherwise could not be constituted. Even KASHISH's corporate sponsors see the festival as an institution with mainstreaming potential. Sponsorship has often come from corporate human relations departments that see their support as contributing to the betterment of employees.[31] Thus, corporations have understood KASHISH's value in terms of public life, and not as an elite, prestigious, or exclusive cultural event. With KASHISH we find a festival that is deeply embedded in the institutional structures of neoliberal human rights and corporate visions of the social, yet is very conscious of its renegotiation of public space. Its programmers interpret the queer film festival as an event with the potential to rework the public sphere, and if the promotional aspects of KASHISH overemphasize self-recognition, we must remind ourselves that very public film festivals such as this one are contesting human rights culture's claim on privacy as a means of protecting queers.

Activist Worlds at Batho Ba Lorato

The Batho Ba Lorato Film Festival, Botswana's first LGBT film festival, courageously turns public spaces into counterpublics, and the event has become significant to anti-homophobia activism in Africa and beyond. The festival in 2013 was supported by what might again seem like a typical human rights mix of sponsors: foreign and domestic NGOs, a university, and a US film distributor. Moreover, its mission statement is savvily pitched toward education and empowerment, claiming "to create a platform for dialogue through the use of film." It continues,

> This film festival, coined Batho Ba Lorato (People of Love) will be bringing together a society divided on views on homosexuality, Trans and Intersex and [aims] to explore interrelated issues that plague the African continent:
> • How Christianity has exacerbated the violence directed at LGBTQ communities.
> • Homosexuality as "UnAfrican" and unnatural.
> • And whether the anti-sodomy laws that persist in Botswana are justifiable.[32]

An activist impulse is in effect here, promising to place into question both state homophobia and wider social mores, as well as to hold Christianity to account for violence against queer people. And yet Lesbians, Gays, and Bisexuals of Botswana (LEGABIBO), the NGO that organizes Batho Ba Lorato, is very careful to insist in its public statements that "the film festival did not seek to promote homosexuality, but rather sought to create awareness and promote love, respect, tolerance, compassion and appreciation between human beings."[33] The festival strikes a delicate balance, locating itself between competing discourses of LGBT subjectivity and worldliness, with potentially high stakes for local participants. Although it is the youngest of our examples, the festival forwards a synthesis of the minoritizing and universalizing impulses of the more established MIX NYC and KASHISH festivals. This hybrid approach resonates in Batho Ba Lorato's local impact (where it has played an essential role in the legal struggles of local activists) and its global perspective (arguing for the relevance of film programming to human rights debates and black internationalism).

The curatorial choices at Batho Ba Lorato illustrate both the difficulties and the potential for activist work embedded in their position. On the one hand, the festival is clearly operating in a human rights environment. For instance, the film *Life Experiences of LGBTI in Botswana* (2013), a "participatory video" produced by the Canadian research group Envisioning LGBT Human Rights in collaboration with LEGABIBO, is, as its title suggests, a human rights-oriented documentary.[34] On the other hand, the festival works against clichés of the Western-influenced queer life as a consumerist and elite one, lived in opposition to African cultural values. Its choice of films instead constructs queerness in the contexts of local, regional, African, and pan-African cultures. Films include the documentaries *Difficult Love* (2010), directed by the photographer and video artist Zaneli Muholi, on the lives of black lesbians in South Africa, and *Voices of Witness Africa* (Cynthia Black and Katie Sherrod, 2009), about the relationships of LGBT Africans with religion. These choices draw on southern African affiliations and wider continental religious traditions to emplace queerness within Africa rather than the West.[35] The festival also screened Dee Rees's *Pariah* (2011) and *Brother Outsider: The Life of Bayard Rustin* (Nancy Kates and Bennett Singer, 2003), suggesting the potential of leveraging intersections between African and African American queer experiences as a form of worldliness that is at once resistant to conservative nationalism and often ignored by neoliberal circuits of globalism and touristic cosmopolitanism.

These curatorial choices, as well as the festival's topics for post-film discussion, must be contextualized within an African politics in which homosexuality is often associated with unwanted Western influence and, in particular, the rapaciously consumerist effects of globalization. Oliver Phillips has outlined the emergence of both gay rights and homophobic discourse across southern Africa from the 1990s onward, tracing the unintended effect of anti-homosexual polemics by Robert Mugabe in promulgating a binary hetero–homo model of sexuality as constitutive of subjectivity. For Phillips, "An analysis of the persecution of homosexuals in Zimbabwe, and the contrary extent of their emancipation in South Africa, indicates how sexuality as a whole, regardless of hetero/homosexuality, comes to be a more significant constituent of subjectivity, and so becomes an increasingly constitutive, but certainly not exclusive, ingredient of national identity."[36] Homophobic laws are justified in terms of national, traditional, or religious values; thus, John McAllister argues, it is crucial for LGBT activists in the postcolonial South to counter the argument that homosexuality is un-African.[37] He argues that precisely because both modern gay identities and universal human rights discourses *are* Western imports, they enable reactionary forms of nationalism to play on complex postcolonial feelings. Like us, McAllister is less interested in arguing about ontology than he is concerned with the geopolitical and experiential situation of articulating queer subjectivities in Botswana today. To resist what is seen as Western influence is a powerful draw, even when that call is made in the name of a religion that also comes from the West.[38]

In this context, Batho Ba Lorato's focus on films about Botswanan and southern African queers offers a rejoinder to the homosexuality-as-foreign argument. We might frame the festival's exhibition practices in terms of Third Cinema. In this way it focalizes collective national struggles of black people across the globe, often screening films by African American filmmakers alongside those by African filmmakers. This may seem like a simple or obvious gesture, but in the context of a CNN globalism, the corrosive force of tourist economies, and neoliberal multiculturalism, asserting these transcontinental and transatlantic affinities forms a powerful retort to the worlds proposed by corporatist cultural relativism and its neocolonial visions for Africa and its diaspora. These curatorial moves present LGBT experience as what McAllister calls "legitimate expressions of an ongoing process of postcolonial adaptation and métissage," or the "tswanarisation of global gay culture."[39] "Tswanarisation" here describes a kind of vernacular modernism but articulated strategically to take back the terrain of the local as a postcolonial queer space. In this context, the festival's choice of a Setswana-language title can be read as an activist strategy of queer worlding.

The festival aimed at outreach to a wider community in Botswana: its Flickr account notes that nightly audiences of up to 150 people included many heterosexuals "who had come to find out more about these sensitive issues." The space was papered with anti-homophobia posters, including the UK charity Stonewall's "Some People Are Gay: Get Over It" and "Different Family: Same

Figs. 2.5 and 2.6: Audience members at the Batho Ba Lorato Film Festival in Gaborone use social media to voice support for LGBT rights.

Love" campaigns. Attendees were invited to pose with a handwritten sign, in a style common in international web-based activism. Signs ranged from "I support and love my gay friends" and "Prejudice is ignorance" to quirkier and queerer messages such as "100% 4 Gayland" and "Fuck homophobia" (figures. 2.5–2.6). There is a striking attention to publicity here, from the carefully worded welcome to a potentially homophobic audience to the social media activism that makes standing up for LGBT rights seem easy and fun. But even if the prominence of a UK-based charity or Canadian government support might give us pause, it is important not to read from that same privileged position. The address to a non-queer audience, for instance, means something quite different here from in Lisbon. Whereas the insistence by Queer Lisboa's director, João Ferreira, that the festival caters to a broad cinephile audience aims to emplace queer film culture in the culturally powerful center of world cinema, Batho Ba Lorato speaks to non-queers from a further marginalized space. The festival leverages social media (alongside traditional paper media, campaigns, etc.) to create a counterpublic, in which the film festival as socially sanctioned cultural event enables and nourishes modes of being in the world that might otherwise be unavailable to Botswanan queers. The Flickr photo stream—along with the post-film discussions and outreach campaigns—aspires to an imagined community that has as much in common with Third Cinema's visions of transnational solidarity and public spaces of education as it does with the Gay International.

These counterpublics alone make a strong intervention into the worlds of queer film festival culture, but what is most significant about Batho Ba Lorato is its direct participation in one of the most potentially consequential legal cases for queer people in the global South. In February 2012, LEGABIBO, the group that organized the festival, applied to the Botswanan government to be registered as an official association. It was rejected on the grounds that "the Botswana constitution does not recognize homosexuals" and the objectives of the organization were contrary to Botswanan law.[40] The group appealed the decision and eventually took its case to the Botswanan High Court. Represented by the international human rights lawyer Unity Dow, LEGABIBO argued for recognition in terms of the democratic values of freedom of association, assembly, and expression. The lawyers for LEGABIBO write, "Freedom of association and expression imposes an obligation on authorities to take positive measures to promote diversity."[41] Thus, while the film festival was creating public spaces for queer association, expression, and diversity in February 2013, its organizers were simultaneously fighting

Fig. 2.7: LeGaBiBo emerges victorious from the Botswanan High Court. Courtesy of Caine Youngman/LeGaBiBo.

a lengthy legal battle for state recognition of their right to exist (figure 2.7). And while LEGABIBO undertakes a range of advocacy activities, the film festival is one of its most prominent public events.

In November 2014, the High Court ruled in favor of LEGABIBO, forcing the Botswanan government to recognize it as a legal entity. The ruling is worth quoting at some length, as it responds powerfully to some of the problems that human rights discourse creates. Judge Terrence Rannowane wrote:

> Section 3 of the Constitution . . . refers to all "persons in Botswana" and since members of LEGABIBO are also "persons" albeit with different sexual orientation, it is difficult to imagine that they are not included in the phrase "all persons" as contained in the above provision. If the framers of the constitution intended that they should be excluded from the enjoyment of those fundamental rights and freedoms I am certain that they

would have done so in clear terms. Consequently, to hold that gay people are excluded from the enjoyment of the fundamental rights and freedoms conferred on "all persons" would amount to cutting down on the scope of such rights by reading into the above provision implicit restrictions contrary to accepted canons of constitutional interpretation.[42]

This resonant and moving passage makes it clear that LGBT people are included in the categories of the human and the citizen and thus are entitled to equal protection under the law. As we will see, human rights discourse has struggled to accord LGBT people this essential humanity, so despite the judge's conservative position on legalizing homosexual acts, the LEGABIBO ruling forms a landmark moment in international queer politics. Some see the judgment as having the potential to create a ripple effect that could bring down anti-gay laws in Botswana. Moreover, because these colonial-era laws are all based on the same statutory language, a challenge in one former British colony could form the legal basis for challenges in all of the postcolonial nations with similarly written laws. Transnational networks of human rights activists and scholars such the Envisioning LGBT Human Rights group, for example, are looking closely at the LEGABIBO decision as a potential model for efforts to fight against Section 377. Batho Ba Lorato demonstrates how proximate queer film festivals are to global LGBT politics and, indeed, how the spaces created by a film festival can participate directly in transforming the world for queer people.

Human Rights and the Non-Human in Festival Posters

In the previous section, we explored how individual festivals create counterpublics or ways for queer people to be in the world. But festivals do engage their audiences not only in their physical spaces but also in their wider paratextual existence. Film festivals' promotional materials extend out into the world, infiltrating public spaces of all kinds, addressing and to some extent constituting their audiences. We are interested in how promotional material imagines the audience, and in particular how the posters for queer film festivals represent, define, and delimit the category of the queer as much as what specific audiences might see on-screen. These materials might be dismissed as a peripheral afterthought, but in analyzing a wide array of posters, we conclude that they are actually highly informative to thinking the relationships among festival audiences, queer communities, and the category of the human.

In the mid-1990s, many LGBT film festivals stopped using decidedly human figures in their promotional imagery and branding. On websites, posters, and programs and in street advertising, images of LGBT humans were exchanged for avatars of queerness: cartoon monsters (figure 2.8), brightly colored everyday objects (figure 2.9), cute animals (figure 2.10). Most often these avatars appeared in groups: a gathering of faceless alien astronauts, an array of cupcakes, or a crowd of penguins.[43] This deceptively simple imagery raises the question of the human through an intriguing evasion of human figures. This evasion asks us to consider both how LGBT politics figures the human and how the queer appears in international human rights debates. The trend toward using nonhumans in queer film festival branding coincides with a rapid expansion of queer filmmaking and film-going in a wider number of regions around the world. Barbara Mennel describes this in her overview of LGBT film history as a period of "intense global proliferation" of queer film.[44] Scholars of film festivals describe this period in similar terms, identifying a fifteen-year period characterized by the growth of "international networks of cultural exchange through which the discourse of gay and lesbian liberation could be deployed in the service of globalization."[45] There is an obvious impetus to read these cute marketing materials as reflecting a certain normalizing rhetoric within globalization, but something suggestive happens when we focus instead on the instability of this promotional iconography in relation to the figure of the human. Rather than reading this imagery as merely epiphenomenal or as superstructural to economic and political pressures, we argue that these images trouble certain assumptions about queer international culture.

A less speculative perspective might acknowledge the practical challenges faced by the designers of these promotional images in the aftermath of earlier debates about the inclusivity of the LGBT movement. The designers no doubt sought to create images that avoid obvious markers of race and ethnicity while proclaiming the multiculturalism of their events. With the rise of queer as a political category and an organizing principle, they also faced the question of how to substantiate the queer's humanity and render it graphically palpable when by its very definition queer is an unstable category that refuses conventional genders, sexual identities, object choices, and bodies. If we were to study each of the festival posters individually, these explanations make the most sense and argue for seeing their figures as human stand-ins. From this perspective, the poster iconography partakes in an old-style liberal humanism in which difference and variety challenge the viewer to remember that we are all human, no matter how different we may look to one another, while trying to accommodate the challenge of the instability of the category "queer."

Figs. 2.8–2.10: Avoiding the explicitly human in queer film festival branding: from top to bottom, Los Angeles (2000), Hong Kong (2011), London (2010).

A broader survey of film festival advertising, however, makes finding the human in these images more difficult. Taking the promotional imagery of several dozen film festivals together reveals a marked reluctance to depict queers as human. In what follows, we explore how these images ask us to recognize their figures as queer while remaining ambivalent about the humanity of those figures. Their representation of the queer—or of groups of queers—comes freighted with an awkward awareness of the precise means by which the human is constituted in contemporary world politics. These images register a resistance toward mobilizing the category of the human in queer politics, on the one hand, and instrumentalizing the LGBT person in the expansion of neoliberal versions of humanism, on the other.

The nonhuman branding trend emerged historically alongside a move by activists within the United Nations to address LGBT rights. New initiatives based in the United Nations argued for the protection of LGBT people via a human rights rationale and for using long-standing human rights treaties as the basis for decriminalizing homosexuality in various parts of the world. The ensuing legal and diplomatic discourse entailed a series of conundrums about whether queerness was human (to which we return shortly). As these debates over whether to recognize queer lives as protectable as human lives unfolded, NGOs and other international charities supplemented their judicial work and political lobbying with a series of cultural initiatives aimed at LGBT communities.[46] When studying LGBT human rights in this period, therefore, it is important to think beyond what is conventionally understood as the work of international politics. When we use the phrase "human rights discourse" later, we signal not only the textual logic of legal debates and United Nations declarations, but also how these initiatives have worked to embed their priorities in everyday life by funding cultural events, community activities, and artworks. When studying queer international cultural practices from this period, it should also be remembered that government programs, intergovernmental agencies, and NGOs have funded LGBT programming as an extension of their international advocacy. This overlay of human rights culture and the expansion of global queer film cultures has entailed specific material conjunctions. In Bolivia, Indonesia, and elsewhere, for example, queer film festivals have incorporated the words "human rights" in their official titles. In Iceland, the Queer Film Festival is held in the Human Rights Institute. Some of the first festivals for queer films in India began as corollaries to recently formed human rights film festivals.

Queer theorists have identified many aspects of contemporary international LGBT culture as complicit with the neoliberal appropriation of the category of the human and as aiding a politics that uses human rights discourse to reassert Western imperialism. In *Global Sex*, Dennis Altman describes "human rights language [as] one of the best examples of epistemological globalization."[47] It is perhaps with such a perspective in mind that David Eng urges, "Queer studies must necessarily approach the question of (homo) sexuality as a critical site for the investigation and negotiation of geopolitics— as a discourse of development, as an emblem of modernity, as a metric for the human, human rights, and human rights abuses."[48] Eng uses the word "geopolitical" to refer to how gay rights are increasingly employed to map the relative political modernity of various regions of the world. Where Gayatri Chakravorty Spivak pointed out the colonial mind-set embedded in human rights culture's social Darwinism, Joseph Massad leverages her critique to accuse LGBT rights discourse of imposing Western models of sexual subjectivity on the world.[49]

Human rights discourse at the start of the twenty-first century performs its progressivism by redeeming the humanity of the queer. To do so, it must invoke the liminality of the queer's relationship to the category of human life. In other words, human rights discourse must first raise the question "Is the queer a human?" in order then to redeem itself by supplying an affirmative answer. It should not surprise us, then, to find those queer cultural practices that imagine they are participating in an international political culture (here, advertising for film festivals) actively grappling with the question of who is the "human" in human rights. In even the most playful and cute manifestations, the promotional iconography of queer film festivals seems to reinvoke the queer's constantly reinscribed status as liminal in relation to humanness. However, in their obstinate refusal to figure queers as human, the promotional images offer a powerful rejoinder to the pattern of denial-of-plus-after-the-fact-confirmation-of the humanity of queers.

Can a cupcake have a species being? The less-than-human and nonhuman figurations of queerness that so frequently populate the promotional imagery of queer film festivals may be organized into three iconographic subsets: avatars, objects, and animals. The first group displays a resolutely indeterminate humanness. Some of these figures remind us of characters associated with the transcendence of physical personhood. They reference familiar icons of fantasy and science fiction, such as the superhero, the extraterrestrial, and the cyborg. The posters for queer film festivals in Jakarta, Melbourne, and Beijing all propose semi-human figures formed from a merger between a face and a movie projector; these composite creatures evoke a technophilic futurism. Other festivals' brand avatars appear to

Figs. 2.11–2.13: Avatars and barely humanoid figures: top, Ljubljana (2001); bottom, left to right, Jakarta (2011), Melbourne (2012).

have jumped from the pages of comic books, maintaining an ambiguous but fiercely independent identity. Like Batman's iconic stance toward Gotham City, the pose of these action figures evokes what it means to face the world alone, whether it is taking on the urban landscape, looking out over the skyline (NewFest–New York), or blithely painting the world pink (Vancouver). These figures are anonymous iconoclasts, sometimes posed with guns, suggesting that they are perhaps spies or terrorists (London, Brussels).

This first group of queer icons reduces the particularities of the body to universalize the identity of the queer (figures 2.11, 2.12, and 2.13). This representational mode of flexible figuration initially asserts a promiscuous pluralism and inclusiveness. Seeming to refuse physiognomy, the figures have empty faces (Chennai, Ljubljana, Barcelona). Odd colors (such as fuchsia) replace skin tones, leaving a blankness that offers the image an amorphous racial identity (Vancouver, Melbourne). The styling of these characters flirts with binary gender categories but refuses to relinquish the body to one gender or another (Brussels). Amid their universalizing flattening of difference, however, many remain coy about the human-ness of the queer body (Jakarta). Taken together, they prompt the question of whether this body is human at all.

Many festivals extend the notion of a de-particularized human form by abandoning the humanoid altogether. These images, which form our second group, represent queerness as a gathering of nonhuman forms (figures 2.14, 2.15, and 2.16). This communal iconography suggests that queerness emerges en masse, assembled via likeness, as in the case of a uniform crowd of rubber ducks (Puerto Rico) that echoes the image of astronauts cited earlier; kernels of popcorn (New York); a prickly pear (Palermo); or petals of a flower (London). Alternatively, these images might define queerness as a grouping that is unusually accommodating to difference, such as an arrangement of fruit (Olympia, Washington), the multicolor layers of a Popsicle (Vancouver), or the similarly divergent strata of a cake (Los Angeles). Still others suggest diversity by showing a gathering of similar forms whose visual appeal emerges in relative differentiation. The cupcakes in the poster for the BFI London Lesbian and Gay Film Festival exemplify this strategy. We might call this approach sameness with sprinkles. This abandonment of the human form enables an intrepid pluralism that escapes the messiness of depicting diversity through the racialization and gendering of bodies. The crowd of small cakes forms a single icon of inclusive collective made possible precisely by banishing from our view the specificity of human physicality.

A third category takes this universalizing nonhuman figuration in a different direction by representing queers as animals (figures 2.17, 2.18 and 2.19). They appear as a lone creature (Lisbon's perpetually plucky duck; Wilmington, North Carolina's brave pink sheep; Warsaw's horse; Chicago's kitten riding a cloud while wearing 3D glasses), a couple (two reindeer locking antlers in the poster for Ankara, Turkey's festival), or a group of animals (Hong Kong's birds happily roosting in a tree that is also decorated with

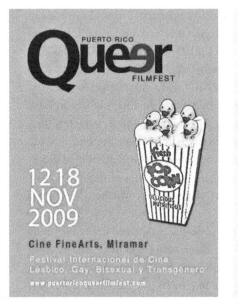

Figs. 2.14–2.16: Objects and foodstuffs: top, from left to right, San Juan (2009), Los Angeles (2013); bottom, London (2011).

underpants; Mumbai's flurry of butterflies). Sometimes these animals nestle against one another as if united in comfortable sameness (Seattle's cats). At other times, various species live happily together in diversity, as in the minimal Tokyo film festival's poster design, which looks almost as though it was drawn from zoological textbook illustrations (figure 2.18). Different animals can also come to form a peaceable kingdom, crowding together on a Noah's Ark–like double-decker bus (London) or cozily coexisting in a poster for South Africa's Out in Africa festival.

Figs. 2.17–2.19: Animals: top, left to right, Istanbul/Ankara (2013), Tokyo (2002); left, Cape Town/Johannesburg (2012).

Alongside the rise of globalized queer film festivals in the 1990s, large-scale international campaigns for the decriminalization of homosexuality began gaining public, governmental, and intergovernmental traction under the rubric of human rights for the first time. The feminist political scientist Rosalind Petchesky suggests that "prior to 1993 sexuality of any sort or manifestation is absent from international human rights discourse."[50] Since then, the question of how to employ human rights law to defend queer people has been prominent, but it has also struggled to find its legal footing and global legitimacy, at times appearing compensatory and overly accommodating in its logic. In the context of international human rights, this logic has tended to extend from one of three rubrics: privacy, autonomy, or special protection.

The United Nations' first major intervention on behalf of sexual minorities draws on the first of these: the human right to privacy. In 1994, the United Nations Human Rights Committee ruled that in criminalizing sodomy, Australia (and Tasmanian law, in particular) was in violation of the human right to privacy as defined in Article 17 of the International Covenant on Civil and Political Rights.[51] How might the promotional iconography of queer film festivals indicate the complications of using privacy rights to protect queer people? The innocuous qualities of the nonhuman trend might seem at first to go along with an arguably coercive privatization of queer identity. Animals snuggling with one another offer perhaps a less controversial portrait of queer intimacy than queer humans touching one another in public. These advertisements could be criticized for using their stand-in nonhuman forms to grant the festival a public image of queerness that can be shown anywhere, whether at a bus stop or in a park near a public toilet. Were we to settle on this reading of the images, we could suggest that these festivals have opted out of addressing questions of queer representation and given in to the climate of homophobic counter-protests, threats, and violence described at the beginning of this chapter. From this perspective, these nonhuman iconographies could be read as a risk-aversion strategy that tells queers to privatize or—in the context of the animal images—domesticate their desires. However, if we think of these images functioning in situ—on mass transit, on public notice boards in parks, and on billboards—they could be seen to subvert the privatization of queer life with their (stealth) innocence. Their bright colors, panoplies of scrumptious desserts (popsicles and cake), and cartoonish characters (animals, superheroes, and astronauts) might very easily appeal to children. Indeed, such images invite the public to join queer activities via a playful iconography not unlike that which appears on boxes of sugary cereal aimed at children. These posters offer no caveats or apologies of any kind, with the words "queer" or "bisexual" appearing as just another cute thing or sweet treat.

The second rubric used to extend human rights to queers is individual autonomy. In 2003, a group of European nations presented the Brazilian Resolution to the United Nations Economic and Social Council. It called for all states to "promote and protect the rights of all persons regardless of their sexual orientation."[52] Although the United Nations never officially adopted this initiative, it was one of the first resolutions to address the lives of queer people and to make possible the inclusion of sexuality in future discussions of human rights. Of course, the resolution was also compromised with its use of the word "orientation," which made its appeal irrelevant to trans people and suggested sexuality as the extension of an autonomous and individualistic personhood. It seems significant, then, that much of the film festivals' nonhuman iconography offers a rendering of collectivity that derails a logic that establishes rights for queers via either privacy protections or the individualist logic of autonomous orientation. The public and communal forms of queerness imagined by the film festivals—gatherings of queers, gaggles of gays—complicate as much as they confirm how liberal politics tailors the life of sexual minorities for human rights discourse. This imagery's refusal of gendered personhood moreover asserts the importance of the very trans identities and genderqueer cultural practices that the word "orientation" would ignore. The 2008 and 2012 revised resolutions continue to use "sexual orientation" but add "and gender identity."[53] However, these resolutions remain open for signature (with opposing statements submitted by non-signing nations) and thus have not been officially adopted by the United Nations General Assembly.

Across the revisions to the resolutions submitted since 2000, a third rubric argues for the extension to LGBT people of protections for groups that are especially vulnerable to violence and oppression. In this respect, the revisions both assert the integrity of the category of human and insist on its modification. They do so in a way that follows the precedent of the Universal Declaration of Human Rights of 1948, which is the foundational document for postwar human rights culture and remains the Ur-text for subsequent international human rights legislation. The logic of this final rubric requires further discussion before we return to the film festival icons.

In a famously vexed passage, the Universal Declaration recognized that certain categories of humans are particularly vulnerable to rights violation. This passage appears in Article 2 and states, "Everyone is entitled to all the rights and freedoms set forth in this Declaration, without distinction of any kind, such as race, colour, sex, language, religion, political or other opinion, national or social origin, property, birth or other status." In a series of revisions—one in 1966, several in the 1980s, and then others in the 1990s—the document has been expanded and modified by subsequent covenants. One avenue of defense has been to read the queer as a person included in the categories named in Article 2 of the declaration, particularly the word "sex" and the words "other status." The website of Amnesty-USA champions efforts to achieve legal inclusion as progressive: "Although the Universal Declaration of Human Rights does not explicitly mention sexual orientation or gender identity, evolving conceptions of international human rights law include a broad interpretation to include the rights and the protection of the rights of LGBT people around the world."[54] The intentions of these efforts to add protections after the fact were no doubt respectable and often even admirable. However, when the Amnesty article suggests that to "evolve" means taking "a broad interpretation," one is tempted to ask: is this rhetorical effort to "broaden" really necessary? Must we read *into* the original declaration to expand the inclusiveness of its conception of the human? This attempt rehearses the problematic move by way of which queers are forced to argue for human rights by demonstrating that queers once were not human. This maneuver comes dangerously close to confirming a logic that excludes individuals from their own species, a logic that may never have functioned so robustly in the first place.[55]

It has been long recognized that the declaration's recognition of special protected categories of humans introduces a crucial conceptual glitch that sets the terms for much of human rights policy since the Second World War and formalized the "or human" logic that continues to haunt much rights work today.[56] While stating that there are no distinctions within the category of the human, the declaration points to existing distinctions. In the very place where it constitutes the category of the human most inclusively, the declaration then also substantiates divisions within that category that would threaten its integrity and its totality. On the one hand, when read sympathetically the declaration can be understood simply to be reminding its readers that such differences do not alter a person's status and rights. On the other hand, the need to single out certain groups reminds readers of the palpable force of those distinctions in everyday life. In doing so, the text inadvertently introduces two categories of subjects: those who distinguish and those who are distinguished. In other words, some of us have always been human, while others of us need to be recognized as human by those who were always already human.

While we might have serious reservations about a queer politics based on the logic of human rights, it could be easily argued that the original text of the United Nations Declaration on Human Rights has *never not* recognized queers as human. The anxious compensatory gesture of correcting past wrongs instantiates exclusions and prejudices that the declaration does not actually commit to print. Thus, it seems important to remain alert to how frequently the critique of contemporary human rights discourse implies that something needs to change about the category of the human to accommodate the queer.

Queer film festivals' posters index these contradictions. They also indicate how these questions have persisted into the twenty-first century. The trans-species collectivism posed by the more zoologically diverse of these posters can be read as mocking this rhetorical glitch. The animals in the advertisements are thus not anthropomorphisms; they are instead refusals of the representational imperative in rights culture of the late twentieth century to assert the humanness of queers. In doing so, they obviate the question of categorical distinctions among humans and pose the nature of the dilemma for human rights discourse since the Second World War. Such discourse must assert the inclusiveness of the category of the human against efforts to dehumanize populations, a tendency that one human rights scholar terms "pseudospeciation."[57] In arguing that certain people's humanity is not self-evident, these initiatives concede to de facto practices of dehumanization.

By sidestepping the ideological work of any after-the-fact inclusions, these images offer an alternative semiotic. The donkeys, rubber duckies, and aliens confront us with a pseudospeciation that, when taken collectively, ironizes the accommodationist (antiqueer) logic described earlier.[58] In this sense, these film festival images are perhaps distinct from other LGBT cultural texts that aim to represent queers for a rights-based political agenda that too frequently enacts exclusions and exceptions, as Jasbir Puar's exploration of homonationalism in a post-9/11 world documents.[59] Puar argues that anti-terrorist rhetoric depends on exempting certain people from the category of the human and that a homonormative culture of gay rights in the West enables a racist and ethnocentric exceptionalism that condemns certain non-Westerners to the category of the subhuman. As she writes, "U.S. exceptionalism may well be articulated by homonationalism globally, and homonationalism is increasingly immanent to some strands of U.S. exceptionalism, especially in the realms of consumption and human and sexual rights discourses."[60] While it would be wrong to suggest that any individual film festival poster forms a fully articulated critique of exceptionalism, this iconography does symptomatically register a dissatisfaction with the continued recruitment of queer bodies in service of posing the question of the human.

The juxtaposition of human rights with cupcakes might feel like a conflation of discourses and a violation of the sacrosanct. Then again, queer politics has had a long-standing interest in interrogating what is considered appropriate to discuss, as well as when and where to discuss it. Queers in politics often trigger snickers and dismissals. The representational overreaching of these film festival logos—their self-conscious metonymy—may strike us as funny, cute, or charming, but this figuration also invites something of a splendid return of the repressed radicalism of queer humanity. These seemingly innocuous and playful figures end up posing a very forceful question to the current international politics of cultural relevance: if we're not human, then what are we? The question "Queer or human?" thus is not tongue in cheek; nor is its provocation simple to resolve. How to claim the category of the human is not self-evident. Does everyone want to be human in the same way? Does everyone want to be human?

Human rights culture tells us that for the rights of queers to count, the category of human needs an after-the-fact reorganization and revision. These film festival images respond precisely to the irrationality of that retrofitting and the other, apparently necessary compensatory rhetorical gestures that accompany it. The metonymy of these promotional images refuses to evacuate the question of the human. In not depicting the human, they draw our attention to human rights culture's wavering on the capaciousness of the category of the human. Avatars, animals, and even cupcakes can capture something about the failure of contemporary human rights discourse to recognize how queers were always human.

Judith Butler has seen the after-the-fact revision of the human in human rights as unavoidable. She writes, "The necessity of keeping our notion of the 'human' open to a future articulation is essential to the project of international human rights discourse and politics."[61] The instability of the category of the human, for her, is a sign of the necessarily contestatory quality of democratic discourse: "International human rights is always in the process of subjecting the human to redefinition and renegotiation. It mobilizes the human in the service of rights, but also rewrites the human, and rearticulates the human when it comes up against the cultural limits of its working conception of the human, as it does and must."[62] Butler argues for keeping the question of the human in human rights a radically unsettled, relational, and immanently revisable category. To reify the human—for Butler, to "presuppose" it—invites oppression and violence.[63] The legal scholar Ben Golder has argued that Michel Foucault's late turn to human rights discourse offers a similarly strategic attempt to transfigure the liberal humanist account of the human. For Golder, Foucault's thought shares with Butler's a tension between critique of the Enlightenment subject and an attempt to form a nonfoundational politics of rights. Foucault, rejecting universalizing humanism, posits "that there are more secrets, more possible freedoms, and more inventions in our future than we can imagine in humanism as it is dogmatically represented on every side of the political rainbow."[64]

In less direct and perhaps less bold ways, these film festival posters enact a critical practice that thinks "the consequential ways in which the human is being produced, reproduced and de-produced."[65] They collectively participate in a process that "rearticulate[s] or resignif[ies] categories of ontology, of being human."[66] Of course, revision does not guarantee greater sensitivity about or recognition of queer ways of living. Butler admits that a history of revision leads to paradox and discomfort but sees the unknowingness of the category as inescapable. Indeed, some efforts to expand the jurisdiction of the United Nations to protect queer lives have led to a further contraction of what it means to live sexually as a human. In this sense, revision may proceed by way of excision from the category of the human as much as by addition to it. Revision might mean that queers have been removed from categories that they previously occupied.[67] Not asking the question of whether this might have taken place forecloses an investigation of how that removal from the human happened in the first place.

These posters are not simply a byproduct of the recent upsurge in queer film festivals. They also respond to increased pressures to understand sexual politics on a global scale. In their semantic richness, these images register the queer's shifting status as human in world culture and track how the queer has shifted world culture's idea of the human. In its most pragmatic-seeming maneuvers of self-promotion, the queer film festival can be said to scrutinize the politics of being human and the question of where queers exist in international space. In this sense, the queer film festival and human rights culture operate in tension as much as they do in concert. The double bind of having to choose to be either human or queer is refigured in the fantastical and whimsical brandings of the festivals to provide a productive, utopian, and at times even resistant mode of being. It would be wrong to say that the anthropomorphizing tendencies here represent a giving up on the category of the human. Instead, by using nonhuman figures, these images draw our attention to the politicization of nature and grant us a denaturalizing perspective on the institutions of our own species being. Not only do these images suggest the queer necessity of doing so. They also rebuke a human rights culture that unnecessarily works overtime to figure out how to accommodate us.

SPEAKING OTHERWISE
Allegory, Narrative, and Queer Public Space

In chapter 2, we argued that cinema creates spaces in which the global presence of queerness can be experienced, and we insisted that the institutional spaces of distribution and exhibition cannot be fully separated from the immaterial spaces of diegesis and spectatorship. The potential of that relationship between on-screen and off-screen movements is clearly manifest in Abbas Kiarostami's *Ta'm e guilass/Taste of Cherry* (1997), a non-queer film that nonetheless engages queer cinematic intimacy as a means of establishing a transnational space through film form. The film's opening scenes and their reception demonstrate the mutual implication of queerness, narrative space, and the global art-house spectator. Mr. Badii, the film's main character, drives around in a Land Rover soliciting younger men to help him with an as yet undisclosed job. The film brings the spectator into the story formally in a series of point-of-view shots and shot/reverse sequences that knot together our space and diegetic space as a mutual zone of

Fig. 3.1: The point-of-view structure in *Taste of Cherry*'s opening echoes a gay pick-up.

ambiguous reaching out and solicitation, one that is clearly understood by some of the men within the narrative as queer (figure 3.1).

When some reviewers noted how easy it is to read this scene as gay cruising for anonymous sex, other critics and fans jumped to defend Badii's heterosexuality, insisting that he is only looking for human compassion. What is interesting in this discourse is the way that, for the latter critics, the homoerotic implications of the scene would foreclose on its universal ethics (of care for the other). Queer bonds here can represent only specific interests rather than the universal concerns needed to see the film as humanist. But some of the film's major critics suggest another way to read this ambiguous space. Laura Mulvey understands the sequence as "illustrat[ing] this crisscross questioning between screen and spectator, playing on different kinds of uncertainty."[1]

Jonathan Rosenbaum has described the aesthetics of Iranian cinema more broadly in terms of an openness in which "open windows invite exchanges with pedestrians, much as moviegoing (as opposed to video watching) generally entails a private experience within a public space."[2] Both Mulvey and Rosenbaum see cinema as an open threshold in which space for an erotics of humanism might be created. Hamid Naficy goes further, insisting that *Taste of Cherry* is not about suicide at all but about the desire for relationships with others. For him, the introduction of homosexual undertones "subverts the officially sanctioned notions of companionship," making queer relationality precisely the thing that can figure universal ethics.[3] Thus, in *Taste of Cherry* humanism is figured as a kind of queer bonding. Same-sex solicitation becomes a means of disorienting both private identifications and public identities.

Kiarostami himself hints at this effect in an interview with the film journal *Positif*. When asked whether he felt critics were reading homosexuality into the scene, his response was problematic, yet fascinating for the correspondences it suggests: "Of course I deliberately produced this impression. These slightly lecherous undercurrents seemed interesting to me. I really like children. I get a lot of pleasure in talking with them. But I know that someone seeing this from the outside might completely misunderstand what's occurring. It pleased me to mislead [*induire*] the spectator like this, and to return him to his own perversion, to his own fantasies."[4] As Kiarostami recognizes, cinematic narration can take misrecognition and turn it into a kind of revised self-awareness. In the opening of *Taste of Cherry*, it is a *cinematic* construction of intersubjective space and queer intimacy that allows such revisions of subjectivity to emerge. And these forms of openness and intimacy leech back into the pro-filmic world: according to Rosenbaum, one of the first gay hookup sites in Iran was called "Where Is the Friend's House?"[5]

This chapter moves into narrative spaces, asking how queerness emerges across the thresholds of public and private that both cinema and queer identities constantly traverse. Indeed, we do not have to move very far from Kiarostami's ambiguous protagonist to find a more definitively queer automotive encounter in Iranian cinema. The beginning of *Aynehaye rooberoo/Facing Mirrors* (Negar Azarbayjani, dir., 2011) leads the audience to believe that an intimacy shared between two people in a car is a moment of lesbianism. Once again, the spectator is misled by the film, although this misrecognition uncomfortably aligns the viewer with the surveilling gaze of the police. The protagonist, Edi, escapes from the police in the taxi driver Rana's car and, as the narrative evolves, reveals that he is trans. This revelation frightens Rana, not because she is transphobic, but because she is not allowed to be alone in a car with a man. She accepts his gender immediately, and it frightens her. Suddenly, the all-too-public private space of the taxi is breaking Iranian religious law, and Edi's trans identity sets off a series of gendered narrative dangers.

The director Negar Azarbayjani has spoken of her film's two incommensurate audiences: queer film festivals and religious conservatives in Iran.[6] The difficulty of speaking at once to both of these groups illustrates the stakes, for queer cinema today, of narrating the public. Trans issues are politically complicated in Iran, where the state response to transsexuality is supportive albeit medicalized, in contradistinction to homosexuality, which is a capital crime.[7] Gender reassignment surgery is sometimes proposed in Iran as a "cure" for homosexuality, overdetermining this narrative misrecognition in different ways. As Rana and Edi talk and drive, however, the film develops a space of caring gazes between them, as their affection becomes more intimate. But the queer nature of this space is redefined, honing a narrational viewpoint for the viewer that overtly disaggregates itself from both the gaze of state control and from a liberal foreign perspective. When in the end Edi flies to Germany, he is escaping forced marriage as a woman and looking forward to transitioning: in some ways, this is a happy ending. Exile is a recurring narrative trope in queer cinema, and especially in trans narrative, as Wibke Straube has argued in her discussion of what she calls "exit scapes."[8] However, the film captures this geography of greater freedom as empty, cold, and strangely lacking in affect. These transnational spaces are haunted by the film's earlier evocations of human relationality and intimacy. Working both with and against the idea of the exit scape, *Facing Mirrors* narrates the need for a queer trans presence both within the national public space of Iran and within the private space of the family.

Facing Mirrors neither advocates Iran's trans policy as an oasis of sexual freedom in an otherwise repressive state nor does it suggest the open liberal arms of Western Europe as a utopia for trans people. Through its allegorical use of space, the film proposes a queer trans politics of gender that cannot be answered by the Islamic Republic's apparently generous policy on medical gender transition. The film's polemic is explicitly feminist in its queer politics: Edi's lack of social mobility and agency is clearly framed by his female gender assignment at birth, which constantly forecloses his movement and constricts the kind of spaces he can occupy. Space, in fact, is deployed across the film as a political problem for queer, nation, and world. The film maps these contested spaces as a means of refusing an easy East–West binary. Across this chapter, we deploy allegory as a framing concept—a practice of spatiality—to draw out queer cinema's resistance to globalization's limiting structure of protected private acts and benign public identity. It is not surprising, then, to find non-Western cinemas struggling to create alternative aesthetic forms that pose queer publicness otherwise.

Saying Something Else in Public

How does cinema narrate queer lives? To pose this question demands that we address the culturally mediated narratives of queerness and publicity.

Wrapped up in the Western optic of coming out is a fraught catch-22 in which queer people are either too closeted or overly blatant.[9] In this context, putting queer people on-screen is a hyperbolic mode of going public. The relationship of public to private spaces is central to queer lives, so the popularity of the coming-out story makes sense as an enduring engine of drama in gay cinema, particularly in the West but also elsewhere. Think, for example, of the British teen drama *Beautiful Thing* (Hettie Macdonald, dir., 1996) or the liberal documentary *Dangerous Living: Coming Out in the Developing World* (John Scagliotti, dir., 2003). Whereas the production of the heterosexual couple is conventionally seen as a basic function of straight narrative (the marriage plot), one might imagine the business of queer narrativity to be the production of the gay subject who comes further and further out. Moreover, films understood as national queer narratives have often functioned as a kind of national coming out, prompting rejection by state authorities, galvanizing LGBT activists, and finding acceptance in the alternative family of LGBT film festivals internationally, as happened with *Fire*.

However, theorists of sexuality and globalization have forcibly rejected the dominance of coming out as a Western model of homosexuality, just as film theory has critiqued the ideological effects of hegemonic forms of narrative. In its representation of gay people, the coming-out narrative forecloses alternative modes of living queerly. Furthermore, in its narrative structure, it reproduces a trajectory that maps disturbingly onto the progress narratives of Western modernity, globalization, and aggressive Westernization in the global South. Queer narrativity, we argue, takes more complex and more critical forms of being public. But if the coming-out narrative is thus a limiting model for queer publicity in the global context, the questions of public and private and of imagining a queer subject do nonetheless underwrite both queer lives and queer narrativity. Thinking beyond Euro-American life worlds, however, the relationship of public and private cannot be determined so easily in advance. The films we address in this chapter turn to allegory as a less deterministic model for figuring queer modes of publicness. Allegory is a narrative form that contains in its very definitions the potential for queer publicity.

Allegory becomes a core concept for thinking queer global visual culture because allegory is literally speaking otherwise in public. From the Greek *allegoria*, the concept's etymology combines *allos* (another, different) with *agoreuein* (speak openly, speak in the assembly), which in turn derives from *agora* (public assembly). Thus, in the everyday understanding of the term, an allegory is a text that says one thing in public but means another. It speaks out loud and sotto voce. Hidden within what it says publicly is a different meaning. Martin Heidegger pointed to the public aspect of allegory in "The Origin of the Work of Art," in which he says, "The art work is, to be sure, a thing that is made, but it says something other than the mere thing itself is, *allo agoreuei*. The work makes public something other than itself; it manifests something other; it is an allegory."[10] Something queer is being articulated here: the allegory elaborates a kind of epistemology of the closet in speaking something other than itself, artfully speaking a truth without saying it directly. This reading could prompt a direct way of thinking about the queer potential of allegory in world cinema. In this version, films speak something that has to remain hidden or closeted, using allegory as a means around censors, perhaps, to gain access to the world stage and allude to forbidden topics. But something else is at work in this mode of allegory. It speaks in the *agora*, in the public sphere, on the world stage, but it speaks otherwise, it speaks about something else. Allegory refuses the liberal public–private distinction, speaking differently in public and reimagining the terms of representation precisely as a question of publicity and even an assertion of worldliness.

Igor Grubić's installation *East Side Story* (2008) offers an illustration of allegory as a mode of representing homophobic violence. The work consists of two video channels presented at right angles to each other and a series of photographs. On the left-hand video is television footage of neo-Nazis and other aggressive protesters verbally and physically assaulting participants in LGBT Pride parades: here, outnumbered riot police try to protect the Pride marchers and both police and queer people are shown brutalized and bleeding. The attacks took place in 2001 in Belgrade, Serbia, and in 2002 in Zagreb, Croatia. Meanwhile, the right-hand video shows a group of dancers retracing movements and gestures of these events in the streets of Zagreb, largely ignored by passersby. The dance performances on the right-hand projection clearly allegorize the events on the left: the juxtaposition of the two projections makes clear that the choreography is referring to the violence, and the dancers' bodies articulate fear, aggression, confrontation, and injury (figures 3.2–3.3). In the classic definition of allegory, the dancers "say" one thing but are really articulating something else. Here, we are reminded that Craig Owens describes allegory as a structure in which one text is read through another, a model of critique centered on textual revision.[11] In this logic, the video of the dancers overwrites the documentary video of the violence, critiquing the political event in another form and thus rewriting it. It

Figs. 3.2–3.3: The video installation *East Side Story* juxtaposes news footage of homophobic attacks on LGBT Pride marches with choreographed gestures in the same city streets of Zagreb.

is precisely at the level of form that we apprehend the allegory: by reiterating gestures divorced from the events that gave rise to them.

This installation demonstrates the complexity of allegory: it is not just that the dancers represent events of homophobic violence in a different medium. Their bodily movements are not exact copies of what happens in the documentary sequences; they are clearly iterative but not transcriptive in any direct sense. For example, the spectator cannot always tell whether the dancers are performing gestures of the Pride participants, neo-Nazis, or police. *East Side Story* sees the transformation of real-world events into something aesthetic via choreography, photography, and video not simply as a second-order representation but as a form of historiography. Pure documentation does only limited work in figuring the relationship of nationalist politics to queer embodiment, so the documentary video on its own is not sufficient critique. We need the dance, not as an elegy or a testimony, but as a mode of writing, an articulation of the event itself and Grubić's and the dancers' response to it. In shifting our attention from one representational mode to another, allegory produces an amplification that creates a different relationship to what a public event means.

And this is a queer rhetoric. *East Side Story*'s iterative form becomes queerly political in its supplementarity. In fact, Owens discusses the idea of allegory as a supplement: for instance, a classical sculpture is already complete before it is named "virtue," so the approach of modern art criticism is to ignore this added meaning and concentrate on the form itself. Thus, "Allegory *is* extravagant, an expenditure of surplus value; it is always *in excess*. Croce found it 'monstrous' precisely because it encodes two contents within one form."[12] Owens does not make them explicit, but we can hear the wickedly queer currents in allegory here—the extravagant, the wasteful, the excessive, the monstrous, and the duplicitous. Each of these terms has a history of association with homosexuality and, in particular, with that which is suspicious in Western aesthetics.[13] *East Side Story*'s dancers might seem meaningless to the passersby in the street or even to the gallery viewer transfixed by the shocking scenes of violence on the left, unsure how to read the more controlled and abstracted bodies on the right. As Dejan Sretenovic has argued, the piece uses choreographed bodies to evoke the corporeal expressivity of queer sex, as well as the physicality of violence and, by contrast, the neutrality of the passersby.[14] Social positions with regard to homosexuality are figured in these bodies, a series of intersecting vectors that can be thought only through both image tracks in combination.

More than simply reinterpreting the violent attacks in dance, *East Side Story* speaks differently in public. As Sretenovic puts it, "Grubić's interventionist aesthetic act in public space in itself exteriorizes the ambiguity of visibility and invisibility attendant on such artistic practice."[15] On the one hand, this strategy could be seen to smuggle political speech into a seemingly innocuous performance. Spectators in Zagreb's public squares probably do not know that this performance refers to queer pride or violence, and they might respond differently to the choreography if they did. In allegorical terms, Grubić uses the abstract gestures of dance to articulate something hidden. But if there is something invisible in the street performance, there is also something that becomes visible in the finished installation. They do not speak either the language of neo-Nazis or that of the Pride marchers; rather, they reassert public space for queer bodies in a way that is not contestatory but participatory in subtle and covert ways. The dancers are "speaking in public," intervening in everyday spaces, in the midst of quotidian flows of ordinary routines and actions. They are highly visible, standing out by doing something quite different from the usual use of Zagreb's streets, yet they appear oddly invisible, ignored in a way that neither the Pride marchers nor the neo-Nazis wish to be. Sretenovic finds Grubić's work to focus consistently on "marginalised social groups that have become victims of the unfulfilled promises of democracy."[16]

East Side Story uses the form of allegory to trouble the relationship between public rights and private behavior, a distinction rarely accorded to queer lives and queer bodies. It undoes the conventional social narration of public and private spaces that underwrites liberal subjectivity and heterosexual privilege. Furthermore, the installation poses queer publicness as a strategy for exposing the political failures of postsocialist politics, but one does not simply stand in for the other: in queer allegory one must always move back and forth from one kind of body, image, performance, and politics to another. In contexts in which homophobic violence is mobilized as nationalist resistance to globalized late capitalism, Grubić's piece opens up a means to rethink queer sovereignty and democratic community.

In this chapter, we use the concept of allegory to interrogate the stakes of narrating queer lives. Moving from Fredric Jameson's contested account of national allegory, we propose allegory as an always worldly and geopolitically charged form. The chapter analyzes a series of non-Western films, all of which use allegory to overwrite Western narratives of otherness. They refuse to install the figure of the queer as an avatar of modernization or as the privileged figure who negotiates between global and local. The sections address a range of films from Guinea, India, Japan, Thailand, China and South Korea, as well as films that could be categorized as art cinema, documentary, popular cinema, and avant-garde. Through these readings, we aim to draw out both the danger and the potential of allegory as a mode of queer worldliness for non-Western cinema.

National Allegory and Queer World Making

Jameson's concept of national allegory forms one of the more influential theories of "Third World literature" and has become a touchstone for narrative theory, harnessing the concept of allegory to the exigencies of the Third World narrative.[17] For Jameson, allegory is necessary to represent the real conditions of the postcolonial nation, since the legacy of colonial oppression alongside the pressures of neo-imperialism do not permit the forms of realist or modernist narratives favored in Western modernity. For critics (and there are many), Jameson's totalizing sweep is itself a colonizing gesture, limiting the complexity of non-Western textuality. Why must *all* Third World narratives do this single thing, asks Aijaz Ahmad?[18] He insists that the so-called Third World is also part of the capitalist system and must, therefore, have experienced some of the separation of public and private that Jameson associates with First World societies.[19] Ahmad therefore refuses a First World–Third World taxonomy, instead considering the world in terms of the global struggles that are legible in all parts of the system. Despite the persistent validity of Ahmad's critique, Jameson's concept nonetheless remains provocative for thinking how texts assert their place in the world.

Jameson's model links the relationship of private and public that defines allegory to the complex geopolitical systems of postcolonial capitalism. For Jameson, Third World texts use the private to allegorize the public, in contrast to the way that private and public operate in Western texts.[20] He asserts that the experiences of neo-imperialism, postcoloniality, and economic subjugation produce a different condition of representability and that the public-private split is one of the places that we can see the effects of this difference. This structure for Jameson includes a split between "the domain of sexuality" and "the public world of classes and the economic."[21] Neither realism nor modernism respond to the particular constrictions of life in the Third World, and an aesthetic analysis must engage with these geopolitical distinctions. This argument enables a queer analysis in its insistence that being in a different relationship to power produces a different way of being public (or private) and therefore a different way of staging this relationship textually. It accounts for the centrality of publicity in constructions of sexual and gender identities and politics, and it addresses the systems of global capital within which identities and politics are negotiated. Thus, the Jamesonian concept of allegory offers a model for understanding the geopolitics of queer narration as at once complexly local and shot through with the exigencies of global power.

It might seem odd to turn Jameson's argument to queer purpose since one of the critiques mounted against national allegory is its unquestioned gender privilege, as Ahmad has suggested.[22] However, one of Jameson's earliest examples of cinematic allegory, *Dog Day Afternoon* (Sidney Lumet, dir., 1975), has queerness and gender transgression at its core. The protagonist of *Dog Day Afternoon*, Sonny, is a queer man who robs a bank to fund his trans lover's gender transition surgery. Jameson ignores this critical narrative vector in his well-known analysis of the film as allegory. Some of Jameson's first thinking on cognitive mapping emerges from his analysis of the film. He argues famously that the characters and locations form an allegorical structure for the viewer, one that reveals something of the new late-capitalist world order; the uncaring and stultifying systemization of value engineered by large-scale multinational corporations that otherwise are unrepresentable. For Jameson, *Dog Day Afternoon*'s allegorization begins to bring the violent totalizing force of these world systems into view. But what we see as the film's remarkably sympathetic depiction of a queer relationship does not seem to factor into the film's topology according to Jameson. Queer intimacy does not have a place on his map.

The significance of this intimacy to the film's allegory can be seen in a crucial scene in which Sonny, played by Al Pacino, makes a phone call to his lover. The film figures the location of queer contact as one that is possible only via cinematic space. In turn, the film deploys that space thematically to bring into question the possibility of queer intimacy. The scene opens in close-up, with Sonny and Leon intercut as they talk. Narrationally, the spectator is almost fooled into thinking that the film is sharing exclusive access to a private moment, but they quickly realize they have been hoping for an intimacy that can never be achieved. As the conversation continues, the film cuts to a wider shot that reveals that the police have been listening the whole time. According to legend, Pacino demanded that this encounter between his character and his gay lover be shot as a telephone scene and not in physical proximity. We could simply read this scene as a subtle articulation of the epistemology of the closet: queers are deprived of true intimacy. In fact, queers never seem to calibrate their privacy "correctly," and our relations, like Sonny and Leon's, are always either restrictively private or too overtly public.

But this scene also turns up the heat on the film's simmering dystopia, and it underscores its pessimism through a crucial and sudden betrayal of the film's narrational relationship to the viewer. The revelation that others are listening represents one of the first times the film has misled us, and the spectator's sudden realization that the lovers' conversation was never private prompts us to feel sad and cheated. The cold face of corporate capitalism is represented diegetically in the violation of privacy but also cinematically in a cruel twist of the film's narration. Like the sinister hospitality represented by the home-baked cookies that Harrison Ford's evil gay offers in the equally conspiratorial world of *The Conversation* (Francis Ford Coppola, dir., 1974), *Dog Day Afternoon*'s false intimacy might force the viewer to reflect back on the destructive powers of late capitalism and how it threatens to reorganize the world in even more inhuman terms. Queerness—and its relationships to publicness and privacy, intimacy and worldliness—transpires to be at the heart of *Dog Day Afternoon*'s allegory of late capitalism. Without Sonny's love and devotion, we have no sense of what global corporate capitalism threatens to eliminate. Sonny's actions in robbing the bank tie queer intimacy to anticapitalist revolt. Although Jameson does not consider it directly, we find queerness to be essential to understanding the film's geopolitical structure.

The centrality of queer bodies to political allegory—and the odd cultural amnesia to which they are subject—is also visible in *V for Vendetta* (James McTeigue, dir., 2005), a film about revolution against a totalitarian state that centers a lesbian love story. As Allison McGuffie has argued, the film enacts a queer critique of repressive social structures and, moreover, closely links queer sexuality with political revolution.[23] Perhaps, given that the film's producers were the trans filmmakers Lana and Lilly Wachowski, it should not be surprising that *V for Vendetta* imagines a rather queer revolution. The film is set in a dystopian future in which a fascistic right-wing regime rules the United Kingdom with military force. The regime insists on conformity and punishes any form of difference, but it is sexuality that emerges as the narrative's decisive difference. The first overt act of refusal comes from Gordon, a gay television presenter with a secret room hiding homoerotic BDSM images and other forbidden objects. By satirizing the regime on his show, he rejects his stringently closeted life and is soon afterward arrested, tortured, and killed.

The central queer story, though, is of Valerie and Ruth. We see their love story in flashback: at first they live an idyllic life in a cottage with a rose garden. Then, during the rise of the oppressive regime, the two women are captured and tortured to death. Their story ends with Valerie, close to death, affirming her love for Ruth, insisting, "But for three years we had roses." The protagonist Evey finds this story written painstakingly on toilet paper, which Valerie had hidden in the wall of her prison cell. Later imprisoned in the same cell, Evey reads the testimony and is spurred to revolutionary action. We learn that V, the masked revolutionary who mentors Evey, was also radicalized by the same story. The history of Valerie and Ruth gave him the courage to burn down his prison (destroying his face in the process) and to take up arms against the state. Thus, the decisive evidence of the state's oppression is its violence against lesbians, and a story (in the past, a gauzy fantasmatic vision) of lesbian devotion figures that which it is worth fighting and dying for.

V for Vendetta has had a powerful afterlife and has been particularly influential on the vernacular of anticapitalist activism. The Guy Fawkes mask worn by V and by the film's revolutionary citizens has been appropriated by the Occupy movement, by the online activists Anonymous, and by other groups centered on anonymous action. The image of V's mask can be seen stenciled on sidewalks in all of the centers of popular resistance to neoliberal capitalism. The film clearly offers a broad—critics would say, unnuanced— allegory of anticapitalist activism. Yet few of those who view the film as political allegory even recall that Evey's and V's revolutionary acts are motivated by a lesbian love story. In the film's climactic scene, Evey sends the dead body of V and a train full of explosives toward the Houses of Parliament covered in red roses, reminding us that queer intimacy is the very symbol of revolutionary commitment. If the film as a whole allegorizes a generic anticapitalism, then within the text roses figure queer bonds, which in turn bespeak the instigation of revolutionary desire. *V for Vendetta*, like *Dog Day Afternoon*, becomes even more queer when read from the perspective of allegory.

Queer politics, it seems, have been hiding in plain sight within some of Anglophone culture's most canonical allegories of global capital. What might happen to the processes of figuring totality if we looked queerly at other national contexts for allegory? In considering queer allegory, then, we aim not to replicate forms of critique blind to queer figuration but to consider what light queer narrativity sheds on the tension between visualizing totality and recognizing difference. The debate over national allegory has been enormously productive for film scholars seeking to account for the transnational logics of "world cinema," and any adoption of these logics, we claim, must include the queerness of world cinema. Jameson enumerates some things that happen in allegorical texts: the staging of a social and historical nightmare, a psychology that must be read in social terms, the problem of narrative closure in a situation with no political solution, and the fabulous becoming more effective than realism to articulate the real. All of these narrative situations speak evocatively to queer experience and begin to limn the possibilities for a queer allegorical text. Jameson's vision of the figurability of the world in national allegory might be more queer than it first appears. As Helen Leung argues, "The question of sexuality has long been present in the politicized cinemas that emerged in the wake of the Third Cinema tradition. It is one of the most powerful allegorical vehicles for the representation of power and its abuses."[24] Or, as John David Rhodes succinctly puts it in relation to contemporary American queer cinema, employing allegory "demonstrates a serious dissatisfaction with available modes of representation."[25] This chapter identifies allegory as a central form of queer narration, one that refuses the relationship of public and private demanded by globalization's subject and offers ways of speaking—and being—otherwise in the world.

The Doubleness of Queer Allegory

The question of allegory is central to *Dakan/Destiny* (Mohamed Camara, dir., 1997), which is widely viewed as the first sub-Saharan African film with a gay theme. In it, Manga and Sori fall in love as high school students but are separated by their families. Manga's mother sends Manga to a traditional healer to be cured of homosexuality while Sori's father insists Sori take over the family business and marry. Sori does get married and has a child. Meanwhile, after years with the healer, Manga enters a relationship with Oumou, a white woman he meets through his mother. Both in some way outsiders, the two forge a bond. When the men see each other again in a bar, though, they immediately recognize their mutual desire. Despite their love for their families and apparently genuine relationships with women, Manga and Sori ultimately leave everything behind to be together. At first glance, then, *Dakan* does not seem to be allegorical at all, at least in terms of sexuality. The film was controversial precisely for its *direct* representation of homosexuality, perceived by many African critics as un-African, sinful, or an unwanted relic of European colonialism.[26]

The tensions between Western gay narratives and postcolonial cinema are set in motion in *Dakan*'s international circulation. Premiered at Cannes and shown at several lesbian and gay film festivals in the West, as well as at the Panafrican Film and Television Festival (FESPACO) of Ouagadougou, *Dakan* fits neatly into some of the "universal" narratives favored by the queer film festival circuit. On its website, the US State Department substantiates its claim to be "Championing Human Rights through Public Diplomacy" by listing the fact that the American Embassy in Guinea hosted a public screening of the film.[27] It is legible as a coming-out story, as well as a politically oriented narrative about demanding space in a homophobic society. And yet, of course, its unique selling point is its national alterity; its status as the first gay sub-Saharan African film. So as much as its circulation depends on similarity, it also depends on difference. Thus, on the website of the film's US distributor, California Newsreel, we find several quotes. One is from *Variety*, which says, "'Coming out' and seeking acceptance is nothing new; but in this small but heartfelt film it is given fresh life. . . . A trailblazer in the African context."[28] Another, from Kwame Anthony Appiah, says, "This fascinating film . . . allows us to see the dangers in supposing there can be a universal gay narrative." In the same moment, the film is packaged as a universal coming-out narrative whose point of novelty is its African setting and as a salutary reminder to American audiences that Western categories of queer publicity are not available to all. In this sense, the film can be seen as simultaneously minoritizing and universalizing along core–periphery geographies. Here, the tension seems to be that of "genrefication," familiar from our discussion of the LGBT film festival. In other words, does the film tell a national story or a universal story? In the African context, this question subtends a history of debate on postcolonial representation.

We might think of *Dakan* as a textbook example of Jameson's national allegory. Although Guinea gained independence from France in 1958, its economic relationship with the Soviet Union for the next three decades, according to Lieve Spaas, led to meager film production and extensive censorship. It was not until 1995, after a period of liberalization, that elections were held and European funding enabled new film production to emerge.[29] Thus, not only can we see 1997 as a relatively early moment in the cinematic articulation of postcoloniality in Guinea, but it is historically overdetermined by the key vectors of twentieth-century geopolitics: colonial France, the breakup of the Soviet Union, democratization movements in Africa, and transnational economic and cultural policies in Europe. *Dakan* would seem like an ideal text to map the Guinean relationship to a complex postcolonial experience. Sure enough, the film responds to several of Jameson's aesthetic stipulations. In the impossible love of Sori and Manga we might read a "social and historical nightmare," in which their psychological pain as characters stands in for the nation's pain in the face of modernization. Moreover, the film's bleak ending is easy to interpret as "the problem of narrative closure in a situation with no political solution." The film ends with the lovers leaving the village forever, in this account, because there is no solution available to Guinea's weak position in the world system.[30]

The problem with extending Jameson's theory in this way is that it instrumentalizes homosexuality, reading it only as a means to an end, the visible part of an allegorical text that actually aims to speak about the nation. This effect is also described by scholars working on representations of queers in North Africa. Writing on *Omaret yakobean/The Yacoubian Building* (Marwan Hamed, dir., 2006), Stephanie Selvick says, "Homosexuality is used allegorically as a tool through which to achieve literary decolonization. Homosexuality becomes synonymous with 'colonial' and 'Western,' therefore, the physical act of eradicating homosexuality also eradicates leftover remnants of coloniality that were necessarily attached. Massad demonstrates how the trope has developed more recently. Sexual deviancy is no longer used in conjunction with postcolonial success, but rather is indicative of postcolonial corruption. Both uses of the trope demonstrate how 'deviant' sexual practices become marked as harmful to Egyptian postcolonial futurity."[31] Queerness here becomes the repository for the negative aftereffects of the colonial situation, burdened with representing its geopolitical instabilities and contradictions. In a pathbreaking essay on homosexuality in Egyptian cinema, Omar Hassan writes, "Homosexuality in effect becomes the morally decrepit part of the relationship between the colonizer and the nationalist. In effect, the only reason that it is permissible within the narrative (or with viewers) is because the manifestation of homosexuality allows for the Egyptian nationalist to physically 'rape' his colonizer, which in a sense allows him to claim back a part of his nationhood (and to an extent his manhood)."[32] Queer desire vanishes, as the conservative voices of "heterosexual Africa" might wish it to do, in favor of a more conventionally political figuration of the postcolonial nation.

Thérèse Migraine-George usefully argues that we need to study *Dakan* in both the global context of international homophobia and the local context of African same-sex histories and practices. She reads the film at the intersection of global and local currents, proposing that it illustrates "how homosexuality inscribes itself in the lives of people who inherit their traditional socio-cultural heritage in a globalizing world. In other words, I wish to examine how their same-sex feelings, desires and experiences are intricately part of their everyday lives at the junction of local and global structures and ideologies."[33] This reading counters what we might see as a vernacular modernist account of world cinema (also seen in *Variety*'s review). Instead, Migraine-George insists that "modernization is more often equated with dehumanizing self-interest, while indigenous traditions appear as a potentially vital and fluid source of change which can lead to renewed African identities."[34] There is something appealing about this analysis, which adroitly collapses the Africa/tradition versus Europe/modernity binary and opens a potential for African queer form. But ultimately there is no such form: Migraine-George returns to the structure of national allegory when she concludes that "homosexuality thus also appears as a trope used by the filmmakers to interrogate the kind of identity that African societies, standing at the junction of local traditions and global ideologies, struggling to redefine themselves, want to construct and/or adopt for themselves."[35] Even for her, then, queer desire is ultimately only a trope, a rhetorical figure that stands in for something of a different order. In this logic, queers have no ontological status.

This is the danger of allegory for queer cinema: too often, in films whose queer content shocks, criticism deploys allegory to erase that troubling of sexual or gendered norms and to redirect meaning elsewhere. The publicity of representing queer life is reversed by the emphasis on unqueer allegorical meaning. Thus, while there is something enabling in the idea of the national allegory, it can break down or become opaque when queers stand at its representational core. Jameson refuses to acknowledge the queerness at the heart of Dog Day Afternoon, and while critics cannot ignore Manga and Sori's homosexuality, they tame its radicalism by reading it as an allegory for something more politically palatable. Must queers only figure more "universal" issues of the nation in postcolonial and postclassical cinema? If the bad kind of allegory uses queer desire merely to point to the more important question of nation, then a more radical queer use of allegory involves a back-and-forth movement, as with East Side Story, from the private to the public and from text to text. It is possible to read Dakan's queer narrative as both gay and postcolonial; indeed, as both in relation. As we shall see, by speaking otherwise in public, Dakan harnesses both cinematic specificity and the condensations of allegory to figure African queerness.

Dakan's US distributor California Newsreel boasts on its website that the film contains "the most sexually explicit opening scene in African cinema." This may seem to be an odd claim, since the scene shows nothing more than two fully clothed men kissing passionately in a car. It is a claim that is clearly designed to promote the film in terms of uncensored sexuality, but it will surely be revealed as overstated when the spectator realizes that the opening is not even the most sexually explicit scene in the movie. Beyond a desire to

Fig. 3.4: *Dakan*'s visioning of sexuality places the lovers in a romantic tableau.

sex up an otherwise rather chaste film, the distributor's claim does make a certain kind of sense: Manga and Sori's embrace is a shocking intervention into a semipublic space. Narratively, we intuit that the couple has nowhere to be private, and what we are seeing is not an assertion of public sex but thwarted privacy. Nonetheless, this opening marks the film immediately as a bold visioning of homosexuality, insisting from the start on the importance of publicity. Viewers expecting homosexuality to be indicated in an allusive and coded fashion are visually accosted with cinematic ontology from the beginning: two male actors kissing in the semipublic space of a film set, and two characters who stage gay desire as part of the African everyday (figure 3.4).

According to *Variety*, the shooting of *Dakan* was disrupted by anti-gay protesters. There is also controversy over the Guinean government's financial support for the project: some sources report that the government withdrew funding when it learned of the topic of the film, but the credits begin with a title listing "the support of the Republic of Guinea." Whatever the case, these very public battles over representation speak to what Alexie Tcheuyap terms "the radical cultural metamorphosis that African societies have experienced since independence: the explosion of sex and its accompanying discourse, its transformation into a public and even political issue."[36] Thérèse Kuoh-

Moukoury argues that African cultures traditionally have understood sex as purely private and not an issue for politics or art, and Tcheuyap sees the rapid overturning of this cultural norm as an epistemic break in postcolonial Africa.[37] *Dakan* exemplifies this shift, making sexuality visible on-screen and insisting that homosexuality is not a private vice but a social issue. The question of whether or not sexual orientation can be a political topic for a film is thus raised: whereas in the West, gay rights might seem an obvious topic for a social problem film, in the African context *Dakan* could be read as a failure to be political. Abdoulaye Dukule argues that if sex is not seen as a public issue, then it cannot be a good subject for cinema, which historically has been used as "a political and social tool."[38] *Dakan* is a challenge to this regime, for it demands not only to educate in the traditions of African political cinema, but also to speak in public about queer sex.

One way to navigate this shift is through Rebecca Romanow's concept of the queer postcolonial body. Romanow argues that in the metropole it is the body that stands in for postcoloniality, not the distant abstraction of the nation.[39] But in the postindependence African nation, too, the body takes on increased significance in which its ability to figure the new discourses of sex stands in contrast to—and often in conflict with—prior modes of figuring the body politic. Making sexuality public involves disfiguring the image of the nation, and while this rhetorical move is connected to the ways that the forces of global capital have been brought to bear on postcolonial African nations, one cannot be simply mapped onto the other. *Dakan* does not simply use homosexuality to allegorize economic modernization: to do so would concur with the idea of homosexuality as "*la maladie des blancs*," an essentially conservative understanding of how postcolonial politics meets queer sexuality. Rather, the film uses the queer body to disfigure prior images of the nation.

Intertwined with the gay love story, *Dakan* features an economic plot. Sori's father is a businessman who considers Manga's family lower class and lacking ambition. He wants Sori to go to college and eventually run his fish-farming business, whereas Sori wants to go to farming school and return to his village to look after the family livestock. Ideas about modernity, sexuality, and economics here form a tight nexus. Sori's father represents economic modernization, even a Westernized vision of capitalist entrepreneurship. In this regard, Sori disappoints not by dint of his "Western" homosexuality but by being overly traditional, wanting not a capitalist relation to livestock but a peasant one. However, rejecting the family (business) in favor of one's individual desires is seen as modern, un-African. Sexuality and business practices crisscross ideologies of tradition and modernity in the father's and son's lives.

Moreover, the contrast between Sori's father's modernity and Manga's mother's tradition is shown to collapse when their sons come out to them. Manga's mother, who is coded as traditional in dress and manner, refuses to accept Manga's homosexuality as a possibility, saying that in all of history it has never happened for a man to love a man. Sori's father seems to take a more modern view, never questioning that his son is gay, but caring only about the effect on the business and Sori's place in society. His more "enlightened" response takes homosexuality itself as read but seeks to avoid social and economic stigma. Like the neoliberal politics that his character embodies, it presents itself as more modern but turns out to be no less oppressive than religious condemnation.

Manga's and Sori's bodies form the center for these crosscurrents of postindependence African culture, not figuring the nation but embodying the queer back and forth between public and private, desire and duty, national and international that weigh on the postcolonial body.

We can see this doubled operation if we examine the film's style, which promotes an allegorical reading in its visual and narrative patterning and its antirealist tableau compositions. Roy Armes says that "Camara treats his subject in a deliberately formalized manner, using explicitly worked-out, patterned dialogue, deliberate paralleling of scenes and incidents, and some very carefully composed visual images."[40] For Armes, this formalism is a problem, preventing spectatorial identification and investment in the characters. It is true that the film lacks interiority and suture, flattening out scenes into tableaux that create emotional effects but not psychological ones. By contrast, we read these patterns as markers of allegory, signals of another meaning visible beyond direct representation. For instance, when Manga tells his mother that he is attracted to a boy, she is sitting in an armchair in the exact middle of the frame, an imposing figure in her traditional dress. Behind her is a window—also centered—with decorative latticework and, on each side, matching shutters. The symmetrical composition and flat blue-and-orange color scheme betrays the naturalism of the story (figures 3.5–3.6). Similarly, both Manga's mother and Sori's father tell their children, "We've put all our hope in you." There is symmetry at the level of scene and dialogue, as well as in mise-en-scène. Allegory here refers the text to other texts: both to the Western compositions of art cinema and to the formalized structures of repetition in West African griot storytelling. Thus, at the level of form, *Dakan* reiterates the narrative question of local and global, traditional and

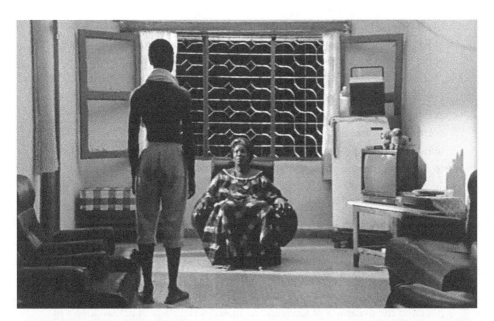

Figs. 3.5–3.6: Manga's mother refuses to accept his sexuality in *Dakan*.

modern, and in both cases it rejects the binary. We shuttle between African and European representational modes as a necessity for figuring the relationships between queer desire, Guinean identity, and economic globalization.

Dakan animates the tension between a conservative allegory that would erase African queerness and the potential for a queer critique of both reactionary homophobia and postindependence modernization. In the final scene, Manga and Sori drive away from their village, their families, and their lives into an unseen future as a gay African couple. *Dakan* not only refuses to represent their future, it actually narrates meta-textually national allegory's "problem of narrative closure in a situation with no political solution." If the film must allegorize Guinean identity, then Manga and Sori have no choice but to walk off-screen because there is no place for them. In this allegorizing move, homosexuality is not a real part of Guinea but a figure; hence, there can be no homosexuals in the national frame. If, however, we read the vanishing lovers as Romanow's queer postcolonial bodies, then they begin to produce a mode of allegory that does not erase homosexuality but, rather, builds queerness into the dynamics of globality. As material signifiers of actual queers in Guinea, their disappearance demands that we do imagine their future, an African future for queer couples. It is in the intersection of these formal modes that the film is able to stage a queer geopolitical critique: only by reading Manga and Sori both as allegory and as direct image of the world can a different geopolitics be imagined—one that has space for queers in its worldview.

Controversy and the Narration of Lesbian Lives

Deepa Mehta's *Fire* (1996) is a canonical text in histories of queer cinema, largely because of the public controversy it provoked. The film tells the story of two Indian women, both married, who fall in love and eventually decide to leave their husbands and be together. Like *Dakan*, *Fire* may not at first strike viewers as allegorical. Instead, it appears direct, courting controversy in the context of Indian cinema through its explicit representation of same-sex desire. We see the protagonists, Sita and Radha, kiss and embrace, and in a dramatic scene they are caught in bed together. However, the controversy stemmed not only from this novel visioning of Indian homosexuality but also from the competing allegories this romance narrative offered to different types of viewer.

From one perspective, the film speaks about diaspora and the emergence of a transnational and cosmopolitan Indian identity. Mehta lives in Canada, and the film was co-produced with Canadian and Indian funding. Since the film could likely not have been produced in India, where homosexuality in

1996 was still functionally illegal under the infamous Section 377 of the Penal Code, its subject matter marked it as a transnational text. *Fire* thus stages a parallel between the women who leave traditional marriages to be together and the film itself, which breaks out of Indian national cinematic convention to represent desire between women. In this allegory, India may appear as oppressively conservative, and Sita and Radha articulate the need for new ways of thinking and feeling that seem to derive from modernity and Western modes of being. If *Fire* uses Indian lesbians as a way to construct a globalized, diasporic vision of Indian identity, the (first) problem is an instrumentalization of sexuality, in which the lived experiences of queer women in India are suppressed in place of a Westernized fantasy of India's coming out into global modernity. As Gayatri Gopinath says, "Within the dominant discursive production of India as anterior to the West, lesbian or gay identity is explicitly articulated as the marker of full-fledged modernity."[41] Here, Sita and Radha perform a limiting allegorical function, articulating something about the world but nothing about women's desire and, in particular, nothing about Indian queers. From this perspective, the film aligns with a liberal worldview in which LGBT films narrate the queer subject as an avatar for the nation coming out into a globalized world. *Dakan* has been seen in the same terms, and we have already discussed the neocolonial potential of the LGBT film festival, which depends on a similar worldview.

But even in such apparently obvious parables, the force of allegory can backfire. As critics such as Jigna Desai and Ratna Kapur have argued, *Fire*'s controversial reception history illuminated a more complicated cultural politics than a liberal vision of global coming out might assume.[42] Whereas some Western critics revealed neocolonial mind-sets when they praised the film at the expense of patronizing India's supposed backwardness, the Indian debate ranged from feminist support to unease at Mehta's status as a non-resident Indian to outright violent attacks by supporters of Shiv Sena, the militant right-wing Hindu nationalist party. Cinemas showing *Fire* were targeted for protests and forced to halt screenings, and national narratives around gender, sexuality, and geopolitics were rapidly exposed. The Hindu nationalist Bharatiya Janata Party opposed the film as part of its campaign against Western imperialism, seeing lesbianism as a Western imposition. Indian lesbian groups counterprotested, asserting the confluence of Indian and lesbian identities; however, Mehta and some Indian feminist groups insisted that the issue was freedom of expression and refused to label the film lesbian. Thus, while both Western liberals and Indian conservatives yoked homosexuality and Western modernity together, the film's own director severed issues of speech and representation from the public assertion of lesbian identity, as though the film could not articulate both things at once.

Gopinath points to allegory's function in this rhetoric: "This liberal humanist defense argues that the film is not about lesbianism at all, given that it refuses to name its heroines as lesbians; rather, this argument holds, lesbian desire in the film functions allegorically and merely stands in for larger, more important issues such as women's emancipation as a whole."[43] Here again, we are confronted with the danger of allegory for queer texts—as with *Dakan*, allegory threatens to erase same-sex desire and queer politics in the name of supposed universalities such as free speech and human rights. The controversy around *Fire* vividly illustrates the problem of a queer narrative strategy that always and inevitably bespeaks something else, and does so particularly for those who might be expected to be allies (i.e., the film's director, feminists, free speech advocates). In this situation, allegory appears to be an operation of closing down meaning rather than proliferating signification. Yet the fact that these debates took place suggests that the film's meanings were mutable and that its queer narrativity forced open spaces for different modes of speaking in public.

Desai argues that *Fire* exposed not only negotiations between the queer subject and the Indian state but also those between globalization and postcoloniality. As with *Dakan*, it seems like the same-sex couple in *Fire* bear a particularly heavy burden of representation, figuring the conflict of tradition and modernity in contemporary India, the conditions of possibility for Indian lesbians, the problems of diaspora, and the discourses of normativity that circulate around postcoloniality and globalization. Moreover, the violence of the protests against *Fire* indicates the specific anxieties engendered by female sexuality and lesbian desire. The threat to patriarchy represented by Sita's and Radha's rejection of marriage and domestic labor intersects with their relationship's threat to heteronormativity. This double threat to marriage and Indian womanhood suggests that lesbian narratives that allegorize geopolitical relations are uniquely unstable. Women are used frequently in cinema as figures of the nation, and in *Fire* the threat *of* the lesbian—who cannot be named as such—becomes visible in its material form as a threat *to* lesbians. It spills into pro-filmic space via attacks on cinemas, but in returning to the text, we can see how *Fire*'s allegorical narration insists on making visible this structure of dangerous gendered instability.

If *Fire* offers a problematic liberal allegory, it also hinges on the relationship of private and public space and the way that bodies can speak in each location. Cinematic space is constantly overdetermined through melodrama, another key mode in which films can say more than they say and disclose through mise-en-scène what they cannot say directly. (We discuss melodrama in more detail in chapter 5.) Many Western critics thought the film was overblown, its use of Indian melodramatic codes rendering it unpleasantly excessive for viewers anticipating an art-cinema discourse of aesthetic restraint. For example, Sita and Radha have several emotionally resonant moments on the roof balcony of their shared home. This space is still private and domestic, yet it is outside, and they are visible to the public street. In fact, the privacy it provides is not from the gaze of the street but from the gaze of Biji, the mute but all-seeing mother-in-law who polices their behavior in the home. In this carefully chosen space of public privacy, the two women watch a wedding parade go by in the street. In a play of looks we see long, lingering shots of their faces in close-up, with a shallow focus that forces our attention toward interiority, intercut with a deep-focus long take of the crowd below partying, enjoying the public nature and unfettered visibility of heterosexual unions. The first real sense of desire between the women is marked with a slowing down of the film's pacing and rhythm and a melodramatic dispersal of desire across the contrasting spaces of the balcony and street. Later in the narrative, the women go to the balcony near the end of a day of fasting. Sita is thirsty, and Radha breaks the rules of the fast by giving her water from her own cup. The lesbian roof is a space where physical need, transgression of prohibitions, and intimate care can be expressed; it is a queer space both inside and outside the home.[44]

The melodrama culminates in the trial by fire that forms the narrative's inevitable climax. The story of *agni pariksha* comes from the Hindu epic *Ramayana*, in which Sita must prove her purity by walking through fire.[45] This is the film's central myth, a patriarchal tale in which fire burns only impure women, and the good wife Sita comes through unscathed but is sent into exile anyway. *Fire* echoes this story repeatedly: the film is made by Trial by Fire productions; the servant Mundu watches the scene from a television production of the *Ramayana*; and Swami-ji and Ashok go to a theatrical performance of the same story. The audience is thus primed for the climactic scene in which Radha confronts her husband, Ashok, and admits she is leaving him for Sita. He is furious, and in the ensuing fight her sari catches fire on the stovetop. She is consumed rapidly in flames while the furious Ashok leaves her to her fate; the image cuts to white, and we learn she has escaped to her true love, Sita, only in the final scene. Here, the space

Fig. 3.7: In the finale of *Fire*, a picturesque mosque provides a public and private space for the lovers to meet.

of a Sufist shrine provides both a public and a private space for lesbianism to flourish (figure 3.7).

Why does the film insist on putting Radha through a trial by fire in which she must be burned before she escapes into presumed exile? The story of Sita has strong resonance for Indian feminism, where it frequently has been used to question patriarchal gender norms and to address domestic violence. Here its repetition insists on the continuation of patriarchal standards for women, laying bare the violence with which femininity and heterosexuality can be enforced in India. Yet it also reinscribes *this* story, *this* myth, as the central one. Radha's survival indicates that she is pure—that the women have done nothing wrong—but only if one accepts the terms of patriarchal violence and duty. As much as *Fire* changes the terms of the story, it cannot entirely escape the Mulveyan sadistic requirement to burn its transgressive heroine. Moreover, as crucial as this feminist critique remains, it tends to limit and divert the terms of the women's transgression from the dangerous combination of sexuality and gender to purely a question of gender, and a stable account of gender at that. Nonetheless, the narrative centrality of the Sita myth indicates that the film, despite its diasporic appearance, locates queer transgression squarely in an Indian cultural space. This use of the *Ramayana* centers Hindu tradition, and simultaneously spaces of Muslim devotion provide venues for lesbian love to exist.

In fact, something unexpected happens in the film's narration of queerness and worldliness. Desai argues, with a resonant phrase, that "homosexuality has become a sign of the global."[46] For *Fire*'s critics from both left and right, this means that a Western, neocolonial version of gay identity has been imposed on postcolonial cultures, demanding that same-sex desire fit into dominant models and linking LGBT rights to the political and economic aims of capital. In a more sympathetic reading, Gopinath finds similarities in how, for the film's critics, both queerness and diaspora are situated as alien: not Indian. Thus, "These critiques of Mehta from commentators from across the political spectrum as foreign and therefore ignorant of Indian 'reality' brings into sharp relief the conflation of both 'queer' and 'diaspora' as inauthentic and alien within nationalist discourse."[47] But the film throws these nationalist discourses into doubt, not only insisting on the Indianness of Sita and Radha's love story but associating global circulation firmly with the sexual transgressions of the hetero characters.

This association begins with the opening sequence, in which Sita and her new husband, Jatin, visit the Taj Mahal. (Notably, from the very beginning of the film, Sita's romantic desires are associated with a devotional Muslim space.) Whereas Sita smiles broadly, rapt with the romantic story, Jatin leans against a wall in the background, eating, unmoved. When he comes over, she asks whether he likes romantic movies, and he says no, he likes kung fu and Jackie Chan. Where Sita likes romantic Hindi narratives, Jatin prefers the transnational and globally circulated spectacles of Hong Kong action cinema. Jatin is not only "traditional" in his patriarchal treatment of his wife, but he is also "modern" and "global" in his preferred narratives. Moreover, he transpires to have a Chinese Indian mistress, Julie, a character often left out of debate on the film. In an odd scene of dinner with Julie's family at a Chinese restaurant, her father talks bitterly about how other Chinese left for the West, but his working-class family went to India. This tale of transnational migration is marginal to the plot and yet marked narratively in the film. It is not the upper-middle-class diaspora of Mehta but a pointedly working-class story of movements across the global South. Meanwhile, Julie feeds Jatin with her chopsticks, revealing that she is just as deferential and submissive as the wives whose lives she rejects.

Another vector of global circulation in the film is the video store. As discussed earlier, video stores feature in many films of queer globalism—an underground video rental store forms a locus of debate around queer rights in *Circumstance* and a more typical rental store in Dhaka sets the opening scene of *Common Gender* (Noman Robin, dir., 2012), which we discuss in chapter 5—because the video store is both a physical index of cinema's international transits and a threshold of public culture and private viewing. Videos circulate both above and below the counter, promising globalized pleasures and censored images of forbidden acts. The video store does not always offer queer films, but it always bespeaks a threat to normativities and a potential for transgressive acts. In *Fire*, it is straight customers who can access sexual transgression in Jatin's video store. When Radha catches the servant Mundu masturbating in front of Biji, he tells her that Jatin has a lot of porn videos he rents to special customers. In response to her anger and threat to fire him, Mundu retorts that the "hanky-panky" between her and Sita is bad for the family name. The video store illustrates the circulatory sexual license afforded to heterosexual men, in contrast to Sita's limited scope for self-expression. In an extension of this male privilege, Mundu can all too easily threaten to expose Sita's sexuality as a transgression of the familial, national order.

In *Fire*, therefore, it is the hetero characters who are globalized, with the global staging precisely the way that heterosexual institutions of capitalism and globalization fold in transgressive modernities with seemingly little friction. The queer does not figure the global as such but instead suggests a very different globalism to the one Jatin so successfully navigates. Sita and Radha, like Manga and Sori, are forced into an invisible world, a global space that cannot be visualized. As with the end of *Dakan*, Sita and Radha's future as a couple is unimaginable in the terms set out by the narrative. The film ends with them reunited, but in a fantasmatic romantic setting of a deserted Muslim shrine—the spectator has no means to imagine what might come next for them. Yet as in *Dakan*, *Fire* does end by insisting on their existence, out there, somewhere, but in India, not in some far-off land. If we reverse the Shiv Sena's fear of the alien and take seriously the idea of homosexuality as a sign of the global, there is a powerful idea of queer worldliness lurking in these texts, in which the "global gay" might not be the white homonationalist but a much more destabilizing figure.

In considering the forms and stakes of queer narrativity in India, it is productive to compare *Fire* with *Taar Cheye Se Anek Aaro/More than a Friend* (Debalina Majumder, dir., 2010), a hybrid drama-documentary film that considers how to narrate lesbian lives in a temporarily post–Section 377 India. At first sight, *More than a Friend* articulates the same problematic as *Fire*: its opening (fictional) sequence introduces an off-screen Ranja, who confesses to her mother that the person referenced in romantic diary entries as Tukai is a girl, not a boy, and that she is not just a friend. The coming out paradigm appears to be central, yet the film quickly resists two dominant aspects of *Fire*'s

Fig. 3.8: The lovers Tukai and Ranja visit a studio to pose for romantic photographs together in *More than a Friend*.

liberal coming-out story. First, the film thwarts the idea of coming out into a hostile, backward society by juxtaposing multiple voices. When it switches to documentary mode, we hear from rabid homophobes but also from scholars of sexuality, open-minded straight people, and a range of different same-sex couples. Second, it transforms the possibility of narrating queer life. One woman, coded seemingly as straight, says, "I'm not saying one person cannot like another. That can happen. But what next?" This is also the question of *Fire*, but it is a question that *Fire* cannot resolve. *More than a Friend* moves beyond imagining same-sex desire to representing lesbian lives and futures.

The film's mix of documentary and fiction poses the nature of the image and the possibility of representation as central to queer narrativity. In an early scene, Tukai and Ranja visit a photography studio, where they have portraits taken in conventional romantic poses (figure 3.8). The studio has pictures of Hindi movie stars on the wall, guiding the proper representational codes of heterosexual desire. When the women pose affectionately, the photographer becomes angry and abusive. Here and elsewhere, the film reveals itself to be very aware of the stakes of the image; how its characters navigate heteronormative and gender normative spaces; and, more important, how the film navigates them. This fictional scene proposes the image as a key place where norms are enforced and contested. We also learn that Tukai is making a film, and the spectator begins to wonder whether the real interviews we have seen are also her fictional ones. There is a simple twist here, in which Tukai is taking control of the means of production and

There can't be any relationship between two men.

Fig. 3.9: *More than a Friend* mixes fiction and documentary in a scene in which Tukai conducts real street interviews.

making her own images, but it is also more complex. The camera is an apparatus for imagining Indian queer identities, but it is also one that intervenes in how women's bodies can be looked at, touched (as one woman relates, a doctor touched her all over), and controlled.

In the next scene, Tukai asks passersby whether they have heard of same-sex relationships. Although she is a fictional character, the actress is asking real people so that the scene is both fiction and documentary (figure 3.9). The sequence is reminiscent of Pier Paolo Pasolini's *Comizi d'amore/Love Meetings* (1964), as its deceptively simple questions open out a complex documentary construction. Like Pasolini, Tukai asks questions that include issues of class at a fundamental representational level, and that concern reflects back into the fictional narrative. Whereas in *Fire* the servant Mundu is sneaky and abusive, in *More than a Friend* Tukai's family servant is privileged narratively: in key scenes we have access to her inner thoughts in voiceover and her point of view. At first she thinks lesbianism is a rich person's issue, but then she remembers that her niece has a close female friendship. Her emotions and reactions are centered once again when the niece commits suicide. Later, she talks with Ranja's mother about her dead niece, giving the mother pause for thought when she describes the dead girl as having "so much love." This sad story is picked up in the documentary strand, which intercuts two women telling stories about queer women who committed suicide after being forced to marry or raped by male relatives. Alongside these stories of violence we hear wryly humorous anecdotes from a couple whose jointly owned house caused familial tension and who nonetheless are navigating relationships with extended families. We cut back from interviews to see the same subject on Tukai's laptop, where Ranja pushes her to turn it off. They snuggle in daylight, talking casually about college. Instead of *Fire*'s melodramatic consummation in stolen moments, we have a much more everyday expression of physical affection. Comparison of these two films testifies to how the conditions of representability have changed from 1996 to 2010, but rather than indicating a progress narrative, the films speak in different ways about allegory's relationship to historicity.

We can see the link between queer allegory and historicity by turning briefly to Walter Benjamin's analysis of the *Trauerspiel*, or German tragic drama, in which he argued that this baroque and largely forgotten form could reveal the radical potential of allegory for a Marxist theory of history.[48] For Benjamin, whereas the symbol can appear to be singular and natural, to speak without mediation and to emerge from the aesthetic experience of the world, the allegory seems mechanistic, old-fashioned, and inauthentic, only able to trade in signs of things. Allegory always points to the gaps and displacements in meaning, and it is thus a potentially radical form. In a queer reading of Benjamin, the symbol might take on the apparent obviousness of heterosexual representation and the allegory the inauthentic superficiality of queer art.

Moreover, Benjamin's revaluation of the baroque allegory insists on the transformative power of the outdated and the apparently unnecessary. The Indian lesbian is both too late (passé for Western tastes) and too soon (entering an economy in which gender is rigidly enforced and sexual violence is still commonplace). This temporal organization is not simply a problem of neocolonial discourse or Indian conservatism; it describes the potential of queer cinema to dislodge reactionary modes of historicity. Both of these films provoke questions of their timeliness: *Fire* is both out of time and out of place, a film whose fascination arises from its baroque propensity to say so much more than it actually says. *More than a Friend* makes clear its necessary inauthenticity and the difficult process of reordering images when lives are undoubtedly at risk. As allegories of queer worldliness, these films set in motion—sometimes violently—performances of exclusion and negotiation and of public and intimate speech.

The "World Exposition of Images"

Jameson's national allegory focuses on realist form; indeed, one of Ahmad's critiques is that it ignores the modernist and avant-gardist writers of Latin America, Africa, and Asia. Ahmad's point also has a validity for cinema, although Jamesonian allegory in film is already associated with a broader range of narrative forms, including the art cinema of Edward Yang and the Third Cinema of Ousmane Sembène, as well as the new Hollywood of *Dog Day Afternoon*. Thinking about experimental film offers a way to gain fresh purchase on queer film allegory, since avant-gardes and underground forms have license to represent lives and experiences that otherwise would go undocumented. We have to think only of the importance of films such as Kenneth Anger's *Scorpio Rising* (1963), Jean Genet's *Chant d'amour* (1950), or Barbara Hammer's *Dyketactics* (1974) to see the documentary power of the queer avant-garde, as well as the mutual influence of experimental and popular forms of queer image. But although experimental film is often considered to be non- or anti-narrative, its alternative modes of representation can critique dominant forms of narrativity and narrate queer lives differently, thus avoiding the pitfalls and nourishing the promises of queer allegory. We turn, therefore, to a key example of experimental cinema to demonstrate the plasticity and expressivity of queer allegory.

Toshio Matsumoto's film *Funeral Parade of Roses* (1969) combines documentary, narrative, and experimental form in an exuberant oedipal melodrama set in the world of Tokyo's "gai bois" or "queens."[49] Eddie is a young queen who works in a gay bar and travels in a mixed hippie scene of drug dealers, Marxist protesters, and avant-garde filmmakers. He is having a relationship with his boss at the bar, Gonda, and the film's climax comes with the discovery that Gonda is the father who abandoned Eddie's family as a child. Horrified by the realization, Gonda commits suicide, and Eddie, in turn, blinds himself. *Funeral Parade of Roses* engages fictionally with the thriving gay scene in Tokyo, in which, as, Mark McLelland tells us, "By the early 1960s, there were estimated to be over 100 establishments employing a staff of more than 400 distributed throughout the former red-light districts of Asakusa, Shinjuku and Shinbashi. Among these establishments was a new style of 'gay bars' . . . where transgendered [*sic*] male hostesses known as 'gay boys' . . . served drinks and provided conversation for customers, often making themselves available for after-hours assignations."[50] The film mixes a fictional narrative about the hostess Eddie with documentary sections interviewing some of the film's actors, as well as gay men on the street. Moreover, the film's star, Peter, was a nonprofessional actor discovered in a show bar. This self-reflexive mixture of documentary and fiction recapitulates the narrative's move between underground scene and public performance—or, in queer allegorical terms, inside and outside.

In fact, Matsumoto's own writing on cinema locates inside and outside as central problems of representation. He is best known as a documentarian, but his films resisted the social realism of canonical Japanese documentary and developed a strongly experimental strain. Abé Mark Nornes has described Matsumoto as a key figure in the critique of realism in postwar Japanese cinema, whose demand for subjectivity in the perspective of filmmakers was an attempt to produce a more politically engaged cinema.[51] In an interview with Aaron Gerow, Matsumoto says,

> Although I found the freedom of avant-garde's uninhibited, imaginative world extremely attractive, it had the tendency to get stuck in a closed world. Documentaries, on the other hand, while intensely related to reality, would not really thoroughly address internal mental states. . . . I asked whether there wasn't a need for documentary to assume a subjectivity that could make visible what was invisible. In that sense, I felt that documentary and the avant-garde have to be connected within a moment of mutual negation.[52]

The logic of allegory echoes in Matsumoto's opposition between the interior, closed world of the avant-garde and the limiting exteriority of documentary's referential domain. Not unlike the way we earlier described allegory as overwriting, Matsumoto's genre hybridity is dialectical: it aims for a "mutual negation" that revises each type of space in relation to the other to create new worlds that are neither purely objective nor purely subjective. For Matsumoto, the problem with the forms is their separation; as Mika Ko puts it, "For Matsumoto the interior is an extension of the exterior and there is nothing that distinguishes them in any clear or absolute manner."[53] Thus, the documentary must include aspects of the avant-garde. It must speak in public but do so differently. This is already a form of allegory, and in *Funeral Parade of Roses*, both the subjective interiorities and the public cultures being articulated are queer in nature. Ko sees *Funeral Parade of Roses* as attempting to do justice to both "visible and invisible social realities," and we argue that the film mobilizes structures of allegory to combine the queer with the political in the global sphere.[54]

Allegory promises to reorder the relationship of inside and outside in part by reconfiguring narrative space. In his writings, Matsumoto anticipates a use of cinema in which insides penetrate outsides, and vice versa. Owens argues that allegorical texts operate by means of referentiality, rereading and critiquing existing texts rather than allowing the spectator to assume a direct relationship of diegesis to external reality. Certainly, *Funeral Parade of Roses* is full of references, explicitly or implicitly citing Oedipus, comic books, Kabuki theater, and much more. But more than just prefiguring B.

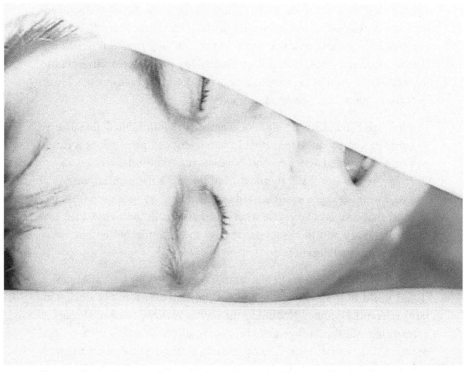

Fig. 3.10: *Funeral Parade of Roses* begins with solarized images of bodies so aestheticized that they are hard to read.

Ruby Rich's "homo pomo" style, the film demands from the outset that we question both the objectivity of the image and the subjectivity of the characters.[55] It opens with a sex scene between what many spectators take to be a man and a woman. The film is solarized, and the images are thus both hard to read in detail and aesthetically beautiful (figure 3.10). Skin and bodily curves fill the screen, fetishizing the body but withholding its gender. Eventually, Eddie's torso moves past the camera, which freeze frames on his male-looking flat chest. This early sequence plays with the cinematic inscription of bodily truths, offering a comedically knowing or shocking reveal to different audiences. This early duplicity is echoed in the film's repeated interest in masks: although the Oedipal plot depends on the material status of Eddie as Gonda's biological child, the operation of gender, sexual, and subcultural performances belies any easy belief in bodily truths beneath the mask. The forms of drag and gender performativity evinced in the queens' lives do not cover but constitute subjectivities. Allegory here is not a substitutive process in which a body looks female but is "really" male. Instead, it sets a dialectic in place between surfaces and depths, both cinematic and bodily.

We can see this troubling of appearance and reality in narrative terms. Allegory does not depend on the straight lines of causal, syntagmatic narrative but creates meanings paradigmatically, one thing speaking of another. Owens sees this effect as a postmodern seriality of structure, in which sequences are "not dynamic, but static, ritualistic, repetitive. It is thus the epitome of counternarrative, for it arrests narrative in place, substituting a principle of syntagmatic disjunction for one of diegetic combination."[56] Matsumoto describes "looking at things in terms of lateral connections," and this refusal of linear narrativity also bespeaks the queerness of the avant-garde.[57] For instance, Homay King argues that Andy Warhol's films conjure a queer temporality in their refusals of narrativity. Warhol's screen tests deflect attempts to narrate: the subject looks at the camera without talking, and the time of the film is determined not by narrative temporality but by the length of a roll of 8 mm film. Something queer is articulated in this evacuation of heteronormative causality; something else is articulated in Edie Sedgwick's awkward performance or Ann Buchanan's unblinking tears.[58] *Funeral Parade* does not evacuate narrative causality in this direct way but fragments it, proliferating the contiguities of each event, combining a melodramatic and campy compression of narration in the Oedipal plot with non-narrative interludes and spectacular digressions. In Sara Ahmed's terms, the film has a queer orientation; it does not move in a straight line.[59]

The narrative is essentially circular: it shows the same scene twice, first from Eddie's point of view at the beginning and then from Leda's near the end. Rather than suspending narrative as Warhol does, or slowing it down like Apichatpong, Matsumoto alternately speeds it up, fractures it, and repeats it. There is a linear story to be reconstructed from the out-of-sequence plot of *Funeral Parade of Roses*, but there are also significant parts of the film that simply do not fit into the story. The film makes use of the Oedipus myth, central to the Western canon and, as Teresa de Lauretis has argued, to patriarchal film narration, but speaks differently with it.[60] Of course, the family romance itself is queered: our Oedipus is a gay boy, a queen; he sleeps with his father, not his mother; and he kills his mother, not his father.[61] But among the shards of this familiar tale are other diegeses, other worlds that can be allegorized among the ruins of Oedipus. The actor who plays Leda is interviewed, as are other gay men—not actors but simply documentary social actors on the streets of Shinjuku. An avant-garde performance group stages a happening in the streets, an event planned by Matsumoto and so in one register part of

Fig. 3.11: *Funeral Parade of Roses* plays with gender in a public restroom.

the fictional diegesis, but in another a real event, with real passersby, documented as a protest, a political intervention in which Eddie the fictional character is the odd man out. Finally, the scene in which Eddie and his gai boi friends visit a public bathroom and then fight comedically with a gang of women is a fragment of drag versus girl power slapstick (figure 3.11), a gender battle over realness that is closer to *Paris Is Burning* (Jennie Livingston, dir., 1990) than Jonas Mekas. This fragmented narrative maps an attempt to speak something else in public.

What does *Funeral Parade of Roses* allegorize that could not be spoken in dominant forms of Japanese film culture? Most obviously, the culture of gai bois was not depicted in mainstream Japanese cinema and was rarely visible in realist documentary. But more important, the film figures queer life as a kind of global visibility, a mode of dissent against Japanese postwar modernity and a specifically Japanese figuration of the global protests of 1968. *Funeral Parade of Roses* was released in 1969 and made in the context of public protest against the renewal of the Japan-US Security Treaty and the international student protest movement. The film does not represent these political currents directly, yet they suffuse its fragmentary structure. The queens work in a bar frequented by rich businessmen, and the economics of sex work figures larger capitalist inequalities. Tokyo's gay bars were influenced by Parisian clubs and, in particular, by the style of Le Carrousel.[62] In fact, Peter was discovered in one such show bar when he was cast in *Funeral Parade of Roses*. Transnational currents of queer economic exploitation are an unspoken but visible foundation for the film.

The film's allegory is a question not just of economics on-screen but of narrative economy. The Oedipal story, for instance, centers on inheritance, and the violent bequest of the father is readable as the rejection by Japanese counterculture of the 1960s of the wartime generation. Eddie cannot bear the discovery that he is having sex with his father and responds to his mother's cruelty and perceived betrayal with an equal measure of shocking violence. This Oedipus narrative takes a Western myth and makes it articulate Japanese historical traumas, in which the Law of the Father demands a radical gesture of refusal. Moreover, the film consistently adapts international narrative forms, placing its representations of a very specific Japanese subculture into a global cultural and political context. It refers repeatedly to New American Cinema and especially to Jonas Mekas, linking its own textual practices self-reflexively to an emerging international avant-garde. This set of associations disturbs easy discourses of American imperialism: at the same time that the student movement decries the Westernizing force of global capital, the interstitial abstractions of experimental film imagine other Americas and create transnational counterculture connections. Just as we can see the New American Cinema as political—even Mekas's very personal work functions as a refusal of industrial cinema—*Funeral Parade of Roses* makes a claim on a different relationship to Japanese cinematic (and economic) institutions. And significantly, it is queerness, the queens, who can make this protest visible.

Mika Ko cites Matsuda Masao's description of the film as a "world exposition of images" because of its wide range of references.[63] Ko sees this appellation as negative, but we can redeploy this insult queerly as a way to think the film's figuration of worldliness. For Ko, the more positive spin is that the film brings the international avant-garde together with something that is culturally specific to Japan. This is true, but we want to focus on the implications of a world exposition of images. The negativity derives from a sense of an arbitrary accumulation of images that lack proper order and a leisure activity in which images are mere spectacle, offering non-productive and unserious pleasures. Each of these terms is ripe for a queer rereading—the digression from proper meaning and order, the postmodern collage, the lazy and leisurely wasted time as opposed to the well-ordered time of rational modernity, and the pleasurable image as superficial spectacle. The film plays with all of these implications to inscribe a different optic of worldliness, shaking up the systems of capitalist globalization to view the world differently, in a fragmented, audiovisually rich, often affective style. The politics of May 1968 and the new family structures of the gay underground are not arbitrarily connected at all, in fact, and the film insists we see the links between these networks.

Ko reads Eddie as "allegorizing the radical student movement of that time; that is, to be functioning as a symbol of modern youth kicking out, or overcoming, 'old' Japan," but she does not connect the queer with the worldly.[64] For her, the film provides a range of loosely connected rejections of the old, including avant-garde form, underground sexuality, and student rebellion. The problem with this account of the film, as with the readings of *Dakan* as a national allegory, is that this equally national reading silences the political potentiality of queerness, using the queer simply as figure of something else. Thus, she reads Eddie's blinding in the final scene as a representation of the extremists in the 1970s, whose activism shocked the public. This account instrumentalizes Eddie's violent blinding, absenting the queer character from his fictional life and using his body as a puppet vehicle for an unconnected topic (figure 3.12). By contrast, we argue that across *Funeral Parade of Roses*, the direct meaning of the image is bound to its allegorical form. Taro Nettleton glosses Japanese response to the film, in which major critics described its effects as dizzying. Nettleton proposes that Peter's on-screen presence is "enrapturing and overwhelming," and his queer sex scene shatters subjectivity.[65] Here, the force of a queer image is not a distraction from but, rather, the vehicle of anticapitalist critique. The allegory form binds queer (direct) speech to worldly (indirect) speech, insisting on a dialectic rather than a replacement.

Nettleton argues that the Shinjuku neighborhood, and Matsumoto's representation of it, enables a queer politics to emerge in *Funeral Parade of Roses*. The question of "who qualified as the city's rightful citizens" turns the visibility of gay culture in the film into a question of public and private.[66] He reads the film's representation of gai bois through Ernesto Laclau and Chantal Mouffe, who insist that transformations in the condition of politicization "tend . . . to dissolve the distinction between the public and the private." *Funeral Parade of Roses*, for him, "intentionally imagines a world in which

Fig. 3.12: *Funeral Parade of Roses* depicts a horrifically blinded Eddie.

these realms are inseparable."[67] Like Grubić, then, Matsumoto mounts a
dialectic of public and private visibility, and he does so in a uniquely contested place and time. The wasteful leisure time that Masao describes is also
a queer culture of loitering that Nettleton describes as under attack by the
increased privatization of hitherto public spaces in Tokyo. As the Japanese
economic miracle overtakes subcultural space, queerness forms both an allegorical figure and a weapon. Matsumoto's film unleashes a global cohort
of homosexuals "growing like a cryptogram, no less, in the shadows of the
culture of over-mature capitalism."[68] Here again, gays are used instrumentally to figure capitalism, but for Nettleton, *Funeral Parade of Roses* is more
sophisticated than its director's words. "Gay boys," he suggests, "represented
an alternative to, and a potential to disturb, Japan's privileging of capital and
GNP growth."[69]

If perversion is a heretical turning away from acceptable public speech,
then *Funeral Parade of Roses* repeatedly stages possible models of perverse
corporeality on the world stage. Matsumoto engages with the avant-garde

critique of capitalism when he says, "In a sense, this kind of rejection of the ordered and arranged world of the dualistic law of perspective I am talking about is a way to start bringing modernity into question."[70] As in Stephen Heath's canonical account of Renaissance perspective in "Narrative Space," a critique of dominant modes of vision in narrative is a prerequisite for the radical undoing of space, place, and gender.[71] What we see in *Funeral Parade of Roses* is a queer refusal to conform to Japanese modernity, even as queen culture is fully inserted into the transnational economic regime of salary-men and showgirls. In both the documentary and the fictional worlds of the film, the gai bois insist, along with the student radicals and experimental dance troupes, on speaking a different form of globality.

Devouring Public and Private

The Thai filmmaker Apichatpong Weeresethakul exemplifies contemporary cinema's queer worldliness in more obvious ways than Matsumoto. The narrative opacity of his films and their frequent reference to Thai folktales suggest that allegory might be a productive way to approach their engagement with politics, yet his films are distributed in the apparently apolitical circuits of world art cinema. For many of the critics who have supported his rise to prominence, Apichatpong's queerness is not important or even remarked on. The majority of his films do not declare their characters as being gay. Only *Hua jai tor ra nong/The Adventures of Iron Pussy* (2003), *Sud pralad/Tropical Malady* (2004), and *Mekong Hotel* (2012) contain obvious LGBT figures, and the qualities that make Apichatpong's films successful in the art-cinema market have more to do with his trademark slow style than with his queerness. Yet it is precisely this apparent disjuncture that needs to be unsettled. Allegory is the trope that enables us to see how Apichatpong combines the sexual, the political, and the aesthetic.

Allegory is a play on the relationship of public to private spaces, and Apichatpong's films riff continuously on the textual and material implications of this binary. Indeed, Jihoon Kim sees his films as structured by a series of binaries, metonymically connected: gay–straight, rural–urban, male–female, traditional–modern, and real–fantasy.[72] For Kim, Apichatpong blurs the boundaries of these categories, asking audiences to immerse themselves in an experience of the interstitial. Most visibly, films like *Sang sattawat/Syndromes and a Century* (2006) have a diptych form, splitting the narrative into two parts, two diegeses that nonetheless mirror and bleed into each other. We might well view this unsettling of binary thinking as a queer strategy, especially when considered in relation to the films' evocation of gay–straight

Fig. 3.13: *Tropical Malady*'s first part ends with a moment of intimacy in which the Thai national flag is visible in the background.

and male–female interstices. *Tropical Malady* narrates a queer love story in these interstices, locating intimacies in between the public spaces of pop concerts, religious shrines, and street markets and the enclosed, subjective spaces of the jungle.

Tropical Malady is also constructed explicitly as a diptych. The first section of the film tells the story of a soldier, Keng, who is stationed in the rural north of Thailand. He meets Tong, a local boy, and the two embark on a romantic relationship. While not especially explicit, the film pushes the limits of Thai censorship in a shot in which the men kiss and lick each other's hands with a Thai national flag flying in the background (figure 3.13). Afterward, Tong walks off toward the jungle, leaving Keng to an exhilarating but melancholic motorbike ride through the town on his own. Shortly after this encounter, the film flickers and vanishes, the screen goes black for thirty seconds, and the image returns with what seems to be a credit sequence for a different film, called *A Spirit's Path*, about a shape-shifting Khmer shaman. In the second part, the same actors may or may not be playing the same parts. Maybe-Keng goes into the jungle to find Maybe-Tong, and in the almost complete darkness of the jungle, he encounters a magical tiger who may or may not want to consume him (figure 3.14). Visual and narrative opacity are combined with a mysterious erotics of the shamanic were-tiger: by allowing himself to be eaten, Maybe-Keng can enter the shaman's world.

This doubled narrative structure practically demands to be considered in terms of allegory. What is the repetition of the gay relationship of the film's

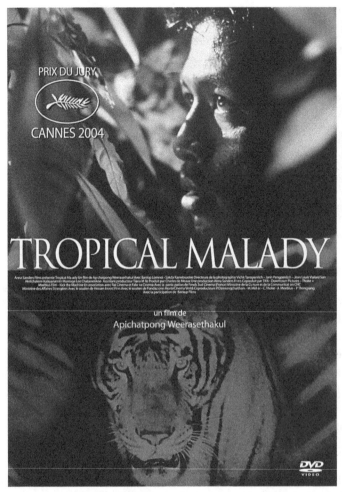

Fig. 3.14: This poster for *Tropical Malady* emphasizes the allegorical qualities of the shamanic tiger spirit.

first half in terms of a man drawn irresistibly to a were-tiger if not an allegorization of non-normative desire in the language of northern Thai folktales? But our conception of allegory can go beyond a simple substitution of one meaning (gay desire) for another (Thai folklore). *Tropical Malady* offers us exactly the kind of syntagmatic disjuncture that Owens considers central to counter-narrative. The film is a series; a diptych of anti-narratives that do not go anywhere but, instead, set events in motion around a structure of queer desire. In this disjunctive structure, the allegorical space repeats the literal one in coded form. Peter A. Jackson notes in a different context that the tiger has a semiotic resonance in Thai sexual cultures: *seua bai* (or bi-tiger) is Thai slang for a masculine man who is attracted to both men and women, and tigers were used in the twentieth century to code dangerous masculinity in the form of gangsters and, on occasion, predatory gay men.[73] The were-tiger that emerges at the end of *Tropical Malady* is a folkloric, ritualistic repetition of the gay lover in the register of Thai subcultural iconography. Thought of this way, something like the same story appears twice: first in global/public and then in Thai/private narrative spaces.

This account of allegory also resonates with recent queer refusals of linear narrative, such as Ahmed's aforementioned concept of queer orientations that deflect, pervert, and turn away from the straight lines of normative textuality.[74] Viewed in this light, the narrative also offers a digressive pathway where a realist account of the possibilities for gay romance in rural Thailand (and for representing it on film in cosmopolitan Thailand) is diverted into a surreal vision of ghosts, mythic creatures, and jungle darkness. In this reading, the film diverts into fantasy at the exact moment that realism is no longer adequate. Owens points to this effect when he says that allegory turns realism into expressionism, "transforming the most objective naturalism into the most subjective expressionism, or the most determined realism into the most surrealistically ornamental baroque."[75] The first part of the film sets up a modern Thai cinematic subject who speaks to the world in the idiom of liberal gay visibility. But when Keng and Tong kiss under the Thai flag, we reach the limits of realism. As the second part of the film begins, the spectator is hurled into the space of allegory; we no longer have the comfort of realist identificatory structures. We are disoriented, in the jungle, listening for tigers.

Here, Apichatpong speaks differently in the public sphere of world cinema. A man being consumed by a tiger spirit is not literal, but neither does the film simply ask us to work out what it is "really" saying. Notions of modernity and folkloric belief, citizenship and being, publicity and privacy, desire and its object, what it means to be human and who might or might not be desirable under that name: all are articulated quite differently in the dark of the jungle. As in *Dakan*, *Tropical Malady*'s queer allegory does not link tradition to homophobia and Western modernity to gay freedom. Indeed, as Benedict Anderson has demonstrated, the Thai tradition of *kathoey*—feminine gay men who speak as women—was well understood in the rural areas in which the film was shot. When he showed the film in this area, audiences recognized its kathoey characters and accepted them as part of village life.[76] So queerness exists both in the public, rational, realist spaces of the film's first half and in the private, folkloric, animal spaces of its strange second part. And it is in the figure of the shamanic tiger that the allegory is at its most powerful. A talking monkey warns Keng of his fate and draws us into the world of animals. To link gay and lesbian people with animals is often a dehumanizing and dangerous rhetoric, but as we saw in chapter 2, queer animal figures can be used to other effects. In *Tropical Malady*, the nonhuman figures the object of queer desire as something rarely beautiful, sublimely threatening, and deeply lodged in Thai culture. "Once I have devoured your soul, we are neither animal nor human," says the tiger, and the film's final sequence is a slow approach to this promise of something other than humanistic selfhood. *Tropical Malady* thus imagines a queer Thailand more radically in this allegorical section than it can do in the realist narrative with which it begins.

Carla Freccero writes that "queer, to me, is the name of a certain unsettling in relation to heteronormativity. It can be thought of, and is akin to, the 'trace' in the field of sexuality."[77] The idea of queer sexuality as a trace, a spectral disturbance in the textual field, allows us to see Apichatpong's allegories as a particular formation of doubling. Apichatpong uses cinematic space here not only to bring two incommensurate diegeses together but to have one overwrite the other. The private space of sexuality is not merely a metaphoric rendition of public or national spaces; rather, the two categories touch in unexpected and often uncanny ways. Apichatpong's *Loong Boonmee raluek chat/Uncle Boonmee Who Can Recall His Past Lives* (2010) figures spectrality directly in the strange body of an ape ghost with bright red eyes who embodies a dead son returned to the family. This memory and that of the princess who has sex with a fish are queer figures from the past—uncanny traces of past moments but also figures who destabilize the human.

We have already addressed the thorny problem some discourses have in imagining queers as human. But both here and in the queer animality we explore in chapter 5, destabilizations of the human are imbued with an unexpected force of refusal. Bliss Cua Lim makes a similar reading of the *aswang* figure in Filipino culture, arguing against dominant accounts of the folkloric monster as that which is excluded from the national. Instead, she suggests, queer variants of the aswang in films such as *Mga bata ng lagim/Children of Terror* (Mar S. Torres, dir., 1964) and *Bakasyon/The Visit* (Raya Martin, dir., 2004) are "kinfolk . . . in the grips of supernatural becoming."[78] With the queer aswang, as with Apichatpong's beasts, the animal-human boundary is traversed with a transgression that is not about bestiality but about altering the constitution of the human subject. That this spectral transgression is linked to queer desire and intimacy is made clear in *Tropical Malady*, in which wanting a man recurs in the fantasmatic desire to be eaten by a tiger. This unfigurable desire (evoking Bersani's fantasy of annihilation) refutes liberal homonormativities with a desire grounded in the material conditions of the northern Thai jungle, a perverse cinematic space of darkness, invisibility, unfamiliar sounds, and ghostly presences.[79] *Tropical Malady* speaks on the public stage of world cinema, but it locates worldliness in the secret spaces of the jungle.

Perverse Allegories

We have seen in these analyses how film narrative can deploy allegory to narrate queer lives outside hegemonic forms. To conclude, we turn to an iteration of that challenge that focuses our attention on the *difficulty* of allegory for queer films.

Allegory's queer mode of articulation has something in common with perversion. Allegory starts by speaking about something else in the public assembly, and there is a proximity between speaking differently (from an explicit public norm) and perversion's turning away (from an implicit moral or social good). Of course, one word is Greek and the other, Latin, and we often invest "perversion" with Freud's use of the term rather than its original, religious one. But both words describe the rejection or traduction of a publicly defined norm. In perversion, the rejection is more explicit—turning away—but it is also a case of directionality, not looking the right way, speaking otherwise, over there, not oriented "correctly." The Freudian perversion is likewise a turning away from proper objects of desire, a willful rejection of heteronormativity that exuberantly eroticizes the "wrong" subjects and objects. Both versions of perversion thus share with allegory a performance of otherness that touches on public life. Both words begin from a public sphere and go on to reframe, reject, or imaginatively remold it. Speaking in the public sphere but not speaking in the terms it demands is a queer act, and allegory could be deemed a form of representational perversion. This intertwining of terms becomes especially visible in allegories of perversion, which are already a doubling, a pressing together of modes of rhetoric that form contiguous ways of creating counterpublics.

Philip Rosen has argued that cinemas are not constantly national but become so in moments of national crisis, and we might similarly propose that in moments of geopolitical crisis (or moments charged with transformative possibility), perverse allegory emerges as a cinematic strategy.[80] Two particularly prominent examples emerge in East Asian New Waves. *Dong gong xi gong/East Palace, West Palace* (Zhang Yuan, dir., 1996) is the first mainland Chinese film to deal directly with gay life. It also tells the story of a BDSM encounter that transpires between a writer and the policeman who arrests him for cruising in a park. According to Chris Berry's analysis of the film, its title is Beijing gay slang that refers to the toilets in Tiananmen Square. This title thus forms a connection between Tiananmen Square as code for queer desire and Tiananmen Square as code for the pro-democracy protests and state massacre that followed in 1989. The square is a powerful repository of Chinese myth, and by linking its name to a story of illegal actions, police interrogation, and violence, *East Palace, West Palace* seems to suggest a national allegorical reading. Does the film speak about the repressive nature of contemporary Chinese society? It surely does, and Berry has argued that the social marginalization of gays and lesbians in China is matched by the inability of artists to work freely and, indeed, is "generalized across Chinese society today, and it is the product of the contradictions that characterize and constitute the contemporary Chinese post-socialist condition."[81]

Thus, the story of the writer being beaten by the policeman is an allegory, in Jamesonian terms, of the Chinese nation and specifically of the post-Tiananmen contradictions of economic openings existing alongside ideological restrictions. But to read the film only in this way is to instrumentalize the perverse relationship, reducing queer desire to an index of geopolitical change. That the relationship is formed of violence, of submission and domination, is also a material signifier. Queer desires signify as themselves, as a historically and culturally specific instance of sexuality that cannot be dismissed as a metaphor for something else. The perversions of the writer and the policeman are queer rewritings of Chinese power dynamics, re-creating the space of the police station as a locus of gay freedom in the center of state violence. Narrating a cop beating a gay artist in terms of sexual pleasure makes viewers uncomfortable, as sadistic scenarios touching on historical instances of actual violence often do. But what is uncomfortable is the demand that we see both scenarios at once. It is impossible to obviate one reading to make the other easier. We cannot have a liberal sympathy for pro-democracy demonstrators when Tiananmen is yoked to sexual perversion and cruising in toilets. Nor can we have a simple gay identity story when desire is so politically edged and perversely articulated. Perversity complicates geopolitics.

Our second example is the South Korean film *Gojitmal/Lies* (Jang Sun-Woo, dir., 1999). *Lies* tells a straight love story that nonetheless unsettles heteronormativity, to use Freccero's term, in various ways. The lovers are of different generations, bringing together an eighteen-year-old schoolgirl and a thirty-something-year-old artist. There is already a strong hint of gender critique here, where the protagonist, Y, chooses an older lover to avoid being raped, as both of her sisters were. The patriarchal cult of the Korean schoolgirl and the rape culture that haunts it are clear targets of the film's feminist claims. (Like Catherine Breillat's À ma soeur!/Fat Girl [2001], Lies suggests that the heteronormative model of sexual initiation for girls is more violent than its alternatives.) Y thus decides to enter into a BDSM relationship with J that escalates beatings with wires and sticks into scatological acts of humiliation. Lies also invites us to read Y and J's perverse relationship allegorically. It can be seen as a feminist allegory, in which the dominant fantasy of the older man desiring the young schoolgirl is parodied and, in this parody, revealed as a fundamentally violent appropriation of women's bodies. In this reading, sadomasochism is a way to envision actual violence, a stand-in for the patriarchal oppression of Korean society. Here, feminism diverges from queerness, and, as has often happened, a feminist reading views sexual perversity and queer desire as symptoms of societal ills.

The film also suggests a geopolitical allegory: Lies is part of the new wave of South Korean cinema that emerged in the late 1990s and early 2000s, which came about in part through the government's policy of supporting the film industry as a strategic entry point into globalized markets. South Korean film became a key method of marketing Koreanness, and in this context Lies performs a kind of internal critique. In this allegory, state power is again embodied in the heavy-handed top, with sexual violence at once parodying the regimented national myths of a neoliberal visual economy and offering an escape from their rules. But again, to read only these allegories is to flatten out the queer potential of the film. Y's pleasures emerge out of refashioning Korean myths and refusing normative subjectivities at the same time that the film is both a part of and a rebuttal to South Korea's entry into world cinema markets. Indeed, while Lies screened internationally, its screenings in downtown New York were preceded by a stern warning by cinema staff that viewing was "on you." The perceived difficulty of viewing the sex acts represented creates another kind of queer transnational public. It is by reading queer perversions both allegorically and directly, experientially, that we can discern a queer iteration of Korean globalization.

The allegorical narratives of this chapter do not just force a spoke into the wheels of heteronormative discourse: they do not merely derail meaning but also reconfigure its terms. The queer figures in these non-Western films refuse to offer up their alterity to the West as a symbol of Otherness; nor does their queerness symbolize the penetration of Western modernity into other regions of the world. At the same time, being otherwise in the world in the way we have defined it in this chapter does not limit itself to the post-colonial gesture of reappropriating the powerless figure of Western fantasy. Speaking otherwise in public involves not only a reference to an elsewhere, a queer fantasy space, but also a reframing of the public itself. *East Side Story* asks audiences to view the urban spaces of Belgrade and Zagreb anew, and *Dakan* insists on imagining homosexuality inside the spaces of postcolonial Guinea. Whether these films are screened at home or abroad, the affective register of world cinema opens up potentialities for queer cathexes that become transnational, reaching out in unpredictable directions. There is surely a utopian vision at work here, for imagining the world differently is at its heart a utopian endeavor. *Fire*'s Sita and Radha might walk off into a sunset toward a new life as fulfilled lesbians, and the gai bois of *Funeral Parade of Roses* are audaciously creating the subcultures that will remake contemporary Tokyo. But this reframing provokes too much retribution to be simply positive, and rejections of liberal gay politics are equally invested in those excluded from state and consumerist visions of citizenship. Queer allegory perverts and destroys as much as it creates.

Dakan either tells a love story that ends with the couple riding off into the sunset or excludes them forcibly from the national space. *Tropical Malady* might present a fantastical consummation or a deluded gay soldier being eaten by a tiger. Utopia is too close to erasure for comfort in these films that refuse liberal progress narratives of coming out into Western values. We might locate the queerness of world cinema in the intersection of these two modes of thinking, charged with a productive, even dialectical tension. It is allegory that enables these modes to coexist, representing both dystopian and utopian gestures at once, speaking on the world stage while also figuratively transforming it.

4

THE QUEER POPULAR
Genre and Perverse Economies of Scale

There is a difficulty in thinking about the popular as a modality of queer cinema, because queerness is often seen to confound the category of the popular. LGBT people are understood as belonging to a permanent minority that perpetually replenishes but never comes close to a majority. Meanwhile, queerness, insofar as it demands to destabilize presiding systems and norms, precisely refuses any aspiration to dominance. As a category and as a practice, queerness defines itself against cultural normalcy: by rejecting the status quo, it seems like an awkward fit with the dominant forms of Bollywood, Hollywood, or Nollywood. Critiques of homonormativity find troubling precisely those places where formerly oppositional LGBT activism has fallen for the trappings of the mainstream, limiting queer aspiration to the same bourgeois citizenship, repressive institutions, and limited lives that hetero society prescribes. The discourses critiquing the Gay International understand this homonormativity as a product of globalization, such that popular representations of out lesbians and gay men read as Western neocolonialism rather than as queer radicality. Moreover, the many instances of homophobic and transphobic violence that persist at the state level (alongside the hate-mongering of xenophobic populist politics) may make the term "popular" seem out of place in a discussion of international queer culture.

Yet popular cinema is a central location for a queer imaginary, an always already queer space in which everyday pleasures and transgressive desires meet and become newly visible. A mass medium that has always been global and from the start has rendered same-sex desire visible in public, cinema offers a particularly rich staging ground for new models of visual pleasure that exploit the popular and reformulate its constituencies. Manifestations of sexual and gender dissidence can be found everywhere in popular cinemas. In Lebanese melodrama *Sukkar banat/Caramel* (Nadine Labaki, dir., 2007), one of the female protagonists is most likely legible to queer audiences as a lesbian. The film is set in a beauty salon, so normative regimes of femininity are central to the mise-en-scène, and Rima's alternative presentation makes a strong statement. In quite a different mode, the Indonesian supernatural comedy *Poconggg juga pocong* (Chiska Doppert, dir., 2011) trades in the punning similarity in Indonesian between "pocong" (meaning a ghost wrapped in a burial shroud) and "bencong" (meaning variously a gay man, transvestite, or transsexual). The transgender ghosts in this film are played as broad comedy stereotypes, but even in this very straight narrative, queerness performs cultural work, haunting the popular ghost genre. Whereas classical Hollywood's representation of gender and sexuality has long been treated as complexly contested in its institutional context, textual address, and spectatorial response, other popular cinemas are not always granted such space for nuance. In addressing the intersection of queerness and popular cinema, this chapter aims to open out the potential of cinema's most public stagings of gender and sexual dissidence.

The apparently impossible intersection of the terms "queer" and "popular" has prompted various critical responses. The first has a significant history in LGBT and queer film scholarship: to read the queerness that was always present in popular culture. This approach finds not only closeted gay and lesbian characters populating classical Hollywood cinema but also views sexuality as the lens through which popular culture can be understood. Queerness is everywhere and has been always; it does not exist only when it speaks its name out loud but is present for anyone who lends an ear to the lilting of a voice or spots the mannishness of a walk. Vito Russo's pathbreaking history of homosexuality in cinema provided a model for reading queer representations in terms of national identities, ideological critique, and the complex relationships among texts and audiences.[1] Russo claimed that gay desire was always on display for audiences, even when it was seen only in glimpses such as the apparent gay bar in the musical *Call Her Savage* (John Francis Dillon, dir., 1932) or the fervent sadism found in women's prison films of the 1950s such as *Caged* (John Cromwell, dir., 1950). This approach crucially unhitches queer film from intentionality, such that a gay film can be made from gay audience readings as much as from an out gay director. Borrowing from the methods of LGBT cultural history, scholars such as Richard Dyer and Alexander Doty theorized the queer pleasures of cross-identification and transgressive desire that cinema has offered throughout its history.[2]

The reading practices demonstrated by Russo and extended in the 1990s by Doty and Dyer are formalized in films such as Mark Rappaport's *Rock Hudson's Home Movies* (1992) and Pratibha Parmar's *Jodie: An Icon* (1996). These texts take Russo as emblematic of viewing techniques practiced by queer viewers since the beginning of cinema: finding evidence of queer desire in films that otherwise constrain, erase, or ignore queer intimacies. From a superficial perspective, this approach seems to allow the viewer to pick and choose what she wants in a text. However, as a more complex practice, "transcoding" demonstrates that many audiences disregard and overwrite the overt themes and messages of films they watch. While much recent film scholarship enjoins us to recognize that different viewers do different things with films, it should be remembered that this approach was an intervention of queer scholars, artists, and filmmakers working with popular entertainment cinema. This mode of reading takes an irreverent stance toward narrative outcomes but reads the surface of the film with what is at times a religious devotion. Like cinephilia, the queer re-reader picks and chooses where to affix her adoration on the image based on a mixture of private and communal desires. This resistant reading practice demonstrates the complexity of the popular film as a text that always exceeds strategies of containment and unleashes counterhegemonic desires.

Part of our project is to extend this way of thinking to world cinemas, where despite some significant literatures in queer cultural studies, not enough comparative work has been done on cinematic representations of queerness. There are some important examples of this type of work that engage with national and regional contexts. For instance, Samar Habib's work on female homosexuality in Egyptian cinema persuasively teases out a history of women's same-sex desire in popular melodramas, comedies, and spy thrillers.[3] Fran Martin analyzes the female homoerotic imaginary in

Chinese popular cultures, including lesbian cinema and television dramas, and Thomas Waugh has written on male homoeroticism in Bollywood.[4] Also useful is David William Foster's writing on Latin American cinema, in which he moves between analysis of explicitly LGBT films and those, such as María Luisa Bemberg's *De eso no se habla/I Don't Want to Talk about It* (1993), in which queerness is a case of destabilizing the rules of hetero attraction.[5] While building on such culturally specific analyses, we stake a claim on the queerness of cinematic globality itself. Throughout the book, we address popular films whose queerness is easy to see if one is looking for it. In other chapters, we have made a conscious decision not to quarantine the popular, considering popular films alongside art-house features and experimental shorts. In this chapter, we examine popular films head-on to consider what cultural work these films might be able to perform in their various viewing contexts. If cinema spectatorship opens doors to non-normative desires and identifications, this is only the more true in a context of global circulation.

Another approach—and the one we consider to be the most significant— is to consider the relatively few occasions when films are both openly queer and genuinely popular with a mainstream audience. Something peculiar and telling happens when queer films "make it big," and that thing has to do with their invocation of a worldliness. Since the late 1990s, a queer popular has emerged that draws on the forms, modes of production and address, and sensual pleasures of popular genres to produce queer counterpublics within the circulatory systems of world cinema. Our aim across this chapter is to map this worldliness through genres of popular cinema, considering the popular as a mode capable of articulating both the political anxieties of being queer in the world and the aspirations of a queer critique.

This chapter's first section draws out the contemporary stakes of the tenuous legitimacy of the homosexual in contemporary Nigerian video films. At once fascinated and disgusted by homosexuality, Nollywood provides an understudied response to the politics of queer visibility. As the chapter progresses, the binary opposition of popular and queer becomes less and less viable. We look at films that offer lessons of tolerance, focusing on comedies such as Bollywood's *Dostana* (Tarun Mansukhani, dir., 2008) and the Serbian film *Parada/The Parade* (Srdjan Dragojević, dir., 2011). These films maintain a certain hetero perspective, navigating how to mainstream LGBT visibility for a mass audience, but they also complicate assumptions about the relationship of queerness to transnational identities and its representation on the world stage. Queerness's apparently inherent alterity may be referenced by these films, but its destabilizing power is refracted through mainstream film form. Such mainstreaming may undermine queerness (and some of our examples demonstrate the pitfalls of popularity), but it can also articulate queerness's narrative correspondence to globalism. Queerness (co-)occupies the space of the masses. Those characters who cannot see the queerness of popular space are reformed, punished by, or expelled from the narrative. The chapter concludes with an analysis of Thai transgender genre films, including *Satree lek/The Iron Ladies* (Yongyoot Thongkongtoon, dir., 2000) and *Biutiful Boksoe/Beautiful Boxer* (Ekachai Uekrongham, dir., 2004), as sites of queer cultural negotiation and ultimately of queer worldliness. When these queer films become popular, they become global, turning queerness into a pleasurable passport.

Homophobia against Gay Internationalism in Nigerian Film

We begin by examining popular films that some may consider the most difficult to claim as queer: explicitly homophobic films made by Nollywood, the massively popular video film industry in Nigeria that is also the second largest in the world. Homosexuality is illegal in Nigeria, with long prison sentences (or death in those states with sharia law) for same-sex sexual acts, same-sex marriage (including for foreign visitors and diplomats), and any advocacy of LGBT rights (from NGOs and activists to owners of gay bars). In this context, homosexuality is officially nonexistent or invisible, yet in the 2000s a cycle of films emerged in Nollywood that directly represented lesbian and gay Nigerians. Martin P. Botha has written about the paucity of African films willing to speak openly about homosexuality, pointing out the ideological resonance in Africa of sex as private and not determining of subjectivity.[6] In this context, the emergence of the Nollywood homosex cycle is all the more remarkable. Films with central gay, lesbian, and bisexual narratives include *Emotional Crack* (Lancelot Oduwa Imasuen, dir., 2003), *Rude Girls* (Saint Collins, dir., 2007), *Sexy Girls* (Rahim Caz Chidiebere, dir., 2009), *Hideous Affair* (Ikenna Ezeugwu, dir., 2010), *Turn Me On* (Frank Rajah Arase, dir., 2010), *Dirty Secret* (Theodore Anyanji, dir., 2010), and *Sexy Game* (John Uche, dir., 2010). Brian Larkin has characterized contemporary Nigerian film narrative in terms of "moral polarities . . . excessive situations . . . with a strong element of the grotesque in elites' extreme sexual and financial appetites," and these qualities are evident in the gay-themed films.[7] As with Nollywood cycles of films concerned with incest, adultery, abuse, and homicide, the homosex cycle offers audiences a voyeuristic view into families and communities upset by a particular pathology, social ill, or breach of community mores.

In one of the few scholarly discussions of Nollywood gay-themed films, Lindsey Green-Simms and Unoma Azuah argue that "because of Nollywood's predilection for both indiscretion and castigation, it is perhaps not surprising that it is the first and only form of African popular culture to produce an entire body of work that addresses the issue of homosexuality."[8] This description already intimates the significance of these Nigerian films for thinking the intersection of world cinema and queer sexualities, and their characterization of "indiscretion and castigation" sets up the unique discursive space of these films. Green-Simms and Azuah find that "the concept of the closet calls attention to the politics and interplay of erasure and exposure that Nollywood films enact."[9] In a context in which homosexuality is not only illegal but is also rarely spoken of in mass culture, the popularity of these gay-themed films presents a conundrum to researchers. The authors conclude from their interviews with filmmakers and audiences that "people were clearly keen to see and make such films—some because they wanted a space to condemn what they felt was a growing normalization of homosexuality and some because they felt film could and should push social boundaries. What we found was that the eager desire—whatever the motivation—to produce and consume the films existed in tandem with the inclination to remain silent or ignorant about both them and the existence of homosexuality in Nigeria."[10] Thus, Nigerian cinema and its audiences are driven to visualize homosexuality, to give space to it in the public sphere and yet, at the same time, to deny its existence. The logics of visibility and publicity become especially knotty in this context. Homophobic moral judgment may be the motivation for representation, yet the popular names a space in which desire can be made public, even despite the overt aims of the filmmakers. In other words, the popular emerges from a fraught present,as a contested space where ambivalences emerge and persist.

The stakes of these ambivalences are vividly illustrated by a short article published on a Nigerian news aggregating website. Here is the item in its entirety:

> Just a couple of months back, the Nigerian Government tagged homos*xual activity is [sic] criminal; now Nollywood producers are exploring their democratic rights by releasing a homosexual movie, this is a movie that will surely make jaws drop in disbelief. After the release of extremely er*tic movies like Bold 5 babes and Room 027, it seems producers are getting even more desperate by the look of things. We remember way back when kissing scenes on Nollywood movies were faked. Now, we

hide under civilization and globalization which seems to have encouraged western culture in Nigeria.[11]

This short article animates some of the key ambivalences surrounding Nollywood's increasingly regular depictions of homosexuality. Like the films it condemns, the piece is rife with internal contradiction. It exhibits a textual version of the closet, using asterisks in terms such as "homo-s*xual" to evade discovery by searches. As if demonstrating the ambivalent and irrational publicity of the closet, the text then uses full words without asterisks—e.g., "homosexual"—in a subsequent sentence. Similarly, the word "er*tic," which implies a prudish resistance to sexual speech, is used alongside the uncensored words "babes" and "kissing." Moreover, the article's own status as a document is unstable given that it appears on various websites devoted to gossip about the Nollywood industry. This agile circulation obscures origin and authorship and suggests it may originate from the impulses of marketing more than those of journalistic reporting or criticism. Most strikingly, the piece links homosexual films with "civilization," "globalization," and "western culture," equating moral judgment of queer sexuality with histories of resistance to colonialism and neo-imperialism. The piece exemplifies Dennis Altman's logic of "reverse orientalism," whereby the West is viewed as sexually deviant, decadent, and promiscuous.[12] By examining two key films in this cycle, we unpack both the relationship of homophobia to globalization and the potential of the Nigerian popular melodrama to destabilize the logics of erasure and exposure.

Men in Love (Moses Ebere, dir., 2010) is one of the best known films of Nollywood's homosex cycle and stars the popular actors Muna Obiekwe, John Dumelo, and Tonto Dikeh. As in many of the films in this cycle, a predatory gay converts a straight man to the hedonistic pleasures of a gay life (i.e., good home cooking, compassion, and anal sex). We are introduced to Charles as he is having an affair with his female secretary. The film uses the heterosexual affair as a way into the ordinariness of his domestic turmoil with his wife, Whitney. But when a boyhood friend of Charles named Alex arrives on the scene, he seems to beguile Charles into spending more and more time with him. Eventually, he drugs and rapes Charles, an act that implausibly leads to a romance. The film's narrative logic seems to require the repudiation of Alex, the predatory gay, through visible punishment. Alex is arrested for homosexuality, and Charles recants his desire, saying, "You know I abhor the act of homosexuality." But for *Men in Love*, these sins are not equal. By the end of the film, a traditional pastor has explained to

Whitney that a demon has possessed her husband. With his philandering, Charles is far from innocent, even if we accept that demonic possession led to his foray into homosexuality. Homosexuality requires a different kind of reformation from adultery—a religious and magical transformation, an exorcism that releases Charles from the demon (Alex).

There are two logical readings of the film's homophobia. First, as the web article quoted earlier describes explicitly, the film understands homosexuality as a moral question that is inseparable from globalization. *Men in Love* suggests that homosexuality carries a peculiar geopolitical weight that both exemplifies and tests Nigeria's democracy. Homosexuality makes plain Nollywood's ambivalence toward the globalizing and modernizing pressures of the West. As Altman argues, "Western derived identities can easily become markers of those aspects of globalization which are feared and opposed."[13] The film appears aware of something like a Gay International as an agent of globalization and an exemplar of the foreign forces that threaten the integrity of Nigeria's autonomous national culture. We can map an allegorical correspondence between the invasion/conquest of Charles's body by demonic possession and gay penetrative sex, on the one hand, and the Nigerian national body's invasion by foreign global capital, on the other. Interestingly, the nation is figured as a male body, whose openness is a site of vulnerability and whose violation must be resolved by the end of the film, bringing back its pristine wholeness. This account echoes the dangerous allegories of chapter 3, in which homosexuality figures some other geopolitical object, but in this case the queer is not only a metaphor but also a metonym of globalization's predatory acts.

The film offers nationalist homophobia as a counter to globalization, here figured through the cosmopolitanism of the homosexual. As in chapter 3, allegory enables *Men in Love* to speak in public about queerness even while claiming to repudiate it. But whereas *Dakan/Destiny* (Mohamed Camara, dir., 1997) figured a gay couple as mediators between the national and the global, *Men in Love* deploys homosexuality to bespeak globalization's threat. Here, homophobia responds to globalization in terms that rhyme with how homonationalism operates elsewhere. Indeed, homophobia is suggested to the audience as a means of insulating Nigeria from homonationalism. The film uses homophobia as a way to distinguish certain forms of Western neo-colonialism from nationalism, anachronistically presenting fundamentalist Christianity and the illegality of same-sex acts as more indigenous than homosexuality. In the logic of the film's conclusion, in which a pastor cures Charles and returns him to his family, Christianity affirms Nigerian cultural values, whereas homosexuality violates them. Although *Men in Love* cues its audience to be concerned about globalization's impact on Nigerian cultural sovereignty, it never represents Christianity or commodity culture as breaches of national boundaries. Only homosexuality plays that role. In a variety of ways, then, the film uses homosexuality as a metonym and scapegoat for globalization's threat to Nigerian national values: homophobia operates as a repudiation of the neocolonial aspects of globalization in the global South.

Another way to read the film is to see it is as a symptom of Nigeria's oppression of LGBT people. Of course, to some degree this reading is inevitable: *Men in Love* represents homosexuality as demonic bondage, and its homophobic scenes can be hard to watch. Given the very real violences that threaten queer people in Nigeria, a visceral response to the film might be shared by queer viewers in Nigeria and abroad. Nonetheless, this reading is linked to particular international interventions. *Men in Love* offers further evidence to NGOs, such as the World Bank, which considered cutting aid to Nigeria when its treatment of gays was seen by the world as homophobic and anti-globalization. This can be linked to the first reading because the film makes a case for Nigeria's cultural distinction from the West and flaunts its lack of fear of being exempt and even excluded from the world financial system. Homophobia offers a mode of exceptionalism that is unafraid of isolationism. Thus, from a "Nigerian" perspective, the suppression and subjection to violence of queer people is seen as preserving national integrity, insulating the country from neocolonial economic manipulation.

Yet despite the powerful forces at play in *Men in Love*'s uncomfortable rhetoric, neither homophobic reading can account for a persistent homophilia made public in and around the film. Take the concise promise of the title alone. The violent disturbances caused by homosexuality in the film's narrative are not captured by the phrase "men in love"; nor are they present in titles of many other Nigerian films featuring lesbian and gay characters, such as *Turn Me On, Reloaded* (Lancelot Oduwa Imasuen and Ikechukwu Onyeka, dirs., 2009), and *Sexy Game*. The posters for *Men in Love* are equally split between homophobic depictions that literally demonize Alex and others that present the gay couple in romantic scenarios with homophilic overtones (figure 4.1). The discursive doubling of these posters promotes *Men in Love* simultaneously by making Alex look like a monster (his face looming with snakelike eyes next to the silhouette of a crow against a stormy sky) and by making him one half of a romantic same-sex couple.

Fig. 4.1: This poster for *Men in Love* insinuates that the gay character Alex is not to be trusted.

The duality of the film's marketing is repeated in the text itself, which incessantly speaks about gay sex in explicit terms and renders invisible desires public. When Alex tells Charles that his friend is gay, he introduces the revelation by saying that the friend cannot get married in Nigeria. Charles's shocked reaction is marked with the melodramatic grammar of the rapid zoom, but homosexuality is first articulated not as demonic possession but as an issue of civil rights. Later, Alex tells Charles that he has nothing to be ashamed of. In this narration, homosexuality cannot be self-evidently evil but must be discursively staged over and over. Moreover, *Men in Love* gives a lot of space to representations of gay life. At Alex's party, for instance, we see a room full of gay men. It may be a clichéd tableau of tight Burberry outfits, open shirts, and campy attitudes, but it is nonetheless a representation of something that is not supposed, officially, to exist at all. Even the melodramatic scene in which Whitney finds her husband fucking Alex offers a titillating and surprisingly revealing perspective of the two men's naked bodies. Queer life is more vividly present in *Men in Love* than in many mainstream LGBT features.

Fig. 4.2: In *Mr Ibu and Keziah*, magical soap has the power to turn women into lesbians.

We find a similar abundance in a well-known Nigerian film with a lesbian plot, *Mr Ibu and Keziah* (Stanley Anaekwe, dir., 2010). Like *Men in Love*, *Mr Ibu and Keziah* draws on what Larkin calls an "aesthetics of outrage." For Larkin, what formally defines the Nigerian video film (and its successors) is an exuberance that deploys melodramatic effects within narratives structured "around a series of extravagant shocks designed to outrage the viewer."[14] The homosex cycle certainly plays sexuality for shock value: *Mr Ibu and Keziah* ramps up the supernatural element in a narrative of witchcraft, infection, and socially unacceptable behavior. Keziah is a beautiful but somewhat naïve young woman whose roommate Monica infects her with lesbianism via magical soap (figure 4.2). Once infected, Keziah spirals out of control, moving from a relationship with Monica to a fling with her friend Mirabelle to a predatory phase of attacking random women on the street. Again, the homophobia is overt, with homosexuality figured as an infection that derives from a dangerous combination of (anti-Christian) witchcraft and (Western) feminism.

Yet even this brief outline reveals the film's potential for against-the-grain reading. The scene in which Keziah innocently washes with lesbian soap could easily make a lesbian camp classic: she looks suspicious for a moment, then non-diegetic romantic music begins, and she lathers enthusiastically,

Fig. 4.3: *Mr Ibu and Keziah*'s lesbian feminist cabal who aim to destroy patriarchy.

almost ecstatically, before getting spooked by her own pleasure and rinsing the soap off. It transpires that Monica is part of a lesbian-feminist cabal who aim to destroy the patriarchy (figure 4.3). Once initiated, Keziah becomes desperate for sex, unable to stop touching herself, and attacks a doctor, a seamstress, and an orange seller. This lesbians-out-of-control narrative is wide open for a camp recovery, but strangely it is the melodramatic form that works to recuperate it for moralizing discourse. Here, the exuberant gestures of melodrama—rapid zooms, omnipresent music—labor to make the audience laugh *at* the lesbian characters, locating the film's affective register firmly on the side of homophobia. The film's melodramatic scores—with their swells and deep chords, their acceleration of pathos via sharp strings and quick drumbeats—bring a sinister inflection to otherwise innocent scenes. In fact, in certain moments the musical score operates as the film's only means of securing its homophobia and inoculating the image against its homophilic tendencies. Without the ominous soundtrack or the constant reminder of the peppy auto-tuned theme song that "You don't leave boys for girls," some of *Mr Ibu and Keziah*'s scenes would simply present loving images of women in bed together (figure 4.4).

This disjunction between sound and image leads to another space of potential homophilic reading practice in the online lives of these films. To

Fig. 4.4: Many scenes in *Mr Ibu and Keziah* can be read against the grain as loving lesbian images.

settle on the Nigerian homosex cycle as homophobic ignores contemporary web practices—such as trailers, clips, fan videos, and mash-ups on YouTube and other video sharing platforms—which reflect the broadening and mainstreaming of queer viewing practices and make visible the instabilities of homophobic popular texts. In fact, in Nigeria it has become common practice to watch fragments of movies rather than complete texts.[15] The global consumption of the Nigerian homosex cycle should be seen in this context of transcoding and online video sharing. *Men in Love*'s studio posted previews for the film (and others) on YouTube (figure 4.5). Even though they were officially produced, these previews anticipate queer readings. They construct mini-narratives organized as gay romance stories, in which the homophobic discourse of the film is largely repressed. For instance, in "John Dumelo Almost Caught," the central gay relationship seems closeted but genuine.[16] Dumelo's YouTube channel hosts the video "John Dumelo's Gay Love Drama," which is a scene from *Turn Me On*, showing two men in a romantic scene on a beach.[17] Similarly, lesbian scenes with Mercy Johnson are excerpted from *Mr Ibu and Keziah* and *Corporate Maid 2* (Ikechukwu Onyeka, dir., 2008), as well as a masturbation scene from *Return of White Hunters* (Afam Okereke, dir., 2010), which emphasizes unconstrained female sexuality as a central pleasure of these micro-narratives.[18]

Fig. 4.5: YouTube clips based on *Men in Love* anticipate queer readings of the film.

Like the online practices (such as slash, fanfic, and shipping videos) that reedit popular films to assert or accentuate queer subtexts, these previews reimagine the films and give more space and credence to reciprocal queer desire. They isolate scenes and liberate them from the overarching hetero-normalizing impulses of the film's narrative structure, giving life to intimacies that are left more submerged in official versions. The Nigerian previews are less disruptive formally than queer fan interventions, but they achieve similar effects by simply excerpting a scene from its context. These video clips also remove or recode the very directive musical score that provides viewers of the full-length films with moral commentary on a character's actions. Where the films' homophobia depends almost exclusively on musical commentary, the previews demonstrate that a different score can flip the images easily toward homophilic readings. (A similar argument can be made about the various stills that circulate with online articles about Nollywood's homosex cycle, including the article quoted earlier.)

The Nigerian homosex cycle thus responds to anxieties over Westernization, religion, national identity, and the global in ways that both reveal and overspill official discourses of homophobic anti-globalism. The online trailers effectively amplify the homophilic elements already present in the texts while containing and even removing homophobic elements. In this, they exemplify modern *global* modes of consuming popular texts privately and then *re-publicizing* them, putting them back into popular circulation. When we consider the online audience for Nigerian cinema, both domestically and in the diaspora, it is not impossible to imagine that Nollywood's homosexual content circulates as much for homophilic purposes as it is corralled for homophobic nationalist Christian purposes.

Of course, that same global image culture locates Nigerian film in a different landscape from older instances of homophobic popular cinema, where audiences of classical Hollywood or Bollywood films may have had little alternative to creative transcoding. Green-Simms and Azuah find that LGBT audiences in Nigeria were more likely to download *The L Word* than to view gay-themed Nollywood films that represent queers as sinful.[19] But the growing international reach of Nollywood has also prompted work by diasporic Nigerians, including very different figurations of queer invisibility and erasure. Sunny King's short film *Unspoken* (2012) responds directly both to Nollywood's homophobia and to the taboo against discussing homosexuality in Nigerian culture. The film, which began life as a web series, narrates a diasporic drama of closeted gay men in London. It clearly has different aesthetic priorities from the Nigerian features: it has higher production values, uses shallow-focus cinematography, and aspires to an international film festival style. The story focalizes a straight bridesmaid who discovers that her fiancé is intimate with the bridegroom. Thus, although the film is sympathetic to the cultural causes of this deception, it is still a narrative of outrage, and our entry point for identification, as with *Men in Love*, is the betrayed woman. What does *Unspoken* tell us about the relationships among Nollywood homophobia, diasporic Nigerian cultures, and globalization? The film is superficially more liberal, aimed at a Western, LGBT-friendly audience, and yet its online publicity refuses to name the titular "unspoken" topic. Its careful dance around the closet suggests that Nigerian homophobia and the Western liberal festival film might be closer than is comfortable for either constituency.

Tolerance and the Popular

As Pier Paolo Pasolini once wrote, "Tolerance is a more refined form of condemnation."[20] Fiercely resistant to middle-class culture, Pasolini saw his role as filmmaker and writer to be to expose society's gestures of accommodation, moments when liberalism proclaims its humanitarianism by measuring its own broad-mindedness. Certainly, the discourse of "tolerance" has remained only one step removed from homophobia in much contemporary political culture.[21] But tolerance becomes a stickier proposition in contemporary queer world cinema, at once offering a vehicle for articulating rapid changes in sexual citizenship and remaining queasily linked to the logics of cultural accommodation. Some of the most successful and popular gay-themed films of the 2000s have addressed LGBT politics in the problematic language of tolerance. Is it fair to equate their liberal gestures with an underlying condemnation? Do the always unstable semantics of popular cinema make the political consequences of tolerance any less certain? Might these films make themselves available to queerer readings? In this section, we examine popular films from two contexts—India and Serbia—to unpack how they depend on narratives of acceptance to speak about international politics and the relationship between East and West.

Dostana was one of the top ten Hindi features in 2008, grossing nearly $18 million worldwide.[22] The film is widely regarded as one of Bollywood's frankest—if problematic—treatments of homosexuality, and Indian film scholars have debated its relation to queer theories alongside its dependence on stereotypes.[23] Meanwhile, in the Western press it was described positively as "a non-preachy plea for tolerance and acceptance."[24] *Dostana* centers on two men, Sameer (Sam) and Kunal, who pretend to be gay lovers so that they are able to rent an apartment with the gorgeous straight woman Neha, to whom they are both attracted. They become friends, and their faked homosexuality leads to comic layers of misunderstanding in which they must "come out" to both family and state. The film's diegesis is a world surprisingly exempt from homophobia. The narrative reforms its only resistance to homosexuality, figured in Sam's tradition-observant mother, through a simple substitution in which she is shown how gay couples are analogous to straight married ones. *Dostana* promises that tradition can be modernized as easily as the mother can be won over; beliefs can be reformed and retrofitted to a gay union, at least outside India. That the film is set in Miami is no coincidence. As Rajinder Dudrah has pointed out, locating *Dostana*'s plot in the United States, even when the film was produced in India, enables a form of queer visibility that would be impossible in a film set in India.[25] Nonetheless, the film's parable of accommodation connects to its testing of the audience's liberalism. It does so both by tracing the outlines of a space for the gay couple within straight films and by providing its narrative space as a testing zone for the aspirant tolerances of its imagined audience.

Following this thread of tolerance, it is not difficult to read *Dostana* as a homonational film. After all, it depicts the closeted same-sex couple simultaneously as a dilemma for traditional non-Western culture and as its cure. When the couple goes public (fully gay), the non-Western can be rid of prejudice and brought fully into modernity. A perspective sensitive to the neocolonial impulses of the Gay International would point out that the film's rehabilitation can take place only by constructing a dichotomy of East and West that depends not only on a simplistic depiction of Eastern patriarchal rigidity (embodied in the figure of Sam's mother) but equally on a fantasmatic version of the West's liberalism. Opposed to apparently closed-off and un-modern Punjabi family values, the Florida of the film is a state that not only protects against discrimination but exists in a fictional America that grants universal privileges to same-sex couples. These protections and rights are part of the film's mise-en-scène: in this land, the gleaming and airy offices of the Immigration and Naturalization Service (INS) actually save the most efficient processing for gay couples, who are fast-tracked through civil union applications. Neither governmental nor social homophobia exists here, as it arguably did in the real Florida circa 2008, where queer people were barred from adopting (even as single parents), could not form any type of legal partnership with their partners, and could be discriminated against at work and by landlords, and where homosexuality was banned from being mentioned in public elementary schools. By contrast, little threat of discrimination comes with assuming a public gay life in *Dostana*'s Florida. Sam and Kunal easily adopt the identity of a gay couple to appear more attractive as prospective renters. They never confront prejudices or encounter the physical violence that many same-sex couples in Florida continue to negotiate in their daily lives, even in Miami. In *Dostana*'s America, economic opportunity, citizenship, and marriage rights go hand in hand with gay rights, as if the Defense of Marriage Act (DOMA), still very much in effect in 2008, did not exist (figure 4.6). Furthermore, these privileges exist as a surplus, just there for the taking. From this perspective, the film's depiction of gay coupling (however fake it may be) provides the narrative with a means of exploring and quantifying the liberties and abundances that the fully modern nation-state has to offer.

Dostana thus vividly models the intolerances built into the logic of tolerance. Despite the fact that the overt discourse of the film teaches audiences to tolerate gays, it repeatedly undercuts the apparent benefits of this tolerance.

Fig. 4.6: *Dostana* posits a fantasy Florida that extends immigration rights to same-sex couples.

As we have seen, its acceptance of homosexuality is built on homonational fantasies of monogamous sexual citizenship. Tolerance here comes at a political price. Moreover, for a "tolerant" film, it notably does not allow the minor characters who are openly gay any narrative prominence or agency, and when the film does depict gay men, it trades in fairly broad stereotypes. There is a back-and-forth slippage between moments when fake-gay characters present a plea for tolerance and those where homosexuality is played for laughs. However, as tempting as it is to decry the musical number in which Sam and Kunal perform gay stereotypes on their imagined hedonistic European trip as *intolerant*, there is something else at work in these representations, something that escapes the tolerant-versus-intolerant binary.

The film asks viewers to look beyond the discourse of tolerance by undercutting heterosexual paradigms of desire. Visually, it is quite comfortable rendering the two men as a couple, either devising narrative excuses to entangle their bodies or simply framing them in tight two-shots. In the final shot of the film, Neha asks the men whether they ever really did anything together, then walks out of the frame, leaving them looking at each other before following her (figures 4.7–4.8). As a final organization of bodies, it knowingly plays out the titillating overlap of homosocial and homosexual around which the film centers. It thus refuses to stabilize the heterosexual identity of either of the two men when they share the screen. *Dostana* flirts with a homophilic viewer, overtly referencing the famously queer appropriations of *Sholay* (Ramesh Sippy, dir., 1975) and continually staging tableaux replete with homosexual to-be-looked-at-ness. T. Muraleedharan has located

Figs. 4.7–4.8: In *Dostana*'s final shots, Neha walks out of frame, leaving the two men alone together.

similarly queer possibilities in the male-male friendships in popular Malayalam films. Although these films do not play so explicitly as *Dostana* with homosexuality, Muraleedharan finds in them a rich vein of queer bonding.[26] Across popular Indian genres, the concept of *dostana*, or friendship, can be read queerly. As Rohit Dasgupta argues, "By acknowledging the slippages between 'real identity' and 'mistaken identity', [films such as *Dostana*] usher in a new queer cinematic discourse within popular Bollywood."[27] Parallel, then, to the voyeuristic shots of John Abraham's muscular torso emerging from the water is the popular appropriation that Dasgupta discusses of the film's songs in Indian diaspora gay bars.

Dostana's narrative and point-of-view structures are also striking in their resistance to containment. The romance plot seems to work toward

Fig. 4.9: *Dostana* constructs a polyamorous point of view with these romantic snapshots of Sam and Neha's date that imply the presence of a third person, probably Kunal.

resolving the standard love triangle through a very unconventional release of sexual and narrative tension. As the story of competition between the two men progresses, the idea of one of them becoming Neha's lover appears less and less plausible. The film's narration even seems to suggest a ménage à trois as a viable solution midway through the conflict. In one strange scene, Sam and Neha go on a date, but the photo album we see of their romantic evening suggests that Kunal came along to take the pictures (figure 4.9). This polyamorous point of view is untroubled by the implication of a male-male-female (MMF) threesome, something that most straight narratives seek to avoid. In other films (*Holiday Inn* [Mark Sandrich, dir., 1942]), the narrative would devise a way to defuse both the homosociality and the competition of the scenario by introducing an additional romantic option, thus allowing two male-female couples to form. This effect could easily have been achieved in *Dostana* through the introduction of another heterosexual woman, but instead the film introduces a third man, Abhi, who eventually wins Neha's heart. While this addition allows Neha to be moved eventually onward toward heteronormativity, it does nothing to recover the heterosexuality of Kunal and Sam. *Dostana* offers no avenue of stabilization to alleviate the pressure of homophilic intimacy.

Dostana illustrates the doubled effect visible in popular queer cinema, in which films at once embody and exceed the limitations of the homonational, homophobic, and tolerant. In a sense, this effect names a key property of popular cinema, which is always at once an inscription of dominant ideologies and a site of contestation and overflow. We find these eruptions of queer representation in popular genres to signal acute moments of historical tension that cannot be reduced to any single frame of reference. When popular films speak about queerness, they engage not only sexuality but also globalization, nationalism, and the intersections of race, ethnicity, and gender. This confluence is not a coincidence, but it demonstrates the ways that sexualities are closely inscribed in contemporary geopolitics.

Whereas *Dostana* articulates the fault lines of tolerance for India and its diaspora, another film serves as a comparable bellwether in South East Europe. *The Parade* is also a tale of tolerance, made by a straight-identified director and aimed squarely at a mainstream theatrical audience in its home country of Serbia. The film focuses on an apparently unsuitable topic for comedy: the violent attacks on LGBT Pride marches in Serbia in the 2000s. Harking back to Dragojević's similarly scabrous comedic take on the breakup of Yugoslavia in *Lepa sela lepo gore/Pretty Village, Pretty Flame* (1996), *The Parade* uses ethnic and sexual stereotypes to parody contemporary Serbia's homophobia. The story involves a gangster and war veteran who is coerced into defending the LGBT Pride parade in Belgrade and rounds up his old wartime comrades and enemy combatants from different parts of the former Yugoslavia to help him protect the gay characters. Post-Yugoslav nationalism and ethnic difference are intertwined in the film's visioning of queer human rights.

Part of what makes *The Parade* such a significant film is its popularity with audiences. What might sound like a niche gay festival film was in fact the number-one film in Serbia and Montenegro in 2011, by some measure. It brought in more than $1.1 million at the domestic box office, compared with the number-two film, *The Smurfs* (Raja Gosnell, dir., 2011), which earned only $600,000, and it easily beat out the other major films of the year, such as *Pirates of the Caribbean: On Stranger Tides* (Rob Marshall, dir., 2011), *The Hangover Part II* (Todd Phillips, dir., 2011) and *Harry Potter and the Deathly Hallows: Part 2* (David Yates, dir., 2011).[28] Indeed, its total box office takings in Serbia are only fractionally smaller than *Avatar* (James Cameron, dir., 2009). For a low-budget comedy about gay politics, *The Parade* was a surprising blockbuster hit in Serbia and was only slightly less popular across the former Yugoslav nations. In stark contrast to the Pride marches represented in the film, which are tiny and show a few brave LGBT people surrounded by aggressively hostile protesters, the film's huge audience conjures an image of a Serbian public keen to engage with gay rights.

This conflict between public acceptance and violent rejection played out across the production and exhibition of *The Parade* in a way that is similar to *Dakan*'s difficult history. *The Parade* had to be shot partly in secret locations

Fig. 4.10: A poster for *The Parade* animates the central conflict between neo-Nazis and LGBT Pride marchers.

because of threats from right-wing nationalist organizations.[29] One crucial scene was shot at the actual 2010 Pride parade, and the sense of threat in this semi-documentary sequence is palpable. Dragojević notes wryly that the scene was shot during "the first 'successful' Pride [parade] in the history of Serbia. The only success was that the participants stayed alive."[30] (This engagement with violently contested public spaces around Pride parades echoes Igor Grubić's video work, discussed in chapter 3. The publicity of the street provides a way to resist violent homophobia across experimental and popular forms.) When *The Parade* was released, both the Orthodox Church and the right-wing press called for a boycott, and even outside the region screenings proved controversial.[31] In Armenia, for instance, a screening of the film was funded by the European Union and the German Embassy, but protests by the nationalist youth group Hayazn led the event to be cancelled out of fear of potential violence.[32] So like *Dakan*, state-sponsored screenings of *The Parade* attempted to fold the film into an international human rights discourse, but in the European context, nationalist extremism trumped Western universalism (figure 4.10).

The Parade uses broad comedy to navigate these difficult waters, explicitly setting up ethnic and homophobic slurs as a way into the film's textual economy. It opens with a lexicon to explain its rich vocabulary of derogatory terms, including *Ustaše* for Croatians, *Chetnik* for Serbs, and *peder* for

Fig. 4.11: In *The Parade*, stereotyped characters come together to watch classic queer cinema.

queers. The logic here is to normalize queerness by bringing gays into an imagined happy family of everyday post-Yugoslav prejudices. True, the main gay characters, Mirko and Radmilo, are a wedding planner and an effeminate vet, but the straight characters are also stereotyped along gender, class, ethnic, and religious lines.[33] Many of the jokes operate both ways: when the gangster Limun is forced to share a bed with Radmilo, Limun's homophobic fears license humor that can be read equally as poking fun at his backwardness or as relying on gay panic responses. Clearly, the film is aware of this equivocation—indeed, it repeatedly plays on it. When Limun discusses his friendship with a Croatian soldier, he jokes that "ass brought me here." The scatological anecdote that follows is not overtly (homo)sexual, but the film leaves open the possibility that macho camaraderie might be more than a little queer. Limun's favorite movie is *Ben Hur* (William Wyler, dir., 1959), which Radmilo gleefully informs him is a gay film. As with the role played by *Sholay* in *Dostana*, classic male-on-male movies take on a pedagogic role for audiences in how to read male-male sociality queerly. But later in the film, that queer reading also schools Limun, who while rewatching *Ben Hur* with a queer audience seems finally to realize the universality of human love and the urgency of his mission to protect the gays (figure 4.11).

Since the films addressed in this section negotiate LGBT rights in the language of tolerance, it is striking that some strongly critical responses to *The Parade* have explicitly centered on tolerance as a problem. One French review argues that the film gains a spurious importance because it treats a hot topic and that because it is from Serbia it gains counterfeit weight as

"world cinema." It might be useful to think about how "world" cinema operates as a category here—where marginality within Europe provides a space
that threatens West European claims to cinematic authority.[34] A more sub-
stantial critique comes from *The Balkanist*, which argues that "the film also
has a darker agenda: It quietly celebrates 1990s-style nationalism under the
guise of promoting 'tolerance.' Here, tolerance is minimal, extending only
to 'useful' gays and considers the gay characters merely instrumental for the
real ethnic argument of the film."[35] The claim that *The Parade* promotes ex-
tremist ethnic nationalism is unconvincing, but the article does capture the
problem with linking gay rights to liberalism.[36] Paul Hockenos, one of the
Western critics accused of being clueless, writes, "In addition to gay rights,
the film affirms the future of the region's states as mutually respecting, tolerant societies, united not by class consciousness or ethnic blood rivalries but
by liberal values."[37] We read *The Parade* quite differently, seeing its value
precisely in its problematization of such an easy reliance on gay liberalism
and that liberalism's rejection of class consciousness.

Thus, as discomfiting as *The Parade*'s broad comedy of stereotypes and
logic of tolerance can be, the film also forges significant linkages. Crucially, it
connects homophobia to capitalism, nationalism, and neoliberalism, queerly
insisting that we cannot conceptualize sexuality without taking these other
terms into consideration. It demands that its spectator think about a relationship between nationalism and protecting queers: the structure of the narrative is that nationalism leads to homophobia and that transnationalism is
needed to protect human rights. Of course, in the Serbian context, "human
rights" has a resonance beyond the protection of sexual minorities, and *The
Parade* forces the spectator to make those connections. In one scene, the
local police commissioner refuses to protect the Pride march, saying, "If
we grant human rights to faggots and dykes, even Gypsies and Albanians
will ask for them." Here, instead of the tactic of pitting queers against racial
minorities that antihomonationalist theorists decry, *The Parade* puts ethnic
and sexual minorities in the same boat, demonstrating how exclusionary
politics operates in contemporary Serbia.

The film self-consciously repeats this figuration of ethnic and sexual exclusion. In one striking shot, the camera pans from a poster for "Alfavil property development," depicting a white and shiny future housing complex, to
the location's shantytown reality. Limun's job in the new Serbia is a legal
version of ethnic cleansing—physically removing Roma residents from the
shantytown so international developers can move in. The rapacious form of
capitalist development that moved into Serbia from Western Europe after

the war leverages anti-Roma racism to create precisely the reorganization of urban space—cleansed of undesirable groups—that sanctions homophobic violence. Dragojević addressed this process when asked in an interview why there is so much homophobia in the Balkans:

> This is a complex development, but if I have to simplify it, it's due to people's fear and bewilderment in the face of the economic situation. Many young people experienced how their parents lost their jobs after the war. At the same time, there's been the development of a nouveau riche class that has bought up companies and the media. To shift the blame away from the glaring redistribution of wealth and the injustice of it all, the nouveau riche fuel their hate on supposedly weak targets, such as gays and lesbians.[38]

In this post-socialist landscape, as in the Nigerian films, homophobia expresses public fears about the encroachment of globalization on national and cultural sovereignty.

A narrative that centers on LGBT rights is ideal for engaging these feelings, because the violent attacks on Pride marches became a subject of public debate in Serbia. Branislav Jakovljević sees the neo-Nazi protesters in class terms: "They neither present an anachronism of the 1990s wars, nor simply an aberrant phenomenon of transition, nor marginal individuals who violently push the periphery into the centre of social life, but rather an extension of violence that finds its basis in capitalism, which nobody in Serbia dares to challenge anymore. They are the armed forces of one particular class and its ideology, which is normalized to the extent that it is hardly visible."[39]

The Parade makes this ideology visible in its final scene, in which Mirko makes an emotional speech that attempts to articulate an alternative vision of Serbia. Mirko's Serbian identity begins from queerness in the manner of Étienne Balibar's *droit de cité*, in which the rights of all are linked to those of the lowermost person.[40] Citizenship derives from the right to exist, to walk freely in the city streets, and in the melodramatic arc of the film's concluding scenes, Mirko can do so only after his death. Both in real life and in *The Parade*, the state fails to protect its citizens, and the violence in the film's climax insists that homophobia is the responsibility not of a few extremists but, rather, of the deliberate inaction of the state.

In contrast to this violent nationalism, then, *The Parade* aligns gay subjects with the transnational. The transnational, however, is highly contested in the Balkan context: it can be seen as progressive in the sense of opposing right-wing extreme nationalism, embracing pan-European cultural identities and leftist internationalism. However, European transnationalism can also imply the neoliberal policies of the European Union, which imposed globalizing forms of capitalism, rapid development, and austerity on the former Yugoslav nations. It is thus possible to read pro-European gay liberalism as naïve or even counterproductive. Mirko's expensive wedding planning business illustrates precisely this conflict between gay rights activism and complicity in a capitalism that is ultimately violently exclusionary. We later learn that he is actually an artist who cannot make a living and hates being a wedding planner. It is the homophobia of Serbian society that allows him no other opportunity to make a living. *The Parade* imagines the transnational not in terms of the European, though, but as a pan-Yugoslav cultural space.

The film is a co-production, funded by almost all of the former Yugoslav nations: Slovenia, Croatia, Macedonia, Serbia, Bosnia and Herzegovina (specifically, the Bosnian Serb Republic), and Montenegro. These sponsors are represented in the road movie narrative, in which Limun and Radmilo travel across the former Yugoslavian space to persuade Limun's old comrades/enemies to help protect the Pride parade. As Limun gets the band back together, the film explicitly draws both humor and transnational sentiment from camaraderie across the ethnic and religious lines of the Yugoslav wars. His group of comrades includes a Muslim, a Catholic, and an Orthodox Christian, with visual jokes, such as the Catholic and Orthodox Christian crossing themselves in opposite directions. Some of the jokes are close to the bone (this is where the Balkanist piece finds nationalist rhetoric in negative stereotypes of Albanians), but most striking from our perspective is the intertwining of ethnic humor and queerness.

The video store recurs as a queer space in *The Parade*, providing, as it does in *Circumstance* and *Fire*, a site of sexual and cultural transgression. We first encounter the Bosnian character Halil in his video store, where a customer is complaining that he has been given gay porn by mistake instead of the straight porn he wanted. To check the problem, Halil plays the tape on the store's monitor, momentarily creating a public gay porn screening. The joke is that this apparently respectable Muslim store owner cheerfully trades in gay porn, but it is also not entirely a joke. The video store normalizes queerness as a way of being in the world, here as in *Circumstance*. In *The Parade*, the stereotypes of a nostalgic pan-Yugoslav identity enable and, indeed, construct a homosocial camaraderie across the former barricades. Yugoslav transnationalism becomes a kind of homosocial affective bond that transcends the homonational couple form and enables the project of defending LGBT human rights.

The film ultimately imagines a utopian transnational queer space that is not dissimilar to the activist concept of "Queeroslavija." Irene Dioli describes the work done by queer activists in the former Yugoslav nations to create networks of queer festivals across national borders. For Dioli, Queeroslavija is characterized as transnational (making material connections across Balkan countries), nostalgic (articulating the affective discourse of leftist Yugo-nostalgia), and utopian (imagining a safe and inclusive space for queer people that Yugoslavia never really provided). Thus, it is "ultimately, a way of finding citizenship in a country that no longer, and does not yet, exists."[41] *The Parade* speaks to a larger audience than the counterpublic produced by the radical queer festival, but it equally deploys transnational, nostalgic, and utopian feelings to redefine the nation and the supranational as queer spaces. The spaces created by Queeroslavija activists are avowedly marginal, creating radical queer counterpublics in a spirit similar to that of the Batho Ba Lorato festival discussed in chapter 2. But as a popular film, *The Parade* leverages the space of cinema differently. Like the video store, it understands cinema as a public sphere and addresses an unrestricted transnational audience to fold queer subjectivities into a utopian/nostalgic vision of post-Yugoslav space.

Thai Genre Films on the World Stage

Our final examples come from Thailand, where gender and sexual dissidence have found unprecedented prominence in popular film genres. In the early 2000s, a wave of genre films with gender dissident, or *kathoey*, protagonists broke box office records in Thailand and were distributed across Asia and beyond. Examples include well-known sports films such as *The Iron Ladies*, which tells the true story of a mostly trans volleyball team who became Thai champions, and *Beautiful Boxer*, which tells another true story, of an internationally famous kathoey Thai kickboxer who transitions and is barred from fighting because women are forbidden to practice this nationally sacred sport. Less famous in the West are films such as *Tat soo foot/ Kung Fu Tootsie* (Jaturong Mokjok, dir., 2007), a martial arts film about a queer gang boss; *Kuu Raet/The Odd Couple* (Nopparat Puttarattamamane, dir., 2007), a serial killer drama; and the bank heist movie *Plon naya/Spicy Beauty Queens of Bangkok* (Poj Arnon, dir., 2004) and its sequels. Thus, the sports films can be located in a broader generic landscape of kathoey films in Thailand—and, indeed, they need to be understood within a Thai national context of gender diversity—but they also open onto various types of transnational mobility and worldly projections. In these films, queerness becomes a passport to the world stage both in textual terms and in terms of distribution and exhibition: just as many of the films' protagonists seek an expanded life world through sports, performance, or crime, these films were highly popular across Southeast Asia, and some circulated significantly in the West. However, the terms of their circulation complicate and, indeed, often refute the singular narrative of the Gay International.

Because the gender category of kathoey has been understood as particularly Thai, these films provide a case study for interrogating what it might mean to think the global contexts in which queer cinema travels. The kathoey film's international circulation presses the universalizing discourses of the global gay up against local forms of gender and sexual identity and the discourse of world cinema up against the politics of representation at local, regional, and national levels. Brett Farmer proposes what he calls "vernacular queerness" in recent Thai cinema, in which popular genre films "function as vital sites for the popular negotiation of modern Thailand's rapidly changing sexual economies."[42] He is interested in ambiguously gay films such as *Rak Haeng Siam/Love of Siam* (Chookiat Sakveerakul, dir., 2007), in which the narrative indeterminacy of orientation and object choice express the changing landscape of gender and sexuality in contemporary Thailand. The kathoey films are much broader in tone, but the concept of vernacular queerness is nonetheless generative when considering how they intersect national with global forms of subjectivity. We argue for a close connection of gender diversity with global engagement in Thai popular cinema, and we propose that these genre films demonstrate a distinct form of queer worldliness that emerges in the promiscuous spaces of popular cinema.

This cycle of films features gender diverse protagonists who can be imperfectly translated in Western terms as transgender, gay, or queer. Before moving further into the films, it is useful to consider briefly why the category of kathoey is so significant in Thai cinema and how it helps us conceptualize the politics of queer world making. Thai culture does not have the sex-gender split that grounds Western discourse on gender and sexuality. Instead of a regime of separate genders and sexualities, Thai culture has *phet*, or what Peter Jackson defines as "eroticized genders."[43] Desire is understood as flowing from gender, and there are traditionally three genders: man, woman, and kathoey. Kathoey as a category once included various forms of non-normative gender and sexual object choice, including those we might translate into a Western register as gay men, effeminate men, transgender women, and butch lesbians. For some critics, the term "kathoey" has connotations similar to those of "queer," offering a way to disaggregate and destabilize binaries of identity and desire. Indeed, for Mila-gros Expósito Barea, "kathoey" operates like "queer" to deconstruct binaries of identity and desire.[44] However, Western concepts of homosexuality have influenced Thai culture radically from the mid-twentieth century onward, and Rosalind Morris argues that there has been a shift away from the tradi-tional three-gender system and toward a Western four-way system of hetero man, homo man, hetero woman, and homo woman.[45] This account fits with Dennis Altman's critique of the imperialist global gay, in which the West-ern category of homosexual has been expanded through globalization.[46] But Jackson offers a more nuanced analysis, arguing that Thai culture has not simply adopted Western discourses wholesale but, instead, has used them to create a proliferating set of phet. As well as man, woman, and kathoey, he now finds *tom* (butch lesbian, based on tomboy), *dee* (femme lesbian, based rather splendidly on lady), *seua bai* (bisexual, with a reference to doubleness and tigers on which Apichatpong's *Tropical Malady* plays), gay king, and gay queen. Thai gender, for Jackson, illustrates the uneven and localizing effects of globalization and its powerful resistances to homogenization.[47] It is this rapid efflorescence of eroticized genders and the concomitant emergence of new public gender discourses that the kathoey genre film negotiates in transnational terms.

Kathoey films inevitably comment on Thailand's relationship to global-ity because gender categories are inextricably linked to the histories and contestations of globalization. Dredge Byung'chu Käng argues that whereas kathoey used to be seen as traditional, it is now being linked to discourses of modernity and foreignness. A conservative strand in Thai politics links kathoey gender to Western influence and degeneracy, rewriting Thai iden-tity to exclude gender non-normativity and making queers the avatars of baleful modernization.[48] Kathoey became more visible in the Thai media after the 2006 coup: the government of the late 2000s was associated with an openness to both the economics and cultures of globalization, and gay rights became an issue politicized along party lines.[49] Cultural conservatives fear that ladyboys define Thai identity on the world stage, and the real Iron Ladies were removed from the Thai national volleyball squad because they were seen as "tarnishing Thailand's reputation."[50] At the same time, the global gay critique focuses on the discourse of self-exoticizing with which Thai ladyboy shows attract Western audiences to view kathoey performances as a minstrel show. Visible gender diversity prompts contradictory anxieties, fantasized at once as a threatening invasion from abroad and the public revelation of na-tional shame. This troubled conjunction of kathoey with worldliness sets in

Fig. 4.12: Nong in *The Iron Ladies* combines butch athletic prowess with aspects of feminine presentation.

motion conflicting narratives of Thai national identity and prompts cultural anxieties about visibility on the world stage. The kathoey genre films both articulate and respond to these anxieties, imagining an identity in which kathoey are both traditionally Thai and globally modern.

These pressures are vividly staged in *The Iron Ladies*, which, in putting together its volleyball team of outsiders, represents genders across the modern Thai spectrum. Wit is closeted, about to be married to a woman, and in thrall to the reproductive expectations of his traditional Chinese family. Nong is very masculine, "built like a buffalo," but he also has sparkly nail polish and a little braid tucked behind his ear (figure 4.12). Jung is a more stereotypical loud, kittenish kathoey who wears makeup and often expresses himself with animated gestures. The film codes the team reserves—April, May, and June—as girlish, and they use feminine pronouns when they refer to themselves in speech. We are introduced to Pia in a Pattaya cabaret, where she works as a showgirl: she has had what she refers to as a "full body overhaul" and can be characterized as a "real kathoey." When we first meet Mon, he asks the coaches whether he has been excluded from the team because he is gay, and when we first meet Coach Bee, the jock players nastily call her a "tom." Gender diversity is the very first way that characters are introduced and, in several cases, in the context of homophobia. This marking out of new types of phet may not be entirely legible to a foreign audience, yet the film asks its audiences to think their way into the Thai gender system. The producer Visute Poolvoralaks says, "Each character has his own fans. And now people from all social levels are coming to see the movie. Why? I think because the audience can connect to each character when they can find it in their society." Here, speaking the nation becomes a process of queer identification. Instead of an East–West logic that pits Western imperialism against conservative nativism, *The Iron Ladies* nests the national inside the global. Moreover, its strategy for constructing these extra-national modes of identification is to engender a queer popular.

By any measure, *The Iron Ladies* was popular in Thailand. It made more than twice its budget just in its domestic opening weekend and more than sixty million baht in its first ten days.[51] The film launched something of a kathoey trend in Thai cinema in the early 2000s, and by 2004, the *Bangkok Post* estimated, 10 percent of the Thai films released featured transgender characters in major roles.[52] This surprising statistic prompts a methodological question: how should we read this kind of popularity? We might start simply by considering what "popular" means in this context: we are referring here both to mode of articulation, film style, and genre and audience reach, box office returns, and international distribution and exhibition. The kathoey cycle centers on popular genres: from rom-coms to martial arts films and horror, many, although not all, with a comedic element. The director Poj Arnon has come to be associated with the genre, having made several of the best-known kathoey films, including *Spicy Beauty Queens of Bangkok*; *Waai Beum Chia Gra-heum Lohk/Cheerleader Queens* (2003), about a trans cheerleading team; *Hor Taew Tak/Haunting Me* (2007), a comedy horror film in which four transgender characters have to exorcise ghosts; *Phuean . . . Ku Rak Mueng Wa/Bangkok Love Story* (2007), a slightly artier gay romance; and *Dtaew Dte Dteen Ra-Bert/Sassy Player* (2009), a return to the sports film, this time a kathoey soccer team.

The audience for these films was not limited to a queer niche—as a feel-good sports movie, *The Iron Ladies* succeeded in diverting broad popular appeal through identification with kathoey characters. *Screen Daily* reports, "With a box-office of around $3.5 million, *The Iron Ladies* has become the second-highest grossing film in Thai history coming second only to the $4 million record set by ghost thriller *Nang Nak*."[53] One might attribute this appeal to the national qualities of the story and its basis in a real-life Thai volleyball team, but *The Iron Ladies* was also massively popular across Asia. It came third in annual Singaporean box office for 2001 and made almost $1 million in Hong Kong in its first week.[54] In terms of exhibition, it was probably the most successful of the cycle of films internationally, with a theatrical release across Asia, Europe, the United States (where it played in cinemas for eight months), and South Africa. When we track the film's movements around the world, we find a fascinating navigation of the story's local specificity and its appeal to a global audience.

In 2001, *Time* magazine ran a story about *The Iron Ladies* (in itself a powerful indicator of a certain mainstream international visibility), saying, "Even if the phenomenon of katoey [*sic*] athletes is uniquely Thai, its appeal seems to be universal: *The Iron Ladies* topped the Hong Kong box office on its release last September, and recently the film opened in Australia, where it was voted most popular movie at Sydney's Mardi Gras Film Festival."[55] Universality is seen as necessary here to justify outsiders' interest in a uniquely Thai phenomenon, and it is evidenced by the mapping of Hong Kong versus Australia (Asian and Anglophone), box office versus film festival (low and high culture), and straight audience versus queer audience. Indeed, the film did circulate in all of these institutional spaces. In addition to mainstream theatrical releases, *The Iron Ladies* traveled in art-cinema circles. It received a special-mention Teddy at Berlin 2001; won for best feature at Out-Takes Dallas; and earned audience awards at the Dublin Gay and Lesbian Film Festival, New York Lesbian and Gay Film Festival, and San Francisco International Lesbian and Gay Film Festival. What did these diverse audiences find pleasurable and translatable in the film?

The film is legible internationally because it deploys the generic devices and stock characters of the underdog sports film: outsider athletes, a mean jock with a bullying coterie, and an inspiring coach. But *The Iron Ladies* queers this traditionally (although, of course, not exclusively) straight male genre by inflecting each of these generic markers with questions of gender or sexuality. The players are marginalized because they are kathoey; the jock is not just arrogant but homophobic; and the coach is not accepted at first because she is a lesbian. If we look at the keywords for the film on the International Movie Database (IMDb), we can see how the sports genre is combined with queerness. The plot keywords include indices of popular sport genre conventions such as team, leader, band of outcasts, pride, inner strength, athlete, competition, triumphant, adversity, and champion. It also includes queer indicators such as queer cinema, homosexual, drag queen, makeup, ladyboy, lesbian, and transvestite. The confluence of these categories is already intriguing, but what is especially notable are how often the terms combine or complicate categories: band of outcasts (because they are a ragtag team, in the style of *The Bad News Bears* [Michael Ritchie, dir., 1976], or because queers are outcasts?), pride (team pride or gay pride?), sensation (shocking news story or queerness as sensuous and pleasurable?), inner strength (as a function of athletic prowess or as courage in the face of transphobia?), prejudice and adversity (again, sporting or social?). Embodying non-normative gender identities in public is folded into becoming famous on the world stage, as sports provide a platform for international publicity. *The Iron Ladies* speaks differently in public, but instead of allegory, the film articulates a popular form of queer publicness that uses genre to speak directly and explicitly.

Another answer for the popularity of *The Iron Ladies* can be found, counterintuitively, in an example of the film's commercial failure. May Adadol Ingawanij and Richard Lowell MacDonald studied its poor box office performance in London, arguing that UK audiences expect foreign films to be sophisticated art cinema, appreciated by connoisseurs; thus, the art-house audience for *The Iron Ladies* was a bad match for its demotic genre pleasures.[56] It could not circulate successfully as art cinema and thus had to find a niche within the context of "world cinema" that was not coextensive with art film. Gay and lesbian film festivals offered one such niche, but another is suggested by the US distributor Strand's publicity for the film. Strand's online catalogue promises, "In the tradition of *The Adventures of Priscilla, Queen of the Desert* and *The Full Monty* comes *The Iron Ladies*. . . . Breaking box-office records across the globe, *The Iron Ladies* has won the hearts of critics and audiences alike." The text proposes a global tradition of queer genre cinema and inserts *The Iron Ladies* into a familiar Anglophone context of gay-friendly, heartwarming comedy. The band of outsiders trope proves crucial for nationally located generic narratives to go global, where queer characters can at once be safely limited to "funny" roles and yet simultaneously provide pleasurable access to geographic and subjective alterity.

Why was *The Iron Ladies* able to articulate such a directly queer narrative in a popular form? One answer is that it built on a small but significant history of kathoey-themed films in Thailand that begins with *Phleng sut-tai/ The Last Song* (Pisal Akkraseranee, dir., 1985), a melodrama about a tragic nightclub singer that was a mainstream success, spawning a chart-topping song and an equally popular remake by the original director in 2006. The mid-1980s saw an earlier spate of kathoey films, notably including *Chan Poochay Naya/I Am a Man* (Bandevanop Devakul, dir., 1987), an adaptation of *The Boys in the Band* (William Friedkin, dir., 1970). *I am a Man* was the highest-grossing film made by its production company and was named by the National Film Archive of Thailand as one of one hundred must-see Thai movies. Oradol Kaewprasert calls these films "queer melodramas," and they helped create an audience for the new cycle of kathoey films in the early

2000s.[57] However, whereas the films of the 1980s closely followed the pattern of tragic queers, excluded from society, the kathoey wave that began with *The Iron Ladies* instead places kathoey characters in uplifting, feel-good stories. The kathoey characters are often comedic, following a different representational convention of playing the sissy for laughs, but unlike classical Hollywood sissies, they are granted agency, desire, and narrative centrality.

If we look beyond the global circulation of *The Iron Ladies* to consider the kathoey wave more broadly, international marketing, distribution, and exhibition demonstrate a complex formation of the genre's queer worldliness. *Kung Fu Tootsie* illustrates the circulation of those films that did not enter Western consciousness quite so much, with distribution more centered in Asia, these films still represent a significant popular presence. *Kung Fu Tootsie* is actually the best-performing kathoey film in Thailand, with a higher total box office than *The Dark Knight* (Christopher Nolan, dir., 2008). On its release in July 2007, it became the first Thai film to top the domestic box office all year, knocking *Harry Potter and the Order of the Phoenix* (David Yates, 2007) out of the number-one spot.[58] It was widely released across East Asia and Southeast Asia, reaching number twenty-five on the worldwide weekly box office.[59] The different posters for kathoey films across Asia reveal the semiotic flexibility (and political sensitivity) of the genre. In Thailand, the poster for *Kung Fu Tootsie* features the film's star, Sittichai Pabchompoo, posed as a tough-faced gangster yet brandishing a feminine fan, and prominent in the cast is Kohtee Aramboy, an actor-comedian famous for playing kathoey parts. The Malaysian version, however, is more conservative, minimizing the kathoey characters in the image and connoting gender dissidence via a kickboxer wearing high-heels. *Haunting Me* illustrates another pattern, of the kathoey film that performs most strongly through its association with another genre—in this instance, horror. The film was very successful across Asia, especially in Hong Kong, where it was marketed strongly as a horror film. The Hong Kong publicity campaign foregrounds fright and features a young female ghost, relegating kathoey characters to a monochrome background, whereas the Thai poster is organized around the four kathoey protagonists and presents the film as a comedy. However, its cross-genre presence is significant in Thailand, too: *Haunting Me* is the tenth-highest-grossing domestic horror film of all time.[60]

The popularity of these films presents a challenge for presiding notions of queer globality: how can we describe the audiences for, and the appeal of, these films? The films are not playing in explicitly queer spaces; nor are they offering a gay- or trans-specific form of narrative identification. Without making any assumptions about the gender identities and sexualities of these audiences, we can discern a transnational queer cinematic space that does not fit well with the critical narratives of the global gay, or homonationalism. Queer pop culture is here not a minoritizing space but enacts other, non-identitarian forms of belonging and pleasure. Spaces of reception here conjure counterpublics that are not fully recognizable in the films' textuality or authorship. The films may not be made by queer-identified directors or addressed to queer-identified audiences, yet they circulate in heterogeneous spaces, creating potentially queer publics in unpredictable ways. The films thus enable us to locate a majoritizing queer space in world cinema—one that might do cultural work very different from that of the LGBT film festival.

This queer popular space can be glimpsed online—for example, on film discussion boards, which construct a certain popular Asian public. On a Thai board, one commenter wrote about *Love of Siam*, "Well some people argue this is a gay movie. . . . It has a love elements between two boys." Another wrote on *Sassy Player*, "I saw it. I laughed. I was entertained. There is something for everyone. Don't think it is only a ladyboy movie or only for gays, it is for everyone. It is in no way whatsoever a gay movie." What does it mean for *Love of Siam* or *Sassy Player* to be read as not gay movies? We might say that these are not gay movies precisely because the homonationalist argument does not apply here: the kathoey genre film does not link gay rights to limiting forms of bourgeois subjectivity, to normalizing state politics, or to the couple form. Instead, kathoey subjectivity is collective and transnational, drawing on local discourse for comedic effect but articulating nationally embedded gender regimes to resistant modes of globalism. We see this kind of resistant globalism in the writing of the Malaysian blogger Jaymee Goh (a.k.a. Jha), who writes about watching *Kung Fu Tootsie* alongside *Hua Mu Lan/Woman General Hua Mulan* (Feng Yueh, 1964), a Thai martial arts film, reading Homi Bhabha and books on Malaysian ethnicity, and writing both lesbian mermaid stories and steampunk fan fiction with recoded genders and races.[61] Jha illustrates explicitly what the other examples do implicitly: that Thai kathoey films intervene in a critical queer counterpublic that imagines the stakes of the transnational differently from the terms offered by homonationalism and global gay discourse.

The Asian circulation of *Beautiful Boxer* provides a telling case study here. The film's premiere in Singapore was a gala with the prime minister's wife, Goh Chok Tong, as the guest of honor. We might read this event as an attempt to co-opt a queer film to present Singapore as a progressive state, thereby covering up not only the country's anti-LGBT hegemony but also the ethnic tensions in which Thai and other non–Chinese Singaporeans historically have felt marginalized by state policies. Countering this interpretation, though, is Kenneth Chan's argument that given levels of censorship in Singapore, queerness is an "impossible presence" that must be rendered visible strategically in the mainstream. For him, *Beautiful Boxer* provides an example of "transgenderism as social resistance."[62] Seen in this way, the repeated description in the Singaporean media of the director Ekachai Uekrongtham as a Thai Singaporean director diverts nationalist rhetoric from its usual pathways, adopting Ekachai's transnational and ethnically Thai identity as a way to queerly disrupt Singaporean national space.

The film also travels to more clearly activist sites. In India, it was screened at Films of Desire: Sexuality and the Cinematic Imagination alongside films by Royston Tan, Richard Fung, and others. Screenings and discussions were run by Creating Resources for Empowerment in Action and the South and Southeast Asia Resource Centre on Sexuality. In Hanoi, the film was screened as part of Viet Gay Pride events in 2013, alongside the gay French rom-com *Comme les autres/Baby Love* (Vincent Garenq, dir., 2008) and a guest appearance by the trans designer Trung Anh from the Vietnamese version of *Project Runway*. The shifting registers of these contexts—from *Project Runway* to Richard Fung in two easy steps—gives a sense of the film's plasticity, but it is not a quality of *Beautiful Boxer*'s textuality so much as the labile space of the queer popular in which kathoey films can speak to the Asian multiplex as comfortably as the queer activist festival.

To conclude, we turn to the films themselves, which stage textually the very address to the world stage that their popular circulation enacts. Aspects of these films certainly are open to criticism as ideologically retrograde; they often present kathoey characters as a minstrel show, or figures of fun, and they arguably participate in the neocolonial discourse of Thailand as an exotic ladyboy exhibit. However, we are concerned that such approaches overly instrumentalize films and limit the potential of analysis. To dismiss non-Western popular films as ideologically imperfect is to grant political and aesthetic complexity only to the products and audiences of Hollywood cinema or those of international art film. It seems that queer films are often burdened in this way; thus, we want to be especially attentive to the potential contained in these popular texts to interrupt the narratives of conservative world making and create queer modes of being in the world that escape liberal gay discourse.

The Iron Ladies and *Beautiful Boxer* construct narratives of worldliness through sport, where national and international competitions form a cul-

Fig. 4.13: *Beautiful Boxer* draws on popular accounts of Thai feminine stage performance and masculine Muay Thai.

turally central entrée to the world stage. Both films take advantage of this existing discourse to move from the national to the international and from privacy to publicity. *Beautiful Boxer* begins by presenting the young Toom's kathoey identity as a mixture of masculine and feminine, with both being strongly identified as Thai. In a scene at a temple fair, she watches two kinds of male bodies perform: Thai boxers with strong, muscular, masculine bodies and then traditional dancers with elegant, sinuously moving feminine bodies. Male masculinity and male femininity are both represented as traditionally Thai (figure 4.13), and Toom's uniqueness is her determination to combine both at once, in the same public performance. She ends the film as a woman in a way recognizable to a Western audience, but for much of the film the category of kathoey enables a much more nuanced and layered expression of gender. With this insistence on the Thai traditional grounding of Toom's identity, and because *Beautiful Boxer* is based on a true story, it is able to assert a claim on Thai national truths.

The film places this national evocation of gender diversity into a narrative that is framed as international from the outset. The first words spoken in the film are in English, and Toom's story is organized by her voiceover narrating her life in English. *Beautiful Boxer* speaks first of all in the global lingua franca, textually asserting Toom's story as one of global interest, and in practical terms, helping the film travel to venues that prefer English-language dialogue. There is also a framing narrative in which an Anglophone journalist interviews Toom about her life story: his accent is hard to place, suggesting a generic Anglophone exoticizing investment in Thai culture. Toom initially learns English to speak to white tourists and to sell them souvenirs. She also flirts with a white man, suggesting the socially overdetermined nexus of Thai globalization with gender. In one dramatic scene, Toom emerges from the shadows to save the journalist from a fight with a souvenir vendor. The setting places the nightclub where Toom sings in a tourist area—a contested zone of Thai globalization—and her kickboxing proposes a spectacular Thai conflation of masculinity and femininity that can save the day for the foreigner. The film does not just tell Toom's international story; it organizes its own articulation and address in transnational terms.

However, the framing narrative of the Anglo journalist works to distance spectators from Toom, locating the spectator as a rapt outsider listening to Toom's story told in flashback. Whereas *The Iron Ladies* asks the viewer to identify *with* kathoey characters and to experience the narrative directly through their perspective, *Beautiful Boxer* deploys the intermediary character of the journalist to place the non-Thai spectator in the perhaps more comfortable role of avid listener. Nonetheless, it does something quite unusual in the genre, which is to play Toom's story entirely as a melodrama. Kathoey representation in contemporary Thailand is conventionally comic relief, so kathoey comedies can be seen as more socially acceptable and less threatening than a drama that asks the viewer to feel deeply for Toom's losses. Even though *The Iron Ladies* does not see its characters as jokes, it trades on public acceptance of kathoey as comedians. In this context, there is something bold in *Beautiful Boxer*'s refusal to see Toom as funny.

The Iron Ladies also closely enmeshes gender and globalism: it narrates its tale of sporting triumph as a victory of modern over reactionary gendering. The film's antagonist is a sexist tournament official who schemes to ensure that the Iron Ladies' team loses. It is striking that his hateful behavior is framed first as sexist: he comments on the appearance of female employees and reads pornography in his office. When Coach Bee confronts him, her speech is also about gender: she points out that it is not only kathoey and toms he dislikes but anyone who does not conform to patriarchy—female governors or astronauts and women in jobs rather than in the kitchen. Queer politics is thus closely linked to feminism, and by including a prominent tom character, the film moves queerness away from being kathoey only and is able to make broad points about gender and publicness. The team's route to victory involves public gender performance: the Iron Ladies lose when they are forced to play without makeup and their redemption begins when they return to the arena in full kathoey style. The centrality of this publicity

Fig. 4.14: Queerness is proposed as a route to international fame in the opening title sequence of *The Iron Ladies*.

is reinforced in the climactic scene. The reactionary official has disqualified the Iron Ladies, but Jung saves the day by turning on a microphone so the entire audience (and those watching on television) hear him say, "Those faggot freaks are out of the competition." Making his hatred public galvanizes the on-screen audience's response: whereas before they had enjoyed the team fetishistically, as an exotic spectacle, now they vocalize their support for the Iron Ladies' right to compete as equals. The film here proleptically figures its own audience, imagining a public for whom cross-gender identification would be both pleasurable and political. The mechanism to make this happen is a kathoey character who makes private speech go public. Whereas traditional Thai culture places a premium on not rippling the calm waters of public life, the strategy of the kathoey is to make homophobia—and its refusal—both audible and visible.

We see this connection right from the outset, when the title sequence humorously condenses queerness, stardom, and globality. Photos of the actors as children are superimposed onto glamorous modes of transnational mobility such as fashion and sport; one places a child onto a newspaper headline "He or She? Become a Superstar," setting up queerness as a route to global fame (figure 4.14). The sequence also includes a cardboard box labeled "Export" and "Warning—Don't Make Them Laugh." In the background are film reels, self-reflexively commenting on the film's own cinematic exportation of queerness. Notably, the labels are in English, understanding the audience as international and, indeed, Anglophone. The Iron Ladies go global as kathoey representatives of their nation in sport, and the narrative's figuration of Thai identity through a team that includes the whole contemporary range of gender identities mediates between the forces of globalization and vernacular ways of being so that kathoey visibility is what stages Thai globality.

The question of translation illustrates how these films assert gender's queer globality. As we saw with *Lilting* (Hong Khaou, dir., 2014) and *Dvojina/Dual* (Nejc Gazvoda, dir., 2013), translation and its difficulty frequently stage queer transnational spaces. Jackson points out how some English words and concepts have been borrowed to describe Thai phet (e.g., gay) but in other areas, such as transgendering, they have not. This difference may reflect the centrality of ideas of kathoey to Thai culture, but it also makes us ask why it is kathoey that centers the films. Thai queer films do not enter the world stage speaking about homosexuality or even about trans experience but about being kathoey. They do not use the most obviously *translatable* category, gay, but instead use the one most foreign to Western audiences and most likely to produce confusion. It is also the most Thai-specific category and can therefore represent an exotic Thainess. But the differences between Thai and Western models of gender/sexuality mean that films based on kathoey characters are ripe for misunderstandings. But even given these dangers, we think it is central to the labor of these films to speak worldliness in the figuration of locality—or, in more queer terms, to demand globality in the very terms of alterity.

If kathoey comedies have the potential to reiterate stereotypes, they are also a significant locus for cultural negotiation. Nguyen Tan Hoang describes the Thai slang *wer*, which derives from the English word "over" and can be used in both positive and negative contexts to imply an over-the-top or exaggerated quality. Although the term is not inherently queer, Nguyen argues that it can carry a queer tonality, where an "over-aesthetic" animates a camp mode of articulation.[63] His examples are experimental and, indeed, they riff ironically on the kinds of popular camp that the kathoey comedies exemplify. But even firmly in the realm of the popular, wer aesthetics are doing queer cultural work. *Spicy Beauty Queens of Bangkok* speaks in a vernacular Thai register, deploying an often presentational theatricality that depends on over-aesthetics for its comedy, yet it still leverages kathoey characters as a way to imagine a cosmopolitan life world. Even though this lower-budget comedy did not access the international audiences of *Beautiful Boxer* or *The Iron Ladies*, *Spicy Beauty Queens of Bangkok* constantly stages gender in the language of the worldly, insisting on the close connection of gender diversity

Fig. 4.15: In *Spicy Beauty Queens of Bangkok*, the gang cross the road in an homage to *Reservoir Dogs*.

with a reimagining of Thai national identity and its renewed positioning in a global cultural field.

In *Spicy Beauty Queens of Bangkok*, a kathoey character robs a bank to fund their gender surgery. The similarity of this plot to that of *Dog Day Afternoon* cannot be missed. As with *I Am a Man*'s remake of *Boys in the Band*, American queer representations of the 1970s are a fruitful reference point for Thai cinema, and *Dog Day Afternoon* is the first of many transnational references in the film. Of course, the registers are completely different. *Spicy Beauty Queens of Bangkok* is a slapstick comedy with ribald humor, but the evocation of *Dog Day Afternoon*'s transgender drama is not the film's only global touchstone. The drag performer Sua is told that the show is traveling to Las Vegas, and if she does not get her top and bottom surgeries done, she will be demoted. Travel in a ladyboy show is one of the few economic opportunities for Thai kathoey, and as limiting as this spectacular labor is, it is an opening onto the world for Sua. As the gang of kathoey robbers cross the street in huge drag costumes, they are framed *Reservoir Dogs*–style, while in the background a Thai flag is visible (figure 4.15). The shot queers the cliché of a cool lineup of criminal outsiders, but it also rewrites it as Thai.[64]

Once inside the bank, the gang is confronted with a rival group of bank robbers who are more conventionally masculine. The mouthiest of the kathoey gang dubs the members of the rival group Beckham, Ronaldo, and Figo, re-ferring back to global sports culture in a quip that both internationalizes the crime spree and eroticizes masculinity. There is something about the sound/image juxtaposition of Prick, with giant drag-queen eyelashes and a revolver, hollering, "Figo!" that encapsulates our majoritizing argument. Who is the ideal spectator for this film: someone who gets camp humor, un-derstands Thai gender, and follows international soccer? The virtual world destabilizes categories in a way that we insist on thinking as queer. (It is also a highly wer moment, in which camp, over-aesthetics, and popular form intermingle promiscuously.) When the queens finally escape from the bank, they relocate rather surprisingly to New Zealand, where Sua buys a sheep farm. The ladyboy show abandoned, worldliness is now reimagined outside the confines of traditional kathoey labor. The bucolic final scene uses the humorous juxtaposition of nature and artifice to locate Thai queerness far beyond the urban spaces of Bangkok.

When the kathoey films became internationally popular, they did so not despite but because of their queer pleasures. J. N. Erni has argued that *The Iron Ladies* is one of a series of transnational queer films that includes *Xi yan*/*The Wedding Banquet* (Ang Lee, dir., 1993) and *Fire* that have projected Asia onto the world stage, demonstrating "an emergent mobility of Asian queer production."[65] The existence of stories on the films in *Time* magazine and other global media shows this mobility. But unsurprisingly, this media attention is double-edged. A BBC story headlined "Transvestites Rescue Thai Movies" purports to address the international success of the Thai film in-dustry, but what makes the story newsworthy is the implicit surprise that "transvestites" should be so popular.[66] Would the success of, say, a series of Thai gangster films have made headlines? Clearly, what makes this story ap-pealing is its queerness, and queerness is not only found in the kathoey: the idea that a transgender-themed film would be popular is itself destabilizing (see figures 4.16–4.19). There is a transphobia, of course, in this exoticizing discourse, the sensational headline, but there is something significant none-theless in the queerness of this mode of global publicity.

The kathoey genre films assert a mode of queer worldliness that is predi-cated on the publicity of the popular. The films can seem to fit into a neolib-eral model of world cinema: *The Iron Ladies* ends with a plea for tolerance by a kathoey audience member, and Wit's decision to leave his fiancée lauds coming out in a Western sense. However, the films' pleasures lie elsewhere, in staging a sensual space of diversely gendered embodiment, in the queer exuberance of their narration, and in the promise of forging transna-

Figs. 4.16–4.19: Popular Thai films include kathoey characters across a range of genres—here, *Haunting Me*, *Kung Fu Tootsie*, *Spicy Beauty Queens of Bangkok*, and *The Last Song*.

tional and transgender bonds. For instance, Pia in *The Iron Ladies* gives a sad speech, saying there are no happy endings for kathoey and referencing tragic queer melodramas such as *The Last Song*. But the film resists that narrative not by presenting happy love stories but by bypassing romance altogether in favor of the bonds of community, team spirit, and worldliness. The films do not fetishize transgender bodies but instead divert and derail the bodily pleasures of the genre film to offer identification across genders and cultures. Although the films sometimes draw on both Thai and international discourses of acceptance and human rights, their intersection of queerness and popular genre reveals different queer pleasures of world cinema in a worldly communalism that is activated when queer films become popular.

World cinema promises to transport the spectator, encoding cross-cultural identification into its institutional DNA. The Thai kathoey genre films illustrate the queer pleasures of cheering for alterity, of allowing oneself to identify with a different system of gender, and of being transported into the desiring point of view of another. These films could travel the world when other Thai genre films could not because queerness creates forms of worldly connectivity. All of these popular films figure responses to globalization, in which sexuality and gender form necessary vectors of global power. Nigerian video films deploy homophobia as nationalist resistance to international gay rights discourse, proposing queers as the agents of neocolonial interference in African sovereignty. Tolerance narratives reconfigure the geopolitics of overdetermined transnational spaces (the Balkans, the Indian diaspora) through the trials of queer publicity. And finally, Thai genre films construct the gender category that is most distinctly Thai as the subjectivity best placed to reimagine Thai cinema in the world. In working through the often contradictory impulses of these films, we place the insights of antihomonational social critique up against the ability of film studies to find more in popular texts than merely their dominant ideological imperatives. Here we view the popular as a crucial domain of contestation in which the relationship of queerness to the world is negotiated and renegotiated. Queer pleasures are a central element of what makes popular cinema popular. It is not simply that queerness can be found submerged in popular cinema, but that the invitation to enjoy gender-fluid identifications and desires is what gives major mainstream cinemas such as classical Hollywood, Hindi genre films, and Hong Kong studio films their rich and seductive appeal. This argument can be expanded to account for the queerness of other world cinema. Queerness is an essential aspect of what makes world cinema pleasurable, and when queer films are popular, these worldly pleasures come vividly to the surface.

political filmmaking and to its futures. The first generation of queer doc-umentary practitioners (including Richard Fung, Pratibha Parmar, Riyan Vinci Wadia, and herself) turned to countercinema practices as a means of undercutting conventional modes of identification and identity and al-lowing forms of living and visibility not otherwise afforded to them.[2] She contrasts this earlier approach with contemporary work, especially the re-instatement in recent Indian LGBT activist videos of a traditional documen-tary understanding of the image as testimonial. Although she appreciates the political intentions of this new queer documentary wave, Ghosh warns that such standard modes of depiction may constrict who counts as queer, excluding more elusive forms of collectivity and radical instances of differ-ence. What these more recent works miss is the vitally intersubjective and unstable sensuality of cinema itself. Ghosh asserts that films such as *Between the Lines: India's Third Gender* (Thomas Wartmann, dir., 2005) provide "not only a mode of seeing but a mode of sensing," in which the cinematic can encode and preserve queerness beyond simply picturing it within the frame. For her, by refusing to reify identities or to objectify otherness, these queer films offer viewers "the exhilarating possibilities of occupying other worlds." Ghosh's ideas resonate with Jacques Rancière's description of a world as "a polemical distribution of modes of being and 'occupations' in a space of possibilities."[3] His well-known concept of the distribution of the sensible is helpful here because it yokes the aesthetic to the unevenly distributed expe-rience of subjectivity in the world and its necessarily geopolitical character.

In this chapter, we mobilize the concept of register to name the ways in which cinema articulates these more elusive, but nonetheless felt, experiences of queerness in and through the cinematic sensorium. "Register" offers an ideal term because it references cinema's mediation of experience, mobiliz-ing intimacies, affects, and sensations. What compels—and, in fact, touches and moves—Ghosh about these films is also what is cinematic about them. In other words, films substantiate queerness via cinema's unique capacity to interweave different modes of being, or what she terms cinema's "incorpora-tion of the sensory." This chapter takes up Ghosh's provocation, identifying the range of registers in which the contemporary queer film speaks.

Of course, genre (and the discourses that surround it) has been and re-mains a central way in which film scholars have mapped the diverse sensual modes of engaging with film's audiovisual sensorium. At the very start of her famous reformation of low genres as "body genres," Linda Williams observes that cultural argument on how to value films often turns on how much of a film is sensual, sensational, or simply gross, a perception that maps along lines of "gender, age, or sexual orientation."[4] Miriam Hansen shares Williams's concern that film studies has largely ignored the sensory impact of the medium. By looking past cinema's central attraction as an affect-generating apparatus, the "totalizing" lens of classicism not only abridged the film-history canon but also "left out, marginalized, or repressed . . . melodrama . . . comedy, horror and pornography which involve the viewer's body and sensory-affective response in ways that may not exactly conform to classical ideals."[5] It could be said that Ghosh's "incorporation of the sensory" exemplifies Hansen's reimagined film history. From its earliest articulations in the 1990s, Hansen's concept of "vernacular modernism" emphasized cinema as a sensorium, both an affect-producing machine and an institution in which virtual and real sensory experiences of modernity could be felt together, reflected on, and even subverted. When Hansen comes to revise the concept for the final time, she argues that genre does not "fully account for the films' affective-aesthetic appeal, broadly understood—whatever it may be that enables them to move viewers . . . across geopolitically disparate spaces and histories."[6] The queer films discussed in this chapter do just this: they generate affective-aesthetic means to move the viewer emotionally and hence to experience geographical and historical othernesss in ways that promise to rework the current geopolitical order.

Reflecting on Ghosh's intervention in the context of Hansen, we find it important to recognize that the nuanced grappling with queerness offered by early and late queer films cannot be described as an intervention in genre. To dismiss the effects she describes as postmodern pastiche, self-reflexivity, or political modernism would be to miss the point. Register provides a more nuanced organization than genre of the subversive sensate engagements offered by queer films, in part because queer films "incorporate the sensory" in ways that often refuse to respect conventional generic distinctions. José Arroyo suggests that queer genres are more porous and citational and therefore have a different relationship to textuality, address, reception, and authorship.[7] Moreover, the geopolitical interventions of queer cinema—its ability to redistribute the sensory potentialities of the world, in Rancière's terms—can get lost when films' affective overages are viewed only through the lens of genre. The idea of register destabilizes genre, cutting across conventional generic categories to think about what we might call a film's "tone." In other words, register involves the tenor of a film: this entails not only its emotional range and affective timbre, but also the proximities suggested by its mode of narration and its terms of engaging us as spectators. Register establishes the spectrum of affective variance for a film, what is referenced in colloquial parlance as its "feel." It encompasses the impressions left by its mise-en-scène, the rhythms of its editing, the attitude of its address, and the evenness of its shifts among emotional octaves. Register references the textual system that manages affect, modulating the film's sensory effects and drawing correspondences among them.

For linguists, register is a type of articulation used in a specific social context and addressed to a particular listener. In other words, as a mode of articulation that privileges the social and that is defined in relation to address and audience, register is intrinsically political. In film analysis, then, attending to register asks us to "listen" differently to a film's formal features, with a particular attention to the ebbs and flows of affect in the cinematic sensorium. To describe a film's register requires acknowledging the film image as a sensory interface, where the social is inscribed in the emotional. Listening to register, then, has much in common with queer reading practices described at the start of the previous chapter, and it is no surprise that registers such as camp and the arch have a long history of association with queer audiences. Queers have often gravitated toward making and consuming texts that shift registers quickly (melodrama, musicals, pornography), and queer films frequently adapt and revise sensory regimes. To recognize and experience these queer registers, we need to listen for tones that might at first seem out of pitch, incommensurate, or wrong.

This chapter explores how cinema produces queer registers of enunciation, which use cinematic means to create experiences of queer belonging. Queer theory has extensively interrogated modes of affect, emotion, and subjectivity, and this literature helps us understand the particular stakes of registering queer feelings. For instance, Sarah Ahmed and Heather Love have outlined the significance of unhappiness for queers; Lauren Berlant discusses "underperformed emotions"; and J. Jack Halberstam has written on failure as a queer practice.[8] Ann Cvetkovich writes that "recognizing affect and desire as the motive for intellectual projects has of course long been central to queer studies."[9] What stands out from our perspective, though, is how often the critiques of affect and queer subjectivity imply a theory of worldliness, of what it means to be queer in this world. We recall that for Cvetkovich, queerness might feel different outside the Western metropolis, and affect might register in the world where identities do not.[10] This is not a problem of making elsewheres legible for the West but, rather, a condition of queer life. Lauren Berlant and Lee Edelman describe "the multiplicities and disjunctures of the affective register within which subjectification is experienced" and find "undoing as such the condition of living in a world that is not our own."[11] Queer cinematic registers make palpable and imaginable other ways of queer belonging in the world, and in doing so they intervene in the politics of queer worldliness.

Queer films invent new registers that both reflect experience and have the capacity to imagine radical forms of social being. To hear these cadences, we must attune ourselves to cinematic tone across and outside of conventional categories of articulation.

These cadences are audible in *L'inconnu du lac/Stranger by the Lake* (Alain Guiraudie, dir., 2013), a French film whose tone shifts from a sultry art-cinematic meditation on a lakeside cruising community to a more suspenseful and ambiguous state when the protagonist Franck witnesses the handsome Michel murder another man in the water. The spectator views the murder through Franck's gaze, in a riveting long take. The way the scene forces us to watch a violent act unfold from a distance recalls how films such as *The Conversation* (Francis Ford Coppola, dir., 1974) and *Blow-Up* (Michelangelo Antonioni, dir., 1966) implicate us in the complex interplay of the desiring look and the concerned eyewitness. In *Stranger by the Lake*, this tension is amplified by the fact that this crucial shot occurs immediately after the film's most explicit depiction of sex.[12] The money shot and the murder shot juxtapose extremes of sensation and emotion, but the death also creates a tear in the film's account of communalism that prompts its complex questioning of queer sociality, intimacy, and belonging.

In its clever play on voyeurism, the film draws on an idiom of contemporary Western European art films that combines the thriller genre with contemporary politics, such as those in Michael Haneke's *Caché/Hidden* (2005). But whereas Haneke's films often address human community in overwrought and obvious figurations (such as television coverage of Middle East conflict appearing in the background of a shot that centers on the anxiety of the bourgeois white subject), *Stranger by the Lake* deploys different types of voyeurism to pose less easily answered questions of belonging. The gaze that grants the viewer access to explicit bodily acts, seen as part of the everyday in the bushes of the cruising ground, is collapsed into the gaze of the ethical bystander, the outside onlooker who has suddenly become an eyewitness. This distribution of looks feels riskier, as if making a whole film in the tone of the ambivalent final shot of *Caché*. *Stranger by the Lake* refuses to settle whom the concept of the social serves, and it implicates the spectator in a questioning of community. Franck knows that Michel is a killer but begins a sexual relationship with him anyway and lies to the police to protect him. His response to the murder asks whether we should apply conventional ideas of community to this group of queer men. Should we expect the men who gather by the lake to act like a community? Do queers need each other, and for what purpose?

The detective asks many of these questions in a hostile tone toward the end of the film, but Franck's desire for belonging exceeds police discourse. The film distances itself from the detective's crude evocation of liberal sociality, killing him off unceremoniously. Despite the uneasy and ambiguous community that remains, his words cannot account for the spectator's experience, our desire for belonging and for union. The narrative of sex that may lead to death can be read as an AIDS allegory, but the film operates more sensitively as a registration of why intimacy persists in danger. *Stranger by the Lake* refuses the detective's crude formulation, framing his judgment and pity as a myopic view of queerness. His condemnation indicates the inability of a straight world to see queer community or even to allow it to exist as a social realm with moral consequence. So while it is true that the men's behavior may not accord with social norms, *Stranger by the Lake* makes felt their impossible relationship to the moral and their exclusion from the social world. The film does not respond directly to the detective's questions, but it uses register as a kind of rejoinder. The co-location of quotidian nakedness and bodies burdened with suspense creates a uniquely ambivalent tone.

What is striking in *Stranger by the Lake*'s tone is its ability to think the belonging of sex and that of community at the same time. It suggests how homosexuals (and other "perverts") are too often punished for exposing the unnatural and exclusive privilege of legitimation in dominant heterosexual bourgeois culture. For lives to count, bodies must belong somewhere, but the spaces and times available for belonging are narrowly delimited. Without clear belonging, queers are left to be bodies without lives, a kind of undead of the social world. It is consequential that these fraught questions of belonging are posed by the film at a sensual level. They would be missed without attention to *Stranger by the Lake*'s register, one that incorporates the sensory in Ghosh's terms and, through its simultaneous deployment of disparate affective regimes, demands that the spectator both experience exclusion from the social and reflect on that experience. The film ends by leaving us in the dark, and the question of belonging hangs potently in that darkness, both in the pitch-black woods of the diegesis and in the movie theater where the film is playing.

The film's darkness confuses looking out for someone's well-being with looking out for someone coming to kill you. Darkness is simultaneously a space of ethical caring and a space of threat and death. *Stranger by the Lake* does not provide us with an adequate mode of queer belonging, but it is valuable because it does present it as a pressing question: what would queer belonging feel like, and can we recognize it? Belonging for us is a way to address the politics of affiliation, relationality, and social being without reifying categories of identity, community, inclusiveness, and diversity. It implicitly demands the need to invent and experience new modes of sociality. Across the chapter, our analyses engage disparate types of film in terms of traditional genre categories, but all of which attempt to register queer belonging textually. We begin with melodrama since this is a register most frequently associated with queer cultural production. From there, we move on to discuss historical romances that describe socially proscribed relationships, seeing these "across the barricades" romances as registering otherwise impossible intimacies. The third section explores affect in more direct terms, through questions of touch and proximity. The final section identifies a queer pastoral mode that links landscape to queer belonging through both subjective experience and geopolitical exclusion.

Trans Melodrama and Human Rights

Melodrama has long been associated with queerness—or, at least, with queers. Gay audiences were a significant part of the cultures of classical Hollywood melodrama, and its broader history includes many directors whose films have a queer appeal (Lino Brocka, Vincente Minnelli, Arturo Ripstein, Douglas Sirk, Luchino Visconti) and gay-identified auteurs (Pedro Almódovar, Rainer Werner Fassbinder, Todd Haynes, Stanley Kwan, François Ozon). Melodrama names "a competing logic, a second voice" that has always been at the heart of popular cinema.[13] It is a mode of filmic articulation that privileges the marginal, locating meaning in mise-en-scène rather than in narrative, in emotion rather than in reason, and in surface rather than in depth. We are interested in how such an established queer register operates globally—how it develops and speaks differently in various cultural contexts, but, more important, how the qualities of melodrama might articulate contemporary conditions of queer worldliness.[14]

The video artist and filmmaker Ryan Trecartin illustrates how melodrama's excess of surface-level signifiers can provide a queer response to globalization by ventriloquizing and amplifying the media-saturated pileup of capitalism's psychotic discursive spaces. Excess, surface, and unmoored emotion articulate the experience of shiny corporate globalism from the perspective of its queer margins. The screaming pitch of Trecartin's work does not subvert staid middle-class sobriety (à la the melodramas of Douglas Sirk). Instead, it replicates and condenses the registers of popular global media genres such as surveillance reality franchises, home shopping channels, corporate/market-infused broadcast journalism, and music videos. Trecartin's videos are extreme, but they do not exaggerate. They simply perform in the register of commodity-driven neoliberalism, combining amphetamine-induced efficiency, compulsive news flashes, narcissistic direct address, and wig-pulling drama to expose the gendered and racialized underbelly of late capitalism's world and the ridiculousness of its compensatory gestures of humanism.

Melodrama also narrates the global in non-Western film cultures. Ravi Vasudevan considers melodrama a "significant structuring force" in Indian culture but argues that "if we are to theorize the validity of the melodramatic mode in the Indian case, it must be in such a way as to reformulate the terms of the modernity within which melodrama emerges."[15] Bhaskar Sarkar goes further, suggesting that globalization itself is experienced as melodramatic in the global South and that melodrama's dominance in Bollywood cinema might be seen as a response to this temporally anxious experience of globalizing modernity. For Sarkar,

> A melodramatic mode, which allows the underdog to have a moral upper hand, often comes into play when a wounded or marginalized subjectivity is the object of representation, whether in developed societies or in the developing world. And since melodrama as a genre provides a space for the symbolic negotiation of social contradictions through formal delays and deferrals, it is not surprising that the genre remains particularly popular in societies that find themselves forever in the waiting room of history.[16]

Sarkar's intervention is crucial in its negotiation of melodrama's apparent global translatability and its necessary cultural specificity. Melodrama is at once a universal register, a form that emerges from and is constantly speaking about modernity, and a site for the articulation of specific and localized feelings.

If we view melodrama as always already a queer register, then it follows that queerness is a constituent part of articulating the political and affective experiences of modernity. And if Sarkar is correct, melodrama in the global South intersects sexuality and geopolitics as sources of marginality and deferred social inclusion. In queer appropriations of South Asian melodrama we see most clearly South Asian cinema's articulation of modernity as a queer experience. Sridhar Rangayan's *Gulab Aaina/The Pink Mirror* (2006) presents itself from the beginning as a queer revision of popular Indian forms. It opens with a drag performance of the song "In aankhon ki

Fig. 5.1: *Pink Mirror* opens with a queer revision of a song sequence from *Umrao Jaan*.

Fig. 5.2: The queer family in *Pink Mirror*.

masti ke" from the popular Urdu film *Umrao Jaan* (Muzaffar Ali, dir., 1981), immediately announcing its debt to and revision of popular Indian cinema (figure 5.1).[17] It also sets up a melodramatic and serial television milieu of excessive style, pure emotion, and queer gender performance (figure 5.2). The film has a comedic aspect, in which two queens, Shabbo and Bibbo, fight over the hunky "driver" Samir. The melodramatic plot emerges around a letter in Shabbo's purse, which transpires to be a notification of HIV-positive status. One of the first significant moments of melodramatic style occurs when the twink Mandy tries to pick up the purse. The image moves to slow motion while booming drum music emphasizes the significance of the object as Shabbo grabs the purse from Mandy and clutches it to her chest. This knowingly over-the-top combination of exaggerated motion and music recurs later in the film when the purse falls on the floor and both Shabbo and Bibbo reach for the letter, which has fallen out. When Bibbo finally opens the letter, we zoom in (also in slow motion), and when she sees its contents, we cut to an extreme close-up of a tear running down her face. Finally, the letter's contents are revealed to the spectator in a rapid zoom into the fateful words, followed by canted angles on Shabbo and Bibbo's horrified reaction shots. *The Pink Mirror* understands melodramatic form as queer expression, a bittersweet assemblage able to articulate the awkwardly coextensive temporalities of queer anxiety and exuberance.

The film tethers these feelings to a queer geopolitics, engaging both Indian and global iterations of sexuality and gender. Vasudevan describes the family as the central term in Indian melodrama's negotiation of the modern individual within traditional structures, and Rangayan's film iterates that drama within the gay family. Bibbo is the plump den mother, and Shabbo is her wayward child. The film plays with stereotypes here, including the queeny bodybuilder and the naïve young gay. These over-the-top figures are not static but constantly rearticulate Indian queer identities. For instance, Bibbo asks Shabbo whether Mandy is her *kothi*, using common Indian slang for a sexual bottom or feminine gay man. But the term is not transparent: Mandy does not understand, so Bibbo explains it as "what we are" and then lists a series of food-related slang terms—"jaggery," "sweet rice," "puffed bread"— and Shabbo jumps in with "queens, drag queens darling." Mandy agrees, saying in English, "Yes, I'm gay." The scene proposes a chain of signifiers that may not mean the same thing at all, depending on cultural context, and what Bibbo picks up on is Mandy's response. She chides him for speaking English ("gay" is the troublesome term here) and starts lip syncing a Hindi song. Hindi slang trumps the global gay, but it is not simply a validation of local identities over global ones. The queens instead often use English as a form of drag, speaking in an exaggerated clipped tone, like British film actresses of the 1940s. The apparent seamlessness of the global "gay" is humorously crosscut with a postcolonial play on the class and gender connotations of a historically embedded English.

The Pink Mirror thus opens onto issues of identity and globalization at the same time that it adds to the subgenre of the AIDS melodrama. But as we saw in chapter 2, Rangayan is also an LGBT activist who founded one of India's first gay nongovernmental organizations (NGO) and organizes events around men who have sex with men, HIV, and human rights. There is something distinct in this combination of highly fictional, emotionally and formally overwrought textuality with socially engaged activism, and it is a combination we see repeatedly in recent South Asian queer filmmaking. Melodrama has always been a key mode of speaking about gender diversity and sexual orientation in India and Bangladesh, and recent films combine popular forms and cultural references with an explicitly activist understanding of cinema as a popular medium. If we look outside the dominant Bombay cinema—for instance, to Tamil visual culture—we find new forms of transgender representation.[18] Recent transgender-themed Tamil films include *Navarasa/Nine Emotions* (Santosh Sivan, dir., 2005), *Thenavattu/Lethargy* (V. V. Kathir, 2008), and *Achchupizhai* (Vignesh, dir., 2007). *Navarasa* is noteworthy for its prominent director, Santosh Sivan, whose films include *Theeviravaathi/The Terrorist* (1999) and *Tahaan/Tahaan—A Boy with a Grenade* (2008), and for the trans actor Bobby Darling, who has acted in several Bollywood films. These films speak across media and languages: the television talk show presenter and radio disc jockey Rose Venkatesan (often called "Transgender Rose") is making her feature directorial debut with *Cricket Scandal*, a film that echoes the Thai *kathoey* cycle by taking sports as its central topic and that also considers the national and international stage sports provide in relation to trans characters. The film is being made in English and dubbed in Tamil, Telugu, and Hindi; multiple versions enable circulation and propose a logic of translatability.

What is striking in these films is the closeness of queer melodrama to political activism. Venkatesan has proposed a political platform to promote women's and LGBT rights, and some LGBT activists have moved into cinema.[19] The trans activist Kalki Subramanian starred in *Narthaki* (Vijaya Padma, dir., 2011), which asserts its status as "the first feature film in the world with a transgender woman in a lead role."[20] Kalki is the editor of a Tamil magazine for transwomen titled *Thirunangai* and a documentary maker. The film's director is a woman (unusual in Tamil cinema, as it is everywhere else in the world). Vijaya Padma came to the topic via her work with an AIDS organization, which led her to meet transgender people and learn about issues of gender-based social exclusion. She decided to make a fiction film rather than a documentary to reach a wider audience.[21] Thus, *Narthaki* begins from an activist understanding of popular cinema. In 2013, the Tamil actress Karpaga was the first trans woman to star in a fully mainstream film, *Paal* (D. Sivakumar, dir., 2013), which means "gender" in Tamil.[22] *Paal* is closer to a melodrama than *Narthaki* in form, but both films tell stories of family rejection, social discrimination, and romantic travails, and both have a clear activist engagement. These films deploy rights discourse alongside melodrama as a mode of visualizing and expanding the spaces available for trans living.

We turn now to a South Asian melodrama that draws on national and regional forms to intervene in human rights discourses around AIDS, sexuality, and transgender/hijra/third sex discrimination. Noman Robin's *Common Gender* (2012) from Bangladesh is in conversation with South Asian television drama, Bollywood-style masala filmmaking, and Bangladeshi genre cinema. Made first as a television drama and then remade as a feature film, *Common Gender* speaks to a wider audience than *The Pink Mirror* and more self-consciously merges popular melodrama with social advocacy. It gained international publicity as the first Bangladeshi film to address the lives of *hijras*, a South Asian gender category that is often thought of as a third sex. Hijras take on aspects of feminine presentation and sometimes remove the male genitals with which they were born, but they do not generally identify in Western terms as trans women. Despite hijras' ancient history as a culture, they face extreme social exclusion and discrimination, and it is telling that this first Bangladeshi film was not made by a hijra director.[23] It opened in just six cinemas at first because it was perceived by its distributor as an art-house film, but it did so well that it expanded to more cinemas and played to packed crowds all summer in Dhaka.[24] So from the outset, something intriguing is happening here: a film that is perceived as addressing a culturally elite group turns out to interpellate a much wider audience, and a melodrama about the lives of queer people overtakes straight romances as a desirable cinematic experience. The film focuses on a family of hijras in Dhaka, with one narrative following the doomed romance of Sushmita and Shonjoy and the other tracing Bubli's separation from her family. Thus, the film draws on romantic and family melodrama narratives, linking both to the marginal social position of hijras in Bangladesh in explicitly human rights terms.

Unlike *The Pink Mirror*, *Common Gender* does not assume a queer spectator position but, rather, works to produce one. The opening scenes move us cannily from a gender normative perspective to a queer one, reminding us that all audiences can form queer attachments. The first scenes show Bubli's parents crying over her gender identity: her mother insists Bubli has a hormonal problem, and her father responds that the neighbors cannot be told that. The problem thus is publicness, a question of honor that makes the family cry. In Sara Ahmed's terms, Bubli is an unhappiness cause. We begin from the unpromising point of view of traumatized normativity, a position that many transgender-themed films adopt—for instance, *El ultimo verano de la boyita/The Last Summer of La Boyita* (Julia Solomonoff, dir., 2009).

The next scene introduces hijras in a conventionally fetishistic way, by showing body parts in pieces. We see ears with long earrings, ankles laden with bracelets, and then a shot of a row of people walking away from the camera in colorful green and pink saris. The sequence uses jewelry and clothing to signal femininity but holds off on showing faces. Next, though, something odd happens: a series of shots of men looking at the camera locates the spectator in the place of the hijra. The sequence sets up hijras in a classical way as feminine objects of the gaze, but it puts the spectator in a more duplicitous position, at once located as the hijra being looked at and as the outsider waiting in suspense for their faces to be revealed. When the hijras turn around they berate the unseen men who whistle; now the spectator is in the position of the obnoxious man who harasses hijras in public and who will be schooled by them. It is a rapid-fire set of position switches as the film triangulates its mainstream viewers. This implication of the spectator further develops in a scene in which the hijras attend a dance performance. The scene centers on the dance itself, in which a glamorous performer looks directly at camera in a series of erotically charged close-ups. This "item girl" is visually distinguished from the hijras who rush the stage to be with her, yet the film refuses to answer a spectator who demands certainty as to whether she is transgender, cisgender, or otherwise gendered.[25] Binary gender is rendered unstable, and the film moves us toward a queerly erotic gaze.

The use of a fetishistic visuality usually associated with the representation of women to represent hijras introduces *Common Gender*'s most radical gesture, which is to disrupt binary gender through a revision of melodramatic form. The film takes codes such as excessive mise-en-scène and emotional performance that have traditionally been used to negotiate female roles in patriarchy and uses them instead to speak of hijras' oppression. Williams argues that melodramas "are deemed excessive for their gender- and sex-linked pathos," and in *Common Gender* pathos is gendered not in terms of perceived cultural femininity but precisely as the pathos of being misgendered, or of having one's gender socially de-legitimated.[26] The film quite explicitly solicits our tears in response to the pathos of hijra gender. We see this adaptation in the argument between Shabnam Mashi and Bindu Mashi as mothers of two rival hijra families. Shabnam tells an increasingly melodramatic story about their mother, who was abused in the marketplace and forced to show her attackers that she had male genitals. Melodrama inheres in the extremes of her facial expression and vocalizing style and in the film's dramatic close-ups, but it also situates these excesses in a story of trauma that has to do with the forced public performance of gender. Through Shabnam's emotions, the scene discloses the excessive social violence involved in being a hijra in public, where the gendered body becomes a site of constant threat.

In one of the film's climactic scenes, Bubli performs precisely "the spectacle of a body caught in the grip of intense sensation or emotion" that Williams considers central to genres of sensation.[27] Rejected by her family, Bubli comes upon a woman on the street feeding a bowl of rice to her young son. Overcome by this display of maternal care, Bubli asks the woman to feed her, too, taking up the position she has lost as a loved and cherished child. The scene builds a melodramatic crescendo with disjunctive overhead shots and a complexly layered soundtrack of music, thunder, church bells, chanting, and Bubli's loud keening. The woman goes along with Bubli's request at first but is scared off by her increasingly hysterical responses. The scene breaks apart formally as the camera angles become unmotivated and non-diegetic music takes over the soundtrack so that we can no longer hear Bubli's cries. Her performance is central here, a bodily display of raw emotion that solicits tears from the spectator.

But, of course, it is the *female* body that experiences intense sensation in Williams's schema, and melodramatic anguish is female emotion. In *Common Gender*, it is the hijra body that suffers, and the film therefore uses *register* to stake a claim on hijras' femininity. It is not only that the characters desire to have their gender recognized in the narrative, but also that the mode of making this claim cinematically—in the public sphere of cinema—is to occupy the feminine position of melodramatic protagonist on-screen. The melodramatic register gives us a mode of experiencing hijra suffering and enables us to read it via pathos, tears, and gendered empathy. (The Italian documentary *Le Coccinelle: Neapolitan Transsexual Melodrama* [Emanuela Pirelli, dir., 2011] evokes similar affects though its representation of trans women who render their struggles into melodramatic songs, which they perform at weddings and other social functions.) Of course, there are risks in this strategy: including hijras as women only to give them access to the same suffering and patriarchal oppression as cisgendered women is not a wholly positive outcome. Also, although hijras present as female, they often consider themselves to be a third sex and not women. As Helen Leung points out, local specificity in trans discourse "should not merely signal local variations on a global theme but also reflect elements that *resist* (and thus

Aren't we human. Can't we even use the toilet?

Fig. 5.3: *Common Gender* melodramatizes human rights in a scene in which hijras are denied access to public restrooms.

have the potential to transform) the theoretical premises of transgender discourse."[28] A globally attentive trans aesthetic might deconstruct or reimagine binary gender forms entirely rather than merely reverse them. Nonetheless, the melodramatic register reworks gendered sensation formally.

Melodrama also becomes the vehicle for the film's human rights discourse, explicitly tethering queer unhappiness to the social hierarchies of gender and sexual oppression that produce it. Whereas classical Hollywood melodramas often speak about patriarchy and capitalism only implicitly, these South Asian films, via melodramatic visual style and soundtracks, redouble the affective register of melodrama by speaking its social critiques in the body of the text.[29] *Common Gender* thus sets up from the outset the precarious social status of hijras, showing the group begging for money from storeowners. The category of the human is introduced when one character rebukes a woman who will not touch her as she gives money, "Why not touching? Aren't I human?" The question of hijras' humanity comes to a crisis when Bubli is thrown out of both men's and women's public toilets and harassed by an angry crowd (figure 5.3). She shouts, "Aren't hijras human?" and when other hijras arrive to fight back, they cry, "I'm hijra. I'm human. Doesn't Allah see us?" Human rights discourse is thus invoked simultaneously with universalizing claims of religion.[30] In Judith Butler's terms, "Embodiment denotes a contested sphere of norms governing who will count as a viable subject within the sphere of politics."[31] Moreover, the activist question of access to public bathroom facilities provides a crossing point for issues of gender, privacy, public life, and the physical body.[32] We might contrast this moment to *Circumstance*'s "fucking is a human right," where a different regime of bodily acts provides a vector for thinking the human.

In the film's unhappy ending we find activism closely linked to melodramatic structures. The film's central romance is between Sushmita, who is a hijra, and Shonjoy, who is a cisgendered man. Shonjoy takes Sushmita to meet his parents, despite her concerns that this might be a bad idea. The meeting does not go well: the parents berate Shonjoy for befriending a hijra and insist that he stop seeing her. Shonjoy tries to use the language of religious equality and intercommunal tolerance, but his father insists that there is no comparison. Insistent non-diegetic music plays as the couple sadly walk away together. Sushmita rejects Shonjoy's attempts to explain his parents' reactions, saying she has been insulted her whole life and accusing him of cowardice for not having disclosed Sushmita's gender to his parents in advance. Her performance becomes unstable, and the scene climaxes with Sushmita threatening to kill Shonjoy if he tries to contact her again and storming off-screen, laughing maniacally. Shortly afterward, the hijras find Sushmita drowned in the communal water tank. *Common Gender* demands Sushmita's suicide because of the intransigent transphobia of the very class that presents itself as socially progressive. There is no place for her in Shonjoy's bourgeois world, and to enable him to live, she has to die.

Melodrama, activism, and human rights discourse come together in the aftermath of Sushmita's disastrous attempt to enter the progressive middle-class family. The grieving hijras take Sushmita's body to the graveyard, but they are turned away. As with the public bathroom, hijras are not given the status of human even in death. As they prepare her body, the film cuts to Sushmita's biological family, from whom she was estranged in life. Her mother desperately wants to see her, but her father forbids it. Eventually, he relents and allows her to go as long as she does not take the chauffeur. The film crosscuts between the hijras crying over Sushmita's body and her mother driving to see her, unaware of her death. In flashback, we see the mother's memories of Sushmita as a little boy and Shonjoy's memories of romance. When Sushmita's mother arrives, she learns that she is too late and will never be reunited with her child. "Too late" is, of course, a classic structure of melodrama, described by Franco Moretti and taken up in film studies by Steve Neale.[33] It is so affective because it is a utopian gesture; it contains not simply the sadness of failure but a utopian desire that it not be too late for the desired meeting. In *Common Gender*, the desired meeting of the hijra with her mother, in other words, is the coming together of gender diversity with the mainstream ideology of family, a shifting of the discourse on family where love and acceptance might save the day. We cry because this cannot happen in the film's diegetic universe, where even the cemetery will not accept Sushmita's humanity. This is also, of course, the political impetus of the melodrama: in Fassbinder's words, we cry because it is so hard to change the world.

Let us return, though, to the surprising popularity of *Common Gender* in Bangladesh. Its distributor misunderstood the film by locating it as an art film aimed at a niche audience. Rather, the film leverages the queer emotionality of melodrama to voice some very direct claims on human rights activism. For the director, Noman Robin, tears are a trigger of social change, and accessing a large popular audience is a form of outreach. The film must navigate between articulating a hijra point of view and addressing a largely cisgendered public in a way that produces a call to action. Reviews picked up on this human rights focus. Alamgir Khan writes, "Awareness raising is urgent for all of us to change our mind-set about [transgender people]. *Common Gender* the film can play an important role in bringing about that necessary change in the country. . . . Our entertainment is not all this film aims to; it is to be seen now what steps our government takes for the transgender people in the country."[34] So the film addresses both the popular audience and the government as potential routes to social change through advocacy, but it also considers melodrama's audience social actors who are able to change the lives of hijras through public and intimate interactions. (In 2013, the Bangladeshi government recognized hijras as a third gender.)

Robin is raising funds for two activist projects that are emerging from the film. One project aims to install digital projectors in rural Bangladeshi cinemas so the film can be shown outside urban centers. The project complicates the class divide of art cinema and popular melodrama with the divide of urban and rural. Melodrama may be a popular mode of film culture in rural Bangladesh, but without the infrastructure of digital conversion, the medium is fast becoming inaccessible. The economics of exhibition, here as in chapter 2, underwrites the potential for queer cinematic experiences. The other project is a fund that uses some profits from the film to set up a transgender cemetery in Dhaka. As in the film, most religious communities in Bangladesh do not allow trans and third gender people to be buried in cemeteries, so people from those communities are forcibly excluded from human dignity when they die. The melodramatic pleasures of the film are leveraged in an attempt to alleviate the same suffering in real life. There is a significant shift here from the queer registers of Fassbinder and Ripstein or even Haynes and Ozon. We might characterize it as a move from the register of modernist melodrama that disrupts formally and affectively the operations of heteronormative capitalism to a register of human rights melodrama that appeals to dominant social structures as agents of change. There is certainly a liberalization in this shift in register, but where human rights melodrama is arguably less politically radical than an earlier model of queer art cinema, it is also more directly engaged in the implications of its representational politics.

Impossible Queer History and Love across the Barricades

The films discussed so far in this chapter use register to create new spaces of queer belonging and ethical obligation. In this section, we turn to historical costume drama, a less obviously queer genre than melodrama but one that shares with it a concern for spectacular surface and emotion. The costume drama is turned to the purpose of making lesbian desire visible and representable, even (or especially) in historical settings in which same-sex love officially has been deemed nonexistent. When the Dubai International Film Festival rejected *The World Unseen* (2007), Shamim Sarif's film about lesbian love in South Africa of the early 1950s, the organizers cited the grounds that "the subject matter doesn't exist."[35] Somehow the film's evocation of an apartheid past proved incompatible with its representation of sexual intimacy between two women. Although the festival may have had other reasons for excluding the film, its supposed anachronism became the official justification. From its title onward, *The World Unseen* refuses to make apologies for imagining something that conventional history would dismiss as impossible. In response to the Dubai festival organizers' critique, Sarif laughed and told *The Guardian*, "You can't have an argument about that, can you?"[36] The film's narrative is entirely structured around the registration of unthinkable bodies, identities, allegiances, and intimacies (figure 5.4).

The World Unseen's main character is Amina, an Indian South African woman who runs a café in Cape Town and whose progressive attitudes toward gender and race, as well as her butch style, mark her as out of sync with the other characters in apartheid-era South Africa. Her romantic attraction to a woman named Miriam centers a web of untimely intimacies, in which the women explicitly reject hierarchies of race and gender. Amina says directly, "I hate apartheid" while putting on a masculine outfit. *The*

Fig. 5.4: *The World Unseen* situates lesbian love in heritage landscapes.

World Unseen is representative of a wider group of films whose depiction of an impossible past is often overlooked because they do not use the tropes of political modernism to respond to the apparent unfigurability of the queer past. They do not, for instance, contain the discontinuities that rupture the historical dieseses of films by John Greyson or Derek Jarman. If the film flirts with anachronism, it does so without the eruptions of heterogeneity associated with counter-cinema. Sarif's reimagining of history instead involves mixing registers drawn from a variety of popular genres such as melodrama, middlebrow docudrama, heritage film, and the women's picture. And unlike that of Fassbinder and even Rangayan, the temporality of her historical narrative never overturns those registers in a critical self-reflexivity. Instead, the film narrates big history through beautiful images of the South African landscape—that in another context would be simply nostalgic—and imagines national racial divisions via diegetic stand-ins, including a black-and-white interracial straight couple. What are lesbians doing in this picture of the past, and what does lesbian desire ignite in this mode of historicity?

This retelling of the past from the perspective of lesbian desire intervenes in the present's politics of difference. *The World Unseen*'s lesbians encode politically difficult bonds, embodying historical intimacies that are often too painful for conventional history to remember. They personify connections that remain otherwise unfigured in both historical and present-day discourses. In this sense, the film's undoing of the repression of same-sex love aims to repair other historical violence by association. The impossibility of love between two Indian South African women serves as an analogy for other kinds of impossibilities: crossing racial divides, believing in the category of the human outside racial categories, and the equality of women to men. In the film's use of conventional history-film tropes (internal flashbacks, stylized retro costuming, long shots of landscape, sepia-tone photographs, emotive score), it positions the forbidden lesbian relationship as more than simply another example of oppression. That relationship's impossibility stands as primary synecdoche for history, figuring sexual violence, racism, and fundamental questions of human community. The film's determination that the cinematic image can make the impossible possible is its central mode of articulating politics, and crucially the figure of the lesbian registers the political as a felt experience.

In fact, without its moments of pent-up lesbian lust or intimacy *The World Unseen* would lose its particularly affective method of expressing politics. Lesbian intimacy remains at the core of the film's humanism, and same-sex love provides the sensual material by which it poses personal desire as the frontier of political change. For example, Miriam rejects both her husband's domestic control and his political affiliations. She goes to work for Amina, where she acts outside of racist norms, forging alliances with black and white South Africans. In addition to this transgression, she develops a romantic relationship with Amina. In one telling scene, Amina feeds Miriam *koeksisters* (South African doughnuts), and the intimate shot of her sharing these treats tethers signifiers of national culture to queer intimacy. While it may appear fairly conservative in its formal mechanisms, the film's emphatic assertion of queer intimacies disrupts conventional registers of national historical narration. Because lesbians belong in the diegesis, the film asserts, they can be assumed to belong in history. Thus, the film's viewers experience a past in which lesbian desire can be seen and felt. In *The World Unseen*, queer intimacies amount to something; they carry an agency, making things forever unlike how they were before.

The World Unseen's impossible love brings us to a group of films in which queer love brings together two otherwise incommensurate political, social, religious, or class communities. We refer to these impossible queers as "across the barricades" lovers. We might think, in the British context, of *My Beautiful Laundrette* (Stephen Frears, dir., 1985), a film in which the representation of a same-sex kiss between white and South Asian characters has become an iconic moment for many audiences. More recently, Israeli films such as *Dhalam/Alata/Out in the Dark* (Michael Mayer, dir., 2012) pose gay love stories between Israeli Jews and Palestinians, and other geopolitical encounters abound, such as that of the white German woman in *Edge of Heaven* who is separated from her Kurdish lover by deportation. The promise of these films is often overlaid with the limitations and contradictions of liberal politics, but no small part of their success is their sensory evocation of queerness as a particular way of occupying the world that renegotiates the relationship between bodies and histories.

Karin Albou's *Le chant des mariées/The Wedding Song* (2008) narrates the friendship of a Muslim woman and a Jewish woman in Tunisia during the Second World War, mapping the shifts in power from French colonialism to Nazi occupation through the social and physical forces exerted on the women's bodies. In a certain reading, the film reiterates an Orientalist gaze at the Muslim woman and an account of Jewish victimhood that feeds into troubling political positions in the present. However, its politics of the female body demands a more nuanced accounting of its historicity: the film insists on intimacy between the Muslim and Jewish women that it nonetheless portrays as anachronistic and out of time. Why does this story need to be situated in the 1940s, and why does the film need to find queer longing in the colonial and Nazi occupations of North Africa to speak to modern histories of race and religion?

It would be easy to read *The Wedding Song* as troublingly Orientalist, providing international lesbian audiences with a titillating perspective on North African women. Albou comes from an Arab and Algerian Jewish family, and the film is a co-production with French as well as Tunisian funding. It was distributed in the United Kingdom by Peccadillo, a largely gay-oriented distributor, and marketed as a lesbian historical drama. Peccadillo's catalogue describes the film this way: "Reminiscent of women-led wartime films such as 'Aimée & Jaguar' and 'The Diary of Anne,' 'The Wedding Song' explores both Jewish and Arab cultures and female sexuality to winning effect." It seems clear that its appeal is to lesbian audiences for whom the setting might be romantically exotic, while also offering the middlebrow pleasures of the historical drama. Brian Whitaker has argued that the French funding allowed Tunisian films to escape strict censorship, which also leads to accusations that the resulting films are aimed at European, not local, audiences.[37] However, an inadvertent Eurocentrism lurks in assuming that "liberal" positions are available only to European audiences and, indeed, that North African filmmakers are so strictly focused on the desires of Europeans.

The film takes place during a crucial tipping point for North Africa's Second World War history, when the French Jewish population lost its colonial power over the Arab Muslim population to the occupying Nazis, who cultivated Muslim support to oust the French. The film depicts French racism as a central motivator of Tunisian anticolonialism—for instance, in a scene in which Nour is thrown out of a dress store and called a "native." The film's Muslim characters conflate this French colonialism with the Jews so that when the owner of a *hamam* (Turkish bath) says, "Let's hope the Germans win and get rid of the French," he is referring to Jewish characters. When Nazi propaganda begins to arrive, it claims that the French are friends of the Jews while the Germans are friends to Muslims. The drama thus focuses on the switch-over from a history of class and colonial oppression of Tunisian Muslims by French Jews to the Jews' quickly becoming victims of the Nazis, and this nexus of historical discourses around European colonialism, religion, and North African politics emerges in the spaces of same-sex affection.

Myriam and Nour spend time together in the hamam, a single-sex Arab space whose otherwise unexceptional nakedness takes on erotic potential in the context of a film branded as lesbian. This erotics is never made concrete in sexual acts, but the hamam does become a space of female solidarity and Muslim solidarity with Jewish women. When the Nazis invade the hamam and take the women without veils, Nour saves Myriam by swearing that Myriam is her sister and a Muslim. Something strikingly similar happens in *Les hommes libres/Free Men* (Ismaël Ferroukhi, dir., 2012), a gay male version of a similar historical affect. *Free Men*, which is based on a true story, centers on French Muslims who helped save Jews in Paris during the Second World War, focusing on the romance of Younes, a young Muslim man who becomes a Resistance fighter and develops a sexual relationship with Salim, who transpires to be a closeted Jew.

As with *Wedding Song*, *Free Men*'s staging of same-sex desire links homosexuality with anticolonial politics in a way that is insistent and yet oblique and muddled. Much of the publicity for *Free Men* (like some for *The Wedding Song*) sells the film as Jewish-themed, entirely omitting its central queerness.[38] Although the films' queer representations are downplayed, they are structurally crucial. The intimacy between Younes and Salim is imagined via sexual tension from the outset, and although the key sex scene occurs off-screen, the film makes a point of showing that a hook-up is taking place. Queerness works in these films to imagine something that otherwise seems unimaginable, to figure Jews and Muslims living in peace and intimacy. We argue that queerness is required in across the barricades films to produce, allegorically, a different version of intercommunal politics—and that it is not at all clear which identity is being used more instrumentally. What is at stake

Fig. 5.5: *The Wedding Song* at once centers Myriam's desiring gaze and Nour's visibility.

in the tentative, but recurrent, emergence of queerness in these middlebrow religious-conflict films?

Free Men is able to visualize gay sexuality relatively directly; lesbian desire in *The Wedding Song* is an altogether stranger thing. The film merely hints at homosexual sex, arguably evading explicit lesbianism. Both women marry men during the course of the film, and although there is a persistently eroticized gaze from the perspective of Myriam, looking down from her balcony at Nour in the courtyard below (figure 5.5), the film relays the desiring look of the lesbian spectator more than it enacts desire within the diegesis. In the hamam, for instance, the spectator is an outsider gazing "under the veil" at Muslim women's bodies. Within the narrative, Nour is never shown as reciprocating Myriam's gaze—indeed, she is represented as desiring a man, Khaled. There is something potentially exploitative about using her as the object of a lesbian gaze. Yet it would misrepresent the film to foreclose on its production of spaces for lesbian desire. Myriam and Nour are repeatedly placed in close proximity, in close-up shots that frame their relationship as physically and emotionally intimate. This framing refutes the shot-reverse-shot structure of the gaze from above. Instead of asking the spectator to look through Myriam at Nour, these shots use frontality and scale to look directly at both women at once, constructing their relationship in terms of touch rather than distanced looking.

The Wedding Song's narrative works perhaps too obviously to negotiate the historical problematics of colonialism, Nazism, and Arab cultures. Its use of shot scale and point of view works in a more nuanced way to create lesbian spaces that inhabit and suffuse this historicity. The film invites the look of the lesbian spectator to animate a certain queer globality, a lesbian cinematic ontology that counters patriarchal looking relations.

The film sets up transgressive acts within the diegesis in which a lesbian look is offered as a privileged mode of spectatorship. This structure is made visible in a scene in which Myriam gives Nour a silky bra and puts it on her. Narratively, there is a strong indication of Myriam's desire for Nour. After a medium shot in which Nour's body forms a spectacle for the spectator, the scene consists predominantly of close-ups and extreme close-ups of Nour's body from Myriam's point of view. The closeness of the shots removes voyeuristic distance and replaces it with an intimate proximity that privileges the textures of clothes and skin. Myriam removes Nour's dress, fastens the bra, breathes on her neck. Lesbian space here is close-up space, designating a lover's viewpoint on the body and excluding the surveillance of the familial, religious, and state patriarchies. Yet if the scene appears to create a purely sensory account of queer space, it also sets up a highly political conflict over Nour's body. Khaled is furious when he sees the bra, insisting on knowing how Nour could afford it and who gave it to her. He insists she remove it, seeing it as whorish. The space between Jewish and Muslim bodies shifts throughout *The Wedding Song* as political violence is repeatedly enacted across gendered bodies.

The synthesis of violence, queerness, and women's bodies emerges most vividly in a scene in which Myriam is prepared for her wedding. She has been set up to marry Raoul, a Jewish man who is much older than she is, so he can pay the levy imposed on Jewish families. Raoul has asked that the bride be prepared in "Oriental style," which, we learn, means the complete removal of her pubic hair. This scene is by some measure the most explicit of the film. It is the only point of nudity, and it reveals Myriam's body in surprising detail. The scene queers this avowedly heterosexual ritual in several ways. First, it provides the pretext for an eroticized proximity between the naked Myriam and Nour, who cradles her head. Nour cares for Myriam, but Myriam's suffering face might easily be viewed as ecstatic. Second, this eroticization of pain can be extended to the position of the spectator, placed in a potentially uncomfortably sadistic position as we watch the older woman kneel between Myriam's legs and knead sugaring paste between her fingers. Most strikingly, the scene, like the bra scene, uses close-ups to produce a textural intimacy and tactile affiliation. Shots include extreme close-ups of the sugaring paste on skin, of Myriam's pubic hair being ripped out, and

Fig. 5.6: In a scene of hair removal, *The Wedding Song* creates a tangible trace of the profilmic as blood wells up on the actor's skin.

of the blood spots that seep up to the surface of the skin (figure 5.6). The film prompts a visceral reaction and shifts us from fictional historical space to the profilmic space of the actress enduring this painful process. Blood spots provide a cinematic ontology, a tangible trace of the body in pain. An indexicality of the female body emerges powerfully here, a bloody violence associated with hetero marriage that nonetheless provides the pretext for a scene of queer intimacy and visceral corporeality.

The ideological force of this scene resonates through the rest of the film. As the hair removal ends, we cut in a series of excessive graphic matches from a close up of what looks like a vulva to Myriam's eye to the scene through a lacy tablecloth as Myriam watches the Nazis violate her home and attack her mother. This scene and its transition constitute an aesthetic rupture, from the style of a tasteful middlebrow historical drama to a disjunctive accretion of shocking images. This formal rupture juxtaposes the bodily closeness of the lesbian image with the bodily violence of the Nazis and the ambivalent collaboration of the Muslims. The shocking cuts, like the bleeding body, create a mechanism for negotiating what the film insists on rendering as impossible desires, both for lesbian sex and for intercommunal solidarity. On Nour's wedding night, blood again plays a central role. After the couple have sex, Khaled slices open her foot to stain the sheet and pretend she's a virgin. But during their intercourse, Nour gets revenge for Khaled's insistence that she exclude Myriam from her life. Even as they consummate their marriage, she starts talking about Myriam as her best friend whom she cannot stop seeing. If marriage is linked closely to bloodshed, *The Wedding Song* inserts queer desire into that most apparently implacable of cultural spaces.

There is a complex historicity to *The Wedding Song*'s imagining of a lesbian bond between a Jew and a Muslim in wartime Tunis. The film begins with a letter from Heinrich Himmler to the Grand Mufti of Jerusalem that talks about removing the Jewish problem from Palestine. Thus, although Albou wanted to speak about Jews and Muslims outside of the overdetermined context of contemporary Israel and Palestine, the film nonetheless addresses the geopolitics of the present. It clearly intends a progressive investment in that present, yet contradictions keep returning from its address to a global audience to its very different treatments of Myriam's and Nour's characters. This historical setting is necessary to the film's construction of a queer globality. The relationship between Myriam and Nour delineates a close proximity between Jews and Muslims that cannot be imagined in the present and is thus displaced into a romanticized past. Yet it is imagined in the exact moment that such a relationship becomes impossible in that very past. In the terms of the film's story line, Myriam and Nour could have lived together in the narrative past, but now, in their narrative present, they cannot because the intervention of the Nazis separates them. The story takes place in the exact moment that their intimacy becomes violently impossible, and the film evokes a lesbian intercommunal space precisely in the act of its suffocation. This impossible relationship thus constructs for the global spectator a queer temporality of belatedness. We can feel queerly because they cannot, and our sensory pleasures are caught up in the necessary historical failure of Nour and Myriam's love story.

Material Practices of Queer Touching

Sarah Ahmed asks what it means to move through the world as a queer person, extending the body into social spaces, and what enables or disciplines this movement.[39] This section reformulates Ahmed's question for queer cinema, asking how queer bodies extend into cinematic space and how films can foreground the sense of touch to register intimacy as political being. This phenomenological question is particularly pertinent for film theory, which has investigated how cinema creates a sense of bodily extension and how individual films deploy the sense of touch. Indeed, Laura Marks grounds her polemic on hapticity and cinema in queer examples. Lesbian artists such as Sadie Benning and Azian Nurudin are central to her account of cinema as a tactile medium that is as erotic as it is sensuous.[40] However, much film scholarship on phenomenology and the haptic brackets sexuality along with other political issues. Even when the examples are queer, cinema as a medium emerges unscathed by queerness. Nonetheless, some film scholars are engaged in thinking the medium in relation to the social location of subjects and objects. Katharina Lindner criticizes phenomenology's false universalism, arguing along with Elena del Rio that philosophy's assumption of a white male body describes an experience of mobility that is hardly available to all.[41] Proposing a queer approach to film phenomenology, she writes, "We are likely to be more open to the tactile or kinaesthetic dimensions of the cinematic experience if we have a particular history of tactile or kinaesthetic engagement with the world—that is, if we have come to embody a particularly tactile or kinaesthetic way of being-in-the-world."[42] If queers develop different ways of being in the world, then queer cinema might elaborate new ways to register and nourish those tactile engagements.

Lindner proposes that queer cinematic pleasures are to be found in "sensuousness and bodily affect" rather than in narrative identifications and story.[43] Although we do not think this claim is intended as a universal rule for queer cinematic pleasure, it does open up a space to consider how the affective regimes of queerness become worldly. To return to Sarkar's argument about melodrama and the global South, we might consider how modes of queer life support peculiarly sensory forms of cinematicity. Marks states that "haptic visuality is itself erotic; the fact that some of these are sexual images is, in effect, icing on the cake."[44] Here she demands that we theorize an erotics of cinematic form, thinking sexuality and the body via sensation and sound-image relations. We can extend this line of thinking to consider how queerness might intersect with the forms of hapticity. A less expansive account of this relationship would simply stipulate that if haptic visuality is intrinsically erotic, then it must contain within itself a space of queer eroticism—a space that is already present in Marks's examples, although it is unremarked as such. There is a broader version, though, in which cinematic hapticity is itself queer: it constitutes a disruption of dominant modes of heteronormative vision and provokes a relationship between spectator and screen that opens up the viewer to unexpected and transgressive intimacies.

We consider film images (and sounds) to be capable of producing not only a queerly embodied experience of cinematic texture but also an aesthetic of political being. Cinema's evocation of touch proposes a fantasy of connection, the surface of the screen an object along which one could run one's fingers, eyes, or tongue. Perhaps we imagine touching fabric or grass; perhaps smooth skin. Either way, we should not exempt these fantasmatic encounters from cinema's recurring questions of subjectivity, power, and pleasure. The formal qualities of film texture and touch speak as much about the political distribution and control of bodies, spaces, and things in the world as they do about how it feels to encounter them. Affects are never neutral, and figuring proximities—between spectator and film as well as between on-screen bodies—has high stakes for queer people. Juan Suárez addresses the queerness of cinematic hapticity when he reads grain as a queer aesthetic, teasing out the radical implications of filmic texture and experimental style.[45] The sensuous properties of film are not "merely" aesthetic here but offer revised ways to understand queer subjectivity and community. Suárez positions our work, alongside that of Lucas Hilderbrand and Sarah Ahmed, as part of a "new materialist turn in queer critique" in which a "non-anthropomorphic view of queerness" enables a consideration of the queer potentialities of nonhuman nature and the environment. He concludes:

> Cumulatively, this body of work examines the (often unspoken) material horizons that subtend sexuality and its representations—be it the thingness of the body, particular objects and substances, or the renderings and distortions unique to various media—and shows that the range of the sexual exceeds interiority, individuality, and anthropomorphic embodiment to affix itself also to textures, surfaces, and things; indeed it is in relation to this material interface that many of the political consequences of queerness arise.[46]

We pursue the political consequences of these cinematic proximities, considering queer touch and closeness as formal registers able to reference forms of relationality that are otherwise deemed socially marginal and unproductive.

The material practices of queer touching are foregrounded in the documentary *Acciones #6* (ca. 1995) by Mujeres Creando, a group of Bolivian feminist, anarchist, and anticapitalist activists who make experimental films. In the short video, the group's founders Julieta Paredes and María Galindo interview members of the public about their attitudes toward sexuality in a way that is not dissimilar to that in Pier Paolo Pasolini in *Comizi d'amore/ Love Meetings* (1964). In provoking speech about homosexuality in public, they do not condemn the interviewees, giving even the most homophobic reactions a space. But the women also stage a series of interventions in which they touch one another and the crowd that has gathered to watch them. Early in the action, one of the women announces, "We're going to talk about something that touches us all and touches you too." The politics of touching in public is always precarious for queer people, and here the members of Mujeres Creando link physical touch with emotional resonance. They create

We are lying down on the floor, in the street, vulnerable to your critics.

Fig. 5.7: Members of Mujeres Creandos make a bed on the street in *Acciones #6*.

a "bed" in the street out of sheets and pillows, which Paredes and Galindo lie down on together amid a not entirely supportive crowd (figure 5.7). This performance of lesbian intimacy in a public square seems astonishingly brave, not least because it insists on belonging. The lesbian couple refuses to be excluded from the community, demanding to be recognized as part of public life.

In another part of the action, Paredes and Galindo hand out roses to the crowd. Here, relationality is destabilized as the gift of the flower mediates queerly between subjects and objects. The women reach out, bestowing a single rose as a lover might, and for those who accept, the flower becomes a token that produces proximity. The transactions are shown in slow motion, revealing nuggets of affect in miniature—from the woman who appears to respond romantically, receiving the flower as if it were intended solely for her, to the older woman who cannot bear to touch the flower by the stem, holding it away from her body by a leaf as if she is afraid of contamination. Gavin Brown notes the importance for radical queer activists of reappropriating public spaces and, like Igor Grubić, Mujeres Creando combines political action, performance, and filmmaking in the space of the agora.[47] However, the group is more engaged than Grubić with the formal qualities of video, using a low-tech aesthetic to redouble the visceral qualities of the street action. The garish colors and jagged lines of video effects refuse any normalizing smoothness. They are the formal correlative of painting a giant red heart, of lying on the ground, of touching rough concrete. Tactility measures the potential for material transformation, and the riskiness of public touching forms both an aesthetic and a political strategy.

Acciones #6 illustrates the centrality of touch and proximity to the invention of queer registers of belonging, and it foregrounds the necessary political histories of such affiliations. To reimagine subject-object relations is to follow through on the promise of queer theory to upset identities, but it also offers the opportunity to examine what this might mean in practice, in worldly contexts in which both identities and anti-identitarian modes of living are overdetermined by multiple sites of struggle. For Mujeres Creando, lesbian and feminist identities are closely entangled, and both take part in the politics of anticapitalism and indigeneity. Thus, the group has created an open house in La Paz, which it calls Casa de Indias, Putas y Lesbianas, and it takes on the problem of the universal subject in an article on neoliberalism in which Galindo writes, "We begin by saying that the 'universal subject' does not exist. It isn't the human being, nor is it the individual, but instead it is the white, male, heterosexual, monogamous, Catholic, healthy investor from the North."[48] Echoing the queer critiques of universality we have highlighted in both human rights discourse and phenomenology, Galindo insists on the geopolitically embodied nature of subjectivity.

Acciones #6 plays out this feminist critique in its opening scene, in which an indigenous woman stands on the roof of a city building and talks about what it means to belong to a community of women. As she talks, she wrings out a cloth, setting up a feminist haptics of women's labor, working by hand, squeezing the material around her fingers (figure 5.8). As she describes the feeling of realizing that she could like other women, she pours water over her body and brushes out her long black hair. Sensuality is attached to lesbian awakening and to feminist consciousness. She describes traditional hetero marriage as a prison for women and asserts that she was not born to stay at home like a prisoner. The roof stages a space of freedom, in which feminine tasks are transformed from domestic labor into self-care.[49] The work of Mujeres Creando speaks to the importance of feminism to our understanding of queer belonging, and it illustrates the necessary intersectionality of queer cinema's new registers. As Qwo-Li Driskill, Chris Finley, Brian Joseph Gilley, and Scott Lauria Morgensen write in a North American context, "Settler colonialism is the historical, institutional, and discursive root of heteronor-

It was beautiful for me to realized that I could like a woman

Fig. 5.8: *Acciones #6* elaborates a feminist critique of heterosexuality and women's labor.

mative binary sex/gender systems on stolen land. . . . To interrogate heteronormativity *is* to critique colonial power, which then necessarily intersects
the work of decolonization pursued by queer Indigenous people."[50] For Mujeres Creando, feminist and queer critique can leverage the colonial gender
discourse that remains stubbornly dominant in Evo Morales's leftist Bolivia,
and lesbian desire revises subjectivities that have long been engrained in
class and racial terms. The group's work produces a register in which queer
proximities are given space to breathe and thereby to create subject-object
relations that have the capacity to embody resistant geopolitics of space.

The force of queer proximity can also be felt in other types of relationality. Connections across species and to the natural world can evoke belonging
and intimacy as easily as they can raise the specter of violence and dehumanization. The prospects of being not-human or forming community with
nonhuman animals offer ambiguous benefits for queers, yet the category of
the animal can exert a powerful force for what Donna Haraway terms "queer
re-worlding." Where "queering has the job of undoing 'normal' categories,"
she argues, "none is more critical than the human/nonhuman sorting operation."[51] We have come across issues of animality before in this book: in
chapter 2, in which a zoological illustration of various animals represents

queer community in a poster for the Tokyo International Lesbian and Gay Film Festival, and in chapter 3, in which *Sud pralad/Tropical Malady* (Apichatpong Weerasthakul, dir., 2004) blurs the boundary between human and tiger ghost in its climactic scene of incorporation/consummation. Indeed, the film's Thai-language title translates as "A Queer Animal."[52] We have discussed the position of queerness vis-à-vis the human–nonhuman binary and have asked what it means for queer culture to deploy visions of queer animality as pleasurable. These examples already demonstrate queer animality's variegated affective regimes. The festival poster is cute and light-hearted: it aims to evoke the pleasures of mixed community and the feeling of a space accessible to all. Apichatpong's tiger, by contrast, speaks to *jouissance* and loss of bodily integrity: the human-animal boundary is mutable, but it might be replaced by the sharper border between life and death. Here animality offers a beautiful and intense form of queer belonging that is mediated by the virtual spaces of cinema.

Animality as a space of queer belonging is suggested in the frequency of the fish tank in queer cinema. Fish tanks are a proximetric in which queers are represented as having an affinity for animals, and, more important, queer subjectivity is dispersed across the screen. As iconography, the fish tank suggests both freedom of movement and captivity, incomprehensible alterity and the ability to perceive the body in a radically new space. In the Filipino melodrama *Walang Kawala/No Way Out* (Joel Lamangan, dir., 2008), a fish tank provides a synecdochic figuration of the incarceration of young gays trafficked in Manila. In Li Yu's *Fish and Elephant* (2001), the fish tank is placed on the very edge of the frame as two lovers sit on the bed smoking. Nothing is centered, and peripheral vision offers a hint of what touching across categories might look like. Of course, there is a danger in reading animals as a metaphor for queer subjects. Mel Chen points to the "vivid links [that] continue to be drawn between immigrants, people of color, laborers and working-class subjects, colonial subjects, women, queer subjects, disabled people, and animals, meaning, not the class of creatures that includes humans but quite the converse, the class against which the (often rational) human with inviolate and full subjectivity is defined."[53] Given this history of linguistic and material violence, it makes sense to be wary of comparing queers to animals. Thinking of animality as a signifier of the limits of the universal subject raises again both the urgency and the limitation of human rights discourse for queer cinema.

The Vietnamese film *Hot boy nổi loạn và câu chuyện về thằng Cười, cô gái điếm và con vịt/Lost in Paradise* (Ngoc Dang Vu, dir., 2011), for example,

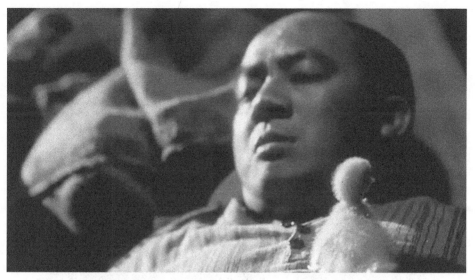

Fig. 5.9: *Lost in Paradise* links queerness to animality and social exclusion,

uses animals to signal an interest in Judith Butler's question of "who counts as human, and . . . whose lives count as lives."[54] The film intertwines the lives of several socially marginal characters: Khoi, a young gay man freshly arrived in Saigon from the country; Tranh, a female prostitute; and Cuoi, a mentally handicapped man who adopts a duckling. Cuoi is a social outsider who lives on a boat by the docks. He steals a duck egg and nurtures it until it hatches, at which point uplifting music accompanies his cries of joy. The film deploys sentimentality to pose a human rights version of intersectional and marginalized subjectivities: the disabled person who is close to nature, the prostitute with a heart of gold, and the naïve and penniless gay in the big city (contrasted with the evil gay) all have a connection that is routed through the duckling. For instance, Tranh defends the duck because she comes from the Mekong and was raised on a duck farm. Internal migration and poverty build a community among the queers, sex workers, and outcasts of Saigon, and the linkage of precarity and care is mobilized in the figure of the duckling. Cuoi lets the creature go with other ducklings in the river, but it returns to him in another sentimental moment. At the end of the film, however, Khoi returns to his hometown; Tranh is imprisoned; and the area habituated by male sex workers is turned into a mall. Only Cuoi's boat remains, as does his companion duck (figure 5.9). Queer life is erased, and animal life provides the sentimental happy ending denied to the queer characters.

Figs. 5.10–5.11: *Fish and Elephant* views its central couple through an elephant's point of view.

Chen argues that, despite the caveats, "animacy can itself be queer, for animacy can work to blur the tenuous hierarchy of human-animal-vegetable-mineral with which it is associated."[55] Queer animality, for him, offers a genre of queer animacy and enables us to see non-normative kinships between humans and animals. This more radical instance of queer animality finds a corollary in *Fish and Elephant*, which, as the title suggests, develops a subtle and extended discourse on the queer affiliations between human and nonhuman animals. Li's film extends both the fish and the elephant as vectors of queer relationality. Fish form a recurring index of the health of Qun and Ling's relationship: the fish tank is always visible in the frame, and one character says, "People who have fish are horny." When Ling is jealous, we see a dead fish floating on top of the tank. Later, the women make up and buy a new fish together. Looking after a fish is a vector of emotional labor that articulates both self-care and care for the other.

The elephant more actively mediates human-animal caring and queer desire. Qun works at the zoo and is a caretaker for an elephant. In a crucial scene in which Ling gives Qun her phone number, their reciprocity is mediated through a striking elephant point-of-view shot (what Fran Martin calls "another space").[56] We see their desire through nonhuman eyes (figures 5.10–5.11). Moreover, the elephant does not like pumpkin, only apples. She is picky and refined and prefers sweet fruit to ungainly vegetables. Her trunk searches out apples like a nonhuman lesbian phallus. The snuffling touch of the elephant's trunk stages a multidirectional embodied hapticity whereby the spectator can feel the shiny apples and the rough, warm caress of the extended extremity. But she can also feel Qun's quickened heartbeat as she accepts Ling's phone number. The sensations of happiness and desire are routed through animality and a queer scenario of care for the other. In *Fish and Elephant*, nonhuman nature is part and parcel of the life world of queer humanity.

The Queer Pastoral

Our final example continues to think about nonhuman environments, as well as proximity and touch. However, in proposing the pastoral as a queer register, it focuses on the relationship between human and nonhuman nature. Visualizing LGBT people in landscapes hitherto imagined as hetero- and gender-normative can constitute a bold political and aesthetic statement. We have already discussed the image of two men kissing in a rural lane in *Tropical Malady*, in which the combination of national flag, jungle setting, and same-sex desire placed queer Thailand on the world stage. In the queer pastoral, rural environments provide spaces for gender identities and sexualities to be reconfigured and for the nation and region to be reimagined. The pastoral as a literary and art-historical form takes as its subject the place of the human in nature. Neither sublime landscape nor human-centered portraiture, the pastoral speaks of the threshold between subject and object, the experience of being in the world, and the cultural and environmental politics of positionality. We argue that in recent queer cinema, pastoral landscapes are not mere temporary escapes from oppressive national cultures. Instead, rural environments nourish transformation, queerly upsetting the nature–culture binary and disrupting both dominant national geographies and world cinema exoticisms.

The clichéd version of queer life is urban, with the country a place to be escaped from, toward the cosmopolitan city. At the same time, dominant versions of visioning the global are also urban. As Ramaswami Harindranath puts it, "There is, thus, a widespread ignorance or neglect of non-metropolitan situations in metropolitan knowledge production on globalization that, ironically, claims to speak for and include the entire globe."[57] Scholars such as J. Jack Halberstam have questioned the class, race, and other hierarchies behind this assumption of the welcoming city, but discourses of queer urbanism remain prominent in the titles of studies such as *Queer Bangkok* and *Gay Bombay*.[58] As important as urban spaces have been to queer cultures, however, there is a countering impulse to locate queerness in the rural environment. We identify two presiding critical discourses on queers and landscape: the homoerotic pastoral and the queer eco-critical. The first discourse is evoked as part of a Western gay intellectual history, arguing that the pastoral form has been suffused with same-sex eroticism from its classical beginnings. Theocritus's *Idylls*, for instance, includes eroticized play among male shepherds.[59] Catriona Mortimer-Sandilands and Bruce Erickson, following David Halperin, have written about how both ancient and Romantic versions of the pastoral included male-male eroticism as a key aspect of nature's "innocent, corporeal plenitude."[60] They describe an influential canon of queerly legible pastoral writing that includes Walt Whitman and Henry David Thoreau, as well as a more marginal literary tradition of lesbian pastoral writing that includes Sarah Orne Jewett and Radclyffe Hall. This discourse enables a (mostly gay male) recuperation of a literary form, but it leaves open the theoretical problems of that form's representational systems. Who gets to frolic in the rural idyll, who labors on the land, and who is not even included in the picture? We will come back to these questions.

The second discourse on queers and nature is the emergence of queer eco-criticism, which seeks to remedy both eco-criticism's blind spot around questions of gender and sexuality and queer theory's blind spots on environmental politics. As Nicole Seymour has argued, queer theory along the lines of Lee Edelman's influential rejection of reproductive futurity forecloses on care for the future in a way that makes it hard to imagine queer environmentalism.[61] Meanwhile, for theorists such as Mortimer-Sandilands and Erickson, the dominant popular discourse of the urban queer focuses on the "pink pound" and imagines gay men as the ultimate consumers. In both cases, queers are imagined as the opposite of environmentalists.[62] These accounts of queerness have been critiqued from many perspectives—not all queers are middle-class, white, gay men with a lot of disposable income— and queer eco-criticism adds to this critique by proposing "the articulation of sexuality and nature as a form of eco-sexual resistance."[63] We suggest that a key part of reimagining queers as environmental stewards is considering queer cultures from a more global perspective, where we can find productive intersections of human and nonhuman nature.

In the analyses that follow, we try to draw out the promise of the queer pastoral as a cinematic form. Queer eco-criticism is not always attentive to questions of representation, but world cinema creates spaces that precisely conjure virtual environments. Thus, a film like the experimental short *Bruce Lee in the Land of Balzac* (Maria Thereza Alves, dir., 2007) imagines an abstract and transnational queer space by juxtaposing an image track of peaceful, "natural" French countryside with a dissonant soundtrack of Bruce Lee fighting. For Alves, a Brazilian filmmaker, European nature is rendered strange by its uncomfortable Others. (Something similar occurs with the entrance of ghosts as a more localized form of queer alterity into Apichatpong's northern Thai locations.) The pastoral thus is never simply a description of a natural setting; rather, it is a mode that imagines nature as a place of escape and pleasure, a utopia of sorts. What happens when the politics of that utopia are complicated, contested, and subverted? Queer pastorals link cinema's ability to imagine fantastical worlds, queer culture's investment in creating counter-publics, and eco-criticism's demand that we reimagine our human relationship to the natural environment. Queers upturn rhetorics of human dominance over nonhuman nature, often by refusing to take part in the nature–culture binary that has proved so destructive for both queer people and the world's ecology. In very different ways, these films articulate a queer nature in which queerness is embedded in local practices and imaginative spaces.

Pojktanten/She Male Snails (2012) is an experimental documentary by the Swedish director Ester Martin Bergsmark. The film is partly a documentary about the transgender activist and artist Eli Levén, but its use of nonhuman nature, rural spaces, and textural detail shifts emphasis from the informative to the immersive and back again. It elaborates a genderqueer aesthetic through textures of proximity, seepage, and transformation of nature, and its close-up shots of snow, forests, fruit, and textiles orient the spectator away from mastery of landscape images and toward sensations of proximity and intimacy. Nicole Seymour understands queer nature through texts that "explicitly link the queer to the natural world through an empathetic, ethical imagination," and *She Male Snails* stages empathy through constructions of cinematic intimacy and care.[64] Moreover, Timothy Morton has argued that the concept of "nature" historically has been a way to establish nationalism, to enforce racial and sexual identities, and to justify violence against the nonhuman environment.[65] *She Male Snails* subverts conventional nature discourse to conjure a radically genderqueer upsetting of this rhetoric.

The film's technology creates a sense of intimacy. As we discussed in relation to the work of Juan Suárez, the texture of the digital video image in *She Male Snails* creates queer intimacies through its use of low light and extreme close-ups on objects. This proximal intimacy is not simply a representation of queer-identified characters; it is, as our reading of Marks suggests, a queer mode of visuality. The film stages the encounter between the author and the director through extended sequences of the two of them in a bath together (figure 5.12). This breaks most conventions of documentary distancing and puts care for the body at the film's center. This care is markedly textural: Ester and Eli shave themselves and each other, and there is a series of close-up shots of foam on legs, shaving, and razor cleaning. We often do not know which body we are looking at— visual distance is replaced with extreme close-ups of isolated body parts, shots that are blurry in part or in whole, and moments of sharp focus that isolate swirls of soap on hairy legs. These intimate gendered grooming rituals recall the sugaring scene in *The Wedding Song*: close-ups of body parts turn skin and hair into oddly erotic textures that resist conventional deployments of the gaze.

Of course, this queer hapticity is not only visual but audiovisual. Sound— and, in particular, voice—is constructed from a close-up auditory perspective that correlates with the film's proximities of vision. *She Male Snails* extensively uses soft-spoken, closely miked voiceover and often offsets speaker and image so that it is unclear who is speaking. In the bathtub scenes, Ester

Fig. 5.12: *She Male Snails* repeatedly shows its protagonists Ester and Eli in a bath.

narrates the history of their relationship together, but we also hear Eli speaking in a similarly intimate tone—for instance, when proclaiming *sotto voce*, "One day, *pojktanten* will rule the world." Although context often makes clear who is speaking, it is not always immediately obvious, and the voices place the listener in a place that is at once intimate and undefined. Natural sounds create an echoing effect: at various moments throughout the film a subtle popping sound recurs, suggesting the crackling of melting snow. Even where the image track provides a longer perspective, the sound track keeps up close, attuned to the soundscapes of Nordic seasonal change. We are not always quite sure what we are hearing, so epistemological uncertainty is tethered to seeping sensual intimacy.

The film combines camp, artifice, gender play, dressing up, and ornamentation (aspects of queerness historically opposed to healthy, masculine nature) with a love for the outdoors, fruit, and fauna. We see one character, Sebastian, as a child and then as a teenager who likes make-up, jewelry, and pretty colors. What is striking is the film's linkage of this gender dissidence to a Nordic nature discourse (figure 5.13). Wild strawberries, mushrooms, and the titular snails abound. The mise-en-scène mixes a camp aesthetic of colorful, plastic, excessively feminine consumer objects with a Nordic aesthetic of being in nature and the sensations of the nonhuman and sublime. Nature and culture are destabilized through a register that privileges sensual touch

Fig. 5.13: In *She Male Snails*, Sebastian is closely associated with nature.

rather than one built on knowledge and visual mastery. Throughout the film, elements of colorful material make their way into nature, whether as ribbons in primary colors, paint on the grass and trees, or elaborated dragged-out figures in the landscape. As Pietari Kääpä puts it in a study of ecology in Nordic cinema, "The centrality of nature for Nordic film culture cannot be underestimated."[66] Nordic cultural discourses of human integration into the *miljø* (non-urban environment) have been used to evoke national identities and to shore up liberal environmental attitudes in the region, both of which have been placed under some critical pressure by eco-critical approaches.[67] Here, the idea of Nordic "nature" is rewritten as a queer structure of feeling.

Moreover, it is important that both nature and culture are genderqueer: snails are natural hermaphrodites, and the objects of everyday life can be resignified to revise or imaginatively reassemble genders (e.g., the baby harness that Ester turns into an elaborate costume for tramping in the countryside). Seymour proposes the category of "organic transgenderism" in which gender transition is at least a partly natural phenomenon, spontaneous and innate, without medical or cultural intervention.[68] In *She Male Snails*, the line between cultural and natural is blurred (figure 5.14), and the liberatory quality of trans subjectivity is about gendered embodiment that is at once natural and homespun. Thus, in one scene, Eli makes a costume from twigs and a plastic spine, foregrounding the homemade and the performative

Fig. 5.14: Nature and artifice are combined in *She Male Snails*.

as forms of self-making that fold nature explicitly into the reconfigured queer body. This trans subjectivity is not "natural" in an assimilationist sense. Rather, it opens a radical conversation between the subject and the natural world that deconstructs the normative biological body. The film's trans aesthetic insists on blurring the nature–culture binary, and it locates these blurred lines firmly in a northern European mytho-cultural sensorium.

Despite the transformative quality of the rural environment in *She Male Snails*, the pastoral can never quite feel utopian for the queer spectator. As Ingrid Ryberg puts it, the film refuses to resolve "a tension between self-realization and self-destructivity. A drive towards liberation and fulfillment is simultaneously a drive towards humiliation and unbecoming."[69] Concern for the safety of the queer child lingers through the film, and this anxiety blooms along with desire in the film's most dramatic scene: an ambiguously erotic encounter with nature. Sebastian hesitantly gets into an unseen man's car. In the woods, the man pushes a naked Sebastian into the trees and to their knees. He pulls their head back and plays a hunting knife down Sebastian's throat. Here, the immersive, up-close qualities of the film create a tension that is painful for viewers. Will this be another tragic story of transphobic violence? But instead, violence is reconfigured into a sublime erotics. The dominant man takes the knife and sticks it into a tree's bark. Replacing it with a metal spile, he pushes Sebastian's head forward so they can drink the sap that pours out. Sebastian is communing with Nordic nature in a direct way, drinking it in. A queer hapticity is here proximate to the most macho of Nordic nature myths. The liquid that pours out of the tree, into their mouth, and down their chest evokes urine or semen as much as it does sap, alluding to other scenarios of erotic exchange and dominance.

She Male Snails is not unique in its reimagining of queer bodies, natural substances, and sticky images. We see something oddly similar in the British filmmaker Campbell X's film *Fem* (2007), in which a femme lesbian with light-colored liquid pouring between her legs fools the viewer into thinking she is seeing urine, when, as the camera travels up the femme's body, we see she is pouring honey over herself. In the director's terms, the honey shot replaces the patriarchal money shot. In *My Dead Brain* (Sarah Stuve, dir., 2009), clichéd figures of femininity revise their own embodiment. A woman who is half Alice in Wonderland doll, complete with stuffing escaping from cloth legs, and a sexy naked robot woman watch raptly as they open their nonhuman bodies and see thick red blood pour over their transformed skin. Wet and sticky textures form a queer erotics in which things are not always what they seem: human and nonhuman nature combine promiscuously, and bodies are not so easily legible as normative regimes of gender might insist.

In Sebastian's case, though, the perversely pleasurable escape into nature is more than a little tinged with bodily danger: they nearly freeze getting back home naked in the snow. Jennifer Barker's idea of the visceral as a deeply embodied level of understanding and experiencing time is appropriate for thinking the strong responses that Sebastian's experience provokes in the spectator.[70] The sex scene in the woods creates a temporality of approaching violence and disaster, prompting visceral anxiety and fear in the queer spectator. When Sebastian is left naked by the roadside, their shivering prompts matching resonances of bodily cold and fragility, and we feel the sheer time they spend out in the cold. The extended temporality of danger and sensory deprivation in this scene breaks the rhythm of the film, which previously had developed a more languid queer temporality, moving promiscuously back and forth between presents and pasts; among Eli, Ester, and Sebastian; and between fiction and fact. The deep pangs of anxiety mixed with desire in the sex scene and its chilly aftermath shift the film's impetus toward loss and coming into being; it implies leaving pasts behind and bringing them with you. It proposes the subject as an impossible yet necessary work of transforming spaces and times.

Being in nature has different stakes for queer people, yet *She Male Snails* ends with a utopian natural tableau of Ester, Eli, and a group of friends relax-

Fig. 5.15: The ending of *She Male Snails* offers a utopian image of a welcoming trans community.

ing by the water, naked and unafraid (figure 5.15). As Butler comments on *Strella/A Woman's Way* (Panos Koutras, dir., 2009), another European trans film, it "opens up possibilities for modes of life which have no intelligible place in the heteronormative structures of kinship."[71] The final shot of *She Male Snails* is a Nordic nature scene par excellence, and it imagines a futurity in which genderqueer pojktanten do indeed rule the world.

Speaking much more clearly in an art-house/festival film aesthetic, *Papilio Buddha* (Jayan Cherian, dir., 2013) is set in southern India and juxtaposes the fetishistic "nature" desires of Jack, a gay white butterfly hunter, with a violently contested rural landscape. The film seems to set up a structure of neocolonial touristic pastoral, in which Jack experiences the Indian landscape as a series of views. Indeed, it draws the viewer in through this familiar (and immediately unsettling) point-of-view structure, in which the spectator is positioned alongside the clueless Jack, taking in India as a pastoral fantasy. This perspective closely relates to the history of picturesque looking relations, in which English aristocrats enjoyed landscapes designed to exclude precisely those who lived and worked in them. Raymond Williams famously argues that the pastoral works to mythologize the actual relations of property and labor in the landscape, and at first *Papilio Buddha* leverages this critique in terms of both racial and sexual hierarchies. Jack employs Shankar, a younger Indian man, as guide and lover. They embrace in bucolic nature, deep in a forested gully. Here nature in the form of butterflies seems to mediate a romanticized view of India, connoting at once the ethereal beauty of the insects and a fantasy of the heroic nineteenth-century scientist who collects specimens and adds to Western knowledge in the hostile environment of the wild and savage South. Shankar helps catch the butterflies, seeming in this opening scene to be entirely an accessory to Jack's self-aggrandizing mission. If Jack's view of India appears neocolonial, the place of queerness is from the start placed under critical question because it seems to exist only in the visual register of colonial fantasy. Is queerness imposed on this environment, or does it already exist here?

However, the film complicates this set-up, insisting that neither the actual nor the visual possession of this landscape is a simple matter. Gradually, another framework emerges for reading the landscape of Kerala—that of indigenous land rights—as the narrative shifts to focalize Shankar, who was previously viewed only as Jack's object of desire. He comes from a landless Dalit community who have lived in this area for centuries but are now regarded as squatting on government land. Shankar's father is a former communist and Dalit activist, and his friend Manju runs a school on the commune. Dalits have faced caste discrimination and political marginalization as a result of their landless status, and the film closely associates the violence done to them with environmental exploitation.[72] The film distributes violence across the land and the bodies of Dalit characters. Shankar is sexually tortured by the police, ostensibly for his illegal butterfly collection, but the film leaves open the possibility that he is disciplined extrajudicially for his homosexual relationship with a white man. Manju is brutally gang raped by a group of higher-caste men. The pastoral is repeatedly subjected to violence, a fall from grace that seems to posit a prelapsarian past. The film's dramatic conclusion is a scene in which the Dalits are driven out by the state; the entire community is dispossessed, and their land is turned over to modernizing forces.

Papilio Buddha reverses the colonial fantasy of the pastoral idyll, flipping the spectator's perspective from that of the wealthy white tourist to that of the marginalized community for whom the landscape is a contested place of labor and precarity, yet also a place of harmonious beauty. Whereas critique of the pastoral often makes simple contrast of false (aesthetic) beauty with true (material) politics, and thus rejects altogether the affective and political potential of the landscape image, *Papilio Buddha* moves the spectator through and beyond this version of what Sedgwick would call a paranoid reading. Instead, the film asks us to envision the Keralan environment as

Fig. 5.16: The Dalit activist Kallen Pokkudan plants mangrove in one of *Papilio Buddha*'s slow cinematic moments.

a space of contestation where perverse allegiances and desires are enabled. *Papilio Buddha*'s queer environmentalism is overtly intersectional: care for the Keralan landscape demands a radical caste critique, which is closely intertwined with a feminist response to the rape of Dalit women, a Marxist analysis of NGO culture, and queer attention to alternative structures of kinship and care. In a return to Mortimer-Sandilands and Erickson's queer eco-criticism, stewardship of the environment focalizes the film's queer representation. Those who nurture the environment are set visibly against those who exploit it. In constructing an indigenous pastoral, the film acknowledges awareness of the colonial dangers of the form, yet it returns to this dangerous register to queer it. It makes a claim on the beauty and value of the landscape by and for Dalits, women, queers, and non-Hindus, insisting that neither the white visitor nor the Hindu nationalist state owns its representation.

As it moves further into Shankar's world, *Papilio Buddha* unfolds a politically activist queer pastoral. Like *She Male Snails*, the film invests in indexical images of real places and real people, using profilmic spaces and material practices to give voice to the environment. Shankar's father is played by the real-life environmental activist Kallen Pokkudan, who works to save the mangrove forest (figure 5.16).[73] There is a kind of typage at work in the film's casting, as well as an engagement with the relationship between humans and the environment that is both material and metaphorical. We see Pokkudan planting in the river, and his movements and gestures as he interacts with the plants are deft and practiced, the result of a lifetime's experience. There are moments of slow-cinematic temporality in which the spectator spends time watching the movement of mangrove stalks, outside of any apparent narrative movement. These scenes provide a documentary view of a

Fig. 5.17: *Papilio Buddha* opens with Shankar framed against a dramatic landscape in long shot.

Fig. 5.18: In *Papilio Buddha*'s final sequence, the Dalit community is forced to leave their land.

traditional farming practice that does not exploit the ecosystem, at the same time embedding a radical process of image making that provides voice and agency for local activists inside the fiction.

Against this embedded, proximate point of view, *Papilio Buddha* also repeatedly constructs the landscape in long shot, placing the human figure as relatively tiny within a composed, nonhuman environment coded as beautiful. The film opens with Shankar embedded in a series of overwhelming landscape compositions (figure 5.17); he is part of the landscape and can move confidently within this landscape, but he is also dwarfed by it. At the outset, it is easy for the spectator to misread this distanced perspective as secure and comfortable. As the film progresses, it uses long shots to disclose the extent to which the Dalit characters who labor in the landscape are unprotected by it. Manju parks the taxi that she drives alongside some other drivers, and immediately the men surround her, threatening her with their physical presence. A high angle shot emphasizes threat, and the point of view suddenly embodies the male gaze in a pure form of hatred. When

Manju flees, we see another long shot of the landscape, with her taxi tiny in the frame. This sequence reminds the spectator of a different valence of human smallness in nonhuman nature: there is nobody to help Manju, and the next scene leads to her gang rape. Pastoral pleasure is destroyed by patriarchal violence, and as the narrative progresses, we see how the female body, the Dalit body, and the queer body bear the brunt of this exploitative system. Violence comes to suffuse the landscape in the final scenes, where the entire Dalit community is dispossessed. The final six minutes of the film consist of a series of long takes of people walking through a landscape in which they now have no place (figure 5.18). The dispossessed people and exploited landscape are paralleled, layering the film's staging of homophobic violence, gendered violence, state violence, and environmental destruction. This long sequence recapitulates the places we have been throughout the narrative as an exodus, staging the end of the pastoral in an image of loss and de-territorialization.

Although very different, the films discussed in this chapter propose forms of queer being in the world whose radical potential is activated in their modulation of the sensory. From melodramas and middlebrow historical dramas to activist documentary and experimental video, queer cinema redistributes the sensible to articulate the stakes of belonging in the world for queer people. Engaging with animals, landscapes, and historical spaces enables queer cinema to evoke affective experiences and politics of community that could not otherwise be so easily spoken. Siegfried Kracauer seems aware of the indeterminacy of nature in cinema, arguing in his canonical *Theory of Film*, "Natural objects, then, are surrounded with a fringe of meaning liable to touch off various moods, emotions, runs of inarticulate thoughts."[74] Across this chapter, we have attempted to take these unstable meanings and to delineate a space of queerness that hitches cinema's inherent abilities to register the sensate textures of the natural world to the geopolitically embedded life worlds of queers. Queer registers offer modes of resistance to the reactionary aesthetic regimes that claim to speak for global humanity.

THE EMERGENCE OF
QUEER CINEMATIC TIME

Stanley Kwan's film *Lan Yu* (2001) is a romantic tragedy set in China during and after the Tiananmen Square massacre. At the end of the film, after discovering that his lover Lan Yu has died, Handong drives in his car through Beijing. Slowing down, he looks out at a construction site and addresses Lan Yu: "Whenever I pass the site where you had the accident, I stop. But my mind is at peace because I feel that you never really left." From here, the film's theme song picks up, a melancholic ballad that provides a musical backdrop of longing to what seemingly is a continuous long take of the cityscape as it passes by the driver's side window of Handong's car. The already highly stylized film thus ends with its most audatious formal gesture. In his indispensable reading of the film, David Eng describes the three-minute long shot as "an elliptical and open ending: the long and continuous flickering blur of the Beijing cityscape."[1] Eng explicitly connects this formal bravura to both queer longing and the geopolitics of late capitalism:

"In constituting homosexuality's expressive desire as a formal problem of visuality—of a queer space and time—Kwan's film presents a battery of aesthetic devices instituting a critical reevaluation of political form: the space of disappearance and emergence; the empty, homogenous time of capitalism; the unreflective march toward 'the end of history.'"[2] Thus, Eng insists that the formalism of *Lan Yu*'s imagery operates as a means of disarticulating hegemonic order.

Here, Eng sets a crucial precedent for reading the formal mechanisms of global queer cinema, and we find particularly compelling the idea that queer temporality contains the capacity to resist the certainty of a neoliberal globalized future. Looking again at the formal features of the final sequence, we find that *Lan Yu dis*integrates conventional cinema time to disaggregate queer subjectivity from capitalist space. The sequence begins with Handong driving slowly so we can see the back and forth between the flat planes of roadside barriers (which block vision) and the spaces between the barriers (which allow sight of a world in depth). As he speeds up, our view begins to fragment space more rapidly, producing a flickering effect, an intermittent motion in which the wholeness of the world exists in the background and in glimpses, as with experimental cinema's appropriation of proto-cinematic effects. Foreground and background move at differing rhythms, as if representing two disjointed temporalities. Sometimes we experience the background as a stubbornly still view. At other times it looks like a slide show of snapshots, flashing different glimpses of the urban landscape. The lack of a smooth, continuous visual narration creates a radical form of ellipsis in which, like the ubiquitous metal panels we see at the beginning, the flow of time appears corrugated or even perforated.

The narrative motivation for the blurring, flickering foreground is clearly Handong's mourning. This formalization of warped time expresses an emotional state of loss, in which the non-synchrony between incoherent foreground and representational background registers how queer longing infects our temporal relationship to modernity's spaces. After about three minutes, Handong's car slows, and the flickering stops. For a moment, we have an unfettered view of the roadside, consisting of only an unremarkable pile of dirt with a dense urbanity lurking behind it. We have barely enough time to register the contents of the shot, then the screen turns black. Seconds later the film reveals its final shot: sepia-tone slow-motion footage of Handong embracing Lan Yu. Time again acquires a warped character, and with the switch to video, the image takes on the quality of a document from the recent past. Queer longing corrupts the spatial articulation of time in *Lan Yu*'s conclusion, turning the film over to visual discontinuities that undo the idea that queerness is late capitalism's handmaiden.

The variegated quality of time that queer desire brings to this film's images will resonate across this chapter. We examine queer cinematic temporalities through textual operations such as anachronism, asynchrony, slowness, inattention, excision, and ellipsis. We consider these inflections of queer temporality to be aligned with what José Muñoz has called "the project of thinking beyond the moment and against static historicisms," which, for him, "resonates with Judith Halberstam's work on queer temporality's relation to spatiality, Carla Freccero's notion of fantasmatic historiography, Elizabeth Freeman's theory of temporal drag, Carolyn Dinshaw's approach to 'touching the past,' and Jill Dolan's recent book on utopian performance. I would also align it with Lisa Duggan's critique of neoliberal homonormativity."[3] We would add to this list film scholars such as David Eng, Bliss Cua Lim, Song Hwee Lim, and Jean Ma, whose reading of Tsai Ming-liang's "queer politics of time" insists on the cinematicity of this critique. Ma describes "a shift in the poetics of queer cinema," and writes "in the spirit of a queer politics that strives to envision alternative habitations of time that might enable different modes of identification and affiliation."[4] These projects of reimagining queer time are also critiques of historicism. *Lan Yu* is also overtly a history film, suggesting that the politics of an infamous moment of political violence and its subsequent censoring are best narrated through queer desire and what it does to time. Temporal disorientation, then, demands to be considered alongside how historicity is narrated. *Lan Yu* supplies the impetus for this chapter because it so vividly proclaims that aesthetics not only can reclaim a space for queers in history but can also reconfigure the subject's relationship to the past.

Utopian Historicities

We find a vivid example of this subjective reconfiguration in the temporal discontinuities of *Proteus* (2003), a film co-directed and co-written by Jack Lewis and John Greyson in an unusual cross-cultural collaboration. The film takes place in eighteenth-century South Africa and is based on archival records of a sexual relationship between a Khoi herdsman Claas Blank and a white Dutch sailor Rijkhaart Jacobsz when the two men were imprisoned on Robben Island. The film is, in the first instance, a cross-cultural co-production between Canada and South Africa; it is also the first gay-themed film made in South Africa after the end of apartheid. But rather than providing a conventional historical drama of gay life in the distant past, *Proteus*

Fig. 6.1: Anachronism functions in *Proteus* to link colonial South Africa with the apartheid era.

proposes a queer approach to the passage of time and our relationship to what came before us: temporality and historicity are mutually imbricated in its disjunctive elaboration of cinematic time.

The film's most visible break with conventional historicity is its overt use of anachronism, a tactic in conversation with other queer filmmakers who have used it to destabilize the heterocentric domination over time telling and history making. Isaac Julien uses it in *Looking for Langston* (1989) to assert African American histories. Derek Jarman consistently deploys anachronism to provoke, most spectacularly in the juxtaposition in *Edward II* (1991) of ACT UP protesters alongside figures from English history, reading Christopher Marlowe's verse as a manifesto for the revolutionary potential of queer love. In *Proteus*, anachronism operates to link colonial South Africa with the apartheid era, overlaying the imprisonment of mostly black workers in the 1800s with that of antiapartheid activists in the 1960s. The historical diegesis is productively seeded with signifiers of the 1960s, including modern buildings, cars, and a policeman with a mustache, wearing sunglasses. Blank is sentenced to ten years of hard labor on Robben Island for being disrespectful to a Dutch citizen, and from the outset the prison is visually linked through anachronism with the modern incarceration there of Nelson Mandela (figure 6.1). Roger Hallas makes clear the boldness of this linkage: Robben Island has become a memorial space for the antiapartheid struggle,

Fig. 6.2: *Proteus* superimposes visually rich images of historical documents with time-lapse sequences of the protea flower.

so to link it with homosexuality is to inscribe queerness into the symbolic heart of the new South Africa.[5] *Proteus* insists that queerness is central to the national imaginary—and, indeed, to the racial systems of colonialism and capitalism from which it has struggled to escape.

This anachronistic style is also visually luxuriant, embracing multiple and interpenetrating subjective capacities, spaces, and temporalities. The opening sequence evokes this decadence in its layering of images: laid-over shots of historical documents are superimposed time-lapse sequences of the sugarbush or protea flower—South Africa's national flower—rising up and blooming (figure 6.2). This juxtaposition first invokes conventional historiography and its cinematic counterpart, proposing the legal documents as a kind of referential accounting of the past and the turning of their pages as a mode of linear historical narrative. In tension with this documentary historicity, the blooms suggest a spectacular and queer flowering. Their bright colors and garish video superimposition are reminiscent of a pop video from the 1980s, and the non-realist speed of their blooming sets up the temporality of queerness as both in sync with and against nature. But, of course, this temporality is ideologically overdetermined. In our first view of Blank, he is running in slow motion: the opposite of the protea flowers, his queerness traps him in a colonial gaze that forecloses on proper human movement. The problem of temporality, then, becomes also a problem of historicity. History is written and rewritten through movement—that is, change captured its most basic form. The first dialogue scene presents three court reporters dressed as secretaries in a 1960s style debating how to translate the Dutch sentence, "I fucked him up the arse." How, the film asks, can we translate sexual acts and queer lives across centuries? Its response is not transhistorical but dialectical.

Proteus constructs its same-sex love story in relation to a discourse on Western scientific knowledge and its implication in racial and sexual oppression. The film sets Blank in relation to a British botanist, Virgil Niven, who asks Blank to tell him the Khoisan names for plants. Blank refuses the role of native informant, telling Niven lewd words instead of proper names, and later inserting the sugarbush plant into traditional folktales to demonstrate useful knowledge and thus keep his safe job with Niven. Meanwhile, Niven is a student of Carl Linneus and works to identify plants within the binomial system that imposes Western taxonomies on South African flora. As Niven explains to Blank, Linneus also provides a racial taxonomy in which Africans are indolent and Hottentots form a bridge between humans and the lower orders. This racialist taxonomy links eighteenth-century scientific knowledge to the systems of racial and sexual hierarchy that lead to apartheid. *Proteus* emphasizes how both the seemingly benign horticultural nomenclature and the obviously violent racializing taxonomy derive from the same epistemology. It also insists that these discursive fields are shot through with homoerotic tension. Immediately after telling Blank that he considers him less than human, Niven gently picks a feather out of Blank's hair, opening up a space of queasy affinities, articulating racist science to queer intimacy. How can we read intimacy between a white man and a black man in eighteenth-century South Africa? As in the apartheid era and, indeed, today, *Proteus* proposes, we cannot read this relationality outside the histories and languages of racial classification. The film's subtitle, "Based on a True Story," is presented in three languages—English, Dutch, and Khoisan—in a self-reflexive play with cross-cultural collaborative authorship and systems of linguistic power.

In *Proteus*, these corrupt systems of knowledge become legible as the mendacious basis for the dominant narratives of both science and history. The film imagines that Linneus stole Niven's work on the protea and passed it off as his own, just as Niven appropriated Blank's tribal knowledge. Nomenclature is corrupt, an exercise of power at all levels. But Blank's queer, black, South African mythology remains nestled invisibly at the core of botanical science, as does Niven's unreported queer labor. This pattern metaleptically repeats the film's central rhetoric, in which the queer relationship between Blank and

Fig. 6.3: *Proteus* proposes an alternate vision of queer kinship and belonging.

Rijkhaart blooms outside the purview of official systems of knowledge, only intersecting with dominant History in its annihilation.

Proteus works from several documents that name Blank and Rijkhaart, all pertaining to their incarceration, trial, and execution. It is one of the truisms of African American writing that one of the few times that enslaved people appear in official records is court documents or chattel records, and this problem of historical recording applies also to the South African history of colonial forced labor. Neither Rijkhaart nor, especially, Blank would be recorded in the genealogical records that could conceive their status as human and their relationships as legitimate. Orlando Patterson demonstrates that slavery's social death is enforced by the breaking of kinship, and *Proteus* illustrates this violence brutally in the scene in which Blank is confronted with a coin purse made from the skin of his mother's breast.[6] The material destruction of social bonds is repeated in history's erasure, but *Proteus*'s originality is to imagine same-sex intimacy blossoming as an alternative source of kinship and belonging (figure 6.3). Rijkhaart and Blank are inevitably killed, but for ten years they maintain an intimate relationship, despite their enslaved conditions of existence. In a utopian fantasy, Rijkhaart imagines that when they are released from jail, he and Blank can acquire a farm and live together by pretending to be master and servant. Such an escape can never happen, but what *Proteus* does make visible is a global politics of queer intimacy, a form of kinship that rejects colonial modes of looking, knowing, and being.

Speaking more broadly, Chris Gittings describes Greyson's oeuvre as "a queer troubling of the tyrannical, heterosexist, and racialized masculinities of empire building," and *Proteus* is certainly all of that.[7] The film stages queer intimacies that pose questions about contemporary geopolitics and that disallow the liberal empathy typical of historical drama to provoke instead experiences of radical alterity. Lewis and Greyson mediate historical and geographical alterity through an erotics that both aestheticizes and politicizes difference, and they turn to cinematic form to animate queer modes of being in the world. We have seen how *Proteus* plays with anachronism and decadence to critique dominant orders of knowledge and power. But more than upsetting dominant racial and sexual histories, the film derails scientific conceptions of natural temporality. The spectator knows in advance that Rijkhaart's plan is a chimera and the two men will never reach his imagined future together. His homonormative progress narrative of property ownership is doomed to failure, but their relationship *can* and does make sense in reverse. The film is constructed as a backward glance: a revision of history that repeats for and in the present and a utopian past that can only be constructed outside and in spite of linear history and its ordering of past and present. This intimacy exists in historical interstices, made beautiful by disjuncture, contamination, the space between the articulated and the lived. The biological temporality of botanical blossoming, reproduction, and death in most films would insist on heterosexual genetic inheritance as the structure of time. But *Proteus* explicitly refuses this logic, showing the protea flower closing again, keeping its queer beauty intact.

These stylistic moves, we propose, help outline contemporary queer cinema's persistent troubling of time. Dissident temporality has been central for recent queer theory, from J. Jack Halberstam's discussion of the emergence of queer temporalities at the end of the twentieth century to Elizabeth Freeman's account of the chrono-normativity enforced by hetero-normative capitalism.[8] Against this force, Freeman proposes "deviant chronopolitics" as a queer mode of imagining "relations across time and between times," and Muñoz articulates the desire for a queer utopian consciousness that is necessarily yet to come.[9] Cinema forms a rich corpus of texts that are able to articulate the non-normative shapes of queer lives, but we argue that it provides more than a series of examples. Cinema's construction of virtual times and spaces enables a political analysis of temporality alongside an affective encounter with queer desires and losses. Moreover, cinema as an institution creates pockets of queer space, time, and experience, delimited by systems of homophobia and repression, elaborating a fractured archive of queer history. In the rest of this chapter, we interrogate the disjunctive temporalities of contemporary queer cinema, following the ripples of queer time across the surfaces of world cinema.

Cinematic Time and the Problem of Hetero-synchrony

It is by now a standard film studies tenet to identify heterosexuality at the core of the Hollywood text. Richard Maltby says, in reference to the Production Code, "Movies have happy endings because part of their function is to affirm and maintain the culture of which they are part. . . . The fact that 85% of Hollywood movies feature heterosexual romance as a main plot device should be seen in light of this regulatory framework. If the movie theatre is a site in which cultural and ideological anxieties can be aired in the relative safety of a well-regulated fiction, we might well ask why we need quite so much reassurance that heterosexual romance is supposed to end happily."[10] Conventional narratives do not simply provide a venue for heterosexual content: heterosexuality is also a significant means by which movies take form. Looking back at David Bordwell, Janet Staiger, and Kristen Thompson's influential descriptions of classical Hollywood cinema, we find the centrality and specificity of heterosexuality articulated in a manner so overt that it is almost denaturalizing for a text written in the early 1980s (especially given the affinities and omissions of Bordwell's later work). For these authors, heterosexuality appears deeply embedded in the narrative structures of Hollywood, giving temporality form through the operations of causality, expectation, and even suspense. They write, "Heterosexual romance is one value in American society, but that value takes on an aesthetic function in the classical cinema (as, say, the typical motivation for the principal line of action)."[11] Moreover, heterosexuality appears as an exemplary insistence for Bordwell, Staiger, and Thompson of how cinema and culture intersect at the level of form—in other words, how social values determine the aesthetic system governing narrative. *Classical Hollywood Cinema* is not a work of queer theory, but it is unexpectedly clear about the role played by heterosexuality in structuring film form.

It is fairly easy to see how linearity and closure are defined by heterosexual consummation. Indeed, some crucial work in queer film studies has developed this line of thinking.[12] Thomas Waugh has argued that gay narratives tend toward open-endedness, displacement, and deferral instead of classical closure.[13] Homay King argues that Andy Warhol's films "make activities that fall outside the logic and temporal progression of heterosexual reproduction into ends or works in their own right."[14] For King, as for Lynn Spiegel, Warhol's refusal of linear and goal-oriented narrative temporality is part of what makes him so important for queer and feminist moving-image scholarship. Spigel regards Warhol as having a queer relationship to televisual time, including the open and endless structure of the soap opera.[15] Taking a more popular corpus of texts, Sara Ahmed has explored the ways in which queers are oriented neither to straight lines of narrative nor to those of life. To be queer is to divert from straight lines, and where queers are forced into classical narrative structures, the results tend to be unhappy.[16] We can see these textual shapes in some of the films we have considered thus far: post-Warholian non-narrative or anti-linearity can be found variously in Ryan Trecartin's videos and *Pojktanten/She Male Snails* (Ester Martin Bergsmark, dir., 2012), and unhappy queers are visible in the classical narrative structures of *Common Gender* (Noman Robin, dir., 2012) and *Three Veils* (Rolla Selbak, dir., 2011).

Linearity and closure are important terms, but we argue that the dissident moves of postclassical world cinema expose another formal structure of conventional films whose systematization of meaning depends upon a heterosexist logic. This structure is narrative synchronicity, or what we call "heterosynchrony": the pleasure of bringing together in harmony several disparate elements, in a coordination of visibly opposing forces, against all odds. As the voiceover wryly intones in the indie rom-com *(500) Days of Summer* (Marc Webb, dir., 2009), "If Tom had learned anything, it was that you can't attribute great cosmic significance to a simple earthy event. Coincidence. That's all anything ever is. Nothing more than coincidence. Tom had finally learned there are no miracles. There is no such thing as fate. Nothing was meant to be. He was sure . . . he was pretty sure." Of course, linearity and closure are not unrelated to heterosynchrony. It is what they aim to orchestrate, and when heterosynchrony occurs, it makes progress pleasurable and provides evidence of closure. Heterosynchrony is crucial to recognize because it remains a prominent mode of organizing meaning in postclassical cinema across both popular and art films. This is true even though many postclassical films do not initially appear to adhere to linear continuity as closely as those that follow the classical Hollywood model. For instance, some films that trade explicitly on their heterosynchronic narrativity include *Eternal Sunshine of the Spotless Mind* (Michel Gondry, dir., 2004), *Go* (Doug Liman, dir., 1999), and *Pulp Fiction* (Quentin Tarantino, dir., 1994). The popular art-house film *Le fabuleux destin d'Amélie*

Poulin/Amélie (Jean-Pierre Jeunet, dir., 2001) is an excellent non-Hollywood example of a heterosynchronic film.

Amélie draws overt parallels between a narrative parable of human intimacy, on the one hand, and a thematic exploration of the photograph's ability to mediate human relations, on the other. Its style has provoked lively debate: many film scholars have disparaged *Amélie* for the disingenuousness of its images, most notably Dudley Andrew, who has called the film "an unctuous feigning of spontaneity."[17] Elsewhere, Rosalind Galt has offered an alternative reading of the film's prettily composed images, linking negative critical responses in France to a rejection of feminine aesthetics.[18] In the context of our current argument, however, the digitally manipulated visuality of the film—including its speeding up of motion, stripping the image of less important details, amplifying certain colors—is bothersome not as a false homage to the French New Wave or as a snub to cinema's indexical realism, but for how it is used to express the *timeliness* of heterosexuality and to endow the consummation of heterosexuality with an almost divine grace. Whereas Galt contrasted the negative response to feminine romance in *Amélie* with the positive critical reception of Jeunet's more conventionally masculine *Delicatessen* (1991), in this regard the films are strikingly similar. The comedic climax of *Delicatessen* comes when all of the actions in a boardinghouse line up *in time* with the rhythms of a straight couple having sex in a squeaky bed. Heterosexuality orchestrates cinematic temporality, and all events happen in perfect narrative time when they synchronize hetero relationality.

From the earliest montage sequences of *Amélie*, the film installs a heterosynchronic logic at a "cellular" level (figure 6.4). In a rapid narration of the protagonist's early life, we begin with a sperm entering an egg, posing heterosexual reproduction as the very prerequisite for the diegesis. The voiceover intones, "*At the same moment*, a sperm with one X chromosome made a dash for an egg in his wife Amandine" (emphasis added). The bilious presentation of wife-as-biological-receptacle is part and parcel of a just-in-time narrative delivery. As the narrative develops, the humor in Amélie's character resides in her perceptive ability to make connections missed by others. So although it appears to present examples of asynchrony, of events not lining up, the film does not see these as something to be resolved, like fixing a broken clock or missing an appointment because of a traffic jam. The actual asynchrony of randomness, digression, and loss is invisible in *Amélie*; it is not useful, relevant, or reproductive. Asynchrony does not matter in the world of *Amélie* because synchronicity always comes to save the day.

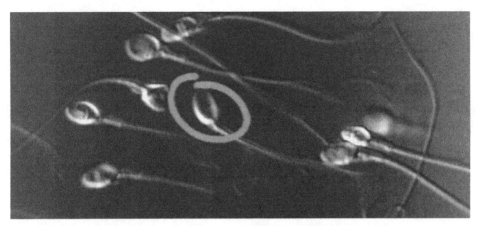

Fig. 6.4: Heterosynchrony in *Amélie* links narrative to the timeliness of reproductive heterosexuality.

Amélie arrives at the exact right moment to help the blind man cross the street, drops her perfume stopper in the exact right place to find the hidden box of memories. Synchronicity gives meaning to an otherwise random set of circumstances and carries with it an ideologically weighted inevitability, a sexual destiny.

The film's charms depend on quirky individualism: Amélie the character loves the feeling of lentils in her hands and interferes mischievously in her colleagues' love lives. But *Amélie* the film explores singularity, the accidental, and the quotidian as a means of emphasizing the sublime qualities of hetero reproduction, the mystical power of genetic variation, and the divine justice that governs chance. Attention to small details and chance meetings allow the mysteries of life to take hold. The quest for a complete self comes to fruition in the wholeness achieved in a union with a person of the opposite sex. Thus, the apparently spontaneous and serendipitous in Amelie's life become meaningful in loving contact; the randomness of life is disambiguated in the opposite sex's touch. The film's complex array of quotidian events, such as the dropping of a photo album, a train crash, and a misconstrued comment turn out to be orchestrated in the name of hetero union. Here, heterosexual desire appears as the force that synchronizes contingency. It gives form to life.

Amélie makes visible the emergent heterosynchronics of postclassical cinema. It does not always tell time with classical Hollywood continuity. In fact, we can associate its temporal structure less with standard cinematic time than with what we might call an intensified synchronicity. The intensified continuity that Bordwell has described as central to postclassical cinema is matched with multiplying forms of narrative synchrony, all of which organize meaning through orchestrating diverse forces into harmony.[19] This duplication of forms is self-reflexively about reproducing reproduction. *Amélie*'s obsession with synchrony is replete with reproductive teleology, a heterosexual cosmology in which straight intercourse enacts a special kind of accident, resulting in a genetic symphony of sorts. This is a kind of popularized iconography of quantum mechanics, in which the interconnectedness of matter, movement, and the meteorological are all organized by heterosexual desire, underwritten by its biological reproductive imperative. Contemporary cinema is anxious about this linkage. Where *Amélie* reiterates heteronormative fantasies of reproduction, Jackie Stacey uncovers in science-fiction fantasies of cloning the cinematic underbelly of this compulsion to formalize reproduction as the sexual encounter of gender difference and biological variance. The threat in these films comes in the form of what Stacey names "the queering of biology."[20]

The sperm-and-egg opening is telling in this regard, for *Amélie*'s view of sex is entirely reproductive. Sexual diversity is dismissed by the film as decadent, boring, and a waste of time. The sex shop where Nino works carries little erotic charge. Indeed, it has no mystique, and the dingy space narratively connotes only boredom and lack of interest. This absence of desiring sexuality is notable in a film that focuses so insistently on creating a sexual relationship. This apparent contradiction reveals how heterosynchronics tend to be romantic or reproductive rather than pleasurable, so that in *Amélie* all desiring sex is ultimately aberrant. It is a highly conservative vision of sexuality that reminds us of the recurring importance of feminist sexual politics to queer analysis. However, such heterosynchronics do not go uncontested, and even the most classical of films can offer moments of queer asynchrony. In *Some Like It Hot* (Billy Wilder, dir., 1959) the narrative transformation of apparently chance encounters into trajectories of heterosexual reproduction is famously uncertain: "Nobody's perfect." When Sugar goes on her first date with Junior (a.k.a. Joe, a.k.a. Josephine), he says, "Do you mind going backward? It might take a little longer." She responds, "It's not how long it takes. It's who's taking you."

Queer Asynchrony

In Dudley Andrew's description of the phases of world cinema, the global phase is signaled by its aesthetic embrace of postponement, non-synchrony, and dislocation. Andrew argues that even in the highly competitive contemporary landscape of screen media, cinema continues to stand out for its ability to provide audiences with a perspective on being in the world, and that account of being in the world is characterized by delay, deferral, and incompleteness. He writes, "In this society of the spectacle, there happily remain films that, while situated in one place and one time, reach viewers elsewhere, all situated differently, all out of phase with themselves and with each other."[21] The intimacies that most move us in *Chun gwong cha sit/Happy Together* (Wong Kar-wai, dir., 1997), for example, are those found not in a lovers' embrace but most exuberantly in the experiences of being out of phase. We might say Wong Kar-wai's poetics invest deeply in the experiences of non-synchrony and dislocation. These experiences form the emotional, experiential, and thematic core of the film. This is arguably what is most queer about *Happy Together*. Along similar lines, Barbara Mennel cites Seung-hoon Jeong's reading of Apichatpong Weerasethakul's films, in which the narrative of the gay couple "rejects expectations of 'romantic progression' " in favor of what Jeong calls "multilayered temporality" and "the postmodern synchronicity of non-synchronous times."[22] In fact, we argue that queer texts are often marked by a troubled temporality in which non-synchronous narrativity throws a wrench in the gears of heterosynchronics. If heterosynchrony manages dominant forms of narrative pleasure, then queer structures of feeling simmer in less synchronous texts.[23]

We have already seen one model of asynchrony in Lewis and Greyson, where anachronism provides a radical refusal of historical linearity, forcing disparate temporalities up against one another and encouraging the present to contaminate the past. Peter Limbrick describes another political version of what he terms "asynchronicity" in the Palestinian filmmaker Kamal Al-jafari's *The Roof* (2006), a film that, he argues, "suggests that the spatializing colonial logic that organizes Palestinians within Israel is also temporal in its practice, and that it queers Palestinians in relation to the normative time of the state."[24] Drawing both on Jasbir Puar to link queerness to a geopolitics of racialization and state violence and on Freeman's insistence that chrono-politics is used to contain populations through biopolitical temporal mechanisms, Limbrick understands asynchrony both as a historical condition ("Palestinians as anachronistic to the modern state of Israel") and as a queer cinematic response.[25] The Lebanese Australian filmmaker Fadia Abboud's short film *In the Ladies' Lounge* (2007) makes a similar claim on a radical historical imaginary. The film's fiction centers on a real historical document: an old photograph of two Lebanese women in masculine suits. The film reconstructs a temporal and spatial continuity in the potential for lesbian

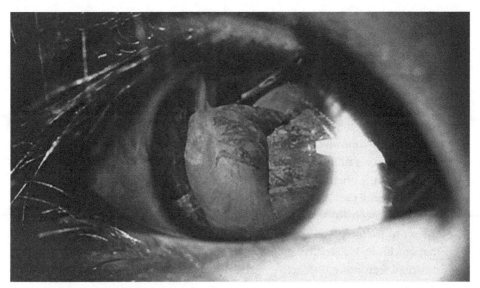

Fig. 6.5: Temporal distortion is attached to subjectivity in *Spider Lilies*.

image making between past and present, the Middle East and the diaspora.[26] In these examples, queer asynchrony forms an overt resistance to national narratives, but it is also located in modes of narration that more subtly decouple same-sex intimacies from dominant forms of cinematic time.

The Taiwanese lesbian director Zero Chou's films repeatedly stage temporality in ways that preclude heterosynchronous orchestrations of time, place, and action (figure 6.5). Chou's *Ci qing/Spider Lilies* (2007) represents lesbian love, but the queerness of that love is something that the film admits is difficult to describe in the language of narrative cinema as we know it. The film centers on a young woman called Jade, who works as a model for a webcam porn company and has been in love with a butch tattoo artist named Takeko since she was very young. After some years apart, Jade meets Takeko once more, but Takeko seems not to remember her. Jade and Takeko have uneven and conflicting access to the past, even though they appear to be invested in the importance of memory. (For instance, Takeko keeps a tattoo journal as a routine practice of accounting for day-to-day events.) The two women do not seem to share key memories of their sexual history together. Any past queer intimacies have been absented from personal history, and queer love leads to a disjointed present in which their affections cannot seem to take hold. Their temporality seems impossible, but, as Lauren Berlant suggests, "Out-of-synchness is not only a drama of negativity but also sociality's great promise."²⁷ Throughout the film they continue to pursue each other without a sense of a shared past or future.

In an expansive reading of Chou as a lesbian auteur, Patricia White indicates that *Spider Lilies* pushes its play with temporality "to the point of confusion."²⁸ Since Jade and Takeko are only a few years apart in age, it makes no sense for Takeko to have forgotten Jade completely. Moreover, in a film that is centrally about memory and its loss (another character suffers from amnesia), the confusing mismatch of Jade's and Takeko's recollections is not accidental but, rather, a central feature of the film's narrativity. This sense of confusion is crucial. In a way, Chou's film might suggest a temporality that is no more radical than Tom Cruise's postapocalyptic sci-fi action film *Oblivion* (Joseph Kosinski, dir., 2013), in which characters' memories are subject to technological alteration. However, *Spider Lilies* makes us aware that synchrony is a structuring device that we have come to expect and that its denial feels more disjunctive to the spectator than the average cyborg/replicant plot twist.

The film refuses what Bordwell, Staiger, and Thompson describe as "temporal integration," a term they borrow from E. H. Gombrich to define "the process of fusing the perception of the present, the memory of the past, and expectations about the future."²⁹ Temporal integration, for these scholars, is the conventional film's overarching framework that allows the viewer to navigate time and invest in causality's telos: "[It] permits the classical viewer to integrate the present with the past and to form clear-cut hypotheses about future narrative events."³⁰ In the narrated memories of queer intimacy in *Spider Lilies*, time refuses to serve in this way as "the vehicle for causality." To understand why this might be so, we turn to Fran Martin's account of the "female homoerotic imaginary" in Chinese public cultures and, in particular, what she describes as the memorial mode of popular narrative. Martin contends, "The memorial narrative of same-sex love between young women proliferates endless repetitions of itself precisely because the social ban on adult lesbianism means that this particular love story cannot be granted closure."³¹ Jade can remember her girlhood love for Takeko, but where closure (narrative, social, corporeal) is not possible in the present, temporal coherence begins to break down.

In fact, *Spider Lilies* never fully clarifies the status of the relationship it depicts in terms of the diegesis or character motivation. Takeko's intermittent amnesia troubles any romantic teleology, and the film remains unclear about whether a scene depicting the two women having sex is a fantasy, a memory, or a reunion. Whatever is consummated in this scene is undermined by a beacon of non-synchrony: in contradistinction to the hetero cosmology of *Amélie*, *Spider Lilies* features a dramatic shot of the moon turning orange and apparently crashing out of the sky. In *Spider Lilies* we have an iconography and narrative structure that directly oppose *Amélie*'s cosmology of grace and serendipity. Chou's film presents us with a *dis*integrating narrative, in which desire and time are unhitched from what Lee Edelman calls "reproductive futurity" and, instead, speak to what Bliss Cua Lim has proposed as a postcolonial cinematic resistance to homogenous time.[32] *Spider Lilies* reveals that the representability of queer intimacy is inextricably linked to cinema's rendering of time. What is so revealing about the film's temporal disjunctures is that its erotics and the affection of Takeko and Jade's relationship are nonetheless clearly offered to the audience. Intimacy persists for us as it remains unsustainable for the film's characters. Thus, the formalism of *Spider Lilies* trains the viewer to see how temporal *dis*integration allows queer desire to present itself. In fact, it is the prerequisite for queer intimacy to appear.

Chou's next feature, *Piao lang qing chun/Drifting Flowers* (2008), presents an even more radical experiment with loosening desire from narrative time. In doing so, it indicates how contemporary queer filmmakers might respond to the trend toward intensified synchronicity. *Drifting Flowers* seems at first glance to set up the kind of intensified synchronicity familiar in postclassical art films such as *Amores perros* (Alejandro González Iñárritu, dir., 2000). It weaves together three stories, each separate but with characters who intersect in a way that, in a conventionally synchronous film, would create a sense of a singular, all-connected narrative world. For instance, the protagonists of the first story, Jing and Diego, are musicians who appear briefly in the second story as performers at the wedding of Lily and Yen. Diego and Lily recur as young lovers in the third story, which happens narratively years before the first one. However, *Drifting Flowers* upsets this sense of synchrony with a series of interstitial scenes in a train, in which characters meet out of time. On the train, some characters appear to have aged, and others have not. Diego exists alongside the elderly version of Lily, even though they have been established as the same age. Refuting the train's metaphorical history of standing in for causal linkage and unidirectional journeys, these train scenes disrupt any sense of a univocal diegetic temporality (figure 6.6). Instead, they figure a lesbian desiring time outside of narratives of loss.

In one way, *Drifting Flowers* is more queer than *Spider Lilies*: it features self-identified lesbian and gay characters, and it deals with LGBT social issues such as familial expectations of marriage, lesbian parenting, AIDS, and

Fig. 6.6: *Drifting Flowers* places characters on a train that seems out of time and out of sync.

elder care. But its queer style emerges in the simultaneous construction and breakdown of these stories, in the offset temporalities that, as with *Spider Lilies*, prompt moments of spectatorial uncertainty. For White, again, "This convergence of the film's multiple temporalities may suggest a disregard for historicizing Taiwan queer culture, a postmodern sense of its rapidly accelerated timeline, or just incompetent plotting." But, she continues, the film's inconsistent temporality forms an "intentional simultaneity" that opens up new intimacies and modes of being. She concludes, "Chou overstuffs her films, it is true, perhaps to make up for lost time, but also to allow each world to multiply." The analyses by both White and Martin help to identify Chou's temporally offset mode of narration as relevant both to her status as a lesbian director and to the transnational quality of her films. By producing queer intimacies through asynchrony, Chou's mode of temporal "overstuffing" constitutes a queer way to tell time.

The Sexual Politics of Slow Cinema

The critical fights that broke out around slow cinema in the early 2010s inadvertently depended on gendered and sexed notions of productive time versus wasted time.[33] What these debates revealed but could not quite resolve was a threatening queer counterproductivity that simmers discursively in the exorbitant slowness of the modern art-house film or festival feature. Karl Schoonover has argued elsewhere that contemporary so-called slow cinema performs an often unnoticed queering of time.[34] Films by Tsai Ming-liang, for example, expose audiences to atemporal leanings: lingering, loitering, waiting, or what Song Hwee Lim characterizes as drifting and stillness.[35] In other words, narrative structure *de*volves in these films as much as it *e*volves. As an emergent form of world cinema, slow cinema is distinguished by a significant attenuation of narrative into expanded temporalities that pervert our usual relationship to cinematic time. Slow cinema wastes our time, asking us to spend time in visibly unproductive ways, outside efficient narrative economies of production and reproduction. As such, slow films are interesting to consider in light of queer theory's debates around negative aesthetics, particularly in how they resist reproductive futurity. Like the willfully unproductive queer, slow cinema refuses to labor along socially sanctioned narrative pathways.

We contend that slowness thus forms a demarcation of queer temporality. Rather than disrupting time through asynchrony and disjuncture, it distends and delays it, creating new modes of subjectivity and provoking sites of risky spectatorial idleness. Time so slowed down as to approach atemporality demands that spectatorship alter its accustomed pathways, orient itself otherwise. André Bazin found many diversions in cinema, not the least of which was its capacity to produce a critical boredom. According to Bazin, the political potential of cinema arises not only in those moments in which an image captures our mind's eye, but also in its "relaxing of attention," which liberates that mind, allowing the viewer's thinking to meander in a constructive manner. Film-induced boredom encourages a loosening of time itself and a consequent freeing of thought. But this freedom might also encourage attention to the others in the theater, to the embodied experience of communal viewing.[36] Slow queer cinema thus attempts to activate Roland Barthes's observation that "the movie house is a site of availability (even more than cruising), the inoccupation of bodies, which best defines modern eroticism."[37] In this section and the one that follows, we counterpose two contrasting versions of slow queer cinema. Our first example is a group of popular independent films that perform slowness without dismantling the normative structures of synchrony described earlier. The section that follows it goes on to analyze a more radical form of temporal distention in the work of Apichatpong. In interrogating these distinct contemporary temporalities, we open out the sexual politics of the slow and boring.

On the surface, films such as the Mexican festival favorite *Mil nubes de paz cercan el cielo, amor, jamás acabarás de ser amor/A Thousand Clouds of Peace* (Julián Hernández, dir., 2003) and the British director Andrew Haigh's art-house success *Weekend* (2011) appear to partake in the world cinema's idiom: they parade the mise-en-scène of art films (empty cityscapes, quotidian details of tarnished modernity, long vistas of traffic jams) and echo the art house's typically humanist stance (expressing concern for the experiences of those who are downtrodden, forgotten, or looked past in contemporary life). Equally, these films initially appear to narrate time with less narrative rigor and to engage with a queer mode of slowness and resistant temporality. But we argue that this surface interest in slowness simply expresses the generic aspirations of the films, which aim to be seen as world cinema rather than "just" gay films. Another example here would be Xavier Dolan's *Tom à la ferme/Tom at the Farm* (2013), which, despite its nod to a long take aesthetic, nevertheless deploys shallow depth of field and rack focus to generate suspense. Whereas these films stylistically seem to involve a loosening of narrative's grip on filmic temporality, in the long run they do not allow critical boredom to take hold. This process of summoning up the idea of slowness and then foreclosing on its risks produces an oddly contradictory address to the viewer. This textual effort both to evoke and to contain the radical potentiality of slowness reveals tensions in the gentrification of gay world cinema. We call this disingenuous stylization of temporality "faux slow," and this trend challenges us to attend more carefully to how we define queer temporality in contemporary cinema.

Both *A Thousand Clouds of Peace* and *Weekend* proclaim their aesthetic commitment to the non-eventful temporality of everyday life while always undercutting the viewer's experience of durée. Whenever either film comes close to depicting time emptied of narrative content, it anxiously undermines its more ambitious aesthetic impulses by overly managing the viewer's gaze, as if scrambling to counteract any wandering of attention. This compensatory eagerness to govern the gaze is reflected in each film's stylistic tics. For example, Hernández's use of shallow focus makes his compositions selective in a directive way (figure 6.7). Most shots impose a focal point on the spectator's gaze, either through strong compositional framing or extraordinarily narrow depth of field. These prescriptive pathways for the gaze threaten to shut down the ambiguity so prized by Bazin in the long take. Moreover, these pathways inhibit critical boredom from ever taking over the narration of the film. One of the main characters in *A Thousand Clouds of Peace* seems always to be waiting, but in this loitering the film never asks us to wrestle with the radical registers of slowness.[38]

Diegetic desire clearly begins to motivate the look here. The look threads together otherwise discordant times and spaces, moving us from one scene to the next and acting as a structuring visual narrator that trumps any tem-

Fig. 6.7: Shallow focus directs the spectator's gaze in *A Thousand Clouds of Peace*.

poral looseness. In that look's domination, the temporalities of the pickup or heartache take over. Unoccupied time suddenly seems to ripen with opportunity or longing. We might think of *A Thousand Clouds of Peace* as *Happy Together* without the circularity, without the ambiguous third male character, without the cartography of absence and transience. *A Thousand Clouds of Peace* also describes desire through a series of missed opportunities and abusive quick fucks, but the film never seems to trust the experiential registers of non-synchrony. We regard the faux slowness of this film's form as a stylistic affect—a kind of troping of art-house temporality—more than as an actual untimeliness.[39]

Like *A Thousand Clouds of Peace*, *Weekend* relies on a stylistic gambit that leads us to believe we are watching a film that would qualify for Andrew's global New Wave: the film's opening sequences use ellipses and passages of dead time to signal quotidian uneventfulness and social dislocation. The film's main character seems out of sync with those around him, and this atemporality makes him appear out of place in his own life. But as the film progresses and the characters divulge their psychological histories, the film begins to renege on its distention of time. Dislocation and non-synchrony, it seems, were simply means for building romantic tension or for indicating the effects of recreational drug use. The film's narrative moves from openness toward closure in a pattern of intensifying concordance. From this perspective, *Weekend* traces the formal outlines of a conventional narrative: the gradually satisfying trajectory from randomness toward an ending with poetic coherence in an arc that merely passes through repetition and coincidence. The increased tautness and synchrony of its romantic narrative quickly dispenses with any actual boredom. The external gestures of world cinema appear here less as aesthetic challenges than as familiar tropes. If, at its start, the film offers encounters with the indecisive rhythms of everyday life, then by its penultimate scene on a train platform, temporality has been disciplined by narrative, and any earlier openness has been co-opted retroactively for the melancholy romantic conclusion. Again, camerawork gives away the film's tendencies from the beginning. The film's repeated use of rack focus suggests a different politics of time and an image that is unwilling to endorse the wandering of attention.

A final example is Ira Sachs's American independent film *Keep the Lights On* (2012), whose style critics linked to *Weekend* and that was released less than a year later. *The Guardian* suggested that together these two films represented something of an Anglo-American queer New Wave or *neorealism* of gay filmmaking. *Keep the Lights On* emulates the naturalism of an older, shot-on-film style of cinema; it apes the grain and particular saturation of warm tones associated with the popularity of Kodak Ektachrome film stock in the 1970s and the looser shooting style of "New Hollywood" cinematographers from that period. The film fetishizes natural light, emulating reverence for the everyday in reflective glares, light flares, heavy diffusion, and other imagistic disturbances that fiction films from the 1970s allowed into the image. Yet this naturalistic imagery covers over a rather conventional narrational system.

On the surface, *Keep the Lights On*'s camerawork gives the impression of a less structured visual narration, using open framings and often refusing shot/reverse shot patterns. Throughout the film, however, the outwardly fluid camerawork refuses to loosen its grip on its central protagonist. So while there are many scenes in which his body does not anchor the majority of the frame composition, the film's cinematography uses telephoto lens shots, narrow depth of field, and rack focus to maintain his subjectivity as the primary focus of our attention. In crucial narrative scenes, these techniques also serve to exclude our identification with the perspectives of other characters, as if they might pose a threat to the flow of narrative. The hyper-subjectivized or even narcissistic point of view that results from this aesthetic counteracts (and, in fact, benefits from) any imbalance or openness to the image.

These faux-slow gay films trope slow-moving narration without cultivating the critical potentials of slowness, and they display nervous tics around unleashing the gaze in time. In these films, the aforementioned camera techniques prevent any undirected wandering of the eye, shutting down the democratic impulses Bazin imagined for a more open image. The popularity of the faux-slow gay film plays out at an institutional level a tension between commercial (heteronormative) impulses toward identification and causality and the gentrification of a certain model of art cinema on the festival circuit. In this regard, we can see in queer cinema the tensions that structure world cinema per se. But this is not simply an issue of contemporary art-cinema style in which textual figurations of sexuality are secondary: to return to Schoonover's claim on slow cinema, slowness is a queer modality of cinematic articulation. Faux slow, therefore, is a style shot through with contradiction; a space of queer cinema whose style undoes the very subjectivity that it attempts to articulate. As such, it provides unique insight into the anxieties of expressing queer subjectivities in the circuits of world cinema.

Slowness as Intimacy

In contrast to these faux-slow films, films by the Thai queer director Apichatpong Weerasethakul encourage a boredom that exposes a variegated temporality. Apichatpong shows us how boredom's "more demanding" modes of attention might offer a means of exploring queer subjectivities. His films both expand our sense of time's relationship to lived experience and identify temporal experimentation as the site of staging alternate modes of intimacy. We already saw something of Apichatpong's queer style in chapter 3, in which we discussed the narrative doubling in *Sud pralad/Tropical Malady* (2004). The diptych's repetition in other terms provides another mode of queer temporal disjuncture—not anachronism but a type of asynchronous proximity and alterity that figures an incommensurable time of queer animality. Apichatpong's films repeatedly figure both queer intimacies and slow temporalities: *Syndromes and a Century* (2006) typifies his staging of slow and lingering, open-ended forms of same-sex relationality. Apichatpong has claimed that for him, queer means that "anything is possible," and in the films, this mode of potentiality is also a temporality in which nothing might happen.[40] To come to grips with this temporality, we focus on *Mekong Hotel* (2012), a particularly aleatory example of Apichatpong's slow style.

Describing Siegfried Kracauer's early theory of boredom, Mary Ann Doane writes that "boredom ensures one's presence, one's refusal to be absorbed into and overcome by regulated time."[41] Such an effect has a history in queer experimental cinema—for instance, in Andy Warhol's durational films. Discussing Warhol's *Haircut (No. 1)* (1963), Matthew Tinkcom writes, "Boredom is not the absence of activity but the seeming insignificance of activities that seem unworthy of attention (and, here, specifically filmic attention); when the figures of this film play with film time and somatic time, they unfold the difference between those two versions of temporality as dominant cinema has sought to exploit it. They, and Warhol, bring a camp inversion to that which is deemed worthy of cinema by making the uncinematic into something worth watching—repeatedly, no less."[42] Recent queer scholarship has explored the potential of Warhol's queer temporalities to produce what Homay King has called "a type of boredom that has restorative potential," offering a newly receptive experience of presence to the spectator.[43] This literature provides an important queer history of cinematic boredom, but Apichatpong's deployment of boredom emerges from a moment quite different from the postwar American avant-garde.

Mekong Hotel ends with a six-minute shot of a river that offers us presence as refusal. To understand *Mekong Hotel*'s deployment of slowness, we must first unpack how the film presents its final shot as a vista. Vistas are views often made possible by outlooks: a riverbank, the edge of a hill, a hotel balcony, and, here, cinema. Critics who champion slow cinema have identified in such vistas a means of reinvesting in the immersive and contemplative qualities of old-fashioned film-going. Slow cinema often uses vistas to accentuate the richness and detail of the projected large-screen image (e.g., the films of Michelangelo Frammartino) and as a rejoinder to the question, Why bother to continue seeing films in cinemas? In the vista, slowness reinvigorates cinema as a medium: in this open space, the film's dilated time can revive the viewer's acuity. For Apichatpong's film, a vista is not *just* a panoramic expanse; it is a *shared* view, a vision seen together and shared together over time.[44] At the *Mekong Hotel*, duration triggers an interpersonal—and perhaps intimate—mode of consumption.

Since the film introduces this final vista through a preceding shot of two male characters looking out at the river, the frame initially strikes us as the unmediated conduit for what the two men are seeing. This is another of Apichatpong's frequent non-heterosexual pairings, and these queer bonds appear with an unexceptional point-blank quality in his narratives. Just before *Mekong Hotel*'s long-take vista, these two men talk openly about being a couple, confirming earlier suggestions by the film that they are lovers. (Even queerer, the film also suggests that these are demons who can switch bodies, so to assign a stable male gender or gay identity to these characters may not be entirely accurate.) Once the film turns its look over to the vista, the men never reappear in the image or on the soundtrack. So while we feel at times vitally connected to this diegetic couple's watching, there are

Fig. 6.8: Time dilates as the protagonists of *Mekong Hotel* discuss their relationship.

other periods in which we feel that our meandering attention abandons their point of view (figure 6.8). The two men, like the demons they represent in the film, haunt our sense of *who* is looking and how many of us are paying strict attention.

As the six-minute shot continues, its complex and variegated temporality confronts the viewer with a tension between individual and collective registers of looking. The shot's most obvious points of interest are four jet skiers who make circles and splashes in the center of the screen. The skiers trace the random patterns of people grabbing the day's last moments. They represent one of the shot's several modes of temporality: an erratic, playful swerving of movement across the image plane. Meanwhile, this is also the time of day when cars are starting to use their headlights, and the unevenness of traffic across the bridge brings an intermittency that—like the skiers— passes through the image with an atomized pacing. About two minutes into the shot, the film introduces a different temporality when a single long boat emerges from the bottom right corner, slowly cutting a diagonal path across the frame. This is an even movement, a more purposeful trajectory. The shot also contains inconsequential and even less noticeable occurrences that betray other durations: someone burns garbage or a small factory sends a gentle cloud of smoke into the sky near the right side of the frame; a greenish lens flare quietly haunts the bottom left of the frame; and the moon gleams so modestly it could be missed.

How are we to read such an open-ended and eventless shot at all, much less read it as queer? We turn to Bazin's "relaxing of attention" and the political productivity of boredom as a mode of spectatorial practice. Every time Bazin watched *Limelight* (Charles Chaplin, dir., 1952) he got bored at some point. After the third time, he recognized in his boredom the potential of cinema to provide alternate modalities of time. Boredom opens up time; time becomes that which we are free to expend however we wish. This sense of boredom can be aligned with Bazin's larger commitment to the democratization of spectatorship through specific formal devices such as the long take, deep focus, and the sequence shot. But when we look more closely at his description of boredom, something slightly different is in attendance:

> Many [viewers] deplore the *longueurs* and talkiness of the first half [of *Limelight*]. . . . It becomes apparent that even the boredom one might experience enters mysteriously into the harmony of the over-all work. In any case, what do we mean by boredom? I have seen *Limelight* three times and I admit I was bored three times, not always in the same places. Also, I never wished for any shortening of this period of boredom. It was rather a relaxing of attention that left my mind free to wander—a daydreaming about the images. There were also many occasions on which the feeling of length left me during the screening. The film, objectively speaking a long one (two hours and twenty minutes), and slow, caused a lot of people, myself included, to lose their sense of time. . . . Time in *Limelight* would be essentially not that of the drama but the more imaginary duration of music, a time that is more demanding on the mind but also leaves it free of the images that nourish it, a time that can be embroidered.[45]

Bazin finds boredom useful in how it reasserts a lived temporality and refuses to relinquish one mode of being to a different temporal regime.

While clearly not describing slow cinema (*Limelight* would hardly fit into that category), Bazin *is* pointing to a critical potential of cinema to resist timeliness. In his idea of embroidered time, Bazin shows us how boredom verifies cinema's capacity to offer alternatives to the hegemonic temporality of causal narration. Boredom offers a mode of temporal variegation, and the word "embroider" suggests the interweaving of various and conflicting temporalities unfolding simultaneously *in* and *in front of* the image.

Using the figure of embroidery, Bazin's language both connects to and contrasts with the descriptions of classical Hollywood continuity to which we have returned in thinking heterosynchrony. Bordwell, Staiger, and Thompson characterize those descriptions this way: "The fundamental plenitude and linearity of Hollywood narrative culminate in metaphors of knitting, linking, and filling." They continue, "Lewis Herman eloquently sums up this aesthetics: 'Care must be taken that every hole is plugged, that every loose string tied up.'" Opposed to the phallic metaphors of completion and the structural integrity of unifying loose ends, Bazin's embroidery thickens the material on which it is applied. It consists of stitches that are supplemental rather than those that strengthen or provide structure. Embroidery complicates and embellishes rather than sutures or mends; thus, it opposes the instrumental synchronics of classical cinema with the potential for individual and non-standard aesthetic articulations of experience.

Returning to *Mekong Hotel*, that long final shot can be read as an extended opportunity for embroidered time. The shot contains such a disparate collection of differently paced micro-events and seemingly inconsequential actions that looking seems unusually individualistic. Slowness may prompt inattention and impatience, foregrounding the idiosyncrasy of our roving gaze. This distraction is decidedly personal, different each time, like Bazin's viewings of *Limelight*. But as much as our experience of boredom is a domain resolutely carved out by the individual subject, it is simultaneously felt as communal. We are aware of sharing a durational observation with other humans onscreen and off. Is it possible to share distraction? To experience boredom collectively?

Much has been made of the collective effects of sensational cinema and comedy, but in watching the end of this slow and experimental art film, we intensely sense our proximity to others. We are returned to our bodies and to an awareness of those other bodies in the theater. The film is quiet enough that we can hear others breathing. We might feel close to them in our impatience and yet also alone in distracted agitation. We worry that our fidgeting might disturb others who are more at peace or attempt to gauge when other audience members would begin to become restless with elapsing time. An odd sense of communality invades us when we are bored in a film. People feel suddenly closer to us, distracting in their physicality. In Barthes's terms, there is an eroticism to this anxious mixture of heightened corporeality, physical constriction, and imaginative freedom.

In this context, it is fascinating that the film uses a queer couple as the basis of its encounter with radical slowness. The couple's looking initiates the film's open-ended conclusion, and the dilation of time seems to be the consequence of their intimacy. If *Mekong Hotel* is a queer film, it is such because it proposes an alternative mode of attention, one that gives space and time to intimacies that exist outside the strictures of heterosynchrony.

Mekong Hotel's final shot refuses to have us forget that the film image in the cinema is always a shared view of one sort or another. This is a vision taken with strangers in the dark. When we lose the communal look that cinema viewing allows, this shot asks, what forms of intimacy will our world lose? This is the difference between Apichatpong's true slowness and the faux slow of Haigh and Hernández. Chris Fujiwara asserts, "If entertainment keeps us waiting, holding out the promise of the new but never fulfilling it, boredom admits waiting to be infinite."[46] Or, as Lim puts it with regard to the durational endings of Tsai's films, they point to "a continuation in some unknown place and some unknown time in the future."[47] For Apichatpong, in more utopian mode, cinema's infinite waiting already creates the possibility of refiguring social relations.

Excision as Queer History

Queers have problems with time. We can never seem to make it work for us, and we often appear outside of it, our milestones not recognized by the conventional intervals of heterotemporality. Most historiographies have been structured in ways that leave out LGBT people or circumscribe the queer movements of our lives. Commercial cinemas (including Hollywood and Bollywood) implemented self-censoring strictures against certain forms of intimacy on-screen. As we saw in chapter 5, hapticity (diegetic and extradiegetic) is freighted with a history of proscribing queer touch. The excision of queer experiences is at once an institutional and a representational politics, whereby feeling our way around the painful absences of the archive becomes a form of queer touching. To read these histories as not only institutional (archival, historiographic, cinematic) but also aesthetic is to observe the gestures of touching that reverse those of excision. What coalesces around these gaps and excisions is a style based on the disjunctive proximity of one temporality to another in a structure of temporal corrugation. In this final section, we propose excision as a mode of queer temporality; a mode in which queer time is precisely what is cut out and where queerness therefore takes root in the splices, the glitches, and the traces of these lost moments.

To animate these issues, we begin with a particularly textured example: the appearance on YouTube of a transferred VHS off-air dub of *Tubog sa ginto/Dipped in Gold* (Lino Brocka, dir., 1971). The film is an early feature from Brocka, one of the best-known Filipino/a directors of his generation, who was also openly gay. Here on YouTube is preserved, if temporarily, one of the most important films representing homosexuality in Filipino film history. *Dipped in Gold* presents all the outward signs of a domestic melodrama, mixed with the preachy aspects of a social problem film and the titillation of soft-core pornography. The marital bliss of Emma, a wealthy Manilan woman, is pierced by the discovery that her husband, Don Benito, has a wandering eye and affairs with men. Emma discovers his covert sex life in a dramatic scene of disclosure that gives the viewer access to an illicit set of intimacies that were rarely seen on-screen in 1971. In purely representational terms, then, the film carries echoes of the exhilarating scale of pathos found in Douglas Sirk's melodramas of the mid-1950s but also anticipates more contemporary films with homosexuality at their narrative centers, such as *Dakan/Destiny* (Mohamed Camara, dir., 1997) from Guinea and *Men in Love* (Moses Ebere, dir., 2010) from Nollywood's homosex cycle.

Although the film could be seen as pathologizing and criminalizing homosexuality, it also provides a candid depiction of homosexual yearning (and it does so from the opening scenes, where the camera witnesses the father's desiring gaze directed at the bodies of semi-naked youth at his son's birthday party). *Dipped in Gold* is seen as belonging to a group of features known as *bomba* films, a category which also included films made by Ishmael Bernal and Celso Ad. Castillo, whose frank representations of sexuality have been seen to reflect the liberalism and turbulence before and during martial law. Bienvenido Lumbera describes bomba as "a subversive genre in which the narrative pretends to uphold establishment values when it is actually intent on undermining audience support for corrupt and outmoded institutions."[48] It is certainly possible to read the melodramatic form of *Dipped in Gold* as at once upholding homophobia and releasing subversive visions of same-sex desire, but to understand its appearance on YouTube we also need to trace a certain institutional history of cinema, sexuality, and the Philippines.

Dipped in Gold was released eighteen months before Ferdinand Marcos declared martial law to avoid the end of his presidency. On September 21, 1972, Marcos shut down Congress while his government worked quickly to assume ownership of media companies, radically limiting the freedom of the press. Censorship reigned, and civil liberties evaporated for most Filipinos in this period. Many who had the means to leave the country did so, leading to a wave of emigration to the United States, Canada, and Europe. The effects of Marcos's coup were transformative of the film industry. Audiences were lost; a range of expression and representation disappeared; and depicting queers (present in Filipino cinema since the 1950s, in, for example

Jack en Jill/Jack and Jill [Mar S. Torres, dir., 1954]) became significantly more difficult.[49] Although the bomba genre was rethought and exploited by the Marcos regime, it is hard not to see in the boldness of *Dipped in Gold* the evanescence of a permissive and dynamic Filipino film culture.

Meanwhile, as rich and varied as Filipino film history has been, the country has lacked a national film archive for decades. Marcos established an archive that lasted for fewer than five years, and not until 2011 was the new National Film Archive of the Philippines created. The existing state collection of films is incomplete; conservation is inadequate; and the archive's acquisition goals are often constricted by large media companies. Bliss Cua Lim assesses the impact of this dire fragility and intermittent preservation, pointing out that "research on Philippine cinema is thus circumscribed by the acute temporal pressures of archival crisis."[50] She estimates that only 37 percent of domestically produced films remain of the nearly eight thousand made since 1897. For Lim, Filipino cinema exists as much in "the anarchive" as it does in an archive. Borrowing Akira Lippit's Derridian terminology, Lim writes, "The anarchive [persists] as the necessary complement to the archive, [it] is the inevitability of loss that shadows forms of historical survival."[51]

In this context, the fact that *Dipped in Gold* and *Jack and Jill* can be viewed on YouTube carries both archival and anarchival significance. The comments posted about *Dipped in Gold* capture simultaneously an archive fever and the evanescence characteristic of Filipino cinema, its "anarchivalist" nature. As one blogger has emphasized, "The end result of having such an active video scene within the immigrant community is the availability of films that would otherwise be absent." The story of *Dipped in Gold*'s appearance on YouTube is overdetermined by the film's relationship to national history (and the ebbs and flows of social mores in official Filipino culture). The film was uploaded from a Betamax tape that was discovered in someone's home in New York. Several posts declare that the film is otherwise inaccessible to them, and some even claim that it exists in no other form. (The film is in fact housed in the National Archive, so there is a kind of inverse archive fever at play in the commenters' desire for its inaccessibility and almost lost status.)

On the YouTube version of *Dipped in Gold*, image and sound are very degraded. As with many films uploaded to YouTube from old VHS recordings taken off-air from television broadcasts, this version of the film is filled with odd interruptions, signal fallout, and other glitches. The stopping and starting of the VCR to avoid advertising breaks may account for some of the glitches; the age of the tape when the film was recorded may explain some others; and the age of the tape when it was uploaded may explain yet more. However, there are also odd ellipses and repetitions that suggest cen-sored content. These glitches mark the space of diaspora, dictatorship, lim-ited access, bootleg circulation, hoarding, used tapes, and perhaps even the wear and tear produced by appreciative viewing practices. Where a viewer has replayed certain scenes or bits of action, the tape quality wears down and the visual signal picks up static. This version of the film thus becomes a distinctive text. As Ramon Lobato argues, "Texts in informal circulation ac-cumulate interference—additions, subtractions, inflections, distractions—as they move through space and time." Or, as he pithily insists, "Distribution is *productive*; it creates meaning and difference."[52]

Lucas Hilderbrand has argued that these formal qualities of degradation provide an alternative history not only of viewership but also of community. He writes, "The aesthetics of videotape are not merely matters of formalist specificity but also engage broader social and cultural issues of circulation, reception, historiography, and regulation."[53] Hilderbrand explores the social (mis)uses of videotape to position bootlegging as an essential historical pro-genitor to contemporary file sharing and crowd sourcing of moving image texts. Unlike its digital counterparts, however, videotape sharing carries the material trace of its circulation, a public history written into its images and sounds. As Hilderbrand writes on the social history of bootlegging Todd Haynes's film *Superstar* (1987), which could not be legally distributed due to a copyright dispute:

> Videotapes of the film . . . inscribe a bootleg aesthetic that exhibits the au-dience's engagement in a clandestine love affair—watching, sharing, and copying the illicit text so that viewers' reception of *Superstar* is histori-cally, perceptually, and emotionally reshaped. Video duplication of the work formally changes the text, so that its thematic concerns—distorted mass media and their relations to subjective and bodily breakdown—become rendered on the surface.[54]

YouTube both expands the reach of the bootlegging impulse, lending it a transnational—if not exactly global—reach. While the platform mitigates certain image fall-out, it introduces other fragmentations, discontinuities, and social commentaries.

The formal aspects of poor quality attest not only to the fragility of na-tional film histories, but also to the experiences of diaspora and the chal-lenges that many types of images with queer content pose to historians and archivists. The quality of a film not only charts the relations and exclusions among various modes of production (big-budget blockbuster versus artisan experimentation), it also maps a film's circulation: where it is able to go and not go; how it is preserved or encouraged to deteriorate; what is available on upscale DVD release and what is left forgotten on an archive shelf or even lost.[55] Discovery of a film once believed lost or thought impossible to imagine brings with it both the thrill of communal rescue (a fan finds an old copy and uploads it) and the shudders of what could have been, what might be out there still, and what is gone that we will never know. YouTube grants its users a means of imagining their redemptive grasp on Filipino films, a stash so complete that it will remedy history's hideous attacks on itself. This apparently degraded archive is also an archive of queer cinema's gaps and excisions.

YouTube's *Dipped in Gold* presents three types of formal disruption: interruption, repetition, and decay.[56] All three types of disruption occur during same-sex intimacy. The first scene of queer touching happens when the husband, Don Benito, is sitting in the front seat of a car with a man to whom he is attracted; he will eventually hire this man, Diego, as his driver and move him into the apartment behind Don Benito's family house. Slowly he moves his hand toward Diego's thigh, then abruptly the image is shattered by an interference pattern skewing the picture as if the tape had been stopped suddenly by whomever was recording it. It then abruptly restarts in the midst of a scene with the wife, Emma, talking to one of her friends. This effect is the equivalent of an in-machine edit, familiar to anyone who has used videotape to record broadcast television programs. In the film's most explicit depiction of same-sex intimacy a more disruptive glitch occurs. In a moment alone in the back apartment, Don Benito strokes the chest of Diego, who lies in front of him on the bed. As Don Benito begins to unbutton Diego's shirt, trying to relax him, the film suddenly repeats this gesture in a loop of dissolves. We see the same caresses, unbuttonings, and crotch gropes twice (figure 6.9). The accompanying soundtrack pulls away from the image, with dialogue falling out of sync. It appears as if the image was censored in its on-air broadcast but in a messy way that actually ends up removing certain touches while extending others.

A final example of the disruption to the image happens in the form of a jump cut that comes later in the same scene. Cutting away from the two men in bed, the film shifts to a long take of Emma walking out the front door and toward the garage. As she passes by Diego's apartment, sexual moans can be heard and a movement in the apartment's window catches her eye. Here the camera follows the direction of her look as she turns to walk closer to the window. Next the film cuts to a close-up of her looking in through the

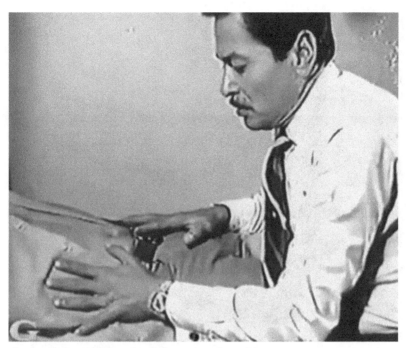

Fig. 6.9: Don Benito gropes his driver in *Dipped in Gold*.

window as the moans get louder and are accompanied by a melodramatic score of tense strings and atonal piano notes: sound and image both cue the viewer to adopt Emma's voyeuristic curiosity, peering into the apartment to see what is causing the moaning. Suddenly, sound and image are interrupted, and there is an odd superimposition of her face onto the curtain and the view of the bedroom. The music cuts disjunctively from a screeching tone to suspenseful chords as if the music was scored in reverse. Her face now reveals the horror of what she has seen, but we have hardly had a glimpse of the enraptured lovers, and with the glitch in the music, we are made to feel we have been left out of the spectacle. In place of a proper eyeline match, a keenly attentive viewer might catch a split-second sight of two bodies, superimposed on the wife's face in close-up framed by the curtains (figure 6.10). What we see is the brief remainder of a dissolve, the second shot of which has been edited out. In this instance, the sound and image signal not only a technical glitch or a possible censorship but also a derailing of the narration.

It is not clear what has prevented us from having full visual access to these scenes of queer touching: a viewer's attempt to re-edit the film, a

Fig. 6.10: The trace of a missing dissolve flashes briefly in *Dipped in Gold*.

television network editing a film for broadcast, or a state censor's actions against the film's content. These disruptions mark not a neutral loss of content but significant events in the history of queer global cinema. The degradations present in *Dipped in Gold* on YouTube suggest the erotics of this engagement with the past and revise cinematic temporality itself. As we saw in our discussion of *Proteus*, the shape of history and its description of lived time are political in nature. The glitches created from what is omitted in *Dipped in Gold* open up a critical space with the capacity to reinscribe queer histories. Otherwise distinct moments share space in the time of viewing online, and YouTube makes these moments contiguous: they touch and rub against each other. They open up a space that not only acknowledges shared obliterations from the record of queer desire but allows for the undoing of such erasures.

The awkward jump cuts that glitch the smooth temporality of the diegesis may not be deliberate stylistic choices, but they nonetheless create a textual effect. Compare these ruptures with Bordwell's description of *Vampyr* (Carl Theodor Dreyer, dir., 1932), where he sees the film's "temporal ellipticality" as "dismantling the stylistic system which presupposes a stable spatio-

In the Brazilian film *Madame Satã* (Karim Aïnouz, dir., 2002), for instance, cinematic space seems to jump erratically in time just as a desiring same-sex gaze is exchanged across a dance floor in an early scene. Queer desire initiates the film's departure from conventional patterns of describing space and time in narrative cinema as bodies and desires intermingle in ways that play tricks with the unfolding of ordinary depiction. Diegetic homosexuality seems to affect the picture itself, producing momentarily disorienting skips in narrative space and time. These ellipses highlight something that has been censored from Brazilian history: the queer tale of Madame Satã, or João Francisco dos Santos, a drag queen, gangster, and capoeira fighter. The child of former slaves, dos Santos embodies histories of economically and racially marginalized countercultures often excluded from official narratives of nation. Like *Proteus*, *Madame Satã* uses formal ruptures in cinematic temporality to enable a queer historicity to come into view, but here the mechanism is excision and rupture rather than anachronism. These mini-ellipses in time are jump cuts inscribed with sexual and political provocation. While it may seem heretical to link a Filipino melodrama from the 1970s that is replete with homosexual panic to a contemporary film imaginatively recovering Brazil's queer past, this comparison demonstrates how recent films register not simply hidden histories (as recovered content) but also the process of hiding history through censorship and omission. We insist on touching these texts across space and time in what we see as a related queer process of revised temporal and worldly contiguity. *Madame Satã* acknowledges how representing queer desires in and for the past is both fervently archival and overtly anarchival. Its ellipses respond to history's excision of queer intimacies; re-eroticizing this history of excisions and reworking the glitches of repressive technologies as poetic form.

We can see examples of this kind of excision across various forms and spaces of recent queer cinema. To return to our opening example, *Lan Yu* uses jump cuts to articulate space expressionistically in relationship to the historical past. The jump cuts come precisely in the moments in which the film interpenetrates queer desire with history, particularly the censored past of the Tiananmen Square uprising. *Soundless Wind Chime* (Kit Hung, dir., 2009), like *Happy Together*, mixes past and present in a fragmentary narrative in which queer migration produces temporal displacements and disjunctures in subjectivity that can be adequately represented only through excised narration. In a different register, the video work of the Indian artist Tejal Shah creates immersive spaces that nonetheless glitch and jump in time. Her installation *Between the Waves* (2012), for example, uses tiny jump cuts to delineate a space overwritten by the temporalities of waste and decay, while in another channel female figures with phallic unicorn horns and plastic dresses interact with a lush forest environment. As with *She Male Snails* (discussed in chapter 5), a queer pastoral offers the potential to reimagine gender, and both texts are ambivalent about human immersion in the nonhuman environment. However, the cuts in *Between the Waves* emphasize the risks inherent in imagining queer subjectivities; indeed, the piece's title foregrounds the temporality of the interstice.[60] Gilberto Blasini has described the "perforations" of time in queer cinema of the 2010s, and the on-again-off-again metaphor of perforation provides another way to conceptualize this same temporal effect.[61]

Although ellipsis has become a standard means by which Hollywood films and television describe time, it is important to distinguish these normative forms from queer discontinuities. At first view, we might simply regard queer excisions as a perfectly conventional means of depicting the intensely experiential, like the drunken subjective camera in *Mean Streets* (Martin Scorsese, dir., 1973), or the semi-conscious haze of concussion in *The Lady Vanishes* (Alfred Hitchcock, dir., 1938), or the narcotic-induced high in *Traffic* (Steven Soderbergh, dir., 2000). Hollywood uses ellipses liberally to cut out boring passages of time in routine actions where the beginning and end are clearly marked (walking upstairs, for example). Ellipses can also be used to the opposite effect, in moments of concentrated action. The fight scenes in *The Bourne Ultimatum* (Paul Greengrass, dir., 2007) are composed of a fury of very brief shots that provide an immersive, white-knuckle ride for the viewer. But even in contemporary cinema's most dynamic editing and frenzied sequences of action, sex, or inebriation, most films keep the viewer oriented in narrative space and keenly aware of individuated bodies as key agents of action over time and space. As Bordwell argues, intensified continuity does more to extend than to pervert classical Hollywood's aims for describing time and space. In doing so, postclassical Hollywood makes time narratively even more efficient (and more efficiently normative) than its classical counterpart.

Queer discontinuity is not simply an extension of Hollywood storytelling and should not be seen as some form of *intensified* continuity. Queer excision, for example, does not amplify an immersion in coherent diegetic space; nor does it intensify synchrony. Instead, it invites the asynchronous, fractures the individual, and displaces linear historicity (which in its normative forms deprives queer desire of social agency and futurity).[62] By drawing together distinct moments from different periods into a new contiguity, these films force us to confront the problems that queerness has posed to traditional modes of historiography. From this virtual network of queer jump cuts emerge non-coincident moments of freedom. These moments contain a potential escape from dominant modes of temporality in which queer relations do not exist, add up to anything, or carry any potential to mark change. Queerness causes linear historicity to lose its way, failing to evolve, refusing to fall into a straight line or unfurl waves of determinism. Instead, history presents itself as an asynchronous series of desires erased and acknowledged.

Recent queer films eroticize elisions that re-charge old films, allowing what was once excised to regain a visibility, however peculiar and incomplete. This work of unexpected linkage also proposes a different shape to world history, in which a Brazilian film might touch a Filipino one outside standard narratives of influence and trajectories of film style. We are thus proposing a queer historiographic project in which style emerges as a means of intervening globally in historicist exclusions. The new forms of rendering intimacy, subjectivity, and historicity via film style constitute what we, following Raymond Williams, call a queer structure of feeling.[63] This structure is an architecture of relationality in which an abstract queer spectator is reoriented to time and space and encouraged to approach history afresh. Queer subjects can thus emerge from periods from which they were once banished as unimaginable or forgotten, and conventional contemporary means of accessing the past are unsettled. In other words, by reworking traditional ways of telling time in film, queer global film style makes a formal and experiential intervention, enacting a queer historicity. Where others long for progression and synchrony, our queer film spectator welcomes the intermittent but boundless embrace of atemporal affections. Where others see jump cuts, the queer film spectator sees queer historicity.

Finally, there is a worldly politics to these queer infractions of conventional time and space. Queer time has a particularly geopolitical bent. Films with queer temporal excisions can depict how globalization fractures the spaces of everyday life and disrupts timekeeping and space making as we understand it. They can use the cinematic as a means of researching modes of time and space that compensate for—but may also resist—capitalist modernity's tasking of the body with specifically sexed and gendered imperatives. Aïnouz's *Praia do Futuro/Futuro Beach* (2014) develops his earlier use of excision in *Madame Satã* into a textual system that can testify to an experience he calls "queer diaspora."[64] The film begins in the northern beach city of Fortaleza, Brazil, where the lifeguard Donato is unable to save a drowning German tourist. After breaking the news to Konrad, the dead tour-

Fig. 6.11: *Futuro Beach* begins in the sharply delineated sunshine of Fortaleza, Brazil.

ist's friend, the two men begin a relationship that eventually takes Donato away from his family to live with Konrad in Berlin. Narratively, the film has many similarities with *Contracorriente/Undertow* (Javier Fuentes-León, dir., 2009), discussed in chapter 1—a South American setting, a drowned man, a conflict between family and gay identity—but *Futuro Beach* resists that film's traditionalist impulses and is more sensitive to the alternative resonances of queer time and space.

The film's most visually striking perforation is between Brazil and Germany: these spaces look radically different, as if they belong to entirely different diegeses. Fortaleza is shot in crisp, saturated colors, with bright top lighting, sharp edges, and graphic compositions (figure 6.11). The sea provides a recurring horizon line, cutting the frame across the middle and emphasizing horizontality. By contrast, Berlin is soft and rainy, shot in a neutral palette of greens, blues, and browns, without extreme contrasts (figure 6.12). In a scene in a park where Donato fights with Konrad about going home to his family, trees form a wavy horizon, with sleet blurring the edges of their figures. Through Donato's transit to Germany, these two spaces are placed up against each other. Queer worldliness brings apparently incommensurate spaces into proximity.

This transnational proximity is not easy. In an emotionally resonant scene early in their time in Berlin, Konrad sings along to "Aline," a French pop song from the 1960s, and Donato joins in, at one point taking a painting of a woman off the wall and using it as a mask. The song seems to reference obliquely some of our/their memories, as its lyrics refer to a lost love, a beach, and crying. But it is sung in French, which neither of the lovers

Fig. 6.12: It then cuts to a softly lit and cloudy Berlin.

speaks as his native language. Like the instances of non-translation in *Lilting* (Hong Khaou, dir., 2014) and *Dvojina/Dual* (Nejc Gazvoda, dir., 2013), it is not clear whether they understand the words, yet they gesture with feeling to this sentimental song. As the lovers twist their bodies in and out of frame, we see patterns of overlapping, lining up and separating, fitting together and moving out of sync, that metaleptically trace their trajectory of adopting the space of another or for another.

Futuro Beach organizes time, space, and belonging around narrative excisions. Aïnouz has described the film as like a carousel of slides, with sharp cuts between individual moments of memory. He shoots many scenes that are cut from the final film in the editing process, so there are indeed actual excisions in the text whose spectral traces remain in the actors' performances and in the irregular movement of narration. For instance, after the dancing scene, the film cuts immediately to the same figures but now about to fuck. The time between these different bodily gestures has been elided: the moment of singing and the moment of fucking flash up one after another. Across the film's narrative space, we see various scales of excision, from small to large edits in space and time, like Aïnouz's carousel of slides.

Small excisions, like those in *Madame Satã*, occur within a single scene, disarticulating space and removing segments of time. For instance, after one sex scene, Konrad gets out of bed and exits the frame, heading for the kitchen. The next shot at first appears to be a match on action, but it is Donato who enters the kitchen, even though the spectator left him lounging on the bed in the previous shot. Nothing important has been cut, but the edit draws attention to this work of removal. In an early scene in which the lovers swim at night in a first attempt to find the body, we do not actually see them jump in the water. Here, excision operates like classical narrative elision, but instead of cutting out unnecessary elements, it is the central action of the scene that is removed. The film consistently withholds those events which would ordinarily be considered consequential. In the scene in which the two men meet for the first time, we cut from Donato offering Konrad a ride home to them fucking. The beginning of their relationship is excised, leaving the spectator unclear about how they moved from grief to desire and making these two affective realms sticky and contiguous. These small excisions prepare us for a more significant one to come.

The film's most radical omission is a massive ellipsis between the second and third chapters, where about a decade of time simply drops out of the film's narration, and the viewer is left to figure out gradually what has happened in the intervening years. The second chapter ends with what appears to be a romantic turning point: a homesick Donato intends to leave Germany for Brazil, but he does not get off the train on the way to the airport. We cut to the couple dancing in a red-hued club, their bodies aligning in the frame as they do in the song scene. After a close-up on Donato's ecstatic face, the film cuts unexpectedly to the intertitle introducing the final chapter, "A German-Speaking Ghost." The next shot is a mist-shrouded Berliner Fernsehturm in Alexanderplatz, and the camera cuts to Donato's younger brother Ayrton, who is now an adult, walking into the frame. The viewer gradually deduces that Donato and Konrad have separated and that the majority of their relationship has been excised, derailing expectations that their romantic trajectory will form the central thread of the film. The third chapter also reveals that Donato has abandoned his family and does not even know that his mother has died in the interim. Years of their lives have been cut out of the narration, just as Ayrton feels that Donato cut off years with his family.

The film's haunting final sequence offers a hesitant rapprochement among the former lovers and the estranged brother. Donato and Konrad take Ayrton on their motorbikes to a strange beach where the sea retreats several kilometers every day, offering a symbolic image of excision in a beach with no sea. As they ride away from the beach, the film ends with a long, rain-soaked shot of the two bikes curving, driving, aligning, and then separating (figure 6.13). As with the singing and dancing sequences that it echoes and extends, there is something very kinesthetic about this shot. It not only depicts fascinating-to-watch objects in motion but also involves the spectator via its movement and its duration, taking us with it as the bikes and the camera's point of view curve, sway, and traverse space in depth. We keep

Fig. 6.13: *Futuro Beach* ends with the protagonists' motorbikes moving apart and together.

expecting a cut away that does not come: as in *Mekong Hotel*, intimacy grows in a durational attention to movement and landscape. We do not know what awaits these characters back in Berlin, but we end with the potential futurity of what we have characterized as atemporal affections, or a communal space of queer longing. In its pattern of riders overlapping and moving apart, the film allows us to experience the characters intertwined as kin, but it never allows us to settle on precisely how their affections will line up.

Marco Berger's *Hawaii* (2013) also deploys slowness to develop intimacy, but when its pent-up passions finally explode, sex is described through a glitchy ellipticism that interrupts any smooth unfolding of time or space. This ellipticism carries a political weight that also hints at the danger of repressed histories. In its brooding art-house aesthetic, which combines the dreamy and the everyday, *Hawaii* operates not unlike a Lucrecia Martel film, exploring the experiential dimensions of dislocation and suggesting that in Argentina, alienation is an experience that is deeply felt in everyday relations. Although this is never directly spoken, the film seems to occur in the wake of the economic crisis, when certain lives are suddenly more precarious. Martin has returned to the village he stayed in as a child, where he is nonetheless homeless. He offers household help to another young man, Eugenio, who is staying at his wealthy family's country house. The film very slowly traces an intense attraction growing between the two men as they are shown completing quotidian tasks. As their affections intensify in an otherwise uneventful narration, the film subtly reveals both a past they share and a present in which only desire connects them socially. For much of the film, their desire builds in direct tension with their disparate relations to class, regional identity, social agency, and property. The closest thing that Martin has to a home is a small pile of possessions in the woods. Meanwhile, Eugenio has more land and space than he knows how to handle. He views his inherited house as a writing retreat and an escape from his otherwise complicated bourgeois life. The film tempts us to view them as sharing "dislocation," but in its careful narration of Eugenio's obliviousness to Martin's situation, the film also cautions us about how such an analogy would only amplify the latter's vulnerability.

When the pair finally has sex, the stability of the image devolves into a disorganized assemblage of jump cuts, ellipses, and abstracted viewpoints. In this scene, the film quickly dispenses with the even, methodical pace that has defined visual revelation throughout the narration prior to this point, but it does not synchronize its time telling to the arc of simultaneous orgasm. The image refuses stasis both in framing and in point-of-view structure. In this intensification of intimacy, it is ambiguous whether queer sex depicts the overcoming of difference, a coupling, or whether we are witnessing a further dislocation.

In its buildup to this moment, *Hawaii* never turns its back on the inequities that the pair's affections must surmount. Their differences have an uneven effect on the escalating erotic tension, sometimes amplifying and sometimes derailing desire. The film marks the differences between Martin and Eugenio as subjective discrepancies and cognitive dissonances: while the working-class Martin clearly remembers Eugenio as his childhood friend, the wealthy Eugenio does not initially realize they ever knew each other. What Eugenio does hold from the past is a View-Master, the twentieth century's plastic version of a stereoscope marketed as a children's toy (figure 6.14). In a metaphor resonant with Aïnouz's vision of filmic narration as like a slide carousel, the lovers' memory is contained in obsolete technology for viewing images. Only when looking together at commercial views showing Hawaii's tourist sites and a pineapple can Eugenio and Martin finally share a moment of remembrance and accept a shared past (figure 6.15). Their ability to hold an image signals an intimacy keyed both to a heightening of erotic tension and to an emergent togetherness. Neither character has actual memories of Hawaii: they were never there together, and it seems neither has ever been there. Yet an intimacy and caring emerges in this sensitive moment of virtual travel, a real memory of a childhood sharing of a prosthetic memory, or a shared hope of escape. It is also an aesthetic experience of a photographic image onto which they project their desire. The View-Master's

Fig. 6.14: The View-Master through which the lovers' memories are contained in *Hawaii*.

Fig. 6.15: *Hawaii*: inside the View-Master is an image of pineapples.

Fig. 6.16: The lovers reclining in long grass in *Hawaii* visually replicate the image of pineapples.

commodified vistas offer a foreign world on which the two men can project their desires, not unlike the Iguazu Falls lampshade in *Happy Together*. This is a far-off space which they once invested with a fanstasmatic identity. Unlike that earlier film's totem, *Hawaii*'s "Hawaii" also belongs to the present and to the space that the two men currently occupy. Even though Martin cannot remember a past with Eugenio, in "Hawaii" he can share a reciprocal past longing that makes their current attraction and intimacy transcend the stark differences between their lives in the present. In the space of the photographic image, that past desire becomes a way not only to experience each other in the present but also to transcend the social and sexual limitations that previously kept them apart (figure 6.16).

Hawaii's allegory of vision illuminates the queer theory of cinema that this book proposes. For us, cinema is never simply a question of content: queerness must be located in the imaginary of the apparatus as much as in the imaginary of the image. The View-Master slide of the pineapple in *Hawaii* does have a specific cadence and identity, but in another way its signified is inconsequential. What matters is how the image allows the two queers to share a memory that was otherwise inaccessible. The particular spaces, desires, and intimacies—virtual and real, remote and local—enabled by the apparatus ignite the potential of queer cinema. Is the View-Master a metaphor for cinema? Like cinema, the toy allows the viewer to transcend her

NOTES

Introduction

1. See Anna Vanzan, "The LGBTQ Question in Iranian Cinema: A Proxy Discourse?" *Deportate, Esuli, Profughe* 25 (2014): 45–55; Shima Houshyar, "Queer and Trans Subjects in Iranian Cinema: Between Representation, Agency, and Orientalist Fantasies." *Ajam Media Collective*, May 11, 2013, http://ajammc .com/2013/05/11/queer-and-trans-subjects-in-iranian-cinema-between -representation-agency-and-orientalist-fantasies.

2. The process of subtitling introduces layers of intertextuality that can be additive as much as distortive and form a constitutive part of the experience of world cinema and its claims for universality. In chapter 1, we address the cinematic spaces created through subtitling more directly. See Abé Mark Nornes, *Cinema Babel: Translating Global Cinema* (Minneapolis: University of Minnesota Press, 2007); Atom Egoyan and Ian Balfour, eds., *Subtitles: On the Foreignness of Film* (Cambridge, MA: MIT Press, 2004).

3. The film's harshest critics have pointed to the American accents with which the lead actors speak Farsi. Again, the film's transnational and de-territorialized production seeps into the text as a politics of authenticity asking who may speak as Iranian.

4. David Damrosch, *What is World Literature?* (Princeton: Princeton University Press, 2003).

5. Jasbir Puar, *Terrorist Assemblages: Homonationalism in Queer Times* (Durham, NC: Duke University Press, 2008).

6. Alexander Doty pursues a similar line of inquiry in *Flaming Classics: Queering the Film Canon* (New York: Routledge, 2000).

7. Laura Mulvey, "Afterthoughts on 'Visual Pleasure and Narrative Cinema' Inspired by *Duel in the Sun*," *Framework* 15–17 (1981): 12–15; Mary Ann Doane, *Femmes Fatales: Feminism, Film Theory, Psychoanalysis* (New York: Routledge, 1991), 24–25. For a discussion of these debates, see Patrice Petro, *Joyless Streets: Women and Melodramatic Representation in Weimar Germany* (Princeton, NJ: Princeton University Press, 1989), 116–17.

8. For a more adjudicating discussion of the figure of the queer in feminist film theory, see Patricia White, "Madame X of the China Seas," in *Queer Looks: Perspectives on Lesbian and Gay Film and Video*, ed. Martha Gever, John Greyson, and Pratibha Parmar (New York: Routledge, 1993), 288–90.

9. Maria San Filippo, "Unthinking Heterocentrism: Bisexual Representability in Art Cinema," in *Global Art Cinema: New Theories and Histories*, ed. Rosalind Galt and Karl Schoonover (New York: Oxford University Press, 2010), 76.

10. Joseph Massad, "Art and Politics in the Cinema of Youssef Chahine," *Journal of Palestinian Studies* 28, no. 2 (Winter 1999): 88.

11. Benigno Sánchez-Eppeler and Cindy Patton, eds., *Queer Diasporas* (Durham, NC: Duke University Press, 2000), 2.

12. Chris Perriam, *Spanish Queer Cinema* (Edinburgh: Edinburgh University Press, 2013), 1, 4, chap. 1.

13. Madhava Prasad, *Ideology of the Hindi Film: A Historical Construction* (New Delhi: Oxford University Press, 1998), 5n14, cited in Gayatri Gopinath, *Impossible Desires: Queer Diasporas and South Asian Public Cultures* (Durham, NC: Duke University Press, 2005), 97.

14. Benedict Anderson, "The Strange Story of a Strange Beast: Receptions in Thailand of Apichatpong Weerasethakul's *Sat Pralaat*," in *Apichatpong Weerasethakul*, ed. James Quandt (Vienna: Synema and Austrian Film Museum Books, 2009), 158–60, 170.

15. Daw-Ming Lee, *Historical Dictionary of Taiwan Cinema* (Lanham, MD: Scarecrow, 2013), 374.

16. Fran Martin, "Introduction: Tsai Ming-liang's Intimate Public Worlds," *Journal of Chinese Cinemas* 1–2 (2007): 84.

17. Harry Benshoff and Sean Griffin, ed., *Queer Cinema: The Film Reader* (New York: Routledge, 2004).

18. Rajinder Dudrah, "Queer as Desis: Secret Politics of Gender and Sexuality in Bollywood Films in Diasporic Urban Ethnoscapes," in *Global Bollywood: Travels of Hindi Song and Dance*, ed. Sangita Gopal and Sujata Moorti (Minneapolis: University of Minnesota Press, 2008); Gayatri Gopinath and Javid Syed, "Desi Dykes and Divas: Hindi Film Clips," presentation at the San Francisco South Asian LGBT Festival QFILMISTAN, 2001.

19. Juan A. Suárez, "Hélio Oiticica, Tropicalism," *Criticism* 56, no. 2 (2014): 295–328.

20. Song Hwee Lim, *Tsai Ming-liang and a Cinema of Slowness* (Hong Kong: Hong Kong University Press, 2014).

21. Rey Chow, "A Phantom Discipline," *PMLA* 116, no. 5 (2001): 1392–93.

22. Teresa de Lauretis, "Queer Texts, Bad Habits, and the Issue of a Future," *GLQ* 17, no. 203 (2011): 244.

23. Deborah Shaw, conversation at Global Queer Cinema workshop, Brighton, April 2013.

24. Andrea Weiss, *Vampires and Violets: Lesbians in the Cinema* (London: Jonathan Cape, 1992), 100; Maria San Filippo, *The B Word: Bisexuality in Contemporary Film and Television* (Bloomington: Indiana University Press, 2013), 125; Ellis Hanson, "Lesbians Who Bite," in *Out Takes: Essays on Queer Theory and Film*, ed. Ellis Hanson (Durham, NC: Duke University Press, 1999), 190–91.

25. Patricia White, *Uninvited: Classical Hollywood Cinema and Lesbian Represent-ability* (Bloomington: Indiana University Press, 1999); Catherine Grant, "Planes of Focus: The Films of Lucrecia Martel," video essay presented at the Queer Cinema and the Politics of the Global workshop, Brighton, May 2012, http://vimeo.com/channels/222321.

26. Ann Cvetkovich, "Public Feelings," in *After Sex? On Writing since Queer Theory*, ed. Janet Halley and Andrew Parker (Durham, NC: Duke University Press, 2011), 173.

27. Eve Kosofsky Sedgwick, *Epistemology of the Closet* (Berkeley: University of California Press, 1990), esp. 1, 40–44, 82–86.

28. Lucas Hilderbrand, *Inherent Vice: Bootleg Histories of Videotape and Copyright* (Durham, NC: Duke University Press, 2009), 71.

29. Seminar on Distrify and queer film distribution at Flare: London LGBT Film Festival, May 2013.

30. Ramon Lobato, *Shadow Economies of Cinema: Mapping Informal Film Distribution* (London: British Film Institute and Palgrave, 2012), 1. See also Barbara Klinger, *Beyond the Multiplex: Cinema, New Technologies, and the Home* (Berkeley: University of California Press, 2006).

31. Lobato, *Shadow Economies of Cinema*, 1.

32. Lobato, *Shadow Economies of Cinema*, 4.

33. It should be noted that much of the research for this project has depended on these informal economies. Furthermore, the personal exchanges and collaborations that led to the completion of this book could be seen as an extension of these queer networks.

34. Lobato, *Shadow Economies of Cinema*, 116.

35. Daniel Herbert, "From Art House to Your House: The Distribution of Quality Cinema on Home Video," *Canadian Journal of Film Studies* 20, no. 2 (Fall 2011): 2.

36. Barbara Mennel, *Queer Cinema: Schoolgirls, Vampires and Gay Cowboys* (London: Wallflower, 2012), 111.

37. Dipesh Chakrabarty, *Provincializing Europe: Postcolonial Thought and Historical Difference* (Princeton, NJ: Princeton University Press, 2000).

38. Romit Dasgupta, "Queer Imaginings and Traveling of 'Family' across Asia," in *Queering Migrations towards, from, and beyond Asia*, ed. Hugo Córdova Quero, Joseph N. Goh, and Michael Sepidoza Campos (New York: Palgrave, 2014), 99–122.

39. OutRight Action International, "Indonesia: LGBT Network Celebrates IDAHO," http://iglhrc.org/content/indonesia-lgbt-network-celebrates-idaho.

40. Robert Kulpa, Joanna Mizielińska, and Agata Stasińska, "(Un)translatable Queer? Or, What Is Lost and Can Be Found in Translation," in *Import—Export—Transport: Queer Theory, Queer Critique, and Queer Activism in Motion*, ed. Sushila Mesquita, Maria Katharina Wiedlack, and Katrin Lasthofer (Vienna: Zaglossus, 2012), 115–45. See also Joanna Mizielińska and Robert Kulpa, ed., *De-Centering Western Sexualities: Central and Eastern European Perspectives* (London: Ashgate, 2011).

41. We are grateful to Victor Fan for pointing out this distinction.

42. Zvonimir Dobrović, in Masa Zia Lenárdic and Anja Wutej, dirs., *Queer Artivism*, documentary film (White Balance, Kosovo, Slovenia, 2013).

43. "Manifesto for the Third Queer Beograd Festival—Kvar, the Malfunction," Queer Beograd Collective, Belgrade, 2006, quoted in Irene Dioli, "Back to a Nostalgic Future: The Queeroslav Utopia," *Sextures* 1, no. 1 (2009): 12.

44. A prominent example of this kind of debate is Joseph Massad, *Desiring Arabs* (Chicago: University of Chicago Press, 2007), which insists that Western gay identities are an imposition in the Middle East. By contrast, Samar Habib argues for both the historic and present-day existence of homosexuality among women in the Muslim world: Samar Habib, *Female Homosexuality in the Middle East: Histories and Representations* (New York: Routledge, 2007). For an overview of these debates, see Christopher Pullen, ed., *LGBT Transnational Identity and the Media* (London: Palgrave Macmillan: 2012), 8–9.

45. Puar, *Terrorist Assemblages*, vii.

46. Penni Kimmel, "In Search of Sensibilities: The International Face of Gays on Film," *Manifest* (June 1983): 45–47.

47. Kimmel, "In Search of Sensibilities, 45.

48. Didier Roth-Bettoni, *L'homosexualité au cinema* (Paris: La Musardine, 2007), back flap copy, 684, 690.

49. Gopinath, *Impossible Desires*, 22; White, *Uninvited*, 194–215.

50. Even for those who do not live on Earth, as Michael Warner points out in his analysis of the heterosexual couple drawn by Carl Sagan and his wife, Linda, to represent our planet when carried into outer space by the US National Aeronautics and Space Administration's *Pioneer 10* spacecraft: Michael Warner, ed., *Fear of a Queer Planet: Queer Politics and Social Theory* (Minneapolis: University of Minnesota Press, 1994), xxi–xxiii.

51. Sarah Schulman, *Israel/Palestine and the Queer International* (Durham, NC: Duke University Press, 2012), 65.

52. Ernst Bloch, *The Principle of Hope*, vol. 1, trans. Neville Plaice, Stephen Plaice, and Paul Knight (Cambridge, MA: MIT Press, 1986), 218–19. For more on queer

theory's relationship to Bloch, see José Esteban Muñoz, *Cruising Utopia: The Then and There of Queer Futurity* (New York: New York University Press, 2009).

53. Rey Chow, *Sentimental Fabulations, Contemporary Chinese Films: Attachment in the Age of Global Visibility* (New York: Columbia University Press, 2007), 22.

54. Sean Cubitt, *The Cinema Effect* (Cambridge, MA: MIT Press, 2004), 338–39.

55. Kwame Anthony Appiah, *Cosmopolitanism: Ethics in a World of Strangers* (London: Penguin, 2006), xiii.

56. Pheng Cheah, "World against Globe: Toward a Normative Conception of World Literature," *New Literary History* 45, no. 3 (2014): 326.

57. Dudley Andrew, "An Atlas of World Cinema," in *Remapping World Cinema: Culture, Politics and Identity in Film*, ed. Stephanie Dennison and Song Hwee Lim (London: Wallflower, 2006), 24.

58. Galt and Schoonover, "The Impurity of Art Cinema," in *Global Art Cinema: New Theories and Histories* (New York: Oxford University Press, 2010), 1–28.

59. Ella Shohat and Robert Stam, *Unthinking Eurocentrism: Multiculturalism and the Media* (London: Routledge, 1994), 104; Fatimah Tobing Rony, *The Third Eye: Race, Cinema, and Ethnographic Spectacle* (Durham, NC: Duke University Press, 1996); Miriam Bratu Hansen, "The Mass Production of the Senses: Classical Cinema as Vernacular Modernism," *Modernism/Modernity* 6, no. 2 (1999): 59–77; White, *Uninvited*, 202; Dudley Andrew, "Time Zones and Jet Lag: The Flows and Phases of World Cinema," in *World Cinemas, Transnational Perspectives*, ed. Nataša Ďurovičová and Kathleen Newman (New York: American Film Institute and Routledge, 2010), 59–89.

60. Andrei Tarkovsky, *Sculpting in Time*, trans. Kitty Hunter-Blair (Austin: University of Texas Press, 1986), 62.

61. Mary Ann Doane, "The Close-Up: Scale and Detail in the Cinema," *Differences* 14, no. 3 (2003): 89–111.

62. Sergei Eisenstein, *Film Form: Essays in Film Theory*, ed. and trans. Jay Leyda (San Diego: Harcourt, 1949), 34–35, quoted in Doane, "The Close-Up," 107.

63. Helen Hok-Sze Leung, *Undercurrents: Queer Culture and Postcolonial Hong Kong* (Vancouver: University of British Columbia Press, 2008), 14.

64. Helen Hok-Sze Leung, "New Queer Cinema and Third Cinema," in *New Queer Cinema: A Critical Reader*, ed. Michele Aaron (New Brunswick, NJ: Rutgers University Press, 2004), 166.

65. Leung, "New Queer Cinema and Third Cinema," 158.

66. Gayatri Gopinath, "Queer Regions: Locating Lesbians in *Sancharram*," in *A Companion to Lesbian, Gay, Bisexual, Transgender, and Queer Studies*," ed. George E. Haggerty and Molly McGarry (Oxford: Blackwell, 2007), 346.

67. Gopinath, "Queer Regions," 344.

68. Sedgwick, *Epistemology of the Closet*, 60–63.

69. André Bazin, "The Festival Viewed as a Religious Order," trans. Emilie Bickerton, in Richard Porton (ed.), *Dekalog3: On Film Festivals* (London: Wallflower, 2009), 15; originally published in *Cahiers du cinéma* (June 1955).

Chapter 1. Figures in the World

1. Teresa de Lauretis, "Queer Theory: Lesbian and Gay Sexualities: An Introduction," *differences* 3, no. 2 (1991): xvi.
2. Cynthia Weber, "From Queer to Queer IR," *International Studies Review* 16, no. 4 (2014): 596–601.
3. Kath Browne, Jason Lim, and Gavin Brown, *Geographies of Sexualities: Theory, Practices and Politics* (London: Ashgate, 2007), 4.
4. Jordana Rosenberg and Amy Villarejo, "Queerness, Norms, Utopia," *GLQ* 18, no. 1 (2012): 1.
5. Roderick Ferguson, "Lateral Moves of African-American Studies in a Period of Migration," In *Strange Affinities: The Gender and Sexual Politics of Comparative Racialization*, ed. Grace Kyungwon Hong and Roderick Ferguson (Durham, NC: Duke University Press, 2011), 119.
6. Roderick Ferguson, *Aberrations in Black: Toward a Queer of Color Critique* (Minneapolis: University of Minnesota Press, 2004), 3; Chandan Reddy, "Homes, Houses, Nonidentity: *Paris Is Burning*," In *Burning Down the House: Recycling Domesticity*, ed. Rosemary Marangoly (Boulder, CO: Westview, 1997), 356–57.
7. Neville Hoad, "Queer Theory Addiction," In *After Sex? On Writing since Queer Theory*, ed. Janet Halley and Andrew Parker (Durham, NC: Duke University Press, 2011), 135–36.
8. For a fuller account of Israeli queer cinema, see Raz Yosef, *Beyond Flesh: Queer Masculinities and Nationalism in Israeli Cinema* (New Brunswick, NJ: Rutgers University Press), 2004. See also Boaz Hagin and Raz Yosef, "Festival Exoticism: The Israeli Queer Film in a Global Context," *GLQ* 18, no. 1 (2012): 161–78.
9. Richard Dyer, *Now You See It: Studies on Gay and Lesbian Film* (London: Routledge, 1990); Vito Russo, *The Celluloid Closet: Homosexuality in the Movies.* New York: Harper and Row, 1987.
10. Dyer, *Now You See It*, 2.
11. Dyer, *Now You See It*, 2.
12. Dyer, *Now You See It*, 275.
13. Dyer, *Now You See It*, 285.
14. Kutluğ Ataman, "Kutluğ Ataman Unplugged," quoted in Barış Kılıçbay, "Queer as Turk: A Journey to Three Queer Melodramas," in *Queer Cinema in Europe*, ed. Robin Griffiths (Bristol: Intellect Books, 2008), 121.
15. Program notes for the screening of *The Last Match* at Flare: London LGBT Film Festival, 2014.
16. Michael Warner, ed., *Fear of a Queer Planet: Queer Politics and Social Theory* (Minneapolis: University of Minnesota Press, 1994), xii.
17. Joseph Massad, "Re-Orienting Desire: The Gay International and the Arab World," *Public Culture* 14, no. 2 (Spring 2002): 85.
18. Inderpal Grewal and Caren Kaplan, "Global Identities: Theorizing Transnational Studies of Sexuality," *GLQ* 7, no. 4 (2001): 663.

19. See, e.g., Daniel Heath Justice, Mark Rifkin, and Bethany Schneider, eds., "Sexuality, Nationality, Indigeneity: Rethinking the State at the Intersection of Native American and Queer Studies," special issue, *GLQ* 16, no. 1–2 (2010); Peter Jackson, "Capitalism and Global Queering: National Markets, Parallels among Sexual Cultures, and Multiple Queer Modernities," *GLQ* 15, no. 3 (2009): 357–95; Nael Bhanji, "Trans/scriptions: Homing Desires, (Trans) Sexual Citizenship and Racialized Bodies," in *Transgender Migrations: The Bodies, Borders and Politics of Transition*, ed. Trystan T. Cotten (New York: Routledge, 2012).

20. Grace Kyungwon Hong and Roderick Ferguson, "Introduction," in *Strange Affinities: The Gender and Sexual Politics of Comparative Racialization*, ed. Grace Kyungwon Hong and Roderick Ferguson (Durham, NC: Duke University Press, 2011), 2.

21. David Eng, *The Feeling of Kinship: Queer Liberalism and the Racialization of Intimacy* (Durham, NC: Duke University Press, 2010), 34.

22. Justin Ocean, "The Reel World," *Out*, May 2011, 54.

23. Benigno Sánchez-Eppler and Cindy Patton, eds., *Queer Diasporas* (Durham, NC: Duke University Press, 2000), 2.

24. Eithne Luibhéid, "Queer/Migration: An Unruly Body of Scholarship," *GLQ* 14, nos. 2–3 (2008): 171.

25. Steve Rose, "Undertow," *The Guardian*, August 5, 2010. http://www.theguardian.com/film/2010/aug/05/undertow-review.

26. Jasbir Puar, *Terrorist Assemblages: Homonationalism in Queer Times* (Durham, NC: Duke University Press, 2008), xiii.

27. Puar, *Terrorist Assemblages*, 28.

28. Jin Haritaworn, Tamsila Tauqir and Esra Erdem, "Gay Imperialism: Gender and Sexuality Discourse in the War on Terror," in *Out of Place: Interrogating Silences in Queerness/Raciality*, ed. Adi Kuntsman and Esperanza Miyake (London: Raw Nerve Books, 2008), 1, 16. We note that this chapter prompted a strong response from white gay figures such as Peter Tatchell, who felt defamed, and the resulting media furor spread far beyond the usual limits of scholarly debate. For a recap, see Stacy Douglas, "On Defending Raw Nerve Books, or the Stuff of Good Feeling," *Upping the Anti*, vol. 11, 2010, http://uppingtheanti.org/journal/article/11-on-defending-raw-nerve-books.

29. Fatima El-Tayeb, *European Others: Queering Ethnicity in Postnational Europe* (Minneapolis: University of Minnesota Press, 2006), 82.

30. Sara Ahmed, *On Being Included: Racism and Diversity in Institutional Life* (Durham, NC: Duke University Press, 2012).

31. See, e.g., Sylvia Wynter and David Scott, "The Re-Enchantment of Humanism: An Interview with Sylvia Wynter," *Small Axe* 8 (September 2000): 119–207.

32. Samar Habib, *Female Homosexuality in the Middle East: Histories and Representations* (New York: Routledge, 2007), 126–29.

33. Eliza Steinbock, "Contemporary Trans* Cinema: Affective Tendencies, Communities, and Styles," paper presented at the Queer Film Culture: Queer Cinema and Film Festivals conference, Hamburg, October 14–15, 2014.

34. Sima Shakhsari, "Transnational Governmentality and the Politics of Life and Death," *International Journal of Middle East Studies* 45 (2013): 341.

35. Elizabeth Povinelli and George Chauncey, "Thinking Sexuality Transnationally, an Introduction," *GLQ* 5, no. 4 (1999): 443.

36. Tamar Jeffers McDonald writes that sexuality is the one factor untouched by radicalizations of the genre in the twenty-first century, noting that "to date there has yet to be a successful mainstream romantic comedy which permits the narrative to focus on a homosexual couple, although there have been several financially profitable independent films which have done so, such as *Go Fish* (Troche, 1994), *Jeffrey* (Ashley, 1995) and *Kissing Jessica Stein* (Herman-Wurmfeld, 2001)." Tamar Jeffers McDonald, *Romantic Comedy: Boy Meets Girl Meets Genre* (Chichester, UK: Wallflower, 2007), 80.

37. Frank Krutnik, "The Faint Aroma of Performing Seals: The 'Nervous' Romance and the Comedy of the Sexes," *Velvet Light Trap* 26 (1990): 57–58.

38. Counter to this critical reading, Shamim Sarif has discussed this structure as deliberate, a bringing into representation of family dynamics often navigated by young lesbians, and an attempt to provide a counterimage to that of Eastern men as abusive and angry: Ellise Fuchs, "It's the Film at Work: An Interview with Shamim Sarif and Hanan Kattan, *Pop Matters*, August 2001, http://www.popmatters.com/feature/144901-interview-with-shamim-sarif-and-hanan-kattan.

39. Rachel Lewis, "Towards a Transnational Lesbian Cinema," *Journal of Lesbian Studies* 16, no. 3 (2012): 277; Habib, *Female Homosexuality in the Middle East*, 331.

40. Elaine Castillo, "Beyond the Promise of Happiness: Rolla Selbak's *Three Veils*," *The F Word*, July 23, 2012, http://www.thefword.org.uk/reviews/2012/07/Three_Veils_Review; see also Sara Ahmed, *The Promise of Happiness* (Durham, NC: Duke University Press, 2010).

41. Ahmed, *The Promise of Happiness*, 89, 96.

42. See Janet Staiger, "Authorship Approaches," in *Authorship and Film*, ed. David A. Gerstner and Janet Staiger (New York: Routledge, 2003), 27–57; Olivia Khoo, "The Minor Transnationalism of Queer Asian Cinema: Female Authorship and the Short Film Format," in *Camera Obscura 2014, Vol. 29, Number 1 85: 33–57*, Patricia White, *Women's Cinema/World Cinema: Projecting Contemporary Feminisms* (Durham, NC: Duke University Press, 2015).

43. Robyn Wiegman, *Object Lessons* (Durham, NC: Duke University Press, 2012), 92.

44. David Martin-Jones, *Scotland: Global Cinema: Genres, Modes and Identities* (Edinburgh: Edinburgh University Press, 2005), 82.

45. Eng, *The Feeling of Kinship*, 31.

46. Daniela Berghahn, *Far-Flung Families in Film: The Diasporic Family in Contemporary European Cinema* (Edinburgh: Edinburgh University Press, 2013), 105, 114–15.

47. Eve Kosofsky Sedgwick, *Epistemology of the Closet* (Berkeley: University of California Press, 1990), 22.

48. Jason Lim, "Queer Critique and the Politics of Affect," in *Geographies of Sexualities: Theory, Practices and Politics*, ed. Kath Browne, Jason Lim, and Gavin Brown (London: Ashgate, 2007), 57–58.

49. Gaurav Desai, "Out in Africa," in *Postcolonial, Queer: Theoretical Intersections*, ed. John C. Hawley (Albany: State University of New York Press, 2001), 140.

50. Lynne Huffer, *Are the Lips a Grave? A Queer Feminist on the Ethics of Sex* (New York: Columbia University Press, 2013), 17.

51. See Heather Love, "Norms, Deviance, and the Queer Ordinary?" paper presented at King's College London, November 13, 2014; Lauren Berlant, "Structures of Unfeeling: *Mysterious Skin*," *International Journal of Politics, Culture, and Society* (March 11, 2015): 1–23.

52. Claudia Breger, "Configuring Affect: Complex Worldmaking in Fatih Akin's *Auf der anderen Seite (The Edge of Heaven)*," *Cinema Journal* 54, no. 1 (Fall 2014): 81.

53. Berghahn, *Far-Flung Families in Film*, 81.

54. Barbara Mennel, *Queer Cinema: Schoolgirls, Vampires and Gay Cowboys* (London: Wallflower, 2012), 110.

55. El-Tayeb, *European Others*, xviii.

56. Gloria Anzaldúa, *Borderlands/La Frontera: The New Mestiza* (San Francisco: Spinsters/Aunt Lute, 1987), 84.

57. Rich understands the subtitling of films as inherently generative of transnational affects and a crucial combatant to the monolingualism of the West. She recognizes the subtitled film as an aesthetic experience that is resistant to a monolingual culture, which she sees as producing "a child-like image of the world, it is an image of the self unwounded by the other, a self uninformed by the other, oblivious to its own status, inured to its needs, cosy in the cocoon of what once upon a time was called ethnocentrism and now, borrowing a term from queer studies in order to change it, might be known instead as imperial normativity": B. Ruby Rich, "To Read or Not to Read: Subtitles, Trailers, and Monolingualism," in *Subtitles: On the Foreignness of Film*, ed. Atom Egoyan and Ian Balfour (Cambridge, MA: MIT Press, 2004), 165.

58. Sedgwick, *Epistemology of the Closet*, 40–41.

59. Rinaldo Walcott, "Outside in Black Studies: Reading from a Queer Place in the Diaspora," in *Black Queer Studies: A Critical Anthology*, ed. E. Patrick Johnson and Mae G. Henderson (Durham, NC: Duke University Press, 2005), 92.

60. Chela Sandoval, "Dissident Globalizations, Emancipatory Methods, Social-Erotics," in *Queer Globalizations: Citizenship and the Afterlife of Colonialism*," ed. Arnaldo Cruz-Malavé and Martin Manalansan (New York: New York University Press, 2002), 21.

Chapter 2. A Worldly Affair

1. Quoted in Ging Cristobal, "'&PROUD' Myanmar's First-Ever LGBT Film Festival," International Gay and Lesbian Human Rights Commission, http://iglhrc .org/content/andproud-myanmar-first-ever-lgbt-film-festival.

2. Cristobal, "'&PROUD' Myanmar's First-Ever LGBT Film Festival."

3. David Archibald and Mitchell Miller, eds., "The Film Festivals Dossier," *Screen* 52, no. 2 (Summer 2011): 249–85, and the continued "Films Festival Debate" in the subsequent issues: see Nikki J. Y. Lee and Julian Stringer, "Counterprogramming and the Udine Far East Film Festival," *Screen* 53, no. 3 (Autumn 2012): 301–9; Roya Rastegar, "Difference, Aesthetics and the Curatorial Crisis of Film Festivals," *Screen* 53, no. 3 (Autumn 2012): 310–17. See also the Film Festival Yearbook series by the St. Andrews Film Studies publishing house, now in its sixth volume. On work concerning queer film festivals, see the four important fora that have appeared in *GLQ*. The first is edited and introduced by Patricia White ("Queer Publicity: A Dossier on Lesbian and Gay Film Festivals," *GLQ* 5, no. 1 (1999): 73–93). The other three are edited by Chris Straayer and Thomas Waugh ("Queer Film and Video Festival Forum, Take One: Curators Speak Out," *GLQ* 11, no. 4 [2005]: 579–603; "Queer Film and Video Festival Forum, Take Two: Critics Speak Out," *GLQ* 12, no. 4 [2006]: 599–625; "Queer Film and Video Festival Forum: Artists Speak Out," *GLQ* 14, no. 1 [2008]: 120–22). Other key essays include Roya Rastegar, "The De-fusion of Good Intentions: Outfest's Fusion Film Festival," *GLQ* 15, no. 3 (2009): 481–97; B. Ruby Rich, "The New Homosexual Film Festivals," *GLQ* 12, no. 4 (2006): 620–25; Marijke de Valck, *Film Festivals: From European Geopolitics to Global Cinephilia* (Amsterdam: University of Amsterdam Press, 2007).

4. André Bazin, "The Festival Viewed as a Religious Order" (1955), trans. Emilie Bickerton, in *Dekalog 3: On Film Festivals*, ed. Richard Porton (London: Wallflower, 2009), 15.

5. Kam Wai Kui and Suzy Capó, interviews London, March 2013.

6. Ragan Rhyne, "Pink Dollars: Gay and Lesbian Film Festivals and the Economy of Visibility," PhD diss., New York University, 2007," vii, chap. 3.

7. Catalogue, Frameline: San Francisco International LGBT Film Festival, 1997, Frameline archive, 24.

8. Frameline: San Francisco International LGBT Film Festival catalog 2006, Frameline archive, 53.

9. Gayatri Gopinath, "Local Sites/Global Contexts: The Transnational Trajectories of Deepa Mehta's *Fire*," in *Queer Globalizations: Citizenship and the Afterlife of Colonialism*, ed. Arnaldo Cruz-Malavé and Martin Manalansan (New York: New York University Press, 2002), 149–61.

10. Jigna Desai, "Homo on the Range: Mobile and Global Sexualities," *Social Text* 20, no. 4 (Winter 2002): 65–89.

11. Manny de Guerre, conversation at Queer Film Culture: Queer Cinema and Film Festivals conference, Hamburg, 15 October, 2014.

12. Jon Binnie, "Neoliberalism, Class, and Lesbian, Gay, Bisexual, Transgender and Queer Political in Poland," paper presented at the Cultural Translation of Sexuality in European Context conference, University of Warwick, June 10, 2013.

13. Sarah Schulman, *Israel/Palestine and the Queer International* (Durham, NC: Duke University Press, 2012), 40–47.

14. Ulelli Verbeke, "Welcome," in *Painting the Spectrum 10 Program,* film festival catalog, Georgetown, Guyana, 2014, 2.

15. Marc Siegel, "Spilling out onto Castro Street," *Jump Cut* 41 (May 1997): 131–36.

16. Martha Gever, "The Names We Give Ourselves," in *Out There: Marginalization and Contemporary Cultures,* ed. Russell Ferguson, Martha Gever, Trinh T. Minh-ha, and Cornel West (New York: New Museum of Contemporary Art, 1990), 191.

17. Hongwei Bao, "Queer as Catachresis: the Beijing Queer Film Festival in Cultural Translation," in *Chinese Film Festival Studies: Sites of Translation*, ed. Chris Berry and Luke Robinson (Basingstoke: Palgrave, 2017), 95.

18. This and subsequent quotes are from two interviews conducted with Stephen Kent Jusick, one on April 2, 2012, at the MIX office in New York, and the other on December 4, 2012, in Brighton.

19. Elena Gorfinkel, "Wet Dreams: Erotic Film Festivals of the Early 1970s and the Utopian Sexual Public Sphere," *Framework* 47, no. 2 (2006): 59–86.

20. "World Clique? Queer Festivals Go Global" panel at MIX film festival, Anthology Film Archive, New York, November 10–20, 1994, transcripts in MIX-NYC archive; see also Robert Reid-Pharr, "MiX-Defying," *Afterimage* 22, no. 6 (January 1995): 3–4.

21. As a film festival, MIX has also steered clear of "monetizing" itself in other ways, refusing to make itself amenable to certain forms of corporate and governmental funding (tourist boards and embassies). The festival has received small amounts of funding from local sources such as New York City's Department of Cultural Affairs and the New York State Council on the Arts and Materials for Arts, but has largely turned away from traditional corporate sponsorship.

22. For more on this urban history, see Sarah Schulman, *The Gentrification of the Mind: Witness to a Lost Imagination* (Berkeley: University of California Press, 2012). In the context of Hamburg, the Right to the City movement links gentrification and rent increases to German and European policies on immigrants and refugees. In both contexts, queer urban spaces are also loci for working-class antiracist politics.

23. Stephen Kent Jusick, "Director's Welcome," program, MIX NYC Queer Experimental Film Festival, 2011, 1.

24. Ger Zielinski, "On the Production of Heterotopia, and Other Spaces, in and around Lesbian and Gay Film Festivals," *Jump Cut: A Review of Contemporary Media* 54 (Fall 2012).

25. Stephen Kent Jusick, "Director's Welcome," program, MIX NYC Queer Experimental Film Festival, 2008, 2.

26. Stephen Kent Jusick, "Director's Welcome," program, MIX NYC Queer Experimental Film Festival, 2010, 3.

27. Conversation with Kam Wai Kui, BFI, London, March 19, 2013.

28. Skadi Loist, "A Complicated Queerness: LGBT Film Festivals and Queer Programming Strategies," in *Coming Soon to a Festival near You: Programming Film*

Festivals, ed. Jeffrey Ruoff (St. Andrews, Scotland: St. Andrews Film Books, 2012), 165.

29. Greyson Cooke, "Interview with Sri Lankan Director," Fridae: Empowering LGBT Asia, October 23, 2014, http://www.fridae.asia/lifestyle/2014/10/23/12725 .frangipani-interview-with-sri-lankan-director.

30. Dhanuka Bandara, "Frangipani: Political Art and Rarified Art," *Ceylon Today*, October 26, 2014, http://www.ceylontoday.lk/96–76347-news-detail-frangipani -political-art-and-rarefied-art.html.

31. Sridhar Rangayan, interview by Karl Schoonover, November 23, 2012, Brighton, UK.

32. "Batho Ba Lorato Mission Statement," quoted on International Lesbian, Gay, Bisexual, Trans and Intersex Association website, http://ilga.org/ilga/en/article /nXMlQzd12L. See also the LeGaBiBo blog, which mentions the festival as the "first annual film festival which explored LGBTI issues. This popular event was held in Gaborone and then toured Botswana, taking in Maun & Francistown and later Palapye": http://legabibo.wordpress.com/events.

33. LeGaBiBo website, http://legabibo.wordpress.com/2013/04/02/batho-ba-lorato -film-festival.

34. Nancy Nicol, Nick J. Mulé, and Erika Gates-Gasse, "Envisioning LGBT Global Human Rights: Strategic Alliances to Advance Knowledge and Social Change," *Scholarly and Research Communication* 5, no. 3 (2014): 1–14.

35. They also address heterogeneous publics. Where Muholi works within a theoretically informed art and academic world, the *Voices of Witness* series is produced by an Episcopal ministry with an activist aim of "healing the rift between sexuality and spirituality in the Church": http://claimingtheblessing.org/about. These films have very different modes of articulation and address, and screening them together constructs a radically revised spectator.

36. Oliver Phillips, "Constituting the Global Gay: Issues of Individual Subjectivity and Sexuality in Southern Africa," in *Sexuality in the Legal Arena*, ed. Didi Herman and Carl F. Stychin (London: Bloomsbury, 2000), 30.

37. John McAllister, "Tswanarising Global Gayness: The 'UnAfrican' Argument, Western Gay Media Imagery, Local Responses and Gay Culture in Botswana," *Culture, Health and Sexuality* 15, no. 1 (2013): 88–101.

38. A fascinating case study of these debates is in a report in the *Guardian* on the Out LGBT film festival in 2015 in Nairobi, which the newspaper ties to President Barack Obama's visit to Kenya and his vocal defense of LGBT rights. The comments section plays out many of the positions at stake in these fraught debates. Some commenters argue that homophobia in Africa is a relic of colonialism and evangelical Christianity or that it is perpetuated by the baleful influence of the church. Others espouse a liberal "white savior" position, suggesting that "we" in the West need to help LGBT Africans, and one commenter, claiming to speak from an African position, argues that homosexuality is not a serious issue for Kenya and interest in it reveals a Western perspective on Africa: Murithi Mutiga, "LGBT Film Festival Celebrates Kenya's Shunned Gay Community,"

September 12, 2015, http://www.theguardian.com/world/2015/sep/12/lgbt-film
-festival-celebrates-kenyas-shunned-gay-community.

39. McAllister, "Tswanarising Global Gayness," 94–95.

40. "Challenging the Refusal to Register LeGaBiBo in the High Court: Factsheet on the Case," Southern African Litigation Centre, February 2014, http://www .southernafricalitigationcentre.org/1/wp-content/uploads/2014/02/Fact-sheet -for-LEGABIBO-case.pdf.

41. "Challenging the Refusal to Register LeGaBiBo in the High Court," Southern African Litigation Centre, http://www.southernafricalitigationcentre.org/1/wp -content/uploads/2014/02/Fact-sheet-for-LEGABIBO-case.pdf, 1.

42. Justice Terrence Rannowane, Botswana High Court at Gaborone, "LeGaBiBo Judgment," November 14, 2014, http://www.southernafricalitigationcentre.org/1 /wp-content/uploads/2014/11/LEGABIBO-judgment-low-resolution.pdf.

43. For a larger selection of these images, see the slide show on the Global Queer Cinema blog, http://reframe.sussex.ac.uk/gqc/.

44. Barbara Mennel, *Queer Cinema: Schoolgirls, Vampires and Gay Cowboys* (London: Wallflower, 2012), 112. The trend could also be understood in the context of New Queer Cinema and its arrival in the mid-1990s as a kind of traveling festival aesthetic, a mobile and transnational quality emphasized in B. Ruby Rich's initial declaration of the category "New Queer Cinema": B. Ruby Rich, *New Queer Cinema: The Director's Cut* (Durham, NC: Duke University Press, 2013).

45. Rhyne, "Pink Dollars," esp. p. 200. See also Ragan Rhyne, "The Global Economy of Gay and Lesbian Film Festivals," *GLQ* 12, no. 4 (2006): 617–19. For more on the geopolitics of film festivals, see Skadi Loist and Ger Zielinski, "On the Development of Queer Film Festivals and Their Media Activism," in *Film Festivals and Activism: Film Festival Yearbook 4*, ed. Dina Iordanova and Leshu Torchin (St. Andrews, Scotland: St. Andrews Film Studies Publishing House, 2012), 49–62; Boaz Hagin and Raz Yosef, "Festival Exoticism: The Israeli Queer Film in a Global Context," *GLQ* 18, no. 1 (2012): 161–78; John Greyson, "Pinkface," *Camera Obscura* 27, no. 2 80 (2012): 145–53.

46. One example is UNESCO's HIV and Health Education website, which champions UNESCO Bangkok's use of films about sexual and gender diversity to redress community stigma and promote human rights: "Tackling Stigma through Creative Media," January 30, 2013, http://www.unesco.org.

47. Dennis Altman, *Global Sex* (Chicago: University of Chicago Press, 2002), 123.

48. David Eng, "The Queer Space of China: Expressive Desire in Stanley Kwan's *Lan Yu*," *Positions* 18, no. 2 (2010): 471.

49. Gayatri Chakravorty Spivak, "Righting Wrongs," *South Atlantic Quarterly* 103, nos. 2–3 (2004): 524, quoted in Joseph Massad, *Desiring Arabs* (Chicago: University of Chicago Press, 2007), 38–39.

50. Rosalind Petchesky, "Sexual Rights: Inventing a Concept, Mapping an International Practice," in *Framing the Sexual Subject: The Politics of Gender, Sexuality, and Power*, ed. Richard Parker, Regina Maria Barbosa, and Peter Aggleton (Berkeley: University of California Press, 2000), 82.

51. For a discussion of the vexed terrain of privacy in queer human legal debates, see Paul Johnson, "'An Essentially Private Manifestation of Human Personality': Constructions of Homosexuality in the European Court of Human Rights," *Human Rights Law Review* 10, no. 1 (March 1, 2010): 67–97.

52. "The Resolution on Human Rights and Sexual Orientation," Economic and Social Council Commission of Human Rights, 59th sess., agenda item 17, April 17, 2003 (E/CN.4/2003/L.92*), http://ilga.org/ilga/en/article/406.

53. "Human Rights, Sexual Orientation and Gender Identity," Human Rights Council, 17th sess., agenda item 8, June 15, 2011 (A/HRC/17/L.9/Rev.1), http://daccess-dds-ny.un.org/doc/UNDOC/LTD/G11/141/94/PDF/G1114194.pdf ?OpenElement.

54. Amnesty-USA, "About LGBT Human Rights," Last accessed May 2, 2016. http://www.amnestyusa.org/our-work/issues/lgbt-rights/about-lgbt-human-rights.

55. Agamben's reading of the refugee is relevant here for how it expresses precisely the exceptionalism at the core of human rights discourse. "The conception of human rights based on the supposed existence of a human being as such, Arendt tells us, proves to be untenable as soon as those who profess it find themselves confronted for the first time with people who have really lost every quality and every specific relation except for the pure fact of being human . . . so-called sacred and inalienable human rights are revealed to be without any protection precisely when it is no longer possible to conceive of them as rights of the citizens of a state": Giorgio Agamben, "Beyond Human Rights," in *Means without End: Notes on Politics*, trans. Vincenzo Binetti and Cesare Casarino (Minneapolis: University of Minnesota Press, 2000), 19–20. And like Agamben's reading of the hendiadys "man and citizen" in the title of the *Déclaration des droits de l'homme et du citoyen* of 1789, we might put pressure on the hendiadys queer and human: Agamben, "Beyond Human Rights," 20.

56. Agamben, "Beyond Human Rights," 20.

57. Jack Donnelly here borrows this term from Erik Erikson: Jack Donnelly, *Universal Human Rights in Theory and Practice*, 2d ed. (Ithaca, NY: Cornell University Press, 2002).

58. Also interesting to consider in this context is the "100% Human" theme of the Jakarta Q Film Festival in 2014, whose posters juxtapose square images of extreme close-ups of human skin in different tones and with different amounts and textures of hair. The promotional materials for the festival stated "we are all 100% human."

59. Jasbir Puar, *Terrorist Assemblages: Homonationalism in Queer Times* (Durham, NC: Duke University Press, 2008), 1–36.

60. Puar, *Terrorist Assemblages*, 67.

61. Judith Butler, "On Being Beside Oneself: On the Limits of Sexual Autonomy," in *Sex Rights: The Oxford Amnesty Lectures 2002*, ed. Nicholas Bamforth (Oxford: Oxford University Press, 2005), 74.

62. Butler, "On Being Beside Oneself," 69.

63. Butler, "On Being Beside Oneself," 74.

64. Ben Golder, *Foucault and the Politics of Rights* (Stanford, CA: Stanford University Press, 2015), 82–83; Michel Foucault, "Truth, Power, Self," in *Technologies of the Self: A Seminar with Michel Foucault*, ed. Luther H. Martin, Huck Gutman, Patrick H. Hutton (London: Tavistock, 1988), 15.

65. Butler, "On Being Beside Oneself," 74.

66. Butler, "On Being Beside Oneself," 77.

67. At the United Nations' Beijing Women's Conference in 2003, for example, the arguments to include women's sexuality in human rights led to protracted debates that resulted in the removal of language that understood women's sexuality as anything outside heterosexual coupling. In other words, in the specification of sexual rights, lesbian and bisexual women lost protection in the convention's resulting declarations: see the discussion in Petchesky, "Sexual Rights."

Chapter 3. Speaking Otherwise

1. Laura Mulvey, "Kiarostami's Uncertainty Principle," *Sight and Sound* 8, no. 6 (June 1998): 25.

2. Jonathan Rosenbaum, "A Few Underpinnings of the New Iranian Cinema," *Senses of Cinema* 21 (2002), http://sensesofcinema.com/2002/feature-articles /new_iranian.

3. Hamid Naficy, *A Social History of Iranian Cinema, Volume 4: The Globalizing Era, 1984–2010* (Durham, NC: Duke University Press, 2012), 215.

4. Michel Ciment and Stéphane Goudet, "Une approche existentialiste de la vie [Interview with Abbas Kiarostami]," (translation ours), *Positif*, no. 442 (1997): 89.

5. Jonathan Rosenbaum, discussion, World Cinemas, Global Networks conference, University of Wisconsin, Milwaukee, April 28, 2012.

6. Negar Azarbayjani, conversation, post screening Q&A, at Flare: London LGBT Film Festival, May 2013.

7. See, e.g., Naficy, *A Social History of Iranian Cinema*, 436.

8. Wibke Straube, "Trans Cinema and Its Exit Scapes: A Transfeminist Reading of Utopian Sensibility and Gender Dissidence in Contemporary Film," PhD diss., Linköping University, Linköping, Sweden, 2014.

9. As Eve Kosofsky Sedgwick puts it, discursive attention to homosexuality "has been impelled by the distinctly indicative relation of homosexuality to wider mappings of secrecy and disclosure, and of the private and the public, that were and are critically problematical for the gender, sexual, and economic structures of the heterosexist culture at large": Eve Kosofsky Sedgwick, *Epistemology of the Closet* (Berkeley: University of California Press, 1990), 71.

10. Martin Heidegger, "The Origin of the Work of Art," in *The Continental Aesthetics Reader*, ed. Clive Cazeaux, trans. Albert Hofstadter (London: Routledge, 2000), 81.

11. Craig Owens, "The Allegorical Impulse: Toward a Theory of Postmodernism," *October* 12 (1980): 69.

12. Owens, "The Allegorical Impulse," 84.
13. We return to the question of the aesthetic in chapter 5. See also Rosalind Galt, *Pretty: Film and the Decorative Image* (New York: Columbia University Press, 2011); Karl Schoonover, "Wastrels of Time: Slow Cinema's Laboring Body, the Political Spectator, and the Queer," *Framework* 53, no. 1 (2013): 65–78.
14. Dejan Sretenović, "The Figuration of Resistance," in *East Side Story Catalogue* (Belgrade: Salon of the Museum of Contemporary Art, 2008), 5.
15. Sretenović, "The Figuration of Resistance," 7.
16. Sretenović, "The Figuration of Resistance," 5.
17. Fredric Jameson, "Third-World Literature in the Era of Multinational Capitalism," *Social Text* 15 (1986): 65–88.
18. Aijaz Ahmad, "Jameson's Rhetoric of Otherness and the 'National Allegory,'" *Social Text* 17 (1987): 4.
19. Ahmad, "Jameson's Rhetoric of Otherness and the 'National Allegory,'" 13.
20. Jameson, "Third-World Literature in the Era of Multinational Capitalism," 69.
21. Jameson, "Third-World Literature in the Era of Multinational Capitalism," 69.
22. Ahmad reveals the silently gendered nature of Jameson's text. "His is, among other things, a gendered text. For it is inconceivable to me that this text could have been written by a US woman without some considerable statement, probably a full-length discussion, of the fact that the bifurcation of the public and the private, and the necessity to re-constitute that relation where it has been broken, which is so central to Jameson's discussion of the opposition between first-world and third-world cultural practices, is indeed a major preoccupation of first-world women writers today, on both sides of the Atlantic": Ahmad, "Jameson's Rhetoric of Otherness and the 'National Allegory,'" 24.
23. Allison McGuffie, "Queering the Revolution: The Political Force of Deviant Sexuality in *Mädchen in Uniform* and *V for Vendetta*," paper presented at the Society for Cinema Studies conference, Philadelphia, March 6–9, 2008.
24. Helen Hok-Sze Leung, "New Queer Cinema and Third Cinema," in *New Queer Cinema: A Critical Reader*, ed. Michele Aaron (New Brunswick, NJ: Rutgers University Press, 2004), 159.
25. John David Rhodes, "Allegory, Mise-en-Scène, AIDS: Interpreting *Safe*." In *The Cinema of Todd Haynes: All That Heaven Allows*, ed. James Morrison, 68–78 (London: Wallflower, 2007), 75.
26. See Marc Epprecht, *Heterosexual Africa? The History of an Idea from the Age of Exploration to the Age of AIDS* (Athens: Ohio University Press, 2008).
27. A similar scenario is outlined in Skadi Loist and Ger Zielinski, "On the Development of Queer Film Festivals and Their Media Activism," in *Film Festivals and Activism: Film Festival Yearbook 4*, ed. Dina Iordanova and Leshu Torchin (St. Andrews, Scotland: St. Andrews Film Studies Publishing House, 2012), 67. Writing about the first queer film festivals in the post-Soviet nations, they describe the support and sponsorship of various "international agencies" and "foreign cultural agencies" (i.e., embassies, institutes, etc.), writing, "With the

prospect of joining the European Union, the governments of the interested countries had to demonstrate their commitment to human rights as detailed by the [European Union]."

28. David Stratton, "Destiny," *Variety*, March 31, 1997, http://newsreel.org/video /DAKAN.

29. Lieve Spaas, *The Francophone Film: A Struggle for Identity* (Manchester: Manchester University Press, 2000), 224.

30. Jameson, "Third-World Literature in the Era of Multinational Capitalism," 71–76.

31. Stephanie Selvick, "Queer (Im)possibilities: Alaa Al-Aswany's and Wahid Hamed's *The Yacoubian Building* and Adaptation," in *LGBT Transnational Identity and the Media*, ed. Chris Pullen (London: Palgrave Macmillan: 2012), 131–45.

32. Omar Hassan, "Real Queer Arabs: The Tensions between Colonialism and Homosexuality in Egyptian Cinema," *Film International* 43 (2011): 18–24.

33. Thérèse Migraine-George, "Beyond the 'Internalist' versus 'Externalist' Debate: The Local-Global Identities of African Homosexuals in Two Films, *Woubi Cheri* and *Dakan*," *Journal of African Cultural Studies* 16, no. 1 (2003): 46.

34. Migraine-George, "Beyond the 'Internalist' versus 'Externalist' Debate," 52.

35. Migraine-George, "Beyond the 'Internalist' versus 'Externalist' Debate," 53.

36. Alexie Tcheuyap, "African Cinema and Representations of (Homo)Sexuality," in *Body, Sexuality and Gender: Versions and Subversions in African Literatures*, ed. Flora Veit-Wild and Dirk Naguschewski (Amsterdam: Rodopi, 2005), 143.

37. Thérèse Kuoh-Moukoury, cited in Tcheuyap, "African Cinema and Representations of (Homo)Sexuality," 143.

38. Abdoulaye Dukule, "Film Review: *Dakan* by Mohamed Camara," *African Studies Review* 44, no. 1 (2001): 119.

39. Rebecca Romanow, *The Postcolonial Body in Queer Space and Time* (Cambridge: Cambridge Scholars Press, 2006), 5–6.

40. Roy Armes, *African Filmmaking: North and South of the Sahara* (Bloomington: Indiana University Press, 2006), 153.

41. Gayatri Gopinath, "On *Fire*," *GLQ* 4, no. 4 (1998): 633.

42. Ratna Kapur, "Too Hot to Handle: The Cultural Politics of *Fire*," *Feminist Review* 64 (2000): 53–64; Jigna Desai, "Homo on the Range: Mobile and Global Sexualities," *Social Text* 20, no. 4 (Winter 2002): 65–89. See also Shohini Ghosh, *Fire: A Queer Film Classic* (Vancouver: Arsenal Pulp Press, 2010).

43. Gayatri Gopinath, *Impossible Desires: Queer Diasporas and South Asian Public Cultures* (Durham, NC: Duke University Press, 2005), 157.

44. Similarly, Gopinath argues for the importance of a spatial analysis to geopolitical concerns. "By depicting the privatized, seemingly sanitized domestic space as a site of intense female homoerotic pleasure and practice, both 'The Quilt' and *Fire* interrogate the teleological Euro-American narrative according to which lesbian sexuality must emerge from a private, domestic sphere into a public, visible identity": Gopinath, "On *Fire*," 635.

45. For more on how the film fits into histories of same-sex relations in Indian culture, see Ruth Vanita and Saleem Kidwai, eds., *Same-Sex Love in India: Readings from Literature and History* (London: Palgrave, 2000), 213–15.

46. Desai, "Homo on the Range," 84.

47. Gopinath, *Impossible Desires*, 132.

48. Walter Benjamin, *The Origin of German Tragic Drama*, trans. John Osborne (London: Verso, 2009).

49. The British DVD translates the Japanese *gai boi* as "queen," which is used as distinct from "drag queen."

50. Mark McLelland, "From the Stage to the Clinic: Changing Transgender Identities in Post-war Japan," *Japan Forum* 16, no. 1 (2004): 6.

51. Abé Mark Nornes, "The Postwar Documentary Trace: Groping in the Dark," *Positions* 10, no. 1 (Spring 2002): 45.

52. Aaron Gerow, interview with Toshio Matsumoto, *Interview Box 9* (1996), http://www.yidff.jp/docbox/9/box9-2-e.html.

53. Mika Ko, " 'Neo-documentarism' in *Funeral Parade of Roses*: The New Realism of Matsumoto Toshio," *Screen* 3, no. 2 (2011): 378.

54. Ko, " 'Neo-documentarism' in *Funeral Parade of Roses*," 380.

55. B. Ruby Rich, *New Queer Cinema: The Director's Cut* (Durham, NC: Duke University Press, 2013), 18.

56. Owens, "The Allegorical Impulse," 72. Drawing from Owens, Rhodes describes the working of queer allegory, writing, "Allegory works via a set of similarities and differences, repetitions and departures. The similarities and repetitions are usually what tip us off in a given text to the operations of allegory; the differences and departures are what give the allegory substance and meaning": Rhodes, "Allegory, Mise-en-Scène, AIDS," 74.

57. Matsumoto, quoted in Taro Nettleton, "Shinjuku as Site: *Funeral Parade of Roses* and *Diary of a Shinjuku Thief*," *Screen* 55, no. 1 (Spring 2015): 19.

58. Homay King, "Girl, Interrupted: The Queer Time of Warhol's Cinema," *Discourse* 28, no. 1 (2006): 98–120.

59. Sara Ahmed, *Queer Phenomenology: Orientations, Objects, Others* (Durham, NC: Duke University Press, 2006), 71.

60. de Lauretis, "Desire in Narrative," in *Alice Doesn't: Feminism, Semiotics, Cinema*. Bloomington: Indiana University Press, 1984, 103–57.

61. The Greek film *Strella* (Koutras, 2009) offers a more optimistic queer reading of Oedipus. Judith Butler and Athena Athanasiou discuss the film in terms of queer self-making, and Butler points out that while some viewers might want it to end in a moment of Oedipal catastrophe (similar to the actual ending of *Funeral*), it continues beyond tragedy to a new form of living: Judith Butler and Athena Athanasiou, *Dispossession: The Performative in the Political* (Cambridge: Polity, 2013), 61. Indeed, Marios Psaras reads the film's Oedipal family reunion as utopian: Marios Psaras, "Family, Nation and the Medium under Attack: Queer Time and Space in the 'Greek Weird Wave,' " PhD diss., Queen Mary, University of London, 2015.

62. McLelland, "From the Stage to the Clinic," 7.
63. Matsuda Masao quoted in Ko, "'Neo-documentarism' in *Funeral Parade of Roses*," 384.
64. Ko, "'Neo-documentarism' in *Funeral Parade of Roses*," 387.
65. Nettleton, "Shinjuku as Site," 14, 16.
66. Nettleton, "Shinjuku as Site," 18.
67. Nettleton, "Shinjuku as Site," 13.
68. Matsumoto, quoted in Nettleton, "Shinjuku as Site," 20.
69. Nettleton, "Shinjuku as Site," 17.
70. Gerow, interview with Toshio Matsumoto, 11.
71. Stephen Heath, "Narrative Space," in *Questions of Cinema* (London: Palgrave, 1981), 19–75.
72. Jihoon Kim, "Between Auditorium and Gallery: Perception in Apichatpong Weerasethakul's Films and Installations," in *Global Art Cinema: New Theories and Histories*, ed. Rosalind Galt and Karl Schoonover (New York: Oxford University Press, 2010), 125–41.
73. Peter Jackson, "Capitalism and Global Queering: National Markets, Parallels among Sexual Cultures, and Multiple Queer Modernities," *GLQ* 15, no. 3 (2009): 372.
74. Ahmed, *Queer Phenomenology*, 67–72.
75. Owens, "The Allegorical Impulse," 74.
76. Benedict Anderson, "The Strange Story of a Strange Beast: Receptions in Thailand of Apichatpong Weerasethakul's *Sat Pralaat*," in *Apichatpong Weerasethakul*, ed. James Quandt (Vienna: Synema and Austrian Film Museum Books, 2009), 158–77.
77. Carla Freccero, "Queer Times," in *After Sex: On Writing since Queer Theory*, ed. Janet Halley and Andrew Parker (Durham, NC: Duke University Press, 2011), 17.
78. Bliss Cua Lim, "Queer Aswang Transmedia: Folklore as Camp," *Kritika Kultura* 24 (February 2015): 178–225.
79. Leo Bersani, "Is the Rectum a Grave?" *October* 43 (Winter 1987): 197–222.
80. Philip Rosen, "History, Texuality, Nation: Kracauer, Burch and Some Problems in the Study of National Cinemas," in *Theorising National Cinema*, ed. Valentina Vitali and Paul Willemen (Berkeley: University of California Press and British Film Institute, 2006), 17–28.
81. Chris Berry, "East Palace, West Palace: Staging Gay Life in China," *Jump Cut* 42 (1998): 84–89.

Chapter 4. The Queer Popular

1. Vito Russo, *The Celluloid Closet: Homosexuality in the Movies*. New York: Harper and Row, 1987.
2. See, e.g., Richard Dyer, *The Culture of Queers* (London: Routledge, 2002); Richard Dyer, "Entertainment and Utopia," in *Only Entertainment*, 2d ed. (London: Routledge, 2002), 19–35; Richard Dyer, "Judy Garland and Gay Men," in *Heavenly Bodies: Stars and Society* (London: Routledge, 2013), 137–91; Richard

Dyer, *Now You See It: Studies on Gay and Lesbian Film*. London: Routledge, 1990; Alexander Doty, *Flaming Classics: Queering the Film Canon* (New York: Routledge, 2000).

3. Samar Habib, *Female Homosexuality in the Middle East: Histories and Representations* (New York: Routledge, 2007). Other national studies include Nick Rees-Roberts, *French Queer Cinema* (Edinburgh: Edinburgh University Press, 2008); Chris Perriam, *Spanish Queer Cinema* (Edinburgh: Edinburgh University Press, 2013).

4. Fran Martin, *Backward Glances: Contemporary Chinese Cultures and the Female Homoerotic Imaginary* (Durham, NC: Duke University Press, 2010); Thomas Waugh, "Queer Bollywood, or 'I'm the Player, You're the Naive One': Patterns of Sexual Subversion in Recent Indian Popular Cinema," in *Keyframes: Popular Cinema and Cultural Studies*, ed. Matthew Tinkcom and Amy Villarejo (New York: Routledge, 2001), 280–97.

5. David William Foster, *Queer Issues in Contemporary Latin American Cinema* (Austin: University of Texas Press, 2004). Other regional studies include Robin Griffiths, ed., *Queer Cinema in Europe* (London: Intellect, 2008); Andrew Grossman, ed., *Queer Asian Cinema: Shadows in the Shade* (New York: Harrington Park Press, 2000).

6. Martin P. Botha, "Queering African Film Aesthetics: A Survey from the 1950s to 2003," in *Critical Approaches to African Cinema Discourse*, ed. Nwachukwu Frank Ukadike (Lanham, MD: Lexington, 2014), 63–86.

7. Brian Larkin, *Signal and Noise: Media, Infrastructure, and Urban Culture in Nigeria* (Durham, NC: Duke University Press, 2008), 184.

8. Lindsey Green-Simms and Unoma Azuah, "The Video Closet: Nollywood's Gay-Themed Movies," *Transition* 107 (January 1, 2012): 35. See also Lindsey Green-Simms, "Hustlers, Home-wreckers, and Homoeroticism: Nollywood's *Beautiful Faces*." *Journal of African Cinemas* 4, no. 1 (2012): 59–79.

9. Green-Simms and Azuah, "The Video Closet," 38.

10. Green-Simms and Azuah, "The Video Closet," 38.

11. "Shocking Photo: Nollywood Releases Gay Movie," *Information Nigeria*, http://empressleak.biz/photo-nollywood-releases-gay-movie; "Nollywood Gay Movie Soon to be Released. Wooh!!" http://www.fabmimi.com/search/label/nollywood#.U3Rp1S8tU2g and https://naijaeast.wordpress.com/tag/nollywood.

12. Dennis Altman, *Global Sex* (Chicago: University of Chicago Press, 2002), x.

13. Altman, *Global Sex*, 98.

14. Larkin, *Signal and Noise*, 172.

15. Our thinking on modes of film consumption follows from our discussions with Connor Ryan and Ilana Emmett, March 2014. See also Connor O'Neill Ryan, "Lagos Never Spoils: The Aesthetics, Affect, and Politics of the City in Nigerian Screen Media," PhD diss., Michigan State University, East Lansing, MI, 2014.

16. "John Dumelo Almost Caught," YouTube video, 1.57, posted by iROKOTV, September 4, 2012, http://www.youtube.com/watch?v=ffJFPsjLbNo.

17. "John Dumelo's Gay Love Drama," YouTube video, 2.37, posted by iROKOTV, April 4, 2012, http://www.youtube.com/watch?v=foe7Iy_1UAI.

18. "Mercy Johnson Seduces Her Madam in Coperate [*sic*] Maid 2," YouTube video, posted by "Nollywood Extracts," 18 April, 2012, https://www.youtube.com/watch ?v=DwnxQRlvSGs; "Mercy Johnson Can't Control Her Sex Urge," YouTube video, 1.41, posted by Mercy Johnson, 13 November, 2014, https://www.youtube .com/watch?v=Alkj-QjgFSI&spfreload=10.

19. Green-Simms and Azuah, "The Video Closet," 46.

20. Pier Paolo Pasolini, "Gennariello," in *Lutheran Letters*, trans. Stuart Hood (Manchester: Carcanet New Press, 1983), 22.

21. Sedgwick argues that tolerance flags a limitation in thinking complexity, insisting that "these defalcations in our indispensible antihumanist discourses have apparently ceded the potentially forceful ground of profound, complex variation to humanist liberal "tolerance" or repressively trivializing celebration at best, to reactionary suppression at worst." This ceding of the space of the political is arguably more dangerous now than when she wrote these words: Eve Kosofsky Sedgwick, *Epistemology of the Closet* (Berkeley: University of California Press, 1990), 24.

22. Box Office Mojo, http://www.boxofficemojo.com/movies/?id=dostana.htm.

23. Rajinder Dudrah, *Bollywood Travels: Culture, Diaspora and Border Crossings in Popular Hindi Cinema* (London: Routledge, 2012); Ajay Gehlawat, *Reframing Bollywood: Theories of Popular Hindi Cinema* (New Delhi: Sage, 2010).

24. Anil Sinanan, "Dostana," *Time Out Los Angeles*, November 17, 2008, http://www .timeout.com/los-angeles/film/dostana.

25. Dudrah, *Bollywood Travels*, 47.

26. T. Muraleedharan, "Queer Bonds: Male-Male Friendships in Contemporary Malayalam Cinema," in *Queering India: Same-Sex Love and Eroticism in Indian Culture and Society*, ed. Ruth Vanita (London: Routledge, 2002), 181–92.

27. Rohit Dasgupta, "The Visual Representation of Queer Bollywood: Mistaken Identities and Misreadings in *Dostana*," *Journal of Arts Writing* 1, no. 1 (2014): 92. For an earlier account of queerness in Hindi cinema, see Shohini Ghosh, "False Appearances and Mistaken Identities: The Phobic and the Erotic in Bombay Cinema's Queer Vision," in *The Phobic and the Erotic: The Politics of Sexualities in Contemporary India*, ed. Brinda Bose and Subhabrata Bhattacharyya (Kolkata: Seagull, 2007), 417–36.

28. Box Office Mojo, http://www.boxofficemojo.com/intl/serbia/yearly/?yr=2011&p =.htm; Phil Hoad, "The Parade Is the Pride of Serbia," *The Guardian*, January 24, 2012, http://www.theguardian.com/film/filmblog/2012/jan/24/the-parade-pride -of-serbia.

29. Paul Hockenos, "Serbia's Brokeback Mountain," *Boston Review*, July 21, 2012, http://www.bostonreview.net/film/serbia%E2%80%99s-brokeback-mountain -paul-hokenos.

30. Srdjan Dragojević, "Srdjan Dragojević's Parada Number One in Home Territories," press release, F&ME, December 4, 2011, http://fame.uk.com/news/Srdjan_Dragojevics_Parada_The_Parade_Number_One_in_Home_Territories.

31. Hockenos, "Serbia's Brokeback Mountain."

32. Alexander Iskandaryan, "Armenia," ECOI.net, 2013, http://www.ecoi.net/file_upload/3256_1371628253_nit13-armenia-3rdproof.pdf.

33. Patricia Bass defends the film's use of stereotype as humor, pointing out that this ironic form has the potential to be productive, as opposed to the Western distanced view of the Balkan wars, which misread them as ethnic spectacle. Thus, she writes, "For example, in regards to Balkan conflict, perhaps laughing at ethnic stereotypes is the only way to swallow the enormity of the violence and oppression of the Yugoslav wars. With regard to homophobic hate crimes, perhaps laughing at the messenger bag of an effeminate veterinarian is the only way to face the horror of a thousand-person public human rights violation": Patricia Bass, "Homophobic Violence and Kitsch: A Match Made in Serbia?" *East European Film Bulletin*, March 2012, http://eefb.org/archive/march-2012/the-parade.

34. Nicolas Bardot, "La Parade," *Filme de Culte*, January 2013, http://www.filmdeculte.com/cinema/film/Parade-La-4677.html.

35. "Revisiting the Parade," *The Balkanist*, September 25, 2013, http://balkanist.net/revisiting-the-parade.

36. For more on debates over Balkan film politics, see Rosalind Galt, *The New European Cinema: Redrawing the Map* (New York: Columbia University Press, 2006).

37. Paul Hockenos, quoted in "Revisiting the Parade."

38. Srdjan Dragojević, interviewed in Hannah Pilarczyk, "Hit Serbian Comedy at the Berlinale: 'I Made a Film for Homophobes,'" *Der Spiegel*, February 15, 2012, http://www.spiegel.de/international/zeitgeist/hit-serbian-comedy-at-the-berlinale-i-made-a-film-for-homophobes-a-815527.html.

39. Branislav Jakovljević, quoted in Daniel Šuber and Slobodan Karamanić, "Symbolic Violence, Landscape and the Normalization Process in Post-Milosevic Serbia," in *Retracing Images: Visual Culture after Yugoslavia*, ed. Daniel Suber and Slobodan Karamanic (Leiden: Brill, 2012), 333.

40. Étienne Balibar, *We, the People of Europe? Reflections on Transnational Citizenship*, trans. James Swenson (Princeton, NJ: Princeton University Press, 2003).

41. Irene Dioli, "Back to a Nostalgic Future: The Queeroslav Utopia," *Sextures* 1, no. 1 (2009): 1–2.

42. Brett Farmer, "Loves of Siam: Contemporary Thai Cinema and Vernacular Queerness," in *Queer Bangkok: 21st Century Markets, Media, and Rights*, ed. Peter Jackson (Hong Kong: Hong Kong University Press, 2011), 98.

43. Peter Jackson, "An Explosion of Thai Identities: Global Queering and Reimagining Queer Theory," *Culture, Health and Sexuality* 2, no. 4 (2000): 407.

44. Milagros Expósito Barea, "From the Iron to the Lady: The Kathoey Phenomenon in Thai Cinema," *Revista de letras y ficción audiovisual* 2 (2012): 191.

45. Rosalind Morris, "Three Sexes and Four Sexualities: Redressing the Discourses of Gender and Sexuality in Contemporary Thailand," *Positions* 2, no. 1 (1994): 15–43.

46. Dennis Altman, "On Global Queering," *Australian Humanities Review*, July 1996, http://www.australianhumanitiesreview.org/archive/Issue-July-1996/altman.html.

47. Jackson, *An Explosion of Thai Identities*, 407. See also Käng, "Kathoey 'In Trend.'"

48. Dredge Byung'chu Käng, "Kathoey 'In Trend': Emergent Genderscapes, National Anxieties, and the Resignification of Male-Bodied Effeminacy in Thailand," *Asian Studies Review* 36 (2012): 475.

49. Käng, "Kathoey 'In Trend,'" 489.

50. Robert Horn, "Sporty Little Number," *Time*, April 2, 2001, http://www.time.com/time/world/article/0,8599,2039820,00.html.

51. "Volleyball's Iron Ladies Strike Box Office Gold," *Golden Scene*, March 14, 2000, http://www.goldenscene.com/ironladies/reviews/latestnews.html.

52. Bangkok Post article, cited in "Transvestites Rescue Thai Movies," BBC, March 23, 2004, http://news.bbc.co.uk/1/hi/entertainment/3558637.stm.

53. Sherman Chau, "Thailand's Iron Ladies Win in Hong Kong," *Screen Daily*, September 14, 2000, http://www.screendaily.com/thailands-iron-ladies-win-in-hong-kong/403618.article.

54. Box office statistics from International Movie Database business reports, http://www.imdb.com/title/tt0263957/business?ref_=tt_dt_bus; Chau, "Thailand's Iron Ladies Win in Hong Kong."

55. Horn, "Sporty Little Number."

56. May Adadol Ingawanij and Richard Lowell MacDonald, "The Value of an Impoverished Aesthetic," *Screening Southeast Asia* 24:2 (Fall 2004): 73.

57. Oradol Kaewprasert, "The Very First Series of Thai Queer Cinemas—What Was Happening in the 1980s?" paper presented at Sexualities, Genders and Rights in Asia: First International Conference of Asian Queer Studies, Bangkok, July 2005, 9.

58. *Screen Daily*, July 29, 2007, http://www.screendaily.com/29-july-2007/78.issue#.

59. Box Office Mojo website, July 20–22, 2007, http://www.boxofficemojo.com/intl/worldwide/?yr=2007&wk=29&p=.htm.

60. Daily Dose of Horror website, 2013, http://www.dailydoseofhorror.com/15-highest-grossing-thai-horror-movies.

61. See http://jhameia.tumblr.com/post/14494141191/ah-i-want-to-know-what-books-youve-read-lately-what.

62. Kenneth Chan, "Impossible Presence: Queer Singapore Cinema 1990s–2000s," in *Queer Singapore: Illiberal Citizenship and Mediated Cultures*, ed. Audrey Yue and Jun Zubillaga-Pow (Hong Kong: Hong Kong University Press, 2012), 169.

63. Nguyen Tan Hoang, "Tropicamp Maladies: Sex, Censorship, and Over-aesthetics in Queer Thai Cinema," paper presented at Global Queer Cinema workshop, Brighton, April 2013, 7.

64. On the version of the film available online, Prick's faux Louis Vuitton dress is blurred out, even as the film circulates easily outside the legitimate DVD market. Clearly, the international trademark division of LV is more frightening than antipiracy forces in the Thai film industry.

65. J. N. Erni, "Queer Pop Asia: Toward a Hybrid Regionalist Imaginary," paper presented at Sexualities, Genders and Rights in Asia: First International Conference of Asian Queer Studies, Bangkok, July 2005, 8–9.

66. "Transvestites Rescue Thai Movies," March 23, 2004, http://news.bbc.co.uk/1/hi /entertainment/3558637.stm.

Chapter 5. Registers of Belonging

1. Shohini Ghosh, "Bearing Witness, Performing Politics: Documentary and the Idea of Intimacy," keynote lecture, Visible Evidence Conference 21, December 13, 2014, Delhi, India.

2. For further discussion of queer documentary history, see Chris Holmlund and Cynthia Fuchs, *Between the Sheets, in the Streets: Queer, Lesbian, and Gay Documentary* (Minneapolis: University of Minnesota Press, 1997), esp. chaps. 2, 5; Michele Aaron, ed., *New Queer Cinema: A Critical Reader* (New Brunswick, NJ: Rutgers University Press, 2004).

3. Jacques Rancière, *The Politics of Aesthetics* (London: Bloomsbury, 2013), 39.

4. Linda Williams, "Film Bodies: Gender, Genre and Excess," *Film Quarterly* 44, no. 4 (Summer 1991): 2.

5. Miriam Bratu Hansen, "The Mass Production of the Senses: Classical Cinema as Vernacular Modernism," *Modernism/Modernity* 6, no. 2 (1999): 64.

6. Miriam Bratu Hansen, "Vernacular Modernism: Tracking Cinema on a Global Scale," in *World Cinemas, Transnational Perspectives*, ed. Nataša Ďurovičová and Kathleen Newman (New York: American Film Institute and Routledge, 2010), 288.

7. José Arroyo, "Film Studies," in *Lesbian and Gay Studies: A Critical Introduction*, ed. Andy Medhurst and Sally Munt (London: Cassell, 1997), 79.

8. Sara Ahmed, *The Promise of Happiness* (Durham, NC: Duke University Press, 2010); Heather Love, *Feeling Backward: Loss and the Politics of Queer History* (Cambridge, MA: Harvard University Press, 2009); Lauren Berlant, "Structures of Unfeeling: *Mysterious Skin*," *International Journal of Politics, Culture, and Society* (March 11, 2015): 1–23; Judith Halberstam, *The Queer Art of Failure* (Durham, NC: Duke University Press, 2011).

9. Ann Cvetkovich, "Public Feelings," in *After Sex? On Writing since Queer Theory*, ed. Janet Halley and Andrew Parker (Durham, NC: Duke University Press, 2011), 173.

10. Cvetkovich, "Public Feelings," 173.

11. Lauren Berlant and Lee Edelman, *Sex, or the Unbearable* (Durham, NC: Duke University Press, 2014), 6, 8.

12. See Emine Saner, "From *Nymphomaniac* to *Stranger by the Lake*, Is Sex in Cinema Getting Too Real?" *The Guardian*, February 21, 2014.

13. Rick Altman, "Dickens, Griffith, and Film Theory Today," *South Atlantic Quarterly* 88, no. 2 (Spring 1989): 345–46.

14. For instance, the Mexican director Arturo Ripstein released *El lugar sin limites/ Place without Limits* (1978), a scathing critique of macho culture in which the queer protagonist dies tragically at the end. Ripstein unpacks the connections between political corruption and masculinity in Mexico. And yet this film makes claims on worldliness, as well. The tragic death of Manuela evokes the impossibility of happy endings for gay people in patriarchal cultures. Most of all, though, it is the mode of melodrama that asserts a global address, where the excessive events, stylistic disjunctures and pure emotions of queer desire, unhappiness, and loss speak not only to a domestic viewer but to an international queer audience.

15. Ravi Vasudevan, *The Melodramatic Public: Film Form and Spectatorship in Indian Cinema* (New York: Palgrave Macmillan, 2011), 35, 42.

16. Bhaskar Sarkar, "The Melodramas of Globalization," *Cultural Dynamics 20*, no. 1 (March 2008): 48.

17. The actress Rehka is also a gay icon in India.

18. For more on the relationship between cinema and trans identities in Tamil Nadu, see S. R. Shanmugavel and Sriram Arulchelvan, "Experience of Exclusion: Tamil Cinema and Male to Female Transgender Community," *Asian Journal of Research in Social Sciences and Humanities* 6/5 (2016): 1112–28.

19. Venkatesan supports LGBT rights, new sex-work legislation, laws to enable greater space for women in the public sphere, and the discouraging of heterosexual marriage and reproduction: see Rituparna Chatterjee, "Rose Venkatesan, the First Transgender to Float a Political Party," *IBN Live*, March 14, 2012, http:// ibnlive.in.com/news/rose-venkatesan-the-first-transgender-to-float-a-political -party/238866-3.html.

20. "Ten Things You Didn't Know about Narthaki," June 17, 2011. https://www .facebook.com/notes/narthaki-the-film/ten-things-you-didnt-know-about -narthaki/193863510664473.

21. Shobha Warrier, "Narthaki: A Touching Film on Transgenders," *Rediff Movies*, May 4, 2011, http://www.rediff.com/movies/slide-show/slide-show-1-south -interview-with-director-vijayapadma/20110504.htm/.

22. *Paal*'s director also is not trans, but the assistant director is. This emerging exploration of transgender lives is a hybrid mode of production with both trans and cisgender participants.

23. *Common Gender*'s director is not a hijra, and the film raises complex issues of ownership, identity, and representation. What does it mean for a cisgendered man to make the first film to engage seriously with hijras as central characters? Robin worked closely with Dhaka's hijra community in researching the film, but he chose to cast non-hijra actors because he felt that casting hijras as themselves could produce an othering spectacle or a pitying charitable gaze. In Bangladesh, it might have been impossible for a hijra director to gain funding for such a project—or, indeed, to exist. We must pay

attention to the absences: the opportunities that are denied and the filmmakers and stars who cannot emerge.

24. Demitri Levantis, "Trans Movie Is Surprise Hit in Bangladesh," *Gay Star News*, July 9, 2012.

25. As Amita Nijhawan says, "Item songs are big-budget dance sequences in Bollywood and arresting examples of how bodies of dancing women in Bollywood, with fusion of traditional and contemporary dance genres construct new sites of sexual desire and identity in India." Item girls are the female singer-dancers who star in these scenes but sometimes do not appear anywhere else in the film's narrative: Amita Nijhawan, "Excusing the Female Dancer: Tradition and Transgression in Bollywood Dancing," *South Asian Popular Culture* 7, no. 2 (2009): 99.

26. Williams, "Film Bodies," 3.

27. Williams, "Film Bodies," 4.

28. Helen Hok-Sze Leung, *Undercurrents: Queer Culture and Postcolonial Hong Kong* (Vancouver: University of British Columbia Press, 2008), 67.

29. Of course, it is not always true that Hollywood film, even classical film, relegates social inequalities to the margins of melodrama. *Imitation of Life* speaks quite explicitly about racism, for instance, and recent melodramas such as *Brokeback Mountain* articulate homophobia as the substantive cause of queer loss.

30. Islam provides both a narrative and a formal mode of thinking equality in the film. In one scene, a group of straight men approach the hijra community. Visibly expecting trouble, the hijras are surprised to learn the straight men are a liberal Muslim group who want to invite them to tea so they can get to know one another. At the formal level, frequent overhead point-of-view shots imply the omniscience of a benevolent deity. Indeed, the film ends with an odd sequence in what might be heaven.

31. Judith Butler, *Undoing Gender* (New York: Routledge, 2004), 28.

32. We might think of political activism around lack of bathroom access for lower-caste women in India or the growth of transgender bathrooms in Thai schools. The ability to perform routine bodily functions safely and privately is a human rights cause at the same time that public bathrooms provide an example of the everyday apparatus of gender binaries.

33. Franco Moretti, "Kindergarten," in *Signs Taken for Wonders: Essays in the Sociology of Literary Forms* (London: Verso, 1983), 157–81; Steve Neale, "Melodrama and Tears," *Screen* 27, no. 6 (1986): 6–23.

34. Alamgir Khan, "Common Gender: A Bold Message," *Dhaka Courier*, July 14, 2012.

35. Rachael Scott, "Having a Gay Old Time," *The Guardian*, April 2, 2009, http://www.theguardian.com/film/2009/apr/02/shamim-sarif.

36. Scott, "Having a Gay Old Time."

37. Brian Whitaker, *Unspeakable Love: Gay and Lesbian Life in the Middle East* (Berkeley: University of California Press, 2006), 106.

38. A. O. Scott, "In French Occupation, a Broader Resistance," *New York Times*, March 16, 2012, C10; Jordan Mintzer, "Free Men: Film Review," *Hollywood Reporter*, August 7, 2011.

39. Ahmed, *The Promise of Happiness*, 12.

40. Laura Marks, *Touch: Sensuous Theory and Multisensory Media* (Minneapolis: University of Minnesota Press, 2002), 1–14.

41. Katharina Lindner, "Questions of Embodied Difference: Film and Queer Phenomenology," *NECSUS* 1, no. 2 (2012): 199–217; Elena del Río, "Film," in *Handbook of Phenomenological Aesthetics*, ed. Hans Rainer Sepp and Lester Embree (Dordrecht: Springer, 2009), 111–17.

42. Lindner, "Questions of Embodied Difference," 201.

43. Lindner, "Questions of Embodied Difference," 201.

44. Marks, *Touch*, 14.

45. Juan Suárez, "Film Grain and the Queer Body: Tom Chomont," paper presented at the Museum of Modern Art in Warsaw, January 10, 2012, http://vimeo.com /37820473.

46. Juan Suárez, "The Kuchars, the 1960s and Queer Materiality," *Screen* 56, no. 1 (2015): xx, 27.

47. Gavin Brown, "Autonomy, Affinity and Play in the Spaces of Radical Queer Activism," in *Geographies of Sexualities: Theory, Practices and Politics*, ed. Kath Browne, Jason Lim, and Gavin Brown (Farnham, UK: Ashgate, 2009), 195–205.

48. María Galindo and Mujeres Creando, "Les exiliadas del neoliberalismo"; our translation. For a range of their collectively written work, see www .mujerescreando.org. Last accessed April 2016. For scholarship on the group, see Elizabeth P. Monasterios, ed., *No pudieron con nosotras: El desafío del feminismo autónomo de Mujeres Creando* (Pittsburgh: Plural, 2006).

49. Women finding spaces of freedom and self-care on roofs is something of a leit-motif in recent lesbian cinema. In *Fire*, the lovers go to the roof to escape from family surveillance; in *Memento Mori*, the roof of the high school is a space free of teachers and rules; and in *Pariah*, a young black lesbian confronts her father on the roof of her girlfriend's apartment building.

50. Qwo-Li Driskill, Chris Finley, Brian Joseph Gilley, and Scott Lauria Morgensen, "The Revolution Is for Everyone: Imagining and Emancipatory Future through Queer Indigenous Critical Theories," in *Queer Indigenous Studies: Critical Interventions in Theory, Politics, and Literature*, ed. Qwo-Li Driskill, Chris Finley, Brian Joseph Gilley, and Scott Lauria Morgensen (Tucson: University of Arizona Press, 2011), 217.

51. Donna Haraway, "Companion Species, Mis-recognition, and Queer Worlding," in *Queering the Non/Human*, ed. Noreen Giffney and Myra J. Hird (London: Ashgate, 2008), xxiv.

52. Peter Jackson, "Capitalism and Global Queering: National Markets, Parallels among Sexual Cultures, and Multiple Queer Modernities," *GLQ* 15, no. 3 (2009): 372.

53. Mel Y. Chen, *Animacies: Biopolitics, Racial Mattering, and Queer Affect* (Durham, NC: Duke University Press, 2012), 95.

54. Butler, *Undoing Gender*, 17.

55. Chen, *Animacies*, 98.

56. Fran Martin, *Backward Glances: Contemporary Chinese Cultures and the Female Homoerotic Imaginary* (Durham, NC: Duke University Press, 2010), 172.

57. Ramaswami Harindranath, *Perspectives on Global Cultures* (New York: Open University Press, 2006), 12.

58. Judith Halberstam, *In a Queer Time and Place: Transgender Bodies, Subcultural Lives* (New York: New York University Press, 2005), 30. See also Kelly Baker, "Conceptualizing Rural Queerness and Its Challenges for the Politics of Visibility," *Platform* 12 (2011): 38–56; Parmesh Shahani, *Gay Bombay: Globalization, Love and (Be)Longing in Contemporary India* (London: Sage, 2008); Peter Jackson, ed., *Queer Bangkok: 21st Century Markets, Media, and Rights* (Hong Kong: Hong Kong University Press), 2011.

59. Theocritus, *Idylls: A Selection*, ed. Richard Hunter (Cambridge: Cambridge University Press, 1999).

60. Catriona Mortimer-Sandilands and Bruce Erickson, eds., *Queer Ecologies: Sex, Nature, Politics, Desire* (Bloomington: Indiana University Press, 2010), 23.

61. Nicole Seymour, *Strange Natures: Futurity, Empathy, and the Queer Ecological Imagination* (Champaign: University of Illinois Press, 2013).

62. Seymour, *Strange Natures*, 22; Mortimer-Sandilands and Erickson, 22.

63. Seymour, *Strange Natures*, 21.

64. Seymour, *Strange Natures*, 1.

65. Timothy Morton, *Ecology without Nature: Rethinking Environmental Aesthetics* (Cambridge, MA: Harvard University Press, 2007), 16.

66. Pietari Kääpä, *Ecology and Contemporary Nordic Cinemas: From Nation-Building to Ecocosmopolitanism* (New York: Bloomsbury, 2014), 1.

67. See, e.g., Gunnar Iverson, Astrid Söderbergh Widding, Tytti Soila, eds., *Nordic National Cinemas* (New York: Routledge, 1998); Sabine Henlin-Stromme "Nature Nation, and the Global in Contemporary Norwegian Cinema," PhD diss., University of Iowa, Iowa City, 2012; Finn Arne Jørgensen, Unnur Birna Karlsdóttir, Erland Mårald, Bo Poulsen, and Tuomas Räsänen, "Entangled Environments: Historians and Nature in the Nordic Countries," *Historisk tidsskrift* 1 (2013), http://www.idunn.no/ts/ht/2013/01/entangled_environments_historians _and_nature_in_the_nordic.

68. Seymour, *Strange Natures*, 36.

69. Ingrid Ryberg, "Sex without Optimism in Swedish Trans* Cinema," special issue, *Lambda Nordica*, forthcoming.

70. Jennifer Barker, *The Tactile Eye: Touch and the Cinematic Experience* (Berkeley: University of California Press, 2009), 120–44.

71. Judith Butler and Athena Athanasiou, *Dispossession: The Performative in the Political* (Cambridge: Polity, 2013), 59.

72. See, e.g., Amita Baviskar, "Tribal Politics and Discourses of Environmentalism," *Contributions to Indian Sociology* 31, no. 2 (1997): 195–223; Ravi K. Raman,
"Environmental Ethics, Livelihood, and Human Rights: Subaltern-Driven Cosmopolitanism?" *Nature and Culture* 3, no. 1 (2008): 82–97; Clifford Bob, " 'Dalit
Rights Are Human Rights': Caste Discrimination, International Activism, and
the Construction of a New Human Rights Issue," *Human Rights Quarterly* 29,
no. 1 (2007): 167–93.

73. Yamini Nair, "The Mangrove Whisperer," *Times of India*, January 8, 2011,
http://timesofindia.indiatimes.com/home/environment/the-good-earth/The
-Mangrove-whisperer/articleshow/7377286.cms.

74. Siegfried Kracauer, *Theory of Film: The Redemption of Physical Reality* (Princeton, NJ: Princeton University Press, 1997), 68.

Chapter 6. Queer Cinematic Time

1. David Eng, "The Queer Space of China: Expressive Desire in Stanley Kwan's *Lan
Yu*." *Positions* 18, no. 2 (2010): 481.

2. Eng, "The Queer Space of China," 482.

3. José Esteban Muñoz, "Thinking beyond Antirelationality and Antiutopianism
in Queer Critique," *PMLA* 121, no. 3 (2006): 826.

4. Jean Ma, *Melancholy Drift: Marking Time in Chinese Cinema*. Hong Kong: Hong
Kong University Press, 2010, 99, 122.

5. Roger Hallas, "Queer Anachronism and National Memory in *Proteus*," in *The
Perils of Pedagogy: The Works of John Greyson*, ed. Brenda Longfellow, Scott
MacKenzie, and Thomas Waugh (Montreal: McGill-Queen's University Press,
2013), 463.

6. Orlando Patterson, *Slavery and Social Death: A Comparative Study* (Cambridge,
MA: Harvard University Press, 1985).

7. Christopher Gittings, "Parsing the Transnational in John Greyson's Queer Cinema: *Proteus, Fig Trees, Covered,* and *Hey Elton*," in *The Perils of Pedagogy*, 2013:
113–34.

8. Elizabeth Freeman, *Time Binds: Queer Temporalities, Queer Histories* (Durham,
NC: Duke University Press, 2010); Judith Halberstam, *In a Queer Time and
Place: Transgender Bodies, Subcultural Lives* (New York: New York University
Press, 2005).

9. Freeman, *Time Binds*, 58, 63; José Esteban Muñoz, *Cruising Utopia: The Then
and There of Queer Futurity* (New York: New York University Press, 2009).

10. Richard Maltby, *Hollywood Cinema*, 2d ed. (Malden, MA: Blackwell, 2003),
16–17.

11. David Bordwell, Janet Staiger, and Kristen Thompson, *The Classical Hollywood
Cinema: Film Style and Mode of Production to 1960* (New York: Columbia University Press, 1985), 5.

12. In a literary context, Judith Roof claims that conventional practices of narrative
are structurally heterosexual and reproductive and demands that sexuality and

narrative must be divorced in order to undermine culture's oppressive social practices: Judith Roof, *Come as You Are: Sexuality and Narrative* (New York: Columbia University Press, 1996).

13. Thomas Waugh, "Cockteaser," in *Pop Out: Queer Warhol*, ed. Jennifer Doyle, Jonathan Flatley, and José Esteban Muñoz (Durham, NC: Duke University Press, 1996), 57.

14. Homay King, "Girl, Interrupted: The Queer Time of Warhol's Cinema," *Discourse* 28, no. 1 (2006): 98–120.

15. Lynn Spigel, *TV by Design: Modern Art and the Rise of Network Television* (Chicago: University of Chicago Press, 2009), 270.

16. Sara Ahmed, *The Promise of Happiness* (Durham, NC: Duke University Press, 2010).

17. Dudley Andrew, "*Amélie*, or Le Fabuleux Destin du Cinéma Français," *Film Quarterly* 57, no. 3 (2004): 38.

18. Rosalind Galt, *Pretty: Film and the Decorative Image* (New York: Columbia University Press, 2011), 22–26.

19. David Bordwell, "Intensified Continuity: Visual Style in Contemporary American Film," *Film Quarterly* 55, no. 3 (Spring 2002): 16–28.

20. See Jackie Stacey, *The Cinematic Life of the Gene* (Durham, NC: Duke University Press, 2010), chap. 1.

21. Dudley Andrew, "Time Zones and Jet Lag: The Flows and Phases of World Cinema," in *World Cinemas, Transnational Perspectives*, ed. Nataša Ďurovičová and Kathleen Newman, 59–89 (New York: American Film Institute and Routledge, 2010), 86.

22. Barbara Mennel, *Queer Cinema: Schoolgirls, Vampires and Gay Cowboys* (London: Wallflower, 2012), 111.

23. Influential accounts of queer film narrativity include D. A. Miller, "Anal Rope," *Representations* 32 (Fall 1990): 114–33; Lee Wallace, "Continuous Sex: The Editing of Homosexuality in *Bound* and *Rope*," *Screen* 41, no. 4 (2000): 369–87. Although they are not about synchrony as such, they do discuss circularity and nonlinearity in classical and postclassical American films, respectively.

24. Peter Limbrick, "From the Interior: Space, Time and Queer Discursivity in Kamal Aljafari's *The Roof*," in *The Cinema of Me: The Self and Subjectivity in First Person Documentary Film*, ed. Alisa Lebow (London: Wallflower, 2012), 102, 109.

25. Limbrick, "From the Interior," 114.

26. We are grateful to Samar Habib for introducing us to this film.

27. Lauren Berlant, in Lauren Berlant and Lee Edelman, *Sex, or the Unbearable* (Durham, NC: Duke University Press, 2014), 56.

28. Patricia White, *Women's Cinema/World Cinema: Projecting Contemporary Feminisms* (Durham, NC: Duke University Press, 2015).

29. David Bordwell, Janet Staiger, and Kristin Thompson, *The Classical Hollywood Cinema: Film Style and Mode of Production to 1960* (New York: Columbia University Press, 1985), 43.

30. Bordwell et al., *The Classical Hollywood Cinema*, 43.

31. Fran Martin, *Backward Glances: Contemporary Chinese Cultures and the Female Homoerotic Imaginary* (Durham, NC: Duke University Press, 2010), 15.

32. Lee Edelman, *No Future: Queer Theory and the Death Drive* (Durham, NC: Duke University Press, 2004); Bliss Cua Lim, *Translating Time: Cinema, the Fantastic, and Temporal Critique* (Durham, NC: Duke University Press, 2009), esp. chap. 2.

33. For interesting summaries of the debates and additional commentary, see Dan Fox, "Slow, Fast, and In Between" *Frieze blog*, posted May 23, 2010, http://blog .frieze.com/slow_fast_and_inbetween/; Vadim Rizov, "Slow Cinema Backlash" *Independent Eye blog*, posted May 12, 2010 (accessed October 22, 2011), www .ifc.com/blogs/indie-eye/2010/05/slow-cinema-backlash.php. Central to these debates is Nick James's contentious editorial "Passive Aggressive" Passive Aggressive. Adrian Martin provides a uniquely rich response to James in "Slow Defence," *Filmkrant*323 (July/August 2010), (accessed October 22, 2011), www .filmkrant.nl/world_wide_angle/7218; Matthew Flanagan provides an interesting account of the slow film's characteristics and suggests a series of effects that the slow image has on its spectator in "Towards an Aesthetic of Slow in Contemporary Cinema" 16:9, no. 29 (November 2008), (accessed October 22, 2011), www.16-9.dk/2008-11/side11_inenglish.htm.

34. Karl Schoonover, "Wastrels of Time: Slow Cinema's Laboring Body, the Political Spectator, and the Queer," *Framework* 53, no. 1 (2013): 65–78.

35. Song Hwee Lim, *Tsai Ming-Liang and a Cinema of Slowness* (Hong Kong: Hong Kong University Press, 2014).

36. "In practical viewing situations [of watching boring films], it's impossible to concentrate entirely either on a film or on one's self": Chris Fujiwara, "Boredom, 'Spasmo', and the Italian System," in *Sleaze Artists: Cinema at the Margins of Taste, Style, and Politics*, ed. Jeffrey Sconce (Durham, NC: Duke University Press, 2007), 243.

37. Roland Barthes, "Leaving the Movie Theatre," in *The Rustle of Language* (New York: Hill and Wang, 1987), 346.

38. For more on Hernández, see Gustavo Subero, "Where Gay Meets Race: Images of Indo-mestizo homosexuality in the work of Julian Hernández" in *Queer Masculinities in Latin American Cinema: Male Bodies and Narrative Representations* (New York: I.B. Tauris 2014), 91–128.

39. The American critic Armond White gives a more positive response to Hernández's queer style, calling him "the most musical, dancelike filmmaker since Max Ophuls": Armond White, "Desire Cinema's Dance Floor," *Out*, August 15, 2014, http://www.out.com/entertainment/armond-white/2014/08/15/.VbUHsprBTVI .gmail.

40. Matthew Hunt, "Exclusive Interview with Apichatpong Weerasethakul," *Encounter Thailand* 2, no. 13 (May 2013): 36–39, http://www.matthewhunt.com /portfolio/exclusiveinterviewwithapichatpongweerasethakul.pdf.

41. Mary Ann Doane, *The Emergence of Cinematic Time: Modernity, Contingency, the Archive* (Cambridge, MA: Harvard University Press, 2002), 162.

42. Matthew Tinkcom, *Working like a Homosexual: Camp, Capital, Cinema* (Durham, NC: Duke University Press, 2002), 94.

43. Homay King, "Stroboscopic: Warhol and the Exploding Plastic Inevitable," *Criticism* 56, no. 3 (2014): 474. See also Parker Tyler, "Drag Time and Drug Time," in *Andy Warhol: Film Factory*, ed. Michael O'Pray (London: British Film Institute, 1989), 92–103, and the reading of Tyler in Juan A. Suárez, "Warhol's 1960s' Films, Amphetamine, and Queer Materiality," *Criticism* 56, no. 3 (2014): 627.

44. Apichatpong's fellow Thai filmmaker Pen-ek Ratanaruang has said, "Our films are slow. Qualities get lost [when they are watched] on the computer or even DVD. You don't even survive [the films], you walk around, clean dust off your book shelves. Our films have to be seen in the cinema in the dark. It's irreplaceable": conversation with Apichatpong Weerasethakul and Pen-ek Ratanaruang led by La Frances Hui, curator of the "Blissfully Thai" film series, Asia Society, New York, May 14, 2011.

45. André Bazin, "The Grandeur of Limelight," in *What Is Cinema?* vol. 2 (Berkeley: University of California Press, 2004), 132.

46. Fujiwara, "Boredom, 'Spasmo', and the Italian System."

47. Song Hwee Lim, *Celluloid Comrades: Representations of Male Homosexuality in Contemporary Chinese Cinemas* (Honolulu: University of Hawai'i Press, 2006), 148–50.

48. Bienvenido Lumbera, quoted in Joel David, ed., *Fields of Vision: Critical Applications in Recent Philippine Cinema* (Quezon City: Ateneo de Manila University Press, 1995), 26. For a discussion of *bomba*'s relationship to sexuality in post-Marcos films, see David, *Fields of Vision*, 112–13. For a more conventional history of *bomba* films, see Bryan L. Yeatter, *Cinema of the Philippines: A History and Filmography, 1897–2005* (Jefferson, NC: McFarland, 2007), esp. 107–10, 113–15.

49. Most of these early representations were of queer men. As David notes, "Lesbians had their share of exposure, but in a different manner" and much later: David, *Fields of Vision*, 27. For a discussion of lesbianism in Filipino films from the early 1980s onward, see David, *Fields of Vision*, 30–31.

50. Bliss Cua Lim, "Archival Fragility: Philippine Cinema and the Challenge of Sustainable Preservation." *Kyoto Center for Southeast Asian Studies Newsletter* (2013): 18.

51. Bliss Cua Lim, "Temporality and Archival Constraint in Philippine Cinema," paper presented at Cinematic Times conference, University of California, Berkeley, November 15, 2013. See also Akira Lippit, *Atomic Light (Shadow Optics)* (Minneapolis: University of Minnesota Press, 2005).

52. Ramon Lobato, *Shadow Economies of Cinema: Mapping Informal Film Distribution* (London: British Film Institute and Palgrave, 2012), 14, 45.

53. Lucas Hilderbrand, *Inherent Vice: Bootleg Histories of Videotape and Copyright* (Durham, NC: Duke University Press, 2009), 16.

54. Hilderbrand, *Inherent Vice*, 163.

55. "As loans or presents, circulated from person to person, bootleg tapes operate within a gift economy, with the material wear and interpersonal resonances such forms of exchange suggest": Hilderbrand, *Inherent Vice*, 189.

56. Of course, other forms of disruption are possible when viewing online video, considering connection and web traffic.

57. David Bordwell, *The Films of Carl-Theodor Dreyer* (Berkeley: University of California Press, 1981), 96, 103.

58. Dudley Andrew, "Cinema and Culture," *Humanities* 6, no. 4 (August 1985): 24–25.

59. Hilderbrand, *Inherent Vice*, 193–94.

60. Experimental film, of course, has a specific history of glitches, jump cuts, and excision. Feminist artists such as Naomi Uman and Peggy Ahwesh have excised the female body from pornographic film, and Carolee Schneemann uses disjunctive editing to revise the erotic potential for showing bodies and sex acts. Although these films emerge from quite different contexts, it is valuable to think across feminist and queer formal experimentation to trace etiologies of response to what patriarchy excises from view.

61. Gilberto Blasini, "The Sounds of Queerness in Contemporary Latin American Cinema," paper presented at World Cinemas, Global Networks conference, University of Wisconsin, Milwaukee, April 28, 2012.

62. See the notion of temporal drag as an alternative to linear historicity, including "retrogression, delay, and the pull of the past upon the present," in Elizabeth Freeman, "Packing History: Count(er)ing Generations," *New Literary History* 31, no. 4 (2000): 728.

63. Raymond Williams, *Marxism and Literature* (Oxford: Oxford University Press, 1977), 130.

64. Karim Aïnouz, conversation, postscreening Q&A, Brighton, UK, May 5, 2015.

BIBLIOGRAPHY

Aaron, Michele, ed. *New Queer Cinema: A Critical Reader*. New Brunswick, NJ: Rutgers University Press, 2004.

Agamben, Giorgio. "Beyond Human Rights." In *Means without End: Notes on Politics*, trans. Vincenzo Binetti and Cesare Casarino, 15–26. Minneapolis: University of Minnesota Press, 2000.

Ahmad, Aijaz. "Jameson's Rhetoric of Otherness and the 'National Allegory.'" *Social Text* 17 (1987): 3–25.

Ahmed, Sara. *On Being Included: Racism and Diversity in Institutional Life*. Durham, NC: Duke University Press, 2012.

Ahmed, Sara. *The Promise of Happiness*. Durham, NC: Duke University Press, 2010.

Ahmed, Sara. *Queer Phenomenology: Orientations, Objects, Others*. Durham, NC: Duke University Press, 2006.

Altman, Dennis. "On Global Queering." *Australian Humanities Review*, July 1996, http://www.australianhumanitiesreview.org/archive/Issue-July-1996/altman.html.

Altman, Dennis. *Global Sex*. Chicago: University of Chicago Press, 2002.

Altman, Rick. "Dickens, Griffith, and Film Theory Today." *South Atlantic Quarterly* 88, no. 2 (Spring 1989): 345–46.

Anderson, Benedict. "The Strange Story of a Strange Beast: Receptions in Thailand of Apichatpong Weerasethakul's *Sat Pralaat*." In *Apichatpong Weerasethakul*, ed. James Quandt, 158–77. Vienna: Synema and Austrian Film Museum Books, 2009.

Andrew, Dudley. "*Amélie*, or Le Fabuleux Destin du Cinéma Français." *Film Quarterly* 57, no. 3 (2004): 34–46.

Andrew, Dudley. "An Atlas of World Cinema." In *Remapping World Cinema: Culture, Politics and Identity in Film*, ed. Stephanie Dennison and Song Hwee Lim, 19–29. London: Wallflower, 2006.

Andrew, Dudley. "Cinema and Culture." *Humanities* 6, no. 4 (August 1985): 24–25.

Andrew, Dudley. "Time Zones and Jet Lag: The Flows and Phases of World Cinema." In *World Cinemas, Transnational Perspectives*, ed. Nataša Ďurovičová and Kathleen Newman, 59–89. New York: AFI/Routledge, 2010.

Anzaldúa, Gloria. *Borderlands/La Frontera: The New Mestiza*. San Francisco: Spinsters/ Aunt Lute, 1987.

Appiah, Kwame Anthony. *Cosmopolitanism: Ethics in a World of Strangers*. London: Penguin, 2006.

Apter, Emily. *Against World Literature: On the Politics of Untranslatability*. London: Verso, 2013.

Archibald, David, and Mitchell Miller, eds. "The Film Festivals Dossier." *Screen* 52, no. 2 (Summer 2011): 249–85.

Armes, Roy. *African Filmmaking: North and South of the Sahara*. Bloomington: Indiana University Press, 2006.

Arroyo, José. "Film Studies." In *Lesbian and Gay Studies: A Critical Introduction*, ed. Andy Medhurst and Sally Munt, 67–83. London: Cassell, 1997.

Baker, Kelly. "Conceptualizing Rural Queerness and Its Challenges for the Politics of Visibility." *Platforum* 12 (2011): 38–56.

Balibar, Étienne. *We, the People of Europe? Reflections on Transnational Citizenship*, trans. James Swenson. Princeton, NJ: Princeton University Press, 2003.

Bao, Hongwei. "Queer as Catachresis: the Beijing Queer Film Festival in Cultural Translation." In *Chinese Film Festival Studies*, ed. Chris Berry and Luke Robinson. Basingstoke: Palgrave, forthcoming.

Barker, Jennifer. *The Tactile Eye: Touch and the Cinematic Experience*. Berkeley: University of California Press, 2009.

Barthes, Roland. "Leaving the Movie Theatre." In *The Rustle of Language*. New York: Hill and Wang, 1987.

Bass, Patricia. "Homophobic Violence and Kitsch: A Match Made in Serbia?" *East European Film Bulletin*, March 2012, http://eefb.org/archive/march-2012/the-parade.

Baviskar, Amita. "Tribal Politics and Discourses of Environmentalism." *Contributions to Indian Sociology* 31, no. 2 (1997): 195–223.

Bazin, André. "The Festival Viewed as a Religious Order" (1955), trans. Emilie Bickerton. In *Dekalog 3: On Film Festivals*, ed. Richard Porton, 13–19. London: Wallflower, 2009.

Bazin, André. "The Grandeur of Limelight." In *What Is Cinema?* vol. 2, 128–39. Berkeley: University of California Press, 2004.

Benjamin, Walter. *The Origin of German Tragic Drama*, trans. John Osborne. London: Verso, 2009.

Benshoff, Harry, and Sean Griffin, eds. *Queer Cinema: The Film Reader*. New York: Routledge, 2004.

Berghahn, Daniela. *Far-Flung Families in Film: The Diasporic Family in Contemporary European Cinema*. Edinburgh: Edinburgh University Press, 2013.

Berlant, Lauren. "Structures of Unfeeling: *Mysterious Skin*." *International Journal of Politics, Culture, and Society* (March 11, 2015): 1–23.

Berlant, Lauren, and Lee Edelman. *Sex, or the Unbearable*. Durham, NC: Duke University Press, 2014.

Berry, Chris. "East Palace, West Palace: Staging Gay Life in China." *Jump Cut* 42 (1998): 84–89.

Bersani, Leo. "Is the Rectum a Grave?" *October* 43 (Winter 1987): 197–222.

Bhanji, Nael. "Trans/scriptions: Homing Desires, (Trans) Sexual Citizenship and Racialized Bodies." In *Transgender Migrations: The Bodies, Borders and Politics of Transition*, ed. Tristan Cotton, 357–95. New York: Routledge, 2012.

Binnie, Jon. "Neoliberalism, Class, and Lesbian, Gay, Bisexual, Transgender and Queer Political in Poland." Paper presented at the Cultural Translation of Sexuality in European Context conference, University of Warwick, June 10, 2013.

Blasini, Gilberto. "The Sounds of Queerness in Contemporary Latin American Cinema." Paper presented at World Cinemas, Global Networks conference, University of Wisconsin, Milwaukee, April 28, 2012.

Bloch, Ernst. *The Principle of Hope*, vol. 1, trans. Neville Plaice, Stephen Plaice, and Paul Knight. Cambridge, MA: MIT Press, 1986.

Bordwell, David. *The Films of Carl-Theodor Dreyer*. Berkeley: University of California Press, 1981.

Bordwell, David. "Intensified Continuity: Visual Style in Contemporary American Film." *Film Quarterly* 55, no. 3 (Spring 2002): 16–28.

Bordwell, David, Janet Staiger, and Kristin Thompson. *The Classical Hollywood Cinema: Film Style and Mode of Production to 1960*. New York: Columbia University Press, 1985.

Botha, Martin P. "Queering African Film Aesthetics: A Survey from the 1950s to 2003." In *Critical Approaches to African Cinema Discourse*, ed. Nwachukwu Frank Ukadike, 63–86. Lanham, MD: Lexington, 2014.

Breger, Claudia. "Configuring Affect: Complex Worldmaking in Fatih Akin's *Auf der anderen Seite (The Edge of Heaven)*." *Cinema Journal* 54, no. 1 (Fall 2014): 65–87.

Brown, Gavin. "Autonomy, Affinity and Play in the Spaces of Radical Queer Activism." In *Geographies of Sexualities: Theory, Practices and Politics*, ed. Kath Browne, Jason Lim, and Gavin Brown, 195–205. Farnham, UK: Ashgate, 2009.

Browne, Kath, Jason Lim, and Gavin Brown, eds. *Geographies of Sexualities: Theory, Practices and Politics*. London: Ashgate, 2007.

Butler, Judith. "On Being Beside Oneself: On the Limits of Sexual Autonomy." In *Sex Rights: The Oxford Amnesty Lectures 2002*, ed. Nicholas Bamforth, 48–78. Oxford: Oxford University Press, 2005.

Butler, Judith. *Undoing Gender*. New York: Routledge, 2004.

Butler, Judith, and Athena Anthanasiou. *Dispossession: The Performative in the Political.* Cambridge: Polity, 2013.

Casanova, Pascale. *The World Republic of Letters,* trans. M. B. DeBevoise. Cambridge, MA: Harvard University Press, 2007.

Chakrabarty, Dipesh. *Provincializing Europe: Postcolonial Thought and Historical Difference.* Princeton, NJ: Princeton University Press, 2000.

Chan, Kenneth. "Impossible Presence: Queer Singapore Cinema 1990s–2000s." In *Queer Singapore: Illiberal Citizenship and Mediated Cultures,* ed. Audrey Yue and Jun Zubillaga-Pow, 161–74. Hong Kong: Hong Kong University Press, 2012.

Cheah, Pheng, "World against Globe: Toward a Normative Conception of World Literature." *New Literary History* 45, no. 3 (2014): 303–29.

Cheah, Pheng, and Bruce Robbins, eds. *Cosmopolitics: Thinking and Feeling beyond the Nation.* Minneapolis: University of Minnesota Press, 1998.

Chen, Mel Y. *Animacies: Biopolitics, Racial Mattering, and Queer Affect.* Durham, NC: Duke University Press, 2012.

Chow, Rey. "A Phantom Discipline." *PMLA* 116, no. 5 (2001): 1392–93.

Chow, Rey. *Sentimental Fabulations, Contemporary Chinese Films: Attachment in the Age of Global Visibility.* New York: Columbia University Press, 2007.

Ciment, Michel, and Stéphane Goudet. "Une approche existentialiste de la vie [Interview with Abbas Kiarostami]." *Positif* 442 (1997): 83–89.

Clifford, Bob. "'Dalit Rights Are Human Rights': Caste Discrimination, International Activism, and the Construction of a New Human Rights Issue." *Human Rights Quarterly* 29, no. 1 (2007): 167–93.

Cubitt, Sean. *The Cinema Effect.* Cambridge, MA: MIT Press, 2004.

Cvetkovich, Ann. "Public Feelings." In *After Sex? On Writing since Queer Theory,* ed. Janet Halley and Andrew Parker, 169–79. Durham, NC: Duke University Press, 2011.

Damrosch, David. *What Is World Literature?* Princeton, NJ: Princeton University Press, 2003.

Dasgupta, Rohit. "The Visual Representation of Queer Bollywood: Mistaken Identities and Misreadings in *Dostana*." *Journal of Arts Writing* 1, no. 1 (2014): 91–101.

Dasgupta, Romit. "Queer Imaginings and Traveling of 'Family' across Asia." In *Queering Migrations towards, from, and beyond Asia,* ed. Hugo Córdova Quero, Joseph N. Goh, and Michael Sepidoza Campos, 99–122. New York: Palgrave, 2014.

David, Joel, ed. *Fields of Vision: Critical Applications in Recent Philippine Cinema.* Quezon City: Ateneo de Manila University Press, 1995.

de Lauretis, Teresa. *Alice Doesn't: Feminism, Semiotics, Cinema.* Bloomington: Indiana University Press, 1984.

de Lauretis, Teresa. "Queer Texts, Bad Habits, and the Issue of a Future." *GLQ* 17, no. 203 (2011): 243–63.

de Lauretis, Teresa. "Queer Theory: Lesbian and Gay Sexualities." *differences* 3, no. 2 (1991): iii–xviii.

de Valck, Marijke. *Film Festivals: From European Geopolitics to Global Cinephilia*. Amsterdam: University of Amsterdam Press, 2007.

Del Rio, Elena. "Film." In *Handbook of Phenomenological Aesthetics*, ed. H. R. Sepp and L. Embree, 111–17. Dordrecht: Springer, 2009.

Desai, Gaurav. "Out in Africa." In *Postcolonial, Queer: Theoretical Intersections*, ed. John C. Hawley, 139–64. Albany: State University of New York Press, 2001.

Desai, Jigna. "Homo on the Range: Mobile and Global Sexualities." *Social Text* 20, no. 4 (Winter 2002): 65–89.

Dioli, Irene. "Back to a Nostalgic Future: The Queeroslav Utopia." *Sextures* 1, no. 1 (2009): 1–21.

Doane, Mary Ann. "The Close-Up: Scale and Detail in the Cinema." *differences* 14, no. 3 (2003): 89–111.

Doane, Mary Ann. *The Emergence of Cinematic Time: Modernity, Contingency, the Archive*. Cambridge, MA: Harvard University Press, 2002.

Doane, Mary Ann. *Femmes Fatales: Feminism, Film Theory, Psychoanalysis*. New York: Routledge, 1991.

Donnelly, Jack. *Universal Human Rights in Theory and Practice*, 2d ed. Ithaca, NY: Cornell University Press, 2002.

Doty, Alexander. *Flaming Classics: Queering the Film Canon*. New York: Routledge, 2000.

Driskill, Qwo-Li, Chris Finley, Brian Joseph Gilley, and Scott Lauria Morgensen. "The Revolution Is for Everyone: Imagining and Emancipatory Future through Queer Indigenous Critical Theories." In *Queer Indigenous Studies: Critical Interventions in Theory, Politics, and Literature*, ed. Qwo-Li Driskill, Chris Finley, Brian Joseph Gilley, and Scott Lauria Morgensen, 211–22: Tucson: University of Arizona Press, 2011.

Dudrah, Rajinder. *Bollywood Travels: Culture, Diaspora and Border Crossings in Popular Hindi Cinema*. London: Routledge, 2012.

Dudrah, Rajinder. "Queer as Desis: Secret Politics of Gender and Sexuality in Bollywood Films in Diasporic Urban Ethnoscapes." In *Global Bollywood: Travels of Hindi Song and Dance*, ed. Sangita Gopal and Sujata Moorti, 288–307. Minneapolis: University of Minnesota Press, 2008.

Dukule, Abdoulaye. "Film Review: *Dakan* by Mohamed Camara," *African Studies Review* 44, no. 1 (2001): 119–21.

Dyer, Richard. *The Culture of Queers*. London: Routledge, 2002.

Dyer, Richard. "Entertainment and Utopia." In *Only Entertainment*, 2nd ed., 19–35. London: Routledge, 2002.

Dyer, Richard. "Judy Garland and Gay Men." In *Heavenly Bodies: Stars and Society*, 137–91. London: Routledge, 2013.

Dyer, Richard. *Now You See It: Studies on Gay and Lesbian Film*. London: Routledge, 1990.

Edelman, Lee. *No Future: Queer Theory and the Death Drive*. Durham, NC: Duke University Press, 2004.

Egoyan, Atom, and Ian Balfour, eds. *Subtitles: On the Foreignness of Film*. Alphabet City, no. 9. Cambridge, MA: MIT Press, 2004.

Eisenstein, Sergei. *Film Form: Essays in Film Theory*, ed. and trans. Jay Leyda. San Diego: Harcourt, 1949.

El-Tayeb, Fatima. *European Others: Queering Ethnicity in Postnational Europe*. Minneapolis: University of Minnesota Press, 2006.

Eng, David. *The Feeling of Kinship: Queer Liberalism and the Racialization of Intimacy*. Durham, NC: Duke University Press, 2010.

Eng, David. "The Queer Space of China: Expressive Desire in Stanley Kwan's *Lan Yu*." *Positions* 18, no. 2 (2010): 459–87.

Epprecht, Marc. *Heterosexual Africa? The History of an Idea from the Age of Exploration to the Age of AIDS*. Athens: Ohio University Press, 2008.

Erni, J. N. "Queer Pop Asia: Toward a Hybrid Regionalist Imaginary." Paper presented at Sexualities, Genders and Rights in Asia: First International Conference of Asian Queer Studies, Bangkok, July 2005.

Expósito Barea, Milagros. "From the Iron to the Lady: The Kathoey Phenomenon in Thai Cinema." *Revista de letras y ficción audiovisual* 2 (2012): 190–202.

Farmer, Brett. "Loves of Siam: Contemporary Thai Cinema and Vernacular Queerness." In *Queer Bangkok: 21st Century Markets, Media, and Rights*, ed. Peter Jackson, 81–98. Hong Kong: Hong Kong University Press, 2011.

Ferguson, Roderick. *Aberrations in Black: Toward a Queer of Color Critique*. Minneapolis: University of Minnesota Press, 2004.

Ferguson, Roderick. "Lateral Moves of African-American Studies in a Period of Migration." In *Strange Affinities: The Gender and Sexual Politics of Comparative Racialization*, ed. Grace Kyungwon Hong and Roderick Ferguson, 113–30. Durham, NC: Duke University Press, 2011.

Foster, David William. *Queer Issues in Contemporary Latin American Cinema*. Austin: University of Texas Press, 2004.

Foucault, Michel. "Truth, Power, Self." In *Technologies of the Self: A Seminar with Michel Foucault*, ed. Huck Gutman, Patrick H. Hutton, and Luther H. Martin, 9–15. London: Tavistock, 1988.

Freccero, Carla. "Queer Times." In *After Sex: Writing since Queer Theory*, ed. Janet Halley and Andrew Parker, 17–26. Durham, NC: Duke University Press, 2011.

Freeman, Elizabeth. "Packing History: Count(er)ing Generations," *New Literary History* 31, no. 4 (2000): 727–44.

Freeman, Elizabeth. *Time Binds: Queer Temporalities, Queer Histories*. Durham, NC: Duke University Press, 2010.

Fujiwara, Chris. "Boredom, 'Spasmo,' and the Italian System." In *Sleaze Artists: Cinema at the Margins of Taste, Style, and Politics*, ed. Jeffrey Sconce, 240–58. Durham, NC: Duke University Press, 2007.

Galt, Rosalind. *Pretty: Film and the Decorative Image*. New York: Columbia University Press, 2011.

Galt, Rosalind. *The New European Cinema: Redrawing the Map*. New York: Columbia University Press, 2006.

Galt, Rosalind, and Karl Schoonover, eds. *Global Art Cinema: New Theories and Histories*. New York: Oxford University Press, 2010.

Gehlawat, Ajay. *Reframing Bollywood: Theories of Popular Hindi Cinema*. New Delhi: Sage, 2010.

Gever, Martha. "The Names We Give Ourselves." In *Out There: Marginalization and Contemporary Cultures*, ed. Russell Ferguson, Martha Gever, Trinh T. Minh-ha, and Cornel West, 191–202. New York: New Museum of Contemporary Art, 1990.

Ghosh, Shohini. "Bearing Witness, Performing Politics: Documentary and the Idea of Intimacy." Keynote lecture, Visible Evidence Conference 21, Delhi, India, December 13, 2014.

Ghosh, Shohini. "False Appearances and Mistaken Identities: The Phobic and the Erotic in Bombay Cinema's Queer Vision." In *The Phobic and the Erotic: The Politics of Sexualities in Contemporary India*, ed. Brinda Bose and Subhabrata Bhattacharyya, 417–36. Kolkata: Seagull, 2007.

Ghosh, Shohini. *Fire: A Queer Film Classic*. Vancouver: Arsenal Pulp Press, 2010.

Gittings, Christopher. "Parsing the Transnational in John Greyson's Queer Cinema: *Proteus, Fig Trees, Covered*, and *Hey Elton*." In *The Perils of Pedagogy: the Works of John Greyson*, ed. Brenda Longfellow, Scott MacKenzie, and Thomas Waugh, 113–134. Montreal: McGill-Queen's University Press, 2013.

Golder, Ben. *Foucault and the Politics of Rights*. Stanford, CA: Stanford University Press, 2015.

Gopinath, Gayatri. *Impossible Desires: Queer Diasporas and South Asian Public Cultures*. Durham, NC: Duke University Press, 2005.

Gopinath, Gayatri. "Local Sites/Global Contexts: The Transnational Trajectories of Deepa Mehta's *Fire*." In *Queer Globalizations: Citizenship and the Afterlife of Colonialism*," ed. Arnaldo Cruz-Malavé and Martin Manalansan, 149–61. New York: New York University Press, 2002.

Gopinath, Gayatri. "On *Fire*." *GLQ* 4, no. 4 (1998): 631–36.

Gopinath, Gayatri. "Queer Regions: Locating Lesbians in *Sancharram*." In *A Companion to Lesbian, Gay, Bisexual, Transgender, and Queer Studies*, ed. George E. Haggerty and Molly McGarry, 341–54. Oxford: Blackwell, 2007.

Gorfinkel, Elena. "Wet Dreams: Erotic Film Festivals of the Early 1970s and the Utopian Sexual Public Sphere." *Framework* 47, no. 2 (2006): 59–86.

Grant, Catherine. "Planes of Focus: The Films of Lucrecia Martel." Video essay presented at the Queer Cinema and the Politics of the Global workshop, Brighton, May 2012, http://vimeo.com/channels/222321.

Green-Simms, Lindsey. "Hustlers, Home-wreckers, and Homoeroticism: Nollywood's *Beautiful Faces*." *Journal of African Cinemas* 4, no. 1 (2012): 59–79.

Green-Simms, Lindsey, and Unoma Azuah, "The Video Closet: Nollywood's Gay-Themed Movies." *Transition* 107 (January 1, 2012): 32–49.

Grewal, Inderpal, and Caren Kaplan. "Global Identities: Theorizing Transnational Studies of Sexuality." *GLQ* 7, no. 4 (2001): 663–79.

Greyson, John. "Pinkface." *Camera Obscura* 27, no. 2 80 (2012): 145–53.

Griffiths, Robin, ed. *Queer Cinema in Europe*. London: Intellect, 2008.

Grossman, Andrew, ed. *Queer Asian Cinema: Shadows in the Shade*. New York: Harrington Park Press, 2000.

Habib, Samar. *Female Homosexuality in the Middle East: Histories and Representations*. New York: Routledge, 2007.

Hagin, Boaz, and Raz Yosef. "Festival Exoticism: The Israeli Queer Film in a Global Context." *GLQ* 18, no. 1 (2012): 161–78.

Halberstam, Judith. *In a Queer Time and Place: Transgender Bodies, Subcultural Lives*. New York: New York University Press, 2005.

Halberstam, Judith. *The Queer Art of Failure*. Durham, NC: Duke University Press, 2011.

Hallas, Roger. "Queer Anachronism and National Memory in *Proteus*." In *The Perils of Pedagogy: the Works of John Greyson*, ed. Brenda Longfellow, Scott MacKenzie, and Thomas Waugh, 462–74. Montreal: McGill-Queen's University Press, 2013.

Hansen, Miriam Bratu. "The Mass Production of the Senses: Classical Cinema as Vernacular Modernism." *Modernism/Modernity* 6, no. 2 (1999): 59–77.

Hansen, Miriam Bratu. "Vernacular Modernism: Tracking Cinema on a Global Scale." In *World Cinemas, Transnational Perspectives*, ed. Natasa Ďurovičová and Kathleen Newman, 287–314. New York: AFI/Routledge, 2010.

Hanson, Ellis. "Lesbians Who Bite." In *Out Takes: Essays on Queer Theory and Film*, ed. Ellis Hanson, 183–222. Durham, NC: Duke University Press, 1999.

Haraway, Donna. "Companion Species, Mis-recognition, and Queer Worlding." In *Queering the Non/Human*, ed. Noreen Giffney and Myra J. Hird, xxiii–xxv. London: Ashgate, 2008.

Harindranath, Ramaswami. *Perspectives on Global Cultures*. New York: Open University Press, 2006.

Haritaworn, Jin, Tamsila Tauqir, and Esra Erdem, "Gay Imperialism: Gender and Sexuality Discourse in the War on Terror." In *Out of Place: Interrogating Silences in Queerness/Raciality*, ed. Adi Kuntsman and Esperanza Miyake, 9–34. London: Raw Nerve Books, 2008.

Hassan, Omar. "Real Queer Arabs: The Tensions between Colonialism and Homosexuality in Egyptian Cinema." *Film International* 43 (2011): 18–24.

Heath, Stephen. "Narrative Space." In *Questions of Cinema*, 19–75. London: Palgrave, 1981.

Heidegger, Martin. "The Origin of the Work of Art." In *The Continental Aesthetics Reader*, ed. Clive Cazeaux, trans. Albert Hofstadter, 80–101. London: Routledge, 2000.

Henlin-Stromme, Sabine. "Nature Nation, and the Global in Contemporary Norwegian Cinema." PhD diss., University of Iowa: Iowa City, 2012.

Herbert, Daniel. "From Art House to Your House: The Distribution of Quality Cinema on Home Video." *Canadian Journal of Film Studies* 20, no. 2 (Fall 2011): 2–18.

Hilderbrand, Lucas. *Inherent Vice: Bootleg Histories of Videotape and Copyright*. Durham, NC: Duke University Press, 2009.

Hoad, Neville. "Queer Theory Addiction." In *After Sex? On Writing since Queer Theory*, ed. Janet Halley and Andrew Parker, 135–36. Durham, NC: Duke University Press, 2011.

Holmlund, Chris, and Cynthia Fuchs. *Between the Sheets, in the Streets: Queer, Lesbian, and Gay Documentary*. Minneapolis: University of Minnesota Press, 1997.

Hong, Grace Kyungwon, and Roderick Ferguson. "Introduction." In *Strange Affinities: The Gender and Sexual Politics of Comparative Racialization*, ed. Grace Kyungwon Hong and Roderick Ferguson, 1–22. Durham, NC: Duke University Press, 2011.

Houshyar, Shima. "Queer and Trans Subjects in Iranian Cinema: Between Representation, Agency, and Orientalist Fantasies." *Ajam Media Collective*, May 11, 2013, http://ajammc.com/2013/05/11/queer-and-trans-subjects-in-iranian-cinema-between-representation-agency-and-orientalist-fantasies.

Huffer, Lynne. *Are the Lips a Grave? A Queer Feminist on the Ethics of Sex*. New York: Columbia University Press, 2013.

Hunt, Matthew, "Exclusive Interview with Apichatpong Weerasethakul." *Encounter Thailand* 2, no. 13 (May 2013), http://www.matthewhunt.com/portfolio/exclusiveinterviewwithapichatpongweerasethakul.pdf.

Ingawanij, May Adadol, and Richard Lowell McDonald. "The Value of an Impoverished Aesthetic." *Screening Southeast Asia* 24:2 (Fall 2004): 73.

Iverson, Gunnar, Astrid Soderbergh Widding, and Tytti Soila, eds. *Nordic National Cinemas*. New York: Routledge, 1998.

Jackson, Peter. "An Explosion of Thai Identities: Global Queering and Re-imagining Queer Theory." *Culture, Health and Sexuality* 2, no. 4 (2000): 405–24.

Jackson, Peter. "Capitalism and Global Queering: National Markets, Parallels among Sexual Cultures, and Multiple Queer Modernities." *GLQ* 15, no. 3 (2009): 357–95.

Jackson, Peter, ed. *Queer Bangkok: 21st Century Markets, Media, and Rights*. Hong Kong: Hong Kong University Press, 2011.

Jameson, Fredric. "Third-World Literature in the Era of Multinational Capitalism." *Social Text* 15 (1986): 65–88.

Jeffers McDonald, Tamar. *Romantic Comedy: Boy Meets Girl Meets Genre*. Edinburgh: Wallflower, 2007.

Johnson, Paul. "'An Essentially Private Manifestation of Human Personality': Constructions of Homosexuality in the European Court of Human Rights." *Human Rights Law Review* 10, no. 1 (March 1, 2010): 67–97.

Jørgensen, Finn Arne, Unnur Birna Karlsdóttir, Erland Mårald, Bo Poulsen, and Tuomas Räsänen. "Entangled Environments: Historians and Nature in the Nordic Countries." *Historisk tidsskrift* 1 (2013), http://www.idunn.no/ts/ht/2013/01/entangled_environments_historians_and_nature_in_the_nordic.

Justice, Daniel Heath, Mark Rifkin, and Bethany Schneider, eds. "Sexuality, Nationality, Indigeneity: Rethinking the State at the Intersection of Native American and Queer Studies." Special issue. *GLQ* 16, no. 1–2 (2010).

Kääpä, Pietari. *Ecology and Contemporary Nordic Cinemas: From Nation-Building to Ecocosmopolitanism*. New York: Bloomsbury, 2014.

Kaewprasert, Oradol. "The Very First Series of Thai Queer Cinemas—What Was Happening in the 1980s?" Paper presented at Sexualities, Genders and Rights in Asia: First International Conference of Asian Queer Studies, Bangkok, July 2005.

Käng, Dredge Byung'chu. "Kathoey 'In Trend': Emergent Genderscapes, National Anxieties, and the Resignification of Male-Bodied Effeminacy in Thailand." *Asian Studies Review* 36 (2012): 475–94.

Kapur, Ratna. "Too Hot to Handle: The Cultural Politics of *Fire*." *Feminist Review* 64 (2000): 53–64.

Khoo, Olivia. "The Minor Transnationalism of Queer Asian Cinema: Female Authorship and the Short Film Format." *Camera Obscura* 29, 1 85 (2014): 33–57.

Kılıçbay, Barış. "Queer as Turk: A Journey to Three Queer Melodramas." In *Queer Cinema in Europe*, ed. Robin Griffiths, 117–28. Bristol: Intellect Books, 2008.

Kim, Jihoon. "Between Auditorium and Gallery: Perception in Apichatpong Weerasethakul's Films and Installations." In *Global Art Cinema: New Theories and Histories*, ed. Rosalind Galt and Karl Schoonover, 125–41. New York: Oxford University Press, 2010.

Kimmel, Penni. "In Search of Sensibilities: The International Face of Gays on Film." *Manifest* (June 1983): 45–47.

King, Homay. "Girl, Interrupted: The Queer Time of Warhol's Cinema." *Discourse* 28, no. 1 (2006): 98–120.

King, Homay. "Stroboscopic: Warhol and the Exploding Plastic Inevitable." *Criticism* 56, no. 3 (2014): 457–79.

Klinger, Barbara. *Beyond the Multiplex: Cinema, New Technologies, and the Home*. Berkeley: University of California Press, 2006.

Ko, Mika. " 'Neo-documentarism' in *Funeral Parade of Roses*: The New Realism of Matsumoto Toshio." *Screen* 3, no. 2 (2011): 376–90.

Kracauer, Siegfried. *Theory of Film: The Redemption of Physical Reality*. Princeton, NJ: Princeton University Press, 1997.

Krutnik, Frank. "The Faint Aroma of Performing Seals: The 'Nervous' Romance and the Comedy of the Sexes." *Velvet Light Trap* 26 (1990): 57–72.

Kulpa, Robert, Joanna Mizielińska, and Agata Stasińska. "(Un)translatable Queer? Or, What Is Lost and Can Be Found in Translation." In *Import—Export—Transport: Queer Theory, Queer Critique, and Queer Activism in Motion*, ed. Sushila Mesquita, Maria Katharina Wiedlack, and Katrin Lasthofer, 115–45. Vienna: Zaglossus, 2012.

Larkin, Brian. *Signal and Noise: Media, Infrastructure, and Urban Culture in Nigeria*. Durham, NC: Duke University Press, 2008.

Lee, Daw-Ming. *Historical Dictionary of Taiwan Cinema*. Lanham, MD: Scarecrow, 2013.

Lee, Nikki J. Y., and Julian Stringer. "Counter-programming and the Udine Far East Film Festival." *Screen* 53, no. 3 (Autumn 2012): 301–9.

Leung, Helen Hok-Sze. "New Queer Cinema and Third Cinema." In *New Queer Cinema: A Critical Reader*, ed. Michele Aaron, 155–67. New Brunswick, NJ: Rutgers University Press, 2004.

Leung, Helen Hok-Sze. *Undercurrents: Queer Culture and Postcolonial Hong Kong.* Vancouver: University of British Columbia Press, 2008.

Lewis, Rachel. "Towards a Transnational Lesbian Cinema." *Journal of Lesbian Studies* 16, no. 3 (2012): 273–90.

Lim, Bliss Cua. "Archival Fragility: Philippine Cinema and the Challenge of Sustainable Preservation." *Kyoto Center for Southeast Asian Studies Newsletter* (2013): 18–21.

Lim, Bliss Cua. "Queer Aswang Transmedia: Folklore as Camp." *Kritika Kultura* 24 (February 2015): 178–225.

Lim, Bliss Cua. "Temporality and Archival Constraint in Philippine Cinema," paper presented at Cinematic Times conference, University of California, Berkeley, November 15, 2013.

Lim, Bliss Cua. *Translating Time: Cinema, the Fantastic, and Temporal Critique.* Durham, NC: Duke University Press, 2009.

Lim, Jason. "Queer Critique and the Politics of Affect." In *Geographies of Sexualities: Theory, Practices and Politics*, ed. Kath Browne, Jason Lim, and Gavin Brown, 53–67. London: Ashgate, 2007.

Lim, Song Hwee. *Celluloid Comrades: Representations of Male Homosexuality in Contemporary Chinese Cinemas.* Honolulu: University of Hawai'i Press, 2006.

Lim, Song Hwee. *Tsai Ming-liang and a Cinema of Slowness.* Hong Kong: Hong Kong University Press, 2014.

Limbrick, Peter. "From the Interior: Space, Time and Queer Discursivity in Kamal Aljafari's *The Roof.*" In *The Cinema of Me: The Self and Subjectivity in First Person Documentary Film*, ed. Alisa Lebow, 96–115. London: Wallflower, 2012.

Lindner, Katharina. "Questions of Embodied Difference: Film and Queer Phenomenology." *NECSUS* 1, no. 2 (2012): 199–217.

Lippit, Akira. *Atomic Light (Shadow Optics).* Minneapolis: University of Minnesota Press, 2005.

Lobato, Ramon. *Shadow Economies of Cinema: Mapping Informal Film Distribution.* London: BFI/Palgrave, 2012.

Loist, Skadi, "A Complicated Queerness: LGBT Film Festivals and Queer Programming Strategies." In *Coming Soon to a Festival near You: Programming Film Festivals*, ed. Jeffrey Ruoff, 157–72. St. Andrews, Scotland: St. Andrews Film Studies, 2012.

Loist, Skadi, and Ger Zielinski. "On the Development of Queer Film Festivals and Their Media Activism." In *Film Festivals and Activism: Film Festival Yearbook 4*, ed. Dina Iordanova and Leshu Torchin, 49–62. St. Andrews, Scotland: St. Andrews Film Studies, 2012.

Loist, Skadi, and Ger Zielinski. "Norms, Deviance, and the Queer Ordinary?" Paper presented at King's College London, November 13, 2014.

Love, Heather. *Feeling Backward: Loss and the Politics of Queer History*. Cambridge, MA: Harvard University Press, 2009.

Luibhéid, Eithne. "Queer/Migration: An Unruly Body of Scholarship." *GLQ* 14, nos. 2–3 (2008): 169–90.

Ma, Jean. *Melancholy Drift: Marking Time in Chinese Cinema*. Hong Kong: Hong Kong University Press, 2010.

Maltby, Richard. *Hollywood Cinema*, 2d ed. Malden, MA: Blackwell, 2003.

Marks, Laura. *Touch: Sensuous Theory and Multisensory Media*. Minneapolis: University of Minnesota Press, 2002.

Martin, Fran. *Backward Glances: Contemporary Chinese Cultures and the Female Homoerotic Imaginary*. Durham, NC: Duke University Press, 2010.

Martin, Fran. "Introduction: Tsai Ming-liang's Intimate Public Worlds." *Journal of Chinese Cinemas* 1–2 (2007): 83–88.

Martin-Jones, David. *Scotland: Global Cinema: Genres, Modes and Identities*. Edinburgh: Edinburgh University Press, 2005.

Massad, Joseph. "Art and Politics in the Cinema of Youssef Chahine." *Journal of Palestinian Studies* 28, no. 2 (Winter 1999): 77–93.

Massad, Joseph. *Desiring Arabs*. Chicago: University of Chicago Press, 2007.

Massad, Joseph. "Re-Orienting Desire: The Gay International and the Arab World." *Public Culture* 14, no. 2 (Spring 2002): 361–85.

McAllister, John. "Tswanarising Global Gayness: The 'UnAfrican' Argument, Western Gay Media Imagery, Local Responses and Gay Culture in Botswana." *Culture, Health and Sexuality* 15, no. 1 (2013): 88–101.

McDonald, Tamar Jeffers. *Romantic Comedy: Boy Meets Girl Meets Genre*. Chichester, UK: Wallflower, 2007.

McGuffie, Allison. "Queering the Revolution: The Political Force of Deviant Sexuality in *Mädchen in Uniform* and *V for Vendetta*." Paper presented at the Society for Cinema Studies conference, Philadelphia, March 6–9, 2008.

McLelland, Mark. "From the Stage to the Clinic: Changing Transgender Identities in Post-war Japan." *Japan Forum* 16, no. 1 (2004): 1–20.

Mennel, Barbara. *Queer Cinema: Schoolgirls, Vampires and Gay Cowboys*. London: Wallflower, 2012.

Migraine-George, Thérèse. "Beyond the 'Internalist' versus 'Externalist' Debate: The Local-Global Identities of African Homosexuals in Two Films, *Woubi Cheri* and *Dakan*." *Journal of African Cultural Studies* 16, no. 1 (2003): 45–56.

Miller, D. A. "Anal Rope." *Representations* 32 (Fall 1990): 114–33.

Mizielińska, Joanna, and Robert Kulpa, eds. *Decentering Western Sexualities: Central and Eastern European Perspectives*. London: Ashgate, 2011.

Monasterios, Elizabeth P., ed. *No pudieron con nosotras: El desafío del feminismo autónomo de Mujeres Creando*. Pittsburgh: Plural, 2006.

Moretti, Franco. "Conjectures on World Literature." *New Left Review* 1 (January–February 2000): 54–68.

Moretti, Franco. "Kindergarten." In *Signs Taken for Wonders: Essays in the Sociology of Literary Forms*, 157–81. London: Verso, 1983.

Morris, Rosalind. "Three Sexes and Four Sexualities: Redressing the Discourses of Gender and Sexuality in Contemporary Thailand." *Positions* 2, no. 1 (1994): 15–43.

Mortimer-Sandilands, Catriona, and Bruce Erickson, eds. *Queer Ecologies: Sex, Nature, Politics, Desire*. Bloomington: Indiana University Press, 2010.

Morton, Timothy. *Ecology without Nature: Rethinking Environmental Aesthetics*. Cambridge, MA: Harvard University Press, 2007.

Mulvey, Laura. "Afterthoughts on 'Visual Pleasure and Narrative Cinema' Inspired by *Duel in the Sun*." *Framework* 15–17 (1981): 12–15.

Mulvey, Laura. "Kiarostami's Uncertainty Principle." *Sight and Sound* 8, no. 6 (June 1998): 24–27.

Muñoz, José Esteban. *Cruising Utopia: The Then and There of Queer Futurity*. New York: New York University Press, 2009.

Muñoz, José Esteban. "Thinking beyond Antirelationality and Antiutopianism in Queer Critique." *PMLA* 121, no. 3 (2006): 825–26.

Naficy, Hamid. *A Social History of Iranian Cinema, Volume 4: The Globalizing Era, 1984–2010*. Durham, NC: Duke University Press, 2012.

Neale, Steve. "Melodrama and Tears." *Screen* 27, no. 6 (1986): 6–23.

Nettleton, Taro. "Shinjuku as Site: *Funeral Parade of Roses* and *Diary of a Shinjuku Thief*." *Screen* 55, no. 1 (Spring 2015): 5–28.

Nguyen Tan Hoang. "Tropicamp Maladies: Sex, Censorship, and Over-aesthetics in Queer Thai Cinema." Paper presented at Global Queer Cinema workshop, Brighton, April 2013.

Nichol, Nancy, Nick J. Mulé, and Erika Gates-Gasse. "Envisioning LGBT Global Human Rights: Strategic Alliances to Advance Knowledge and Social Change." *Scholarly and Research Communication* 5, no. 3 (2014): 1–14.

Nijhawan, Amita. "Excusing the Female Dancer: Tradition and Transgression in Bollywood Dancing." *South Asian Popular Culture* 7, no. 2 (2009): 99–112.

Nornes, Abé Mark. *Cinema Babel: Translating Global Cinema*. Minneapolis: University of Minnesota Press, 2007.

Nornes, Abé Mark. "The Postwar Documentary Trace: Groping in the Dark." *Positions* 10, no. 1 (Spring 2002): 39–78.

Owens, Craig. "The Allegorical Impulse: Toward a Theory of Postmodernism." *October* 12 (1980): 67–86.

Pasolini, Pier Paolo. "Gennariello." In *Lutheran Letters*, trans. Stuart Hood, 17–48. Manchester: Carcanet New Press, 1983.

Patterson, Orlando. *Slavery and Social Death: A Comparative Study*. Cambridge, MA: Harvard University Press, 1985.

Perriam, Chris. *Spanish Queer Cinema*. Edinburgh: Edinburgh University Press, 2013.

Petchesky, Rosalind. "Sexual Rights: Inventing a Concept, Mapping an International Practice." In *Framing the Sexual Subject: The Politics of Gender, Sexuality, and Power*, ed. Richard Guy Parker, Regina Maria Barbosa, and Peter Aggleton, 81–103. Berkeley: University of California Press, 2000.

Petro, Patrice. *Joyless Streets: Women and Melodramatic Representation in Weimar Germany*. Princeton, NJ: Princeton University Press, 1989.

Phillips, Oliver. "Constituting the Global Gay: Issues of Individual Subjectivity and Sexuality in Southern Africa." In *Sexuality in the Legal Arena*, ed. Didi Herman and Carl F. Stychin, 17–34. London: Bloomsbury, 2000.

Povinelli, Elizabeth, and George Chauncey. "Thinking Sexuality Transnationally, an Introduction." *GLQ* 5, no. 4 (1999): 439–49.

Prasad, Madhava. *Ideology of the Hindi Film: A Historical Construction*. New Delhi: Oxford University Press, 1998.

Psaras, Marios, "Family, Nation and the Medium under Attack: Queer Time and Space in the 'Greek Weird Wave.'" PhD diss., Queen Mary, University of London, 2015.

Puar, Jasbir. *Terrorist Assemblages: Homonationalism in Queer Times*. Durham, NC: Duke University Press, 2008.

Pullen, Chris, ed. *LGBT Transnational Identity and the Media*. London: Palgrave Macmillan: 2012.

Raman, Ravi K. "Environmental Ethics, Livelihood, and Human Rights: Subaltern-Driven Cosmopolitanism?" *Nature and Culture* 3, no. 1 (2008): 82–97.

Rancière, Jacques. *The Politics of Aesthetics*. London: Bloomsbury, 2013.

Rastegar, Roya. "The De-fusion of Good Intentions: Outfest's Fusion Film Festival." *GLQ* 15, no. 3 (2009): 481–97.

Rastegar, Roya. "Difference, Aesthetics and the Curatorial Crisis of Film Festivals." *Screen* 53, no. 3 (Autumn 2012): 310–17.

Reddy, Chandan, C. "Homes, Houses, Nonidentity: *Paris Is Burning*." In *Burning Down the House: Recycling Domesticity*, ed. Rosemary Marangoly, 355–79. Boulder, CO: Westview, 1997.

Rees-Roberts, Nick. *French Queer Cinema*. Edinburgh: Edinburgh University Press, 2008.

Reid-Pharr, Robert. "MiX-Defying." *Afterimage* 22, no. 6 (January 1995): 3–4.

Rhodes, John David. "Allegory, Mise-en-Scène, AIDS: Interpreting *Safe*." In *The Cinema of Todd Haynes: All That Heaven Allows*, ed. James Morrison, 68–78. London: Wallflower, 2007.

Rhyne, Ragan. "The Global Economy of Gay and Lesbian Film Festivals," *GLQ* 12, no. 4 (2006): 617–19.

Rhyne, Ragan. "Pink Dollars: Gay and Lesbian Film Festivals and the Economy of Visibility." PhD diss., New York University, 2007.

Rich, B. Ruby. "The New Homosexual Film Festivals." *GLQ* 12, no. 4 (2006): 620–25.

Rich, B. Ruby. *New Queer Cinema: The Director's Cut*. Durham, NC: Duke University Press, 2013.

Rich, B. Ruby. "To Read or Not to Read: Subtitles, Trailers, and Monolingualism." In *Subtitles: On the Foreignness of Film*, ed. Atom Egoyan and Ian Balfour, 153–69. Cambridge, MA: MIT Press, 2004.

Romanow, Rebecca. *The Postcolonial Body in Queer Space and Time*. Cambridge: Cambridge Scholars Press, 2006.

Rony, Fatimah Tobing. *The Third Eye: Race, Cinema, and Ethnographic Spectacle.* Durham, NC: Duke University Press, 1996.

Roof, Judith. *Come as You Are: Sexuality and Narrative.* New York: Columbia University Press, 1996.

Rosen, Philip. "History, Textuality, Nation: Kracauer, Burch and Some Problems in the Study of National Cinemas." In *Theorizing National Cinema,* ed. Valentina Vitali and Paul Willemen, 17–28. Berkeley: University of California Press and British Film Institute, 2006.

Rosenbaum, Jonathan. "A Few Underpinnings of the New Iranian Cinema." *Senses of Cinema* 21 (2002), http://sensesofcinema.com/2002/feature-articles/new _iranian.

Rosenberg, Jordana, and Amy Villarejo. "Queerness, Norms, Utopia." *GLQ* 18, no. 1 (2012): 1–18.

Roth-Bettoni, Didier. *L'homosexualité au cinéma.* Paris: La Musardine, 2007.

Russo, Vito. *The Celluloid Closet: Homosexuality in the Movies.* New York: Harper and Row, 1987.

Ryan, Connor. "Lagos Never Spoils: The Aesthetics, Affect, and Politics of the City in Nigerian Screen Media." PhD diss., Michigan State University, East Lansing, 2014.

Ryberg, Ingrid. "Sex without Optimism in Swedish Trans* Cinema." Special issue. *Lambda Nordica,* forthcoming.

Sánchez-Eppeler, Benigno, and Cindy Patton, eds. *Queer Diasporas.* Durham, NC: Duke University Press, 2000.

Sandoval, Chela. "Dissident Globalizations, Emancipatory Methods, Social-Erotics." In *Queer Globalizations: Citizenship and the Afterlife of Colonialism,"* ed. Arnaldo Cruz-Malavé and Martin Manalansan, 20–32. New York: New York University Press, 2002.

San Filippo, Maria. *The B Word: Bisexuality in Contemporary Film and Television.* Bloomington: Indiana University Press, 2013.

San Filippo, Maria. "Unthinking Heterocentrism: Bisexual Representability in Art Cinema." In *Global Art Cinema: New Theories and Histories,* ed. Rosalind Galt and Karl Schoonover, 75–91. New York: Oxford University Press, 2010.

Sarkar, Bhaskar. "The Globalization of Melodrama." *Cultural Dynamics* 20, no. 1 (March 2008): 31–51.

Schoonover, Karl. "Wastrels of Time: Slow Cinema's Laboring Body, the Political Spectator, and the Queer." *Framework* 53, no. 1 (2013): 65–78.

Schulman, Sarah. *The Gentrification of the Mind: Witness to a Lost Imagination.* Berkeley: University of California Press, 2012.

Schulman, Sarah. *Israel/Palestine and the Queer International.* Durham, NC: Duke University Press, 2012.

Sedgwick, Eve Kosofsky. *Epistemology of the Closet.* Berkeley: University of California Press, 1990.

Selvick, Stephanie. "Queer (Im)possibilities: Alaa Al-Aswany's and Wahid Hamed's *The Yacoubian Building* and Adaptation." In *LGBT Transnational Identity and the Media,* ed. Chris Pullen, 131–45. London: Palgrave Macmillan, 2012.

Seymour, Nicole. *Strange Natures: Futurity, Empathy, and the Queer Ecological Imagination*. Champaign: University of Illinois Press, 2013.

Shahini, Parmesh. *Gay Bombay: Globalization, Love and (Be)Longing in Contemporary India*. London: Sage, 2008.

Shakhsari, Sima. "Transnational Governmentality and the Politics of Life and Death." *International Journal of Middle East Studies* 45 (2013): 340–42.

Shohat, Ella, and Robert Stam. *Unthinking Eurocentrism: Multiculturalism and the Media*. London: Routledge, 1994.

Siegel, Marc. "Spilling out onto Castro Street." *Jump Cut* 41 (May 1997): 131–36.

Spaas, Lieve. *The Francophone Film: A Struggle for Identity*. Manchester: Manchester University Press, 2000.

Spigel, Lynn. *TV by Design: Modern Art and the Rise of Network Television*. Chicago: University of Chicago Press, 2009.

Spivak, Gayatri Chakravorty. *An Aesthetic Education in the Era of Globalization*. Cambridge, MA: Harvard University Press, 2012.

Spivak, Gayatri Chakravorty. "Righting Wrongs." *South Atlantic Quarterly* 103, nos. 2–3 (2004): 523–81.

Sretenovic, Dejan. "The Figuration of Resistance." In *East Side Story Catalogue*. Belgrade: Salon of the Museum of Contemporary Art, 2008.

Stacey, Jackie. *The Cinematic Life of the Gene*. Durham, NC: Duke University Press, 2010.

Staiger, Janet. "Authorship Approaches." In *Authorship and Film*, ed. David A. Gerstner and Janet Staiger, 27–57. New York: Routledge, 2003.

Steinbock, Eliza, "Contemporary Trans* Cinema: Affective Tendencies, Communities, and Styles." Paper presented at the Queer Film Culture: Queer Cinema and Film Festivals conference, Hamburg, October 14–15, 2014.

Straayer, Chris, and Thomas Waugh, eds. "Queer Film and Video Festival Forum, Take One: Curators Speak Out." *GLQ* 11, no. 4 (2005): 579–603.

Straayer, Chris, and Thomas Waugh, eds. "Queer Film and Video Festival Forum, Take Two: Critics Speak Out." *GLQ* 12, no. 4 (2006): 599–625.

Straayer, Chris, and Thomas Waugh, eds. "Queer Film and Video Festival Forum: Artists Speak Out." *GLQ* 14, no. 1 (2008): 120–22.

Straube, Wibke. "Trans Cinema and Its Exit Scapes: A Transfeminist Reading of Utopian Sensibility and Gender Dissidence in Contemporary Film." PhD diss., Linköping University, Linköping, 2014.

Suárez, Juan A. "Film Grain and the Queer Body: Tom Chomont," paper presented at the Museum of Modern Art in Warsaw, January 10, 2012, http://vimeo.com /37820473.

Suárez, Juan A. "Hélio Oiticica, Tropicalism." *Criticism* 56, no. 2 (2014): 295–328.

Suárez, Juan. "The Kuchars, the 1960s and Queer Materiality." *Screen* 56, no. 1 (2015): 25–45.

Suárez, Juan. "Warhol's 1960s Films, Amphetamine, and Queer Materiality." *Criticism* 56, no. 3 (2014): 623–51.

Suber, Daniel, and Slobodan Karamanic, "Symbolic Violence, Landscape and the Normalization Process in Post-Milosevic Serbia." In *Retracing Images: Visual Culture after Yugoslavia*, ed. Daniel Suber and Slobodan Karamanic, 313–36. Leiden: Brill, 2012.

Subero, Gustavo. *Queer Masculinities in Latin American Cinema: Male Bodies and Narrative Representations*. London: I. B. Tauris, 2013.

T., Muraleedharan. "Queer Bonds: Male-Male Friendships in Contemporary Malayalam Cinema." In *Queering India: Same-Sex Love and Eroticism in Indian Culture and Society*, ed. Ruth Vanita, 181–92. London: Routledge, 2002.

Tarkovsky, Andrei. *Sculpting in Time*, trans. Kitty Hunter-Blair. Austin: University of Texas Press, 1986.

Tcheuyap, Alexie. "African Cinema and Representations of (Homo)Sexuality." In *Body, Sexuality and Gender: Versions and Subversions in African Literatures*, ed. Flora Veit-Wild and Dirk Naguschewski, 143–56. Amsterdam: Rodopi, 2005.

Theocritus. *Idylls: A Selection*, ed. Richard Hunter. Cambridge: Cambridge University Press, 1999.

Tinkcom, Matthew. *Working like a Homosexual: Camp, Capital, Cinema*. Durham, NC: Duke University Press, 2002.

Tyler, Parker. "Drag Time and Drug Time." In *Andy Warhol: Film Factory*, ed. Michael O'Pray, 94–103. London: BFI Publishing, 1989.

Vanita, Ruth, and Saleem Kidwai, eds. *Same-Sex Love in India: Readings from Literature and History*. London: Palgrave, 2000.

Vanzan, Anna. "The LGBTQ Question in Iranian Cinema: A Proxy Discourse?" *Deportate, Esuli, Profughe* 25 (2014): 45–55.

Vasudevan, Ravi. *The Melodramatic Public: Film Form and Spectatorship in Indian Cinema*. New York: Palgrave Macmillan, 2011.

Walcott, Rinaldo. "Outside in Black Studies: Reading from a Queer Place in the Diaspora." In *Black Queer Studies: A Critical Anthology*, ed. E. Patrick Johnson and Mae G. Henderson, 90–105. Durham, NC: Duke University Press, 2005.

Wallace, Lee. "Continuous Sex: The Editing of Homosexuality in *Bound* and *Rope*." *Screen* 41, no. 4 (2000): 369–87.

Warner, Michael, ed. *Fear of a Queer Planet: Queer Politics and Social Theory*. Minneapolis: University of Minnesota Press, 1994.

Waugh, Thomas. "Cockteaser." In *Pop Out: Queer Warhol*, ed. Jennifer Doyle, Jonathan Flatley, and José Esteban Muñoz, 51–77. Durham, NC: Duke University Press, 1996.

Waugh, Thomas. "Queer Bollywood, or 'I'm the Player, You're the Naive One': Patterns of Sexual Subversion in Recent Indian Popular Cinema." In *Keyframes: Popular Cinema and Cultural Studies*, ed. Matthew Tinkcom and Amy Villarejo, 280–97. New York: Routledge, 2001.

Weber, Cynthia. "From Queer to Queer IR." *International Studies Review* 16, no. 4 (2014): 596–601.

Weiss, Andrea. *Vampires and Violets: Lesbians in the Cinema*, London: Jonathan Cape, 1992.

Whitaker, Brian. *Unspeakable Love: Gay and Lesbian Life in the Middle East*. Berkeley: University of California Press, 2006.

White, Patricia. "Madame X of the China Seas." In *Queer Looks: Perspectives on Lesbian and Gay Film and Video*, ed. Martha Gever, John Greyson, and Pratibha Parmar, 275–91. New York: Routledge, 1993.

White, Patricia. *Uninvited: Classical Hollywood Cinema and Lesbian Representability*. Bloomington: Indiana University Press, 1999.

White, Patricia. *Women's Cinema/World Cinema: Projecting Contemporary Feminisms*. Durham, NC: Duke University Press, 2015.

White, Patricia, ed. "Queer Publicity: A Dossier on Lesbian and Gay Film Festivals." *GLQ* 5, no. 1 (1999): 73–93.

Wiegman, Robyn. *Object Lessons*. Durham, NC: Duke University Press, 2012.

Williams, Linda. "Film Bodies: Gender, Genre and Excess," *Film Quarterly* 44, no. 4 (Summer 1991): 2–13.

Williams, Raymond. *Marxism and Literature*. Oxford: Oxford University Press, 1977.

Wynter, Sylvia, and David Scott. "The Re-Enchantment of Humanism: An Interview with Sylvia Wynter." *Small Axe* 8 (September 2000): 119–207.

Yeatter, Bryan L. *Cinema of the Philippines: A History and Filmography, 1897–2005*. Jefferson, NC: McFarland, 2007.

Yosef, Raz. *Beyond Flesh: Queer Masculinities and Nationalism in Israeli Cinema*. New Brunswick, NJ: Rutgers University Press, 2004.

Zielinski, Ger. "On the Production of Heterotopia, and Other Spaces, in and around Lesbian and Gay Film Festivals." *Jump Cut: A Review of Contemporary Media* 54 (Fall 2012).

INDEX

Note: Italicized numbers indicate a figure; n indicates an endnote

activists and activism, 87, 97, 106, 171, 175, 202, 220–21. *See also* human rights

affect: affective actions, 37, 39; affective engagement of audience with those on screen, 68, 72–73, 74, 76, 213; affective registers, 6, 50, 212–16, 225; affective spaces and communities, 16, 25; capture of desire through, 226–27, 266, 273–75, 294, 299–301; family and kinship as affective forces, 56, 66; food as carrier of, 66; political of melodrama, 33, 156, 178, 218, 224–25, 228; queer cinematic, 11, 13–14, 75, 230, 232, 237–38, 257, 296; queerness as an affective force, 50, 66, 77, 242, 313n48, 332n53; slow-motion capture of, 239; transnationalism as basis for affective homosocial bonds, 75, 76, 122, 192, 313n57

Africa: African and pan-African films, 98; African concept of sex as private, 137, 171; Batho Ba Lorato Film Festival, 87, 97–101, 316n31; *Dakan (Destiny)*, 32, 132–40,

321n28, 321n33, 321n38; documentaries concerning lives of LGBT Africans, 98; Gaurav Desai on representations of African queerness, 69; homosexuality as unAfrican and unnatural, 97, 99, 132, 210, 316–17nn36–37; human rights and LGBT activism in, 98–99, 101–3, 133; LEGABIBO (Lesbians, Gays, and Bisexuals of Botswana), 97–98, 101–3, 316n36, 317nn39–41; Migraine-George on tradition and modernity in, 134–35, 321n33; modernity and modern behaviors, 137–39, 140; modernization in, 134–35; Nollywood homosex cycle of films, 171–72, 324n8; North Africa, 134, 231–32; Out in Africa South African Gay and Lesbian Film Festival, 81, 110; Panafrican Film and Television Festival (FESPACO), 132; postcolonial concerns, 132, 133, 313n49, 316n35, 320n26; Romanow on postcolonial African body, 137, 140, 321n39; scholarship on African

anachronism: as a temporality used in queer cinema, 174, 231, 261, 272; function of in *Proteus*, 262–63, 266, 333n5; tfunction of in *The World Unseen*, 228–29

Anderson, Benedict, 161, 306n14

Andrew, Dudley, 25, 269, 271–72, 293, 309n57, 309n59, 334n16, 334n20, 337n57

animality: as a space of queer belonging, 242, 245; as a tool for queer reworlding, 241, 242, 281; in cinematic allegory, 162–63; in human rights discourse, 116, 242–43; queer self-representations as animals in film festival posters, 104, 107, 109–12, 115; queer self-representation through animals as a political act, 162–63, 241–42, 257

Anzaldúa, Gloria, 73–74, 313n56

apartheid, 228–29, 261–62, 264

Appiah, Kwame Anthony, 24, 133, 309n55

Argentina: *De eso no se habla (I Don't Want to Talk about It)*, 170; *El favor (The Favor)*, 82; *Hawaii*, 300–304; Julia Solomonoff (director), 223; Lucía Puenzo (director), 85; Lucrecia Martel (director), 12, 18, 300, 307n25; Marco Berger (director), 300; María Luisa Bemberg (director), 170; *Mujer sin cabeza, La (The Headless Woman)*, 12; Pablo Sofovich (director), 82; strong sense of alienation among queers in, 300; *Ultimo verano de la boyita, El (The Last Summer of La Boyita)*, 223; *XXY*, 85

Armenia, 188, 326n32

Armes, Roy, 138, 321n40

Arroyo, José, 213, 328n7

art films, 14–15, 33, 215, 268, 275, 277–78, 285

assimilationism, 47, 61, 67, 251

asynchrony, 33, 261, 271–73, 276, 277, 281, 295–96

audiences: accessibility of to queer films, 17, 29–30; as a concern for scholars of queer cinema, 44; *Acting Out: 25 Years of Film and Community in Hamburg* (documentary), 3; adoption and re-coding of mainstream films by queer, 9, 168–69; as an influence on global mobility of films, 44–46, 188; bootlegging and covert sharing of films by, 16–17, 181, 289; cinematic assumptions of, 121, 152; cinematic control of audience experience of time, 271–72, 276–77, 285; cinematic experiences of gender dissidence for, 38, 168–69, 172, 189, 197, 199–201, 222, 230; culturally-embedded, internationally popular films, 133, 158, 166, 187, 193, 196–97, 206; culture as an influence on audience receptivity and comprehension, 161–62, 172, 175, 197–99; desire of for more cosmopolitan experiences, 81; diasporic, 16; film festivals as reworlding experiences for, 3, 32, 79–80, 82, 84–97, 99–103; filmmaking as a redefinition of time and space for, 29–30, 34; filmmaking for foreign, 8, 181, 182–83, 231, 236; films that address diverse, 62, 221, 222, 227; films that address incommensurate, 121–22; films that amplify the affective engagement of, 67–68, 200–201, 205; genres that address sub-populations, 57, 64, 168, 287–88; global versus local, 44–45; impact of film festival on film distribution, 44–45, 46, 198; international, 16; for lesbian films, 68, 181, 231; minoritized, 15; neoliberal and films perceived to be exotic, 46–48; popular cinema as a source of queer pleasures for, 6–7, 168–69, 170–71; privileged cinematic viewpoint, 47, 76, 275; queer, 8, 214, 217, 329n14; *Queer Artivism* (documentary), 3, 308n42; register and the cinematic audience, 214; subtitling for, 81; voyeurism, 40–42, 171

Australia: audiences in, 198; Australian filmmakers, 272; Fadia Abboud (director), 272; *In the Ladies' Lounge*, 272; James McTeigue (director), 130; legal prohibitions in, 112; queers in, 73, 327n46; Stephan Elliott (director), 199; *The Adventures of Priscilla, Queen of the Desert*, 199

Austria: *Caché (Hidden)*, 215; Michael Haneke (director), 215

auteurs, 8, 82, 217, 274

denaturalization, 8, 29, 117, 267. *See also* naturalization

Denmark: Carl Theodor Dreyer (director), 292; *Dual*, 75–76

Desai, Gaurav, 69, 313n49

Desai, Jigna, 83, 141, 142, 145, 314n10

diaspora: black diasporic queers, 78, 99, 181, 313n59; diasporic experience, 5–6, 43, 58, 68, 142, 145, 210, 289; diasporic lesbians as film protagonists, 31, 57–68, 141, 144; diasporic romantic comedy (rom-com), 58–61, 68; films and videos addressed to diasporic audiences, 16, 23, 181, 289; films produced by diasporic individuals, 26, 140, 145, 181; queer diasporic cinema, 28, 31, 185–87, 296, 311nn23–24, 312n46; South Asian diasporic queers, 306n13, 307n18, 321n43, 325n23. *See also* migration

Dioli, Irene, 193, 308n43

diptych narrative formats, 158, 159, 160, 281

discrimination: against queer individuals, 85, 183, 221–22, 227–28, 254; caste, 254, 333n72. *See also* prejudice

Distrify, 16, 307n29

diversity: as a priority of film festivals, 82, 83–84, 85, 96, 109–10, 115, 242; belonging and, 217; gender, 193–96, 203, 206–8, 212, 221, 227, 317n45; global gay versus local practices as a false dichotomy, 49, 50; governmental responsibility for, 101–2; liberalism, multiculturalism, and, 53, 68–69, 311n30; subjectivity and, 70; theoretical concepts of versus real-life, 69

Doane, Mary Ann, 27, 281, 306n7, 309n61, 335n40

Dobrovic, Zvonimir, 21, 308n42

documentaries: about queer film festivals, 3; *Acciones #6* (Bolivia), 238; *Dangerous Living: Coming Out in the Developing World* (United States), 123; *Difficult Love* (South Africa), 98; documentary elements in *East Side Story* (Croatia), 124–25, 126; documentary elements in *More than a Friend* (India), 146, 147–48; documentary elements of *Funeral Parade of Roses* (Japan), 150–51, 153, 154, 158,

322n53; documentary elements of *Papilio Buddha* (India), 255; documentary elements of *The Parade* (Serbia), 188; Ghosh on experimental queer, 211–12; *Jessica's Journey* (Guyana), 85; Kimmel on gay, 22; *Le Coccinelle: Neapolitan Transsexual Melodrama* (Italy), 224; *Life Experiences of LGBTI in Botswana* (Botswana), 98; Matsumoto on, 151; Movies that Matter Foundation, 94; *Pojktanten (She Male Snails)* (Sweden), 248; queer avant-garde, 150; queer documentary filmmakers, 212; at queer film festivals, 82, 85, 91, 96, 98; *Sade's Story* (Guyana), 85; scholarship on queer, 308n42, 322n51, 328n2, 334n23; *Taboo Yardies* (Jamaica), 85; *The Pearl of Africa* (Sweden), 16; *Venus Boyz* (Switzerland; United States), 85; *Voices of Witness Africa* (United States), 98; *Will This Change?* (Bangladesh), 96; *Yang ± Yin: Gender in Chinese Cinema* (China), 9

Doty, Alexander, 6, 169, 306n6

drag: gender performativity, 152; performers, 207–8, 218; queens, 66, 194, 198, 220, 294; queen versus Japanese *gai boi*, 322n49

dramas: *Beautiful Thing* (United Kingdom), 122–23; coming-out story in gay cinematic, 122–23; *Contracorriente (Undertow)* (Peru), 44–48, 74, 297, 311n25; cross-cultural, 74; documentary-dramas, 146; German tragic *(Trauerspiel)*, 149, 322n48; *Girlfriend, Boyfriend* (Taiwan), 13; *Hei yan quan (I Don't Want to Sleep Alone)* (Taiwan), 20; historical, 13, 228, 231, 261; *Lilting* (United Kingdom; Cambodia), 74–75; *Memento Mori* (South Korea), 20; *Mixed Kebab* (Belgium), 50–51, 53, 55, 69; *My Beautiful Laundrette* (United Kingdom), 50; *My Brother the Devil* (Muslim), 50, 54–57; Nigerian diasporic, 181; Nigerian gay, 179, 325n17; *Nina's Heavenly Delights* (India), 58–59, 63–68; *Proteus* (Canada; South Africa), 261–66, 292, 294, 333n5, 333n7; romantic, 20, 50; that stage sociocultural confluences, 31, 50, 170, 257; *Taar Cheye Se Anek Aaro (More than a*

excision (*continued*)

in *Futuro Beach*, 298–300; institutional of the queer experience, 286, 293; jump cuts and ellipses that produce cinematic, 294–96, 337n59; in *Madame Satã*, 294, 296, 298; narrative, 298–99; obscenity standards as a tool for cinematic, 17; of queer cinema from public records, 17. *See also* censorship

experimental film: *Bara no sôretsu (Funeral Parade of Roses)* (Japan), 32, 150; based on the human body, 337n59; *Bruce Lee in the Land of Balzac* (Brazil), 247; in cinematic hapticity and filmic texture, 238; documentation of lives and experiences by, 61, 150, 211–12, 238–39; experimental imaging, 15; experimental queer documentary, 211; experimental realist narration, 34; experiments with boredom, 281; *Kajitu (Some Days Ago)* (Japan), 10; *Mekong Hotel* (Thailand), 281; MIX NYC Queer Experimental Film Festival, 86, 87–90, 92–93; *Piao lang qing chun (Drifting Flowers)* (Taiwan), 275; *Pojktanten (She Male Snails)* (documentary; Sweden), 248; proto-cinematic effects, 260; transnational counterculture and, 155, 158; work of Apichatpong Weerasethakul (Thailand) with temporality and slowness, 281; work of Pratibha Parmar (India), 61; work of the Mujeres Creando (Bolivia), 238–41; work of Toshio Matsumoto (Japan), 150–54

Facebook, 16, 87, 90, 329n20

family: as a heteronormalizing institution, 19, 45–46, 132, 137–38, 174–75, 196, 308n38; cinematic tension between family and sexual desire, 50, 65, 70–71, 137–38, 297, 299; in *Dakan*, 132–40; diasporic in cinema, 58–60, 63–66, 68, 145, 182; familial love and acceptance as a topic of queer cinema, 226–27; family honor as a source of tension, 222, 226; family rejection as a topic of queer cinema, 221–26; happy coexistence of family

ties and erotic bonds as a utopian future, 67–68; multiculturalism and family in romantic comedies, 58, 59, 60, 63, 231; in *My Brother the Devil*, 54–57; in *Nina's Heavenly Delights*, 63–67; queer-bonded families, 189, 219–20, 222; and queer experiences of loss in *Lilting*, 74–75; queer film festival as a source of familial belonging, 92–93, 99–100, 123; in queer-taken-for-granted narratives, 70–71

Farmer, Brett, 194, 326n42

Fassbinder, Werner, 18, 217, 227, 228, 229

faux-slow: as a disingenuous stylization of temporality, 278–81, 286; *A Thousand Clouds of Peace* as an example of, 277, 278–79; *Keep the Lights On* as an example of, 280; *Weekend* as an example of, 277, 278, 279–80

feminism: authorship and, 60–61, 312n42; cinematic examinations of women's rights, 121–22, 164–65, 240–41, 255, 327n6, 337n59; colonialism and neoliberalism as concerns of, 78, 241; feminist film theory of cinema as an apparatus of desire, 11, 38, 322n60; feminist film theory of the gendered gaze, 6–7, 306nn7–8; feminist responses to *Fire*, 141–42, 144, 321n42; human rights discourse as a concern of, 111; and patriarchy, 177–78; queer politics, lesbianism, and, 177–78, 204, 240, 271, 313n50; Western, 69; women-of-color, 43, 49; work of Mujeres Creando, 238–41, 331n48. *See also* lesbian identities

Ferguson, Roderick, 36–37, 43, 310nn5–6, 311n20

film festivals: Bazin on, 310n69; Cannes Film Festival, 8, 81, 132; cultural practices of, 32; Dubai International Film Festival, 228; internationalization of, 80, 314n3; New York Museum of Modern Art (MoMA), 8. *See also* queer film festivals

Fire (India): allegory in, 32, 140–43, 145–46, 149; controversy over, 83, 123, 140–42, 145, 146, 321nn41–2; lesbian desire in, 19, 83, 140–49, 166, 321n44; melodrama in, 143–44, 149; patriarchy in, 142, 143, 144;

global South: fight for human rights in the, 101; as having different gendered and sexual life worlds from the global North, 5; migration and diaspora in the, 145; neocolonial attitudes of the global North toward the, 40, 42, 44, 123, 175; Sarkar on the melodrama of globalization in the, 218, 237

Gopinath, Gayatri: on cinematic lesbian identity, 141, 142, 145, 309n66, 314n9, 321n41, 321n44; on cinematic spectators, 9, 23, 28–29, 306n13, 307n18; on queer diasporic cinema, 28–29

grabbiness, 22–24

Grant, Catherine, 12, 307n25

Great Britain. *See* United Kingdom

Greece: *Idylls*, 246, 332n59; Panos Koutras (director), 253, 322n61; *Strella (A Woman's Way)*, 253, 322n61; Theocritus, 246, 332n59

Green-Simms, Lindsey, 172, 181, 324n8

Grewal, Inderpal, 43, 311n18

Greyson, John: films of, 33, 84, 229, 261, 266, 272, 317n44; *Proteus*, 261–66, 292, 294, 333n5, 333n7; use of asynchrony by, 266, 272

Guinea: controversy over homosexuality in, 134, 136; *Dakan (Destiny)*, 32, 132–40, 321n28, 321n33, 321n38; Mohamed Camara (director), 32, 132, 138, 174, 287, 321n38; post-colonial, 133–34, 166

Gutiérrez Alea, Tomás, 27

Guyana: *Antiman*, 85; Gavin Ramoutar (director), 85; *Jessica's Journey* (documentary), 85; the nation-state of as a guardian of heterosexual normativity, 85; Painting the Spectrum festival, 85, 315n14; *Sade's Story* (documentary), 85; Society against Sexual Orientation Discrimination (SASOD), 85

Habib, Samar, 53, 60, 169, 308n44

Halberstam, Judith Jack, 214, 246, 261, 266, 328n8, 332n58

Hansen, Miriam Bratu, 26, 213, 309n59, 328nn5–6

hapticity, 236–38, 240, 245, 248–49, 251–52, 286

Haraway, Donna, 241, 331n51

Hassan, Omar, 134, 321n32

Heidegger, Martin, 124, 319n10

Herbert, Daniel, 17–18, 308n35

Herzegovina, *Go West*, 82

heterocentrism, 7, 262, 306n9

heteronormativity: as an assumption belied by the diversity of human lifestyles, 69, 180, 186, 237; the cinema as a force that institutionalizes, 19, 36, 45–46, 48–49, 271, 281; colonialism as a force that institutionalized, 37, 241; family as a force of institutional, 19, 253; patriarchy as a complement to, 142, 164–65; queer behaviors and lifestyles as challenges to, 142, 147, 153, 162–66, 227–28

heterosexuality: as a basis for circumscribing personal conduct, 143, 147, 184, 319n9; as a basis for narrative synchronicity (heterosynchrony), 268–71; as a justification for anti-queer violence, 144, 148; as an assumption that naturalizes its own dominance, 21–23, 127, 143, 146–48, 216, 267, 308–9n50, 333n11; as an underlying assumption of cinema, 18, 28, 266, 267–68; assumption of underlying romantic comedy, 57; and colonial assumptions of otherness, 37, 266; failure of to acknowledge differences among human beings, 77; female rights and feminism as challenges to, 144, 240–41, 319n66; heterosexual patriarchy, 23; heterosexual transgression as more tolerable than queerness, 146, 173–74; influence of on concepts of family, 66; marriage and, 329n19; monogamous, 37, 45, 68, 240; as nationalism, 134, 320n26; and neoliberal assumptions of otherness, 49; outreach of Batho Ba Lorato for heterosexual participation, 99; queerness and heterosexuality in *Taste of Cherry*, 119–21; taken-for-granted queer as a refutation of assumed cinematic, 73

heterosynchrony, 268–71, 272, 273, 284–85, 285–86

hijras: Alamgir Khan on, 227, 330n34; as a South Asian culture, 222; *Common Gender* as a study of the plight of, 145, 222–27, 268, 329–30n23, 330n30, 330n34; discrimination against, 223–26; exclusion of from mainstream cultural spaces, 96; familial formations among, 222, 223; femininity of, 222–24; history and typologies of South Asian, 222; human rights discourses concerning, 222, 223; self-perception of as a third sex, 222, 224; violence against, 223–24; *Will This Change?* (documentary), 96. *See also* trans identities

Hilderbrand, Lucas, 16, 238, 289, 293, 307n28, 337n54

Hindi cinema: audiences, 87; Bollywood references in *Nina's Heavenly Delights*, 64, 66, 67; discourses concerning identity as a topic of, 185; *Dostana*, 170, 182–87, 189, 325n27, 325nn22–23, 325nn22–27; item songs and item girls, 223, 330n25; male homoeroticism in, 170; melodrama as a popular genre for, 218; queerness in, 9, 64, 306n13, 307n18; scholarship on, 307n18, 324n4, 325n23, 325n27, 329n18; the transnational elements of, 66, 325n23, 325n27; self-censuring by, 286. *See also* India

Hindus and Hindu traditions, 141, 143, 144, 255

historicity: excision and restoration of gay content, 293, 296; linear history, 263, 266, 295–96, 337n61; queer, 296. *See also* temporality

Hoad, Neville, 37, 310n7

Hollywood: audience perspective dictated through films, 6–7; cinematic intensified continuity, 295; classical melodramas, 217, 225; classical representations of gender and sexuality, 168, 267; communication of desire in cinema, 6, 307n25; directors of early melodrama, 217; "New Hollywood" cinematographic style, 280; popular films with queer appeal, 217; presence of gay protagonists in popular cinema, 168, 210; self-censoring of films by, 286;

social inequality and homophobia as film subjects, 330n29; temporality in classical cinema, 267, 268, 270, 284–85, 333n10, 334n28; use of ellipsis in cinema, 295. *See also* United States

homogenization, 5, 23, 48, 69, 195

homonationalism: antihomonationalism, 48, 62, 190, 210; complicity of with neoliberal capitalism, 5; debates concerning, 26, 31; homophobia as a reaction to the homonationalism of the global gay, 146, 174; neoliberal tolerance and, 183, 184, 186; queer film festivals and, 80; in queer films, 59, 61, 62–68, 192; and racism, 48, 52, 53, 115, 306n5

homonormativity: antihomonormative queerness and politics, 32, 62; association of with neoliberal globalism and consumerism, 69, 115, 167–68, 261; queer challenges to, 48–50, 59, 60, 66–67, 163, 266. *See also* gay identities

homophobia: as a cause of human rights violations, 175, 188, 326n33; as a deterrent to the screening of queer cinema, 17, 188; as a moral judgment, 172–74; antihomophobic politics, 19, 30, 69, 97, 98–101, 266–67, 316–17n37; as a reaction against Westernization and globalized capitalism, 127, 173–74, 177, 181, 191; as a topic in queer cinematic narratives, 51, 61, 140, 147, 238, 257, 287, 330n29; as a topic in queer cinematic narratives of the Balkans, 187–91, 196–98, 326n33, 326n38; Christian, 97, 173–75, 177, 181, 188; construed as an element of nationalism, 84, 127, 174–75, 181, 188, 190; *East Side Story* as a commentary on homophobic violence, 124–27; ethnic queer as a target in homonormative environments, 49, 72; film festivals screening queer films as targets of homophobic violence, 83–84, 112; homophobic melodrama, 15, 177–78, 180; homophobic violence against LGBT Pride parades, 124–26, 187–88; institutionalized, 18, 84, 98–99, 175, 191; International Day against Homophobia

(IDAHO), 19; kathoey as a confrontation of, 196, 205–6; in Latin America, 44–45; Muslim, 51, 53; neo-Nazi, 124–26; Nigerian Christian melodrama as actively homophobic, 33, 177–78, 181; Nollywood-made homophobic but queer cinema, 171–81, 210; *Papilio Buddha* as a commentary on homophobic violence, 255–57; queer activism against, 19, 21, 77, 97–101; sanctioned by fundamentalist religion, 84, 98–99, 175; scholarship concerning, 30, 134–35; screening of queer films as a means of challenging, 99–101, 112, 132–33, 161, 188; in Serbia, 187–88, 192; in southern Africa, 98–99; state-sanctioned, 18, 53, 77, 98–99, 168, 171, 183; tolerance and, 182, 210. *See also* human rights; violence

homosexuality: as a condition that can be corrected medically, 121–22, 132; as a creation and concept of the West, 13, 99, 107, 126, 132, 134, 141–42, 194–95; activist work of LEGABIBO, 97–99; as a natural state of being human, 97–99, 136–37, 140, 146, 166, 188–89, 194–95; as an unnatural, disavowed, or tabooed subject, 23, 97, 99, 138, 140, 171–72, 228, 294; as a product of colonialism, 134, 174, 254, 316–17n37, 321n32; as a product of modernization and of globalization, 107, 145, 146, 174–75, 308n44, 316–17n37; and cinematic allegory, 132–35, 140–42, 156, 161; cinematic taken-for-granted queer, 73, 206; closeting and coming-out as Western concepts of, 123; criminalization of, 93, 112, 121–22, 140–41, 171, 172, 287; in *Dakan*, 32, 132–40, 141, 142, 146, 156, 161, 166; decriminalization of, 32, 106, 111; as demonic bondage, 174–76, 177–78; in diasporic romantic comedies, 59–60; discrimination, persecution, and violence against homosexuals, 99, 263–65; *Dostana* as a study in tolerance and, 181–87; in *Fire*, 83, 140–44; gender realignment surgery as a cure for, 122; human rights discourses concerning, 133, 318n50; Kiarostami on

readings of in *Taste of Cherry*, 119–21; Nollywood's treatment of, 170, 171–78, 181; in non-Western societies, 13, 136–37, 171–72, 238–39, 259–60, 286–88; religious censorship of, 46, 97, 174–75; Russo on in cinema, 168–69, 310n9; Sedgwick on, 76, 319n9; as un-African, 99, 132, 137; universalizing-minoritizing debates concerning, 76; and Western neoliberal, capitalist voyeurism, 22, 40–44; in world cinemas, 169–71, 254–57, 321nn36–37, 335n37, 336n46

Hong, Grace Kyungwon, 43, 310n5

Hong Kong: *Chūn guāng zhà xiè (Happy Together)*, 272, 279, 294, 303; Feng Yueh (director), 201; *Gam chi yuk yip (Who's the Woman, Who's the Man?)*, 82; *Gei Lo Sei Sap (A Queer Story)*, 82; *Hua Mu Lan (Woman General Hua Mulan)*, 201; Kei Shu (director), 82; Kit Hung (director), 29, 294; *Lan Yu*, 259–61, 294, 304, 317n47; Peter Hosun Chan (director), 82; Stanley Kwan (director), 9, 217, 259, 260, 317n47; Wong Kar-wai (director), 272; *Wusheng feng ling (Soundless Wind Chime)*, 29, 294; *Yang ± Yin: Gender in Chinese Cinema* (documentary), 9. *See also* China

horror films: *Hor Taew Tak (Haunting Me)* (Thailand), 197, 200; *Memento Mori* (South Korea), 20; sensory impact of, 213

human: Appiah on the value of the individual human life, 24; defining "Other" as a means of denying the status of, 80, 242, 332n53; denials and assertions of status, 80, 114–17, 318nn54–57; government biases against recognizing queers as, 102–3; the LEGABIBO battle for recognition, 101–3; neoliberal appropriation of the category of, 106–7; queer festival posters concerning the human status of queers, 107, 318n57; race as irrelevant in defining who is, 230; racist, anti-terrorist rhetoric as a basis for a subhuman category, 115; vulnerability of LGBT persons to marginalization and abnormalization, 80, 113. *See also* utopian aspirations; worlding

International Gay and Lesbian Human
  Rights Commission, 80, 314n1
internationalism, 5, 21, 33, 42, 82, 94, 98,
  191–92
intimacy: as a motivating element of
  cinematic narrative, 131, 186, 215, 274–75,
  285–86; belonging and, 241; censorship of
  on-screen, 286, 289–90; cinematic depictions of same-sex, 9, 13, 47, 159, 248–49,
  275, 290–91, 301; cinematic in *Dog Day
  Afternoon*, 129–30; cinematic in *Facing
  Mirrors*, 121–22; cinematic in *Proteus*,
  264–66; cinematic in *Taste of Cherry*,
  119–21; cinematic in *The Wedding Song*,
  231–36; cinematic in *The World Unseen*,
  228–30; cinematic in *Tropical Malady*,
  159, 162–63; cinematic registering of
  touch, 236–38, 248–50, 286; cinematic
  slowness as, 281, 285–86, 300; communal
  of queer film festivals, 91; in environments of racial prejudice, 228–30, 231–36,
  264–66, 311n21; erotic consumption,
  289–93; excision of queer from some
  histories, 294; formed through spectatorship, 20, 285–86, 300; Ghosh on the
  imperceptible elements of queer, 211–12;
  illegality of same-sex in some countries,
  85; memory and longing as bases for,
  301, 303; performance of in *Acciones #6*,
  238–39; queer structure of feeling, 296.
  See also privacy
Iran: Abbas Kiarostami (director), 119, 121,
  319n1, 319n4; *Aynehaye rooberoo (Facing
  Mirrors)*, 121–22; *Circumstance*, 1–4, 145,
  192, 226; diasporic Iranian protagonist in
  Three Veils, 58; homosexuality in, 121–22;
  Iranian cinema, 305n1, 319n2; Maryam
  Keshavarz (director), 1, 2; Negar Azarbayjani (director), 121; plight of the Iranian lesbian protagonist in *Unveiled*, 50,
  52–55; *Ta'm e guilass (A Taste of Cherry)*,
  119–21; underground DVD markets in, 16
Iron Ladies, The (Satree lek): characters
  and narrative of, 193, 196, 204–6, 210;
  popularity and significance of, 19, 171,
  195–200, 202, 208, 210, 327nn51–54

Islam, 49, 51, 54, 60, 122, 330n30; Islamophobia, 2, 49. *See also* Muslim identities
Israel: *Dhalam/Alata (Out in the Dark)*,
  230–31; Eytan Fox (director), 37; *Ha-
  Buah (The Bubble)*, 37; *Ha-Sippur shel
  Yossi (Yossi)*, 37; Jewish-Muslim and
  Israeli-Palestinian cinematic love stories,
  59, 230–31; Michael Mayer (director),
  230; scholarship on Israeli queer cinema,
  310n8; Schulman on "pinkwashing", 84,
  309n52; settler-colonial films, 34; state
  funding of film festivals, 84
Italy: *Barbarella*, 88; *Blow-Up*, 215;
  boredom and the Italian system of
  film viewing, 335n35; *Comizi d'amore
  (LoveMeetings)*, 148, 238; *Comizi d'amore
  (Love Meetings)*, 148, 238; Emanuela
  Pirelli (director), 224; Ferzan Özpetek
  (director), 7; *Hamam (Steam: The Turkish Bath)*, 7; *Le Coccinelle: Neapolitan
  Transsexual Melodrama* (documentary),
  224; Michelangelo Antonioni (director),
  215; *Mine Vaganti (Loose Cannons)*, 7;
  Pier Paolo Pasolini (director), 18, 148,
  181–82, 238, 325n20
Ivory coast. *See* Côte d'Ivoire

Jackson, Peter A., 160–61, 194–95, 206,
  311n19, 326nn42–43, 332n58
Jakovlevic, Branislav, 191, 326n39
Jamaica: Selena Blake (director), 85; *Taboo
  Yardies*, 85
Jameson, Fredric: Ahmad's critiques of the
  nationalist allegory of, 128–29, 149–50,
  320n18, 320n22; on allegorical texts,
  131–32, 320n17; on allegory in *Dog Day
  Afternoon*, 129, 135; on allegory in *East
  Palace, West Palace*, 163–64; Jamesonian
  cinematic treatments, 133–34, 164; on
  national allegory, 127–29
Japan: *Bara no sôretsu (Funeral Parade of
  Roses)*, 32, 38, 150–58, 166, 322n53, 322n57,
  322nn53–54, 323n63; *Fukujusô (Pheasant
  Eyes)*, 19; *gai bois*, 150–54, 156–58, 166,
  322n49; Jirô Kawate (director), 19; *Kajitu
  (Some Days Ago)*, 10; Nakamura Takehiro

(director), 10; Nobuko Yoshiya (novelist), 19; post-World War II, 154–56, 157, 322n50; Toshio Matsumoto (director), 18, 32, 150–51, 153, 156–58, 322n57, 322nn52–53

jump cuts: as the products of censorship, 291, 294–95; as the products of the communal sharing and viewing of taped films, 291–93; as tools for creating queer historicity, 296; as tools for provoking desire and longing, 290–93, 337n59; as tools for refashioning time and space, 294, 296; use of in *Dipped in Gold*, 290, 292; use of in *Lan Yu*, 294; use of in *Madame Satã*, 294. *See also* ellipsis

Jusick, Stephen Kent, 88, 90, 91

Kaplan, Caren, 43, 311n18

Kapur, Ratna, 141, 321n42

KASHISH Mumbai International Queer Film Festival, 86, 87, 93–97, 98

kathoey: Barea on, 195, 326n44; *Biutiful Boksoe (Beautiful Boxer)*, 171, 193, 201–4, 206; the concept of *phet*, 194, 195, 196, 206; cultural repositioning of in modern Thailand, 194–96; definition of, 161; *Hor Taew Tak (Haunting Me)*, 197, 200, *209*; international popularity of kathoey genre films, 193–94, 195, 197, 199–201, 205–6, 208–10; Jah (Jaymee Goh) on, 201; Käng on, 195, 327nn47–48; kathoey cinema as vernacular queerness, 194, 195, 199, 200, 201, 205–6, 208–10; Poj Arnon (director), 193, 197; *Poochay Naya (I Am a Man)*, 199; *Satree lek (The Iron Ladies)*, 171, 193, 196–200, 202, 204–5, 206–10, 327nn51–54; scholarship on kathoey cinema, 326n44; scholarship on kathoey identity, 327nn47–48; *Spicy Beauty Queens of Bangkok*, 193, 197, 206–9. *See also* gender; Thailand; trans identities

Kenya, 316–17n37

Khan, Alamgir, 227, 330n34

Kim, Jihoon, 158, 323n72

Kimmel, Penni, 22, 23, 308n46

King, Homay, 153, 267–68, 282, 322n58, 336n42

kinship, 67, 73, 74, 245, 253, 265–66, 311n21

Kombugu, Cleopatra, 16

Ko, Mika, 151, 155–56, 322n53

Kracauer, Sigfried, 257, 281, 333n74

Krutnik, Frank, 58, 312n37

Kui, Kam Wai, 81, 314n5

Kulpa, Robert, 20, 308n40

language: availability of queer cinema in local language-based markets, 16; dubbing in *Circumstance*, 3–4; human rights language as epistemological globalization, 107; multilingual cinematic presentations, 96, 264; of tolerance, 182, 189, 226; political functions of, 99, 203, 206–7, 221, 264, 319n66; subtitling, 81; translation as a cultural redefining of concepts, 52, 242; translation of in *Lilting*, 74–76; the variety of available at queer film festivals, 96; variety of foreign films available through Distrify, 16

Larkin, Brian, 171, 177, 324n7

Lebanon: *Circumstance*, 1–4; *In the Ladies' Lounge*, 272–73; Nadine Labaki (director), 168; *Sukkar banat (Caramel)*, 168

lesbian identities: act versus identity, 39; as a force for remaking the world and redefining the human, 24–25, 62–66, 72–74, 97–98, 109, 130–31, 229–30; assertion that lesbians are a product of the modern Western world, 39, 141, 145; black, 12, 98; butch, 12, 62, 194–95, 196, 228, 273; cinematic portrayals of the politics of lesbianism, 2, 20; diasporic, 31, 50, 52–54, 57–68, 141–42, 144–45, 273; documentary and documentary-fiction cinematic studies of the lives of, 147–49, 3282; dykes, 150, 190, 307n18; eroticized depictions of, 11–12, 179, 232, 234, 252; femme, 12, 62, 82, 195, 252; film festivals, 81–84, 91, 104, 132, 198, 199, 314n6, 314nn1–3; governmental denials of the existence of, 171, 228; issues of freedom of expression, 141–42, 238–40, 272–73; issues of marriage, maternity, and family, 59, 60, 66, 140–41, 148, 233,

mise-en-abyme, 67

mise-en-scène: as a complement to narrative, 138, 168, 183, 249; allegory and, 322n56; as a self-reflexive device, 67–68; as a visual statement, 143, 217; in faux-slow films, 277–78; in melodrama, 143, 223; national and locational iconographies, 45, 63, 64; register and, 213–14

MIX festivals: MIX Aalborg, 91; MIX Aarhus, 91; MIX Brasil, 81, 91; MIX Copenhagen, 92; MIX Mexico, 91; MIX NYC, 86, 87–93, 98, 315nn20–21, 315nn23–25

Mizielińska, Joanna, 20, 308n40

modernism, 15, 128, 149, 213, 228, 229. *See also* vernacular modernism

modernity: as a topic addressed by melodrama, 218–19; conflict between tradition and, 137–38, 142; homosexuality and queerness as markers of, 59, 141–42, 195; queer behaviors that challenge capitalist, 154, 155–56, 158, 260, 296; Western self-identification with, 49, 58, 107, 123, 135

monolingualism, 76, 313n57

montage, 11, 27, 29, 53, 66, 211, 269

Morris, Rosalind, 195, 327n45

Mortimer-Sandilands, Catriona, 246, 247, 255, 332n60

Morton, Timothy, 248, 332n65

Mulvey, Laura, 6, 7, 120, 144, 306n7, 319n1

Muñoz, José, 50, 261, 266, 309n52, 333n3

Muraleedharan, T., 184–85, 325n26

music: as a complement to the narrative environment, 64, 259; used for melodramatic effect, 177–78, 180, 219–20, 224, 243; use of non-diegetic to underscore dramatic breakdown, 226, 291

Muslim identities: the cinematic study of racialization and the personhood of, 49–51; diasporic, 49–57, 58–59; European, 49, 232; *Fremde Haut (Unveiled)*, 50–55; *I Can't Think Straight*, 58–60, 62, 64, 67, 68; Jewish-Muslim, Israeli-Palestinian cinematic romances, 231–36; lesbian, 53, 58–60, 231n36, 308n44; lesbian filmmakers, 31; liberal Muslims in *Common Gender*, 330n30; *Mixed Kebab*, 50–51, 53,

55, 69; multiculturalism and, 49, 51, 52, 53, 54, 57–58, 69; Muslim homophobia, 51, 53; Muslim queers, 49–52; *My Brother the Devil*, 50, 54–57; *The Wedding Song*, 231–36; *Three Veils*, 58–60, 62, 68, 69, 268, 312n40; treatment of hijras by some, 222–27. *See also* Islam

Myanmar (Burma), 80, 314n1

Naficy, Hamid, 120–21, 319n3

narrative: allegory, 32, 123–24, 127, 134–35, 140–42, 149–51, 153, 158–62; asynchronic, 33, 261, 271–73, 276, 277, 281, 295–96; the coming out, 123, 133; counternarrative and allegory in *Funeral Parade of Roses*, 150–58; documentary elements combined with fictional, 147–48, 150–51; exile as a narrative trope in queer cinema, 122, 140, 144, 146; figuration through, 37; the gender masquerade in *Unveiled*, 52–55; heterosynchronic, 268–72; historical and linear narratives recontextualized as queer, 28, 153, 158–61, 229–36, 260–66, 272–73, 300–301; influence of cultural values on the aesthetics of, 267; interruptions to, 11, 153, 154, 255, 260, 268, 295–96, 298–99; intersecting narratives, 20; in *Tropical Malady*, 158–62; the in *Undertow*, 45–47; marriage plot, 123; melodrama in, 177, 218, 222, 224; the memorial narrative, 274–75; narrative closure, 46, 59, 131–32, 133–34, 140, 267–68; narratives of acceptance, 182–84; narratives of outrage, 177, 181; narratives of tolerance, 182–87, 210; narrative synchronicity, 268, 271; national allegory, 128–29, 131–32, 134, 140, 149–50; Nigerian film, 171, 173–74, 175–76, 177; political in *Dakan*, 132–40; political transnational of *The Parade*, 187–93; progress narratives, 76, 95, 123, 127, 166; queer narratives, 19, 131–33, 146–50, 157–58, 163, 165–68, 334n22; queerness and tolerance of in *Dostana*, 182–87; register and, 213–15; restrictive natures of coming-out and progress plots, 123; romance in *Fire*, 140–46, 321n44; romantic comedy, 57–59, 68; sexual fulfillment for women as a structuring principle for, 57–60; sexuality as a force in, 129, 130, 267, 287, 312n36, 333n11; slowing of, 153, 277–78; sounds and imagery as framing devices in, 64; split narratives, 158, 159, 160, 275, 281, 294; taken-for-granted queerness as a realigning force for, 70–73; temporality and, 153, 229, 268, 272–78, 284–85, 294, 298–99; the transnational appeal of kathoey narratives, 194–210; universal narratives, 132–33; voyeuristic narratives, 40; Western concept of otherness as a basis for, 127, 132. *See also* queer temporality

narrativity: anti- and non-narrativity in experimental films, 150; cinematic rejections of linear, 153, 268; queer, 123, 131, 142, 146–47, 334n22; temporality and, 153, 272, 274

nationalism: as a complement to homophobia, 84, 99, 174, 190, 191; as a justification for damaging the environment, 248; as a rejection of Westernization in the global South, 99; and the geopolitics of human rights, 187, 190; globalized queer experience as a challenge to, 98; links between queer behavior and rebellious, 13; tolerance as an act of, 190, 191–92

naturalization, 23, 27, 42, 44. *See also* denaturalization

Nazis: neo-Nazis in modern Croatia and Serbia, 124, 126–27, 188, 191; in World War II Tunisia, 231–33, 235–36

neocolonialism: the capitalistic qualities of, 44, 99; fears of, 5, 175, 210; as the imposition of Western neoliberal ideas and attitudes, 12, 44, 48, 85, 141, 145, 167–68; limitations of as a global influence, 25, 85, 149; voyeuristic, touristic qualities of, 42, 202, 253, 254. *See also* colonialism and coloniality; postcolonialism and postcoloniality

neo-imperialism, 14, 44, 77, 128, 173

neoliberalism: as a homogenizing force, 44–48, 165; anti-neoliberal critiques that

follow the logic of, 48; capitalism and, 26, 43–44, 131, 138, 190, 218; cinematic taken-for-granted queer as a refutation of, 73; globalization and, 5, 45, 47, 48, 99, 192, 260; homonationalism as complicit with, 5, 31, 42, 190, 261; human as defined by, 106–7, 240; queer bonds as a means of remaking the world vision of, 73–74, 78, 93, 96–97, 98; racialization as a means of asserting neoliberal power, 43–44, 99, 218; world film culture and, 19, 42, 44, 45–48, 58, 190. *See also* globalization

Netherlands, The: Amsterdam Transgender Film Festival, 81, 94; Dutch protagonists, 261, 262, 264; Movies that Matter, 94

Nettleton, Taro, 156–57, 322n57

New Queer Cinema (NQC), 6, 27–28, 82, 185, 309n64, 317n43, 322n55, 328n2

Nigeria: Afam Okereke (director), 179; *Corporate Maid II,* 179; *Dirty Secret,* 171; *Emotional Crack,* 171; Frank Rajah Arase (director), 171; *Hideous Affair,* 171; Ikechukwu Onyeka (director), 175, 179; Ikenna Ezeugwu (director), 171; John Uche (director), 171; Lancelot Oduwa Imasuen (director), 171, 175; *Men in Love,* 173–76, 177, 179, 180, 181, 287; Moses Ebere (director), 173, 287; *Mr Ibu and Keziah,* 177–79; Rahim Caz Chidiebere (director), 171; *Reloaded,* 175; *Return of White Hunters,* 179; *Rude Girls,* 171; Saint Collins (director), 171; Stanley Anaekwe (director), 177; Theodore Anyanji (director), 171; *Unspoken,* 181; *Sexy Game,* 171, 175; *Sexy Girls,* 171; *Turn Me On,* 171, 175, 179. *See also* Nollywood

Nollywood: censorship in, 172–73, 181; homophobia in homosex cycle films, 173–75, 177–81; the Nigerian Christian melodrama genre, 33, 177, 181; the Nigerian film industry, 171, 181; the Nigerian homosex cycle of films, 171, 173, 175, 181, 324n8, 324n11, 325n18; Nigerian policies regarding gender and sexuality, 171, 172, 174; online sharing of homosex cycle films, 180–81; predilection of for indiscretion

227–28, 318n54, 318n60; identity, 5, 8, 10, 36, 62, 104–7, 111–17, 232–33, 319n63; individual differences and, 5, 30, 266, 332n53; influence of on sexuality, 7, 317–18n49; inherently political nature of cinema, 7, 20, 141–42, 155, 326n36; inherently political nature of queerness, 21, 162, 164, 331n47; melodrama and queer, 218–28; migration as an influence on, 44, 315n22, 318n54; non-Western lesbian, 4, 61, 141, 204, 229–36, 238–41; of cinematic affect versus depiction, 12–13, 313n48, 328n8; of erasure, 32, 228; the of otherness, 36, 37, 331n50; of queer world making, 20–21, 25, 72–73, 140, 155–56, 194–95, 214–17; of temporality, 33, 261, 266–67, 272, 277; of tolerance, 182–84, 186–87, 189–93, 204, 210; of touch, 33, 238–39, 286, 296; overlap of queer and national politics, 21, 81, 83–84, 141, 195, 210, 245–46; overlap of queer and world cinema, 4, 68–69, 81, 132, 218, 305n3; overlap of sexuality and, 1, 20, 136–38, 325nn26–27; political furor over *Fire*, 141–42, 321n42; public-private dichotomy, 156–62, 166, 238–39; queer cinema as a challenge to conventional history and, 28, 48, 229–36, 245–46, 265–66; queer world, 2, 29, 48, 62, 104; questions raised in *Circumstance*, 1–2; of recognition, 70; of representation, 10–11, 194, 286; transgenderism as a political issue, 54, 122; transnational, 58, 201, 312n34; Western coming out, 4; Western gay, 2, 42–43, 70; of world cinema, 5, 20, 29–33, 79, 309n57; of worldliness, 28–29, 68–69, 76–78, 92–93. *See also* geopolitics; racism

pornography, 204, 213, 214, 287, 337n59

Portugal: queer film festival poster imagery in, 109; Queer Lisboa film festival, 20, 80, 101; *The Last Match*, 40–44, 310n15

postcolonialism and postcoloniality: allegory in postcolonial texts, 32, 135, 165–66; anticolonialism, 78, 232; cosmopolitics, 78; creolization, 73; *Dakan* and the politics of, 132–40; decolonization, 134, 241; *Fire*

and the politics of, 140; Jameson's concept of national allegory, 128–29, 133–34, 149–50, 320n18, 320n22; postcolonial cinema, 32; racial and sexual violence in postcolonial environments, 61; reactionary nationalism in postcolonial environments, 99, 145, 173, 316–17n37; reworlding in environments of, 18, 308n37, 309n63, 313n49, 313n60, 321n32, 321n39; sexuality and sexual citizenship as concerns of, 43, 137–38, 140, 142, 145; the tswanarisation of postcolonial environments, 99. *See also* colonialism and coloniality; neocolonialism

posters: as allegory, 160; as an element of cinematic mise-en-scène, 64, 65, 190; animality in film festival, 109–10, 112–15, 241–42; as critiques of the hypocrisy of exceptionalism, 114–15; cultural context as an influence on depictions in, 175–76, 200; for the decriminalization of homosexuality, 111; de-particularization of the human form in film festival, 109; human rights and queer film festival, 103–7, 112–17; the iconography of film festival, 104, 107–9, 112–13, 115, 117; less-than-human and nonhuman figurations in, 107, 117; participant-made film festival, 99–101; pluralism as a topic of, 109–10; as political statements, 99–101, 188, 318n57; use of avatars in, 104, 107–8, 116, 127, 141

Povinelli, Elizabeth, 56, 312n35

power: cinema as a tool to challenge existing, 44, 73, 101, 130, 132, 149–50, 210; colonial, 231–32, 241; inequality as a product of power relations, 43; knowledge and nomenclature as sources of, 264; power relations inherent to sexual identities, 43, 317–18n49; queer film festivals as institutions that challenge existing, 80, 97, 99; queerness as a means of redefining and realigning relationships of, 128–29, 146, 165, 170–71, 195; universalizing concepts that reiterate existing power structures, 14; worldliness as a recalibrating influence on, 25, 164, 166, 241; world-making

power (continued)
  power of cinema, 34, 36, 47–48, 66,
    237–38
Prasad, Madhava, 8, 306n13
prejudice, 101, 114, 183, 189, 198–99. See also
    discrimination
privacy: African concept of sex as private,
    137, 171; as a human right, 111–12, 318n50;
    as a means of protecting queers, 97, 111–12,
    113, 122; blend of public and private in
    video stores and video circulation, 146;
    cinematic blending of public and private,
    3, 90, 120, 205; cultural concepts of, 128,
    137, 138, 171, 319n9, 320n22, 321n44; fa-
    milial, 122; public access as an exercise in
    personal, 226, 330n32; public and private
    spaces in cinematic allegory, 158, 161, 162;
    public privacy, 121, 143, 144; public-private
    distinctions, 90, 124, 128, 132; relationship
    between public rights and private be-
    havior, 127, 156–57; thwarted, 136; viewer
    cinematic transcoding, 169, 179, 180–81;
    violations of, 129–30. See also intimacy
Puar, Jasbir, 6, 22, 48–49, 53, 56, 115, 272,
    306n5
public spaces: absence of queer images from
    some, 17; accessibility to queer media
    in, 17–18, 172, 193; allegory as a means of
    bypassing the public-private dichotomy,
    123–24, 127, 163; exposed private spaces,
    142–43; private experiences in, 120,
    135–36, 159; privatization of once, 157;
    queer film festivals as reimaginings of, 32,
    85, 88, 94–97, 101, 103, 315n19; recognition
    and respect in, 122, 224, 239; redefini-
    tion of through thwarted privacy, 135–36;
    violently contested, 187–88

queer: the ethnic, 49, 51, 52; queerness
    as something that has always existed,
    168–69; the term (linguistic signifiers
    for), 20–22
queer desire and longing: as an influence on
    cinematic temporality, 259–61, 266–67,
    275, 294, 300, 303–5; in cinematic alle-
    gory, 160–61, 162–63; and communal film

viewing, 3; in melodrama, 329n14; non-
  Western, 2, 20, 29, 134–35, 140, 160–61,
  165; in queer diasporic cinema, 28, 68; as
  revolutionary hope, 13, 164; transnational,
  29, 47–48, 74, 76; viewer transcoding and
  unearthing of cinematic, 169, 180–81, 279,
  292–93; world-making power of, 33, 48,
  211, 231, 235–36, 245, 332n58
queer film festivals: &Proud LGBT Film Festival (Yangon), 80, 314nn1–2; Amsterdam
  Transgender Film Festival, 81, 94; Batho
  Ba Lorato Film Festival (Gaborone),
  86, 97–103; Beijing Queer Film Festival,
  86, 315n17; BFI Flare: London LGBT Film
  Festival, 40, 109; as capitalist, globalizing
  entities, 84; Dublin Gay and Lesbian Film
  Festival, 198; Frameline (San Francisco),
  81–82, 93, 96, 314nn7–8; Hamburg
  Lesbian and Gay Film Festival, 84, 91;
  Jakarta Q Film Festival, 318n57; KASHISH
  Mumbai International Queer Film Festi-
  val, 86, 87, 93–97, 98; as locations for the
  assertion of human rights entitlement,
  106; London Transgender Film Festival,
  81; Mardi Gras Film Festival (Sydney), 198;
  MIX, 86–93, 98, 315nn20–21, 315nn23–25;
  MIX NYC Queer Experimental Film Festival, 86, 87; New York Lesbian and Gay
  Film Festival, 198; OUT Festival (Nairobi),
  316–17n37; Out in Africa South African
  Gay and Lesbian Film Festival, 81, 110;
  Out-Takes Dallas, 198; Painting the
  Spectrum, 85, 86; posters as statements
  for the decriminalization of homosexuality, 111; posters as statements of
  queer identity, 108; posters as statements
  regarding human pluralism, 109–10;
  posters as statements regarding human
  rights, 103–7, 112–17; Q! Festival (Jakarta),
  83, 107, 108, 109, 318n57; Queer Beograd
  Festival, 21, 308n43; queer film distribution, 307n29; Queer Lisboa, 20, 80, 101;
  Queer Sarajevo, 84; Queer Zagreb, 21;
  San Francisco International Lesbian and
  Gay Film Festival, 22, 45, 81–82, 84, 198,
  307n18; San Francisco South Asian LGBT

queer temporality (*continued*)
276–77, 281–86, 300, 307n20; as tool for disruption and redefinition, 273, 295–96, 304, 333n8; tunstable relationships of past, present, and future in, 252; use of by Andy Warhol, 153, 267–68, 281–82, 282, 322n58, 334n12, 336n42; use of in *Drifting Flowers*, 275–76; use of in *Futuro Beach*, 296–300; use of in *Hawaii*, 301–4; use of in *Lan Yu*, 259–61, 294; use of in *Madame Satã*, 294, 296, 298; use of in *Mekong Hotel*, 282–83, 285–86, 300; use of in *Proteus*, 261–66, 292, 294, 333n5, 333n7; use of in *She Male Snails*, 252, 268; use of in *Spider Lilies*, 273–75; use of temporal drift by Tsai, 10. *See also* narrative

queer theory: as a complement to world cinema, 5–6, 15, 26, 33, 36, 182, 214, 303–4; challenges of to neoliberal economics, 5; concerns of, 26, 35–37, 43, 56, 69, 73, 106–7, 240; debates concerning negative aesthetics, 277; environmentalism and, 247; global reorientation of, 5–6, 37, 42–43, 76, 78, 309n52; outmoded, Westernized version of, 20, 37, 42; temporality as a concern of, 266

race theory and practice: in Asia, 201, 228–31, 253–57, 333n72; in the black diaspora, 61–62, 73, 78, 310n6, 313n59; creolization, 73; homonormativity and, 115; as irrelevant to defining who is human, 230; in Latin America, 44, 73, 78, 238–41; of Native Americans, 73, 78, 311n19, 331n48

racism: anti-immigration rhetoric that justifies, 51; anti-terrorist rhetoric that justifies, 48, 49, 115, 311n28; capitalist development as a basis for acts of, 190–91, 248, 315n22; colonialist attitudes of, 232, 253, 263–64, 272; film as a means of problematizing, 37, 68, 190, 231–32, 266, 294, 330n29; gender and sexual regulations as justifications for racist practices, 37; liberal tolerance and, 43, 51–52, 59, 84, 218, 311n30, 311nn19–20; norms and normalities as bases for, 37,

43, 242, 332n53; queer romantic comedies as intersection points for gender, sex, and race, 57–59, 61, 66, 69; queer stances against racialization and, 21, 72–73, 78, 87, 109, 230, 241; racialization as a tool for legitimizing racist behaviors, 26, 31, 37, 49–51, 253, 263–64; racist, ethnic-based, and caste-based violence, 254–57, 333n72; segregation, 229. *See also* ethnicity; politics; stereotypes and stereotyping

Rancière, Jacques, 212, 213, 328n3

Reddy, Chandan, 37, 310n6

register: affective registers, 50–51, 178, 214–15, 216; capacity of queer films to invent new registers, 214, 240–41; cinematic, 28, 33, 212, 214, 215, 217; cinematic intimacy as a register of political being, 236, 237, 238, 240–42, 249–50; as cultural context, 161, 194, 206–7, 214, 217–18, 224, 254; definition of, 213–15; experiential, 91, 230, 260, 283, 294–95; historical costume drama, 228, 230; linguistic, 214; melodrama, 217–18, 224–25, 228; multiple registers contained within a film, 28, 96, 153–54, 202, 229; multiple registers in which a film can be read, 95–96, 228; multiple registers of imagery, 106, 115, 117; queer, 217, 228, 230, 240–42, 245, 255, 257

religion: as a cinematic symbol and agent of unqueering, 46, 54, 58, 60–61; Catholics and Catholicism, 46, 192, 240; Christians and Christianity, 33, 46, 177, 181, 192, 240; documentaries on LGBT Africans and continental religions, 98; homophobia as a moral judgment, 172; homophobia perpetrated by some established religions, 84, 99, 174; Jewish protagonists, 231–32, 234, 236; Muslim homophobia, 51; Muslim religious laws, 121; Nigerian Christian melodrama, 33, 174, 181; religious difference as a narrative tool, 59, 60, 82, 230, 232–34; religious discrimination against queer individuals, 227–28; religious fundamentalism, 84

restrictions, 14, 17, 61, 67, 103, 164

retrospectatorship, 23, 26, 28

Rhodes, John David, 132, 320n25, 322n56
Rhyne, Ragan, 81, 314n6, 317n44
Rich, Ruby, 76, 313n57, 314n3, 317n43
rights: activist advocacy of LGBT, 171, 221, 318n53, 329n19; free speech, 142, 238; LGBT rights as a concern of the United Nations, 106; LGBT rights as a topic of queer film festivals, 84, 96, 100–101; LGBT rights as a Western discourse, 58, 107, 145, 191, 316–17n37; privacy, 97, 112–13, 318n50
romance films: *Common Gender* (Bangladesh), 222–27, 268, 329–30n23, 330n34; *Fire* (India), 19, 83, 140–49, 166, 192, 314n9, 321nn41–44, 331n49; *Funeral Parade of Roses* (Japan), 32, 38, 150–58, 166, 322n57, 322nn53–54, 323n63; heterosexuality of Hollywood, 267; *Hommes libres, Les (Free Men)* (France), 232–33, 331n38; *Lan Yu* (Hong Kong), 259–61, 294, 304, 317n47; *Le chant des mariées (The Wedding Song)* (Tunisia; France), 231–36; Oedipal romance, 153; *Pariah* (United States), 62, 98, 331n49; *Phuean ... Ku Rak Mueng Wa (Bangkok Love Story)* (Thailand), 197; *The World Unseen* (South Africa), 228–30; *Three Veils* (United States), 58–60, 62, 268; *Tropical Malady* (Thailand), 32, 158–63, 166, 195, 242, 245, 281
Romanow, Rebecca, 137, 140, 321n39
romantic comedy (rom-com): the assumption of coupling in, 59; diasporic, 58, 59, 61; lesbian, 57–60, 61, 62–63; multiculturalism in, 57, 58, 61; queer, 57, 60, 61, 68, 197, 202, 268; scholarship on queer, 312nn36–37; traditional, heterosexual, 59, 60, 61, 68. *See also* comedies
Rony, Fatimah Tobing, 26, 309n59
Rosenbaum, Jonathan, 120–21, 319n2
Rosenberg, Jordana, 36, 310n4
Rosen, Philip, 163, 323n80
Rose, Steve, 46–47, 311n25
Roth-Bettoni, Didier, 23, 308n48
Russo, Vito, 38, 168–69
Ryberg, Ingrid, 251, 332n69

Sánchez-Eppeler, Benigno, 7, 43, 306n11
Sandoval, Chela, 78, 313n60
San Filippo, Maria, 7, 306n9, 307n24
San Francisco, 22, 45, 81–82, 84, 198, 307n18, 314nn7–8
Sarif, Shamim, 58, 228–29, 312n38, 330n35
Schulman, Sarah, 23, 84, 309n51, 315n22
Scotland, 58, 64–67, 312n44
Screen Daily, 197, 327n53, 327n58
Second World War. *See* World War II
Sedgwick, Eve Kosofsky: on the differences among people, 24–25, 30, 69; on the incommensurability of acts and identities, 39; on the need to resist dichotomies of subjectification, 70, 76–78, 254–55; on tolerance, 325n21; on universalizing and minoritizing discourses of homosexuality, 14, 69, 76–78, 319n9
self-reflexivity, 68, 150, 155, 205, 213, 229, 264, 271
Selvick, Stephanie, 134, 321n31
semiotics, 9, 11, 115, 160–61, 200, 322n60
Senegal: *Black Girl (La Noire de . . .)*, 25; Ousmane Sembene (director), 25, 150
sensuality: food as a sensual force, 66; popular cinema and queer, 170; register and cinematic, 212–13, 216, 230, 236, 237–38, 240, 248–50, 331n40
Serbia: concept and term for "queer" in, 21; Gay Pride parade in Belgrade (2001), 124, 187; Gay Pride parade in Belgrade (2010), 188; *Lepa sela lepo gore (Pretty Village, Pretty Flame)*, 187; nation-state of as guardian of heteronormativity in, 192; neo-Nazi homophobic violence in, 191; *Parada (The Parade)*, 3, 32, 170, 187–92, 192, 325–26nn28–39, 326n35; public debates over gay pride parades in, 191; queer film festivals in, 21; Srđan Dragojević (director), 3, 170, 187, 188, 191, 326n30, 326n38
sex acts, 11–12, 39, 71, 165, 174, 337n59
sexuality: affect and, 13; as an element of human subjectivity, 35–36, 68–69, 77, 98–99; as a topic of human rights discourse, 107, 111–13, 222–28, 317–18nn49–53,

sexuality (*continued*)
319n66; as a vehicle for cinematic allegory, 130, 132, 137–38, 141; cinematic hapticity and, 236–40; cinematic narrative and, 333n11; cinematic staging of, 11; cinematic taken-for-granted queerness as a negation of the importance of, 70–74; and environmental politics, 247; interactive relationship of to space and geographies, 35–37; interplay of cinematic subjectivity and, 37–39, 141, 168, 187, 194–95; interplay of movement, mobility, and translocation with, 43–44, 311n18, 312n35; and Jameson's model of public and private, 128–29; melodrama as a means of articulating issues of sexuality globally, 217–22; politicizing of through queer film festivals, 82–86; politics and, 1, 3, 22, 27–28, 30, 141, 164, 190; politics as an influence on, 7, 240–41, 287; queer, 52, 54, 56, 60, 130, 162, 198, 311n19; in queer cinema, 11, 14, 162, 206–10, 218; religion and, 60–61, 174–75, 316n34; Western globalizing assumptions regarding, 82, 194–95, 311n28; Western theories of, 15, 123. *See also* gender
Seymour, Nicole, 247, 248, 250, 332n61
Shakhsari, Sima, 54, 312n34
Shaw, Deborah, 11, 307n23
Shohat, Ella, 26, 309n59
shots: brief, immersive, 295; combinations of deliberately blurred or sharply focused, 248; the crucial sequence shots in *Stranger by the Lake*, 215; deep focus, long take, 143, 284; designed to preserve the subjectivity of the protagonist, 280; early revelation shots in *Common Gender*, 222–23; for environmental capture, 297; final, 51, 184–85, 215, 253, 260, 282, 299; the floating bed in *I Don't Want to Sleep Alone*, 71–72; frontality and scale to depict a relationship of touch, 233; high-angle, 256; of iconographic national sites, 63; intimate, 159, 230, 234; in *Lan Yu*, 259, 260–61; layered-over, 263; long, 211, 230, 256, 257, 284; mirror, 55; of the moon

turning and moving in *Spider Lilies*, 275; in *My Dead Brain*, 252; open-ended concluding, 259; overhead, 224, 330n30; pan and panning, 64, 190; queer lineup in *Spicy Beauty Queens of Bangkok*, 207; rapid zoom, 220; sequence, 284; shallow-focus, 278; shooting through glass, 10; shot-reverse shot framing, 119, 233, 280; shot scale, 233, 234; shots to effect revelation, 129, 291; six-minute river shot at the close of *Mekong Hotel*, 282–84, 285–86; slow-motion, 260–61; that direct the spectator's gaze, 278; three-minute, 259; two-shots, 47, 184; vista, 256, 282; voyeuristic, 185, 215. *See also* close-up shots; point of view
Singapore: *Biutiful Boksoe (Beautiful Boxer)*, 171, 193, 201–4, 206; censorship and homophobia in, 197, 201–2, 327n62; Ekachai Uekrongtham (director), 171, 202
Slovenia: Anja Wutej (director), 3, 308n42; *Dual (Dvojina)*, 75–76, 206, 298; filmmaking in, 192, 308n42; Ljubljana, 75, 108, 109; Masa Zia Lenárdic (director), 3, 308n42; Nejc Gazvoda (director), 75, 206, 298; *Queer Artivism* (documentary), 3; Slovenian films, 75–76; *The Parade*, 32, 170, 187–92, 192, 325–26nn28–39, 326n35
slow motion, 11, 220, 239, 260, 263
sodomy, 97, 112
sound: as a cinematic worlding tool, 163, 249; as a framing device, 64, 291; as a reworlding tool for the queer sensorium, 80, 227n60; disjunction of from images as a statement, 178–79, 208, 247, 248–49; interplay of with images in *Circumstance*, 3–4; interplay of with images in *Soundless Wind Chime*, 29, 294; juxtaposition of voices, 75, 147; in melodrama, 178, 224–25; sound-image interplay to stimulate viewer sensation, 237–38, 248; videotape sound as a material trace of usage, 288, 289, 290, 291; voiceovers, 64, 148, 203, 248, 268, 269
South Africa: apartheid, 228, 261–62, 264; *Difficult Love*, 98; homosexuals in, 99;

transnational queer space, 29, 86, 193, 201, 247, 276
transnational spaces, 119, 122, 206, 210
transvestites, 6, 168, 198, 208, 327n52
Trauerspiel, 149
Tropical Malady (Sud pralad), 32, 158–63, 166, 195, 242, 245, 281
Tsai, Ming-liang, 3, 8, 10, 20, 71, 261, 276, 286, 306n16, 307n20
Tunisia: anticolonialism and French racism in World War II, 231–32; *The Wedding Song*, 231–36
Turkey: audience interests versus filmmaking in, 40; Çakırlar, Cüneyt, 27, 29–30; diasporic Turks as protagonists, 50, 53, 72, 84; *Edge of Heaven*, 72–73, 231, 313n52; Ferzan Özpetek (director), 7; *Hamam (Steam: The Turkish Bath)*, 7; Kurdish protagonists, 72, 231; Kutluğ Ataman (director), 40, 310n14; *Lola + Bilidikid (Lola and Billy the Kid)*, 40; *Mine Vaganti (Loose Cannons)*, 7; term for "queer" in, 20–21

unhappiness: as an element of queer film narratives, 60–61, 222–23, 225, 226, 268, 329n14; as a topic of queer theory, 214
Union of Soviet Socialist Republics: the economic relationship of with Guinea, 133; film festivals in post-Soviet nations, 320–21n27; Sergei Eisenstein (director), 18, 27, 309n62
United Kingdom: Alfred Hitchcock (director), 295; Andrew Haigh (director), 277, 286; audience expectations of foreign films in the, 199; *Beautiful Thing*, 123; Black queer individuals, 61, 62; British Indian protagonists, 58, 63; Campbell X (filmmaker), 11, 62, 252; colonization of Botswana by, 103; David Yates (director), 187, 200; Derek Jarman (director), 229, 262; *Edward II*, 262; *Fem*, 12, 252; film releases and premiers in the, 40, 45, 231; *Full Monty, The*, 199; *Harry Potter and the Deathly Hallows: Part II*, 187; *Harry Potter and the Order of the*

Phoenix, 200; Hettie Macdonald (director), 123; Hong Khaou (director), 74, 206, 298; *I Can't Think Straight*, 58–59, 62–63, 64, 67, 68; immigration restrictions in the, 40, 130, 231; Isaac Julien (director), 262; *Jodie: An Icon*, 169; *Lady Vanishes, The*, 295; *Lilting*, 74–75, 206, 298; London as the setting for *Limelight*, 284–85, 336n44; *Looking for Langston*, 262; Matthew Warchus (director), 81; *My Beautiful Laundrette*, 50, 68, 230; *My Brother the Devil*, 50, 54, 54–57, 55–57; *Nina's Heavenly Delights*, 2–3, 58–59, 63–68; Peter Cattaneo (director), 199; Pratibha Parmar (director), 3, 58, 61, 67, 169, 212, 306n8; *Pride* (2014), 81; representations of Britishness, 63–64, 66; Sally El Hosaini (director), 50, 54; Shamim Sarif (director), 58, 228–29, 312n38, 330n35; Stephen Frears (director), 50, 230; the Stonewall charity, 99, 101; Stonewall charity, 99; *Stud Life*, 11–12, 62; Sunny King (director), 181; *The Hunger*, 11; in *Three Veils*, 58–59; Tony Scott (director), 11; *Unspoken*, 181; *V for Vendetta*, 130–31, 320n23; *Weekend*, 277, 278, 279–80; working class protagonists, 56, 62; *World Unseen, The*, 228–30
United Nations, 87, 93, 106, 112–14, 117, 319n66
United States: *(500) Days of Summer*, 268; Alice Wu (director), 57; Amnesty-USA, 113–14, 318n53; Andy Warhol (artist, director), 89, 153, 267–68, 281–82, 322n58, 334n12, 336n42; Ang Lee (director), 208; *Avatar*, 32, 187; *Bad News Bears*, 198; Barbara Hammer (director), 150; *Ben Hur*, 189; Bennett Singer (director), 98; Billy Wilder (director), 271; *Bourne Ultimatum, The*, 295; *Boys in the Band, The*, 199, 207; *Brother Outsider: The Life of Bayard Rustin*, 98; *Caged*, 169; *Call Her Savage*, 169; Charles Chaplin (director), 284; Charles Herman-Wurmfeld (director), 312n36; Cheryl Dunye (director), 2; Christopher Ashley (director), 312n36;

Christopher Nolan (director), 200; *Circumstance*, 1–4, 145, 192, 226; Cynthia Black (filmmaker), 98; *Dangerous Living: Coming Out in the Developing World* (documentary), 123; *Dark Knight, The,* 200; Dee Rees (director), 62, 98; *Dog Day Afternoon*, 32, 129–31, 135, 150, 207; Dorothy Arzner (director), 18; *Do the Right Thing,* 64; Doug Liman (director), 268; *Dyketactics*, 150; *Eternal Sunshine of the Spotless Mind,* 268; Florence Vigner (director), 68; Francis Ford Coppola (director), 130, 215; gay rights post 9/11, 48; Gene Kelly (dancer; director), 68; *Go,* 268; *Go Fish*, 312n36; Gus Van Sant (director), 1, 54; *Haircut (No. 1),* 281–82; *Hangover Part II,* 187; *Harry Potter and the Deathly Hallows: Part II,* 187; *Harry Potter and the Order of the Phoenix,* 200; *Holiday Inn,* 186; homonationalism in the, 58, 59, 60, 63, 182, 197–98; Ilene Chaiken (producer), 181; *Invisible Man, The,* 47; Ira Sachs (director), 280; Jack Smith (director), 10; James Cameron (director), 32, 187; James Whale (director), 47; *Jeffrey,* 312n36; Jennie Livingston (director), 154; John Cromwell (director), 169; John Francis Dillon (director), 169; John Scagliotti (director), 123; Joseph Kosinski (director), 274; Kathy Greenberg (producer), 181; Katie Sherrod (director), 98; *Keep the Lights On,* 280; Kenneth Anger (director), 150; *K.I.P.,* 293; *Kissing Jessica Stein,* 312n36; *Limelight,* 284–85, 336n44; *Lips,* 68; Marc Webb (director), 268; Mark Rappaport (director), 169; Mark Sandrich (director), 186; Martin Scorsese (director), 295; Maryam Keshavarz (director), 1, 2; *Mean Streets,* 295; Michael Ritchie (director), 198; Michele Abbot (producer), 181; Michel Gondry (director), 268; *Milk,* 1, 3–4; *My Dead Brain,* 252; Nancy Kates (director), 98; Navid Sinaki (artist), 9; Nguyen Tan Hoang, 206, 293; Noman Robin (director), 145, 222, 227,

268, 329–30n23; *Oblivion,* 274; *Pariah,* 62, 98; *Paris is Burning* (documentary), 154; Paul Greengrass (director), 295; *Pirates of the Caribbean: On Stranger Tides,* 187; *Pop!,* 9; *Pulp Fiction,* 268; queer film festivals in the, 94; Quentin Tarantino (director), 207, 268; Raja Gosnell (director), 187; *Reservoir Dogs,* 207; Rob Marshall (director), 187; *Rock Hudson's Home Movies,* 169; Rolla Selbak (director), 58, 268, 312n40; Rose Troche (director), 312n36; Ryan Trecartin (artist; filmmaker), 217–18, 268; Sarah Stuve (director), 252; *Saving Face,* 57; *Scorpio Rising,* 150; sexuality in the, 35–36; Sidney Lumet (director), 32, 129; *Singin' in the Rain,* 68; *Smurfs, The,* 187; *Some Like It Hot,* 271; Steven Soderbergh (director), 295; *Superstar,* 289; *Taboo Yardies* (documentary), 85; *The L Word,* 181; *Three Veils,* 58–60, 62, 68, 69, 268, 312n40; *Watermelon Woman, The,* 2; Spike Lee (director), 64; Stanley Donen (director), 68; *The Conversation,* 130, 215; *The Hunger,* 11; Todd Haynes (director), 217, 228, 289, 320n25; Todd Phillips (director), 187; *Traffic,* 295; *Venus Boyz* (documentary), 85; *V for Vendetta,* 130–31, 320n23; *Voices of Witness Africa* (documentary), 98; *Wedding Banquet, The,* 208; William Friedkin (director), 199; William Wyler, 189. *See also* Hollywood

Universal Declaration of Human Rights, 113–14

universalism: as an apparatus of cinema, 33, 133, 189, 225, 305n2; assumptions underlying, 14, 39; avoiding or synthesizing universalizing-minoritizing dichotomies, 40, 73, 76–78, 84, 87, 98, 194; Foucault on, 116; potential of for promulgating human rights, 77, 87, 95, 109, 198; racializing, homogenizing potentials of, 42, 51, 70, 237; Sedgwick's concept of universalizing and minoritizing discourses of homosexuality, 14, 69, 76; versus cultural relativism, 39, 51, 52, 56, 73, 99; vulnerabilities

33, 42, 82, 94, 98, 191–92; melodrama as a means of articulating queer worldliness, 217, 329n14; as the ongoing construction of new worlds, 5; queer, 26, 29–34, 48–50, 93, 99, 241, 331n51; queer worldliness as a challenge to racialized and sexualized global hierarchies, 31, 68, 73–74, 78, 149, 171, 217, 297; transnationalism, 43, 66, 190, 191, 192; travel and worldliness, 43; world making, 5, 25, 34, 90, 128–32, 194, 200–202, 214–15. *See also* cosmopolitanism; human; utopian aspirations

World War II, 114, 115, 231, 232

Wynter, Sylvia, 51, 311n31

YouTube: as a site of cinematic preservation, 286–88, 290; cinema clips on, 179–80, 288, 290, 292; John Dumelo on, 179, 324–25nn16–17; queer cinema on, 16, 325n18; viewer cinematic bootlegging and, 289; viewer usage of queer cinema on, 178–79, 286–88, 289

Yugoslavia: *Lepa sela lepo gore (Pretty Village, Pretty Flame)*, 187; post-Yugoslavian politics, 21, 187, 189, 192–93

Zielinski, Ger, 92, 317n44, 320–21n27

Zimbabwe, 99

zooms, 176, 178, 220